Foreign Policy of India in the 21st Century

Foreign Policy of India in the 21st Century

By

Biswaranjan Mohanty

Assistant Professor,
Department of Political Science,
School of Open Learning, University of Delhi, Delhi

New Century Publications
New Delhi, India

NEW CENTURY PUBLICATIONS
4800/24, Bharat Ram Road,
Ansari Road, Daryaganj,
New Delhi – 110 002 (India)

Tel.: 011-2324 7798, 4358 7398, 6539 6605
Fax: 011-4101 7798
E-mail: indiatax@vsnl.com • info@newcenturypublications.com
www.newcenturypublications.com

Editorial office:
LG–7, Aakarshan Bhawan
4754-57/23, Ansari Road, Daryaganj,
New Delhi – 110 002

Tel.: 011-4356 0919

First Published: **July 2012**

ISBN: **978-81-7708-318-7**

Published by New Century Publications and printed at Salasar Imaging Systems, New Delhi

Designs: Patch Creative Unit, New Delhi

PRINTED IN INDIA

About the Book

Foreign policy of any country is not a static phenomenon and this is certainly true of a huge and complex country like India, getting ready to emerge as a major global player in the 21st Century. Jawahar Lal Nehru—India's first Prime Minister—provided the ideological framework from which continuities and changes in foreign policies can be dissected and inferences drawn on the ideological or pragmatic shifts.

India has showcased itself not only as a matured democratic polity but also as an equally matured economy. It has stood tall and robust as a mammoth amidst the domineering global financial meltdown and an equally contagious disease—authoritarianism—in the neighbouring developing world. There is an intense support to Nehru's passionate implementation of ethics and morality in India's policy-making. Whatever be the nature of engagement with Nehru's legacy in India's foreign policy-making, that distinct Nehruvain flavour to India's foreign policy is retained.

Despite compelling circumstances like the Iraq war or the war in Afghanistan and India's Nuclear Deal, India has striven to maintain her Non-aligned stance. Similarly, conflicts in the territories of immediate neighbours have called for a much more serious and responsible role to be played by India. Under such circumstances an intermix of a hesitant shift from the Nehruvian legacy as well as an attempt to utilise it as a marker of India's distinct foreign policy making remains a reality.

The present book provides deep insights into the various dimensions of India's foreign policy, focusing on recent developments. It dishes out variegated perspectives on India's foreign policy underscoring the importance of regional co-operation—especially among South Asian countries—and engaging insightfully with the debate over the Nehruvian legacy.

Author's Profile

Dr. Biswaranjan Mohanty is presently Assistant Professor, Department of Political Science, School of Open Learning, University of Delhi, Delhi. He is a former alumnus of Jawaharlal Nehru University (JNU), New Delhi. He received his M.Phil. and Ph.D. degrees from the School of Social Sciences of the same University. Specializing in international relations, he has published a number of books and regularly contributed articles in national and international journals. He visited the Upasala University, Sweden while working on a research project.

Contents

Preface

Professing and practicing non-alignment has been the hallmark of India's foreign policy since Independence in 1947. The initiative for Non-aligned Movement (NAM)—the biggest independent and informal association of countries on a *sui generis* basis—came from three nations, viz. India, Yugoslavia and Egypt, represented by the three statesmen Jawaharlal Nehru, Joseph Tito and Gamal Abdel Nasser respectively. From its modest beginnings at the Belgrade Conference in 1961 with a participation of 25 nations, the NAM expanded to include 119 members at the Sharm El Sheikh (Egypt) Conference in July 2009.

In the words of Nehru, "non-alignment was not being neutral or being passive but entailed staying away from military alliances of the superpowers geared against each other and their camps".

The fall of the Berlin Wall and the collapse of the Soviet Union ushered a new era in Indian economy and polity and consequently in India's foreign policy. India unveiled the *Look East* policy in 1991. East Asia—including Japan, China, South Korea and ASEAN—are today India's largest trading partners, ahead of EU and the US.

India's foreign policy posture in recent years—particularly towards the region of West Asia and North Africa (WANA)—has been a subject of intense debate. India's growing relationship with the US and Israel, and its *lukewarm stand* on Iraqi crisis and Iranian nuclear issue is seen as a fundamental shift in the Indian foreign policy exercise. Critics have accused the succeeding Indian Governments, during the past two decades, of abandoning its *independent* foreign policy, of deviating from Nehruvian national consensus in foreign policy matters, and towing the pro-American line. Others have argued that the radical shift in the orientation of Indian foreign policy in terms of its pro-American tilt bears the mark of *realism* and *pragmatism* that is dictated by the demands of globalisation.

It is in the face of this undeniable veracity of the protean visage of international relations that the present work carves out its niche. Engaged in etching out the continuities, rifts and the consequent shifts in foreign policy, the book puts forth motley of ideas that effectively permeate existing gulfs and unseen crevices.

Pandit Jawaharlal Nehru—the First Prime Minister of Independent India—was the embodiment of spirit and ideals of democracy, socialism, secularism, nationalism, equality and social justice.

As the first Minister for External Affairs, Nehru was responsible for developing an independent foreign policy for the country. Reviewing the problem of Cold War and bi-polar politics, Nehru designed the equi-distance concept towards big powers while engaging with them in all possible fronts. Nehru played a crucial role in shaping the policy of non-alignment and institutionalized the Non-Aligned Movement.

When viewed from contemporary international system, the past policies may look irrelevant but during the Cold War era those were very practical and dynamic policies. Unlike Pakistan, India did not join any military camp and could pursue an independent foreign policy. India also contributed to the UN efforts in peace-keeping by sending its forces to many war-torn areas.

It is also not clear as to who would have advised Nehru in taking up the Kashmir problem to the UN Security Council. Again, Nehru ordered the stopping of Indian army's surge towards the Pakistan Occupied Kashmir. The much promised plebiscite on Kashmir has become a non-starter. The Kashmir imbroglio continues to affect both India and Pakistan. Significantly, it has complicated the domestic politics of the two countries.

Foreign policy of any country is not a static phenomenon and this is certainly true of a huge and complex country like India, getting ready to emerge as a major global player in the 21st Century. Jawahar Lal Nehru—India's first Prime Minister—provided the ideological framework from which continuities and changes in foreign policies can be dissected and inferences drawn on the ideological or pragmatic shifts.

The 1998 nuclear test provided the defining movement when India shed its Nehruvian baggage. Moreover, in the post-Nehruvian context, India's commitment to non-alignment and Third Worldism became more of a ritual.

West Asia continues to be fulcrum of world politics. Its significance—in terms of its geo-strategic, geo-political and geo-economic richness primarily centred on hydrocarbon resources—hardly requires any elaboration. It is for these reasons that the region has been hotbed for the global power politics since the beginning of 19th Century. The discovery of oil in the region in the beginning of 20th Century further intensified the intervention of external powers at unprecedented level in the region. Though the region represents merely 2 percent of world surface and contains 2 percent of the world's population, it plays a key role in the world's economic structure on account of its vast hydrocarbon resources. The vast proven reserves of oil and natural gas, and high levels of income and consumption have made this region a *highly contested space*. The leading powers of the world seek to influence and control the region as it provides the critical leverage to the respective powers to assert their position in the global power politics. Following the incident of 9/11, the region has attracted the global scholarship and media attention mainly in terms of rise of Islamic militancy, violation of human rights, Gulf War, institutionalized authoritarianism, atrocities of Israel and plight of Palestinians, Iranian nuclear programme, securitization of region etc. These developments mostly concern the external dimensions of the region. However, the global pressure on the region over the years has deeply affected the process of change and development in the region.

I take this opportunity to place on record my deep sense of gratitude to the following scholars for their help and encouragement: Professor Manoranjan Mohanty (formerly, University of Delhi); Professor Aswini Ray (formerly, JNU); Dr. George Mathew, Director, Institute of Social Sciences; Dr. Bidyut Mohanty (ISS); Professor Niraja Gopal Jayal, JNU; Professor S.D. Muni, (JNU), Professor C.P. Bhambri (formerly JNU); and Justice Ranganath Mishra (formerly Chairman of NHRC and Chief Justice of India).

June 2012
New Delhi

Dr. Biswaranjan Mohanty

1

Indian Foreign Policy: Historical Settings and Current Status

India's foreign relations reflect a traditional policy of nonalignment the exigencies of domestic economic reform and development, and the changing post-Cold War international environment. India's relations with the world have evolved considerably since the British colonial period (1757-1947), when a foreign power monopolized external relations and defence relations. On independence in 1947, few Indians had experience in making or conducting foreign policy. However, the country's oldest political party, the Indian National Congress had established a small foreign department in 1925 to make overseas contacts and to publicize its freedom struggle. From the late 1920s onwards, Jawaharlal Nehru, who had the most long-standing interest in world affairs among independent leaders, formulated the Congress stance on international issues.

1.1 Post-Independence Foreign Policy at a Glance

The foundations of India's foreign policy were laid during the freedom movement when our leaders, even when fighting for independence, were engaged with the great causes of the time. The principles of India's foreign policy, that emerged then, have stood the test of time: a belief in friendly relations with all countries of the world, the resolution of conflicts by peaceful means, the sovereign equality of all states, independence of thought and action as manifested in the principles of Non-alignment, and equity in the conduct of international relations.

Under the leadership of Jawaharlal Nehru, India was the founder member of the Non-aligned Movement (NAM). India has played an active role in strengthening the Movement and making it an effective voice in representing the collective aspirations and interests o the developing countries on such vital issues as development, peace and stability. India hosted the 7th NAM Summit in New Delhi in 1983. In recent years, after the end of the Cold War, our foreign policy has been focused on strengthening the Movement by redefining its priorities in keeping with the changing times.

India has also been in the forefront of the world community in the struggle against colonialism. Indeed, the Independence of India itself played the role of a catalyst in removing the vestiges of colonialism in other parts of the developing world, particularly in Africa. India was also the first country to raise the question of racial discrimination in South Africa in 1946. It was at India's initiative that the AFRICA (Action for Resistance to Invasion, Colonialism and Apartheid) Fund was set up at the 8th NAM Summit in Harare in 1986. India was the Chairman of the AFRICA Fund Committee, which wound up in 1993.

A notable feature of Indian foreign policy has been its strong advocacy of general and complete disarmament, with nuclear disarmament being accorded the highest priority. Towards this end, India has taken several initiatives within the United Nations and outside. In 1988, India presented to the 3rd Session of the UN General Assembly devoted to Disarmament an Action Plan for Ushering in a Nuclear Weapons Free and Non-Violent World Order. In order to highlight international concern about the unprecedented nuclear arms race, India was also a member of the Six-Nation Five-Continent joint Initiative in the 1980s. But while India has, and will, remain committed to nuclear disarmament, to be achieved in a time-bound framework, it has consistently and in a principled manner opposed such discriminatory treaties as the Nuclear non-Proliferation Treaty (NPT) and Comprehensive Nuclear Test Ban Treaty (CTBT) and has refused to give up its nuclear options until all countries in the world including nuclear weapon states embrace the idea of nuclear disarmament in a phased manner.

As a founder member of the United Nations, India has been firmly committed to the purposes and principles of the United Nations and has made significant contributions to its various activities, including peace-keeping operations. India has been a participant in all its peace-keeping operations including those in Korea, Egypt and Congo in earlier years and in Somalia, Angola and Rwanda in recent years. India has also played an active role in the deliberations of the United Nations on the creation of a more equitable international economic order. It has been an active member of the Group of 77, and later the core group of the G-15 nations. Other issues, such as environmentally sustainable development and the promotion and protection of human rights, have also been an important focus of India's foreign policy in international forums.

Commensurate with national interests and security, the improvement of bilateral relations is an important component of any foreign policy, and India has succeeded in establishing a network of mutually beneficial relations with all countries of the world.

In particular, the improvement of relations with our neighbours has always been one of the pillars of India's foreign policy. India played an historic and unique role in the liberation of Bangladesh which emerged as a sovereign nation in 1971. Through the implementation of the 1964 and 1974 Agreements, the issues of the stateless people of Indian origin in Sri Lanka were resolved. In 1988, India helped preserve the integrity of Maldives by coming to the assistance of that country and preventing an attempted take over by armed mercenaries. The Indian government has taken recent initiatives to further strengthen ties with our neighbours, which have won international appreciation. These initiatives are based on five clear principles: First, with neighbours like Bangladesh, Bhutan, Maldives, Nepal and Sri Lanka, India does not ask for reciprocity but gives all that it can in good faith and trust. Secondly, no South Asian country should allow its territory to be used against the interests of another country of the region. Thirdly, none will interfere in the internal affairs of another. Fourthly, all South Asian countries must respect each other's territorial integrity and sovereignty. And finally, they should settle all their disputes through peaceful bilateral negotiations.

These tenets have paid rich dividends. A landmark Treaty has been signed with Bangladesh on the sharing of waters of the Ganga. With Bhutan and Nepal, major projects of economic collaboration have been advanced. Our relations with Sri Lanka have shown steady improvement. With Pakistan, India ha consistently pursued a policy seeking to improve relations under the framework of the Shimla Agreement signed in 1972 which provided for the resolution of outstanding issues peacefully and bilaterally and for establishing durable peace in the Sub-continent. Bilateral discussions with Pakistan have resumed recently and India would continue efforts to have good neighbourly relations with Pakistan.

An important achievement of India's foreign policy has been the strengthening of regional co-operation. India is an active member of the South Asian Association for Regional Cooperation (SAARC) which was launched in December 1985. With India's full support, SAARC has recently taken significant steps in accelerating the pace of economic co-operation. The South Asian Preferential Trade Arrangement (SAPTA) became operational in December 1995. At the 9th SAARC Summit in Male in May 1997, which was chaired by India, a historical decision has also been taken to strive for a South Asian Free Trade Area (SAFTA) latest by the year 2001 AD. The emergence of the Indian Ocean Rim Association for Regional Co-operation (IOR-ARC) in March 1997, as a major instrument of cooperation in the larger region, has also had the active support of India.

India's foreign policy has always regarded the concept of neighbourhood as one of widening concentric circles, around a central axis of historical and cultural commonalties. From this point of view, it has always given due priority to the development of relations with South East Asia. In 1947, India organized the Asian Relations Conference. It chaired the International Control Commission in

1954 and was a major player in the organization of the Bandung Conference in 1955. Today, India is implementing a 'Look East' policy which is underpinned by important economic considerations. Some significant steps in the pursuance of this policy have been taken with the admission of India as a full dialogue partner of ASEAN and a member of the ASEAN Regional Forum, in 1996.

An attribute of a dynamic foreign policy is the ability to respond to changing developments. The emergence of the Central Asian Republics in the aftermath of the break up of the Soviet Union was one such recent development, and India, given the strategic and economic importance of this region, has been quick to strengthen its bilateral relations with each of these Republics. The shift in recent years by the countries of Central and East Europe to political pluralism and market-oriented structures has also seen India trying to build upon existing business and institutional linkages so as to further strengthen the traditional ties of friendship with the countries of this region.

The countries of the Gulf have a political and strategic importance for India. The region is a major market for Indian exports. Three million Indians are employed in these countries. The strengthening of ties with this region, therefore, has been a priority of India's foreign policy.

With China the aim of Indian foreign policy has been of developing a relationship of friendship, cooperation and good neighbourliness, exploiting the potential for favourable growth wherever it exists, even as we seek to find a fair, reasonable and mutually acceptable solution to the outstanding border issue. Towards this aim, a series of high level visits have been exchanged, bilateral trade and economic cooperation is growing, and an Agreement on Confidence Building Measures, as part of a wider dialogue on security, has been signed.

India values its bilateral relations with the US. As democracies, both countries have many shared ideals. Relations have also continued to grow with the 15 countries of the European Union, and with Japan. These countries are important economic partners of India, especially in the wake of our economic reforms. However, in pursuing bilateral relations, we have sought to preserve the independence of our viewpoint and protect our national interests from the pressures of conformity.

Our relations with Russia have grown over the years to constitute an important foreign policy priority for both countries. There is a recognition in both counties to the strategic dimension of our multifaceted ties. The considerable goodwill for India in Russia has been further cemented in recent years.

Economic diplomacy has been a key component of India's foreign policy. Apart from long established Divisions in the Ministry to deal with economic issues, an Investment Publicity Unit (IPU) was specifically set up in 1990 with a view to disseminating economic information and coordinating the economic and commercial activities of Indian Missions abroad in the light of the recent economic reforms underway in the country. One aspect of economic diplomacy has been the promotion of South-South Cooperation. The Indian Economic and Technical Cooperation (ITEC) Program was established in 1964. Today it extends to 110 countries in Asia, East Europe, Africa and Latin America and facilitates the training of as many as 1000 foreign candidates in Indian institutions each year.

As many as 20 million people of Indian origin live and work abroad and constitute an important link with the mother country. An important role of India's foreign policy has been to ensure their welfare and well being within the framework of the laws of the country where they live.

The strength of any foreign policy depends also on the professional abilities of those who implement it, both at Headquarters and in the field. With a view to ensuring this, the Foreign Service Institute was established to undertake specialist training for entrants into the Indian Foreign Service, and conduct several other specialist courses for Indian and foreign diplomats.

It is difficult to enumerate the achievements of a country's foreign policy in exactly quantifiable terms. With this as a qualification, it would be a fair assessment to make that Indian foreign policy has sought to preserve, with conviction and consistency, the principles that were enunciated by the founding fathers of the Republic, both in the development of bilateral relations, and in international forums, where our views have won recognition and respect. A significant factor underlying this achievement has been the consensus, cutting across political divides, within the country, on what the basic aims and objectives of Indian foreign policy should be.

1.2 Determinants of Foreign Policy

The foreign policy of a country is influenced by so many factors that it is not possible to enumerate all of them here. Some of the important factor which influence the foreign policy of a country or constitute the inputs of the foreign policy are given hereunder. Broadly speaking these factors fall into two categories. viz. internal and external.

1.2.1 Internal Factors:

1. **Size:** In the first place the size of a state's territory as well as its population greatly influences it foreign policy. Generally the leaders and people of countries with small territory and population do not expect their country to carry great weight in international affairs. On the other hand the leaders and people of large countries are ready to assume special responsibilities.

2. **Geography:** The geography of a country, including its fertility, climate, location in relation to other land masses, and water-ways, etc. also influence the country's foreign policy. It is a major factor in determining self-sufficiency of a country.
3. **Culture and History:** The cultural and historical traditions of a country also deeply influence the foreign policy. Generally, people possessing a unified common culture and historical experience can pursue an effective foreign policy because of the support of all sections of society who share the same values and memories. On the other hand, a country which is culturally and historically fragmented cannot pursue an equally effective foreign policy.
4. **Economic Development:** The stage of economic development which a country has attained also has its impact on its foreign policy. Generally, the industrially advanced countries feel more deeply involved in relations with other countries because they have to import different kinds of raw materials and commodities from other countries. They are also on the look out of latest knowledge and technical know-how. Therefore they maintain intimate trade relations with their trading partners.
5. **Technology:** Advancement in technology, which effects the military and economic capabilities of a state, also exercise profound influence on the foreign policy. However, this factor influences the foreign policy only in an indirect manner, viz., by influencing other sources of foreign policy.
6. **National Capacity:** The national capacity of a state also exercises profound influence on the foreign policy of a state. National capacity of a state depends on its military preparedness, its technological advancement and economic development.
7. **Social Structure:** The social structure of a society also exercises profound influence on its foreign policy. A society which is sharply divided on the basis of wealth, religion, regional imbalances, etc. cannot pursue effective foreign policy on account of division and lack of co-operation among various groups. On the other hand a homogenous society possessing strong sense of national unity can pursue a more effective foreign policy.
8. **Public Mood:** Public mood is another important determinant of a country's foreign policy. Though it is generally held that the public mood usually follows rather than guides the foreign policy making process, it can exercise lot of influence on the determination of a foreign policy of basic realignment in the prevailing great power structure takes place and the state becomes more involved or more isolated from the world affairs.
9. **Political Organization:** The political organization found in a country also greatly influences the foreign policy. Generally, under authoritarian systems

quick foreign policy decisions are possible because the decision making power rests with an individual assisted by his clique. But as the leaders under this system are isolated from the operational environments and the subordinate policy makers provide the information which is perceived by the superiors, there is every possibility of a discrepancy between the psychological and operational aspect of the foreign policy.

Within the democratic system itself the difference in political structure has its impact on foreign policy. For example, under a parliamentary system of government based on co-operation between the Legislature and the Executive, the cordial relations between the two wings have an impact on country's foreign policy. On the other hand, under presidential system based on the principle of separation of powers, the relation between the two wings are likely to be more strained which affect the ambiguity or continuity of foreign policy.

10. **Role of Press:** The press also plays a vital role in the foreign policy formulation process. The press contributes to this process by supplying factual information on the bass of which the people take decision; by publishing specialized articles on current international developments which enable the people to understand the significance of developments in their country in relation to the past developments, and by analyzing the policy of the government in regard to foreign affairs. The press also plays an important role in publicizing the foreign policy of the country.
11. **Political Accountability:** The nature of political accountability prevailing in a system also greatly influences the foreign policy of the country. Generally, in an open political system, the demands of citizen and groups get articulated and transmitted to foreign policy formulators.
12. **Leadership:** The leadership also plays a vital role in the shaping of a country's foreign policy.

1.2.2 External Factors: In addition to the internal factors which influence a country's foreign policy discussed above, a number of external factors also exercise considerable influence on the foreign policy of a country. In our time the world has become so inter-linked that incidents in other countries have their immediate impact on other countries. Thus, a coup d'etat in neighbouring country, or nationalization of oil companies in Middle East or release of a proposed arms control agreement are evens which influence the actions of leaders in other countries.

1. **Power-Structure:** The great power structure prevailing in the world politics also greatly influences the policy of a country. In this regard three possibilities can be envisaged. First, a number of powers may enjoy great

power status and their relations may be based on balance of power system. Secondly, there may be only two powers which dominate the world scene and the other states are compelled to side with one or the other. Thirdly, more than two states attain great power status and the two powers at the poles are less able to command strict allegiance of those in the orbit (the system is known as loose bipolar). The nature of power structure prevailing in the world has a substantial impact on the foreign policy of a country.

2. **International Organization:** The contemporary international organization also greatly influences the foreign policy of a country. While formulating its foreign policy the country has to take note of the international law, treaties and contracts. No country can ignore these factors without jeopardizing its own interests.
3. **Reaction of Other States:** While formulating its foreign policy a country has to take note of the reaction of other states to its various actions. No country can afford to pursue interests which are fundamentally against the interests of the other states because any policy based on narrow national interests is likely to evoke strong reaction from the concerned state and produce disastrous consequences.
4. **Alliance:** Alliances concluded by various states also greatly influence the foreign policy. The states parties to alliance have to respond to the requests and demands of their allies stand refrain from formulation policies or taking actions which are offensive to them.
5. **World Public Opinion:** The world public opinion also exercises profound influence on the foreign policy of a country. It is true that the world public opinion influences the foreign policy of a country only occasionally and is not a factor. Further, it is able to exercise influence on the foreign policy of a state only if it is supported by the domestic public opinion.

1.3 Distinct Features of Indian Foreign Policy

Analysing all these, the following distinctive features of India's foreign policy come to the fore:

1. **Non-alignment:** India was the chief initiator of the policy of non-alignment. The policy of non-alignment means detachment from military blocs and a faith in solving all international disputes through cooperation. She adopted this policy because she wanted to play a more dominant role for the cause of world peace. Opposing the policy of alignment Nehru said, "By aligning ourselves with any one power, you surrender your opinion, give up the policy you would normally pursue because somebody else wants you to pursue another policy. I do not think that it would be a right policy for us to adopt.

We will neither be following the policy based on our ideals inherited from our past or the one indicated by our present nor will be able easily to adopt ourselves to the new policy consequent on such alignment."

Geographical consideration also demanded that India should follow a policy of non-alignment. She has two leading communist powers on or near her border—China and Soviet Union. As a result military alliance with the Western bloc were ruled out because it would be viewed as an unfriendly act by the two communist powers. An alliance with the Communist countries was not possible because India by her traditions could not approve the revolutionary ideology of communism.

It must be noted that nonalignment does not mean that friendly cooperation is not possible with other countries. Further, nonalignment also does not mean neutrality. Neutrality as a policy has little meaning except in times of war.

Thus it would be wrong to designate the foreign policy of India as policy of 'neutrality' because a country which adopts policy of neutrality has no positive opinions on issues which divide the blocs. India on the other hand has spoken clearly and with conviction on the various international issues. For example she considered the march of North Korean troops into South Korea as 'aggression', she condemned the British and French invasion of Suez as a 'naked aggression', she condemned though after much waiting, the Soviet interference in Hungary; she was very critical of US bombardment in Vietnam.

2. **Opposition to Imperialism and Colonialism:** Another feature of the India's foreign policy is that it is opposed to imperialism and colonialism. The government has consistently championed the cause of the exploited nations against the colonial and imperial powers. In a speech before the UN General Assembly on November 3, 1948 Nehru said: "We in Asia who have ourselves suffered all these evils of colonialism and of imperial domination, have committed ourselves inevitably to the freedom of every other colonial country. There are neighbouring countries of ours in Asia with whom we are intimately allied. We look to them with sympathy: We look at their struggle with sympathy. Any power great or small, which in that way prevents the attainment of the freedom of these peoples does an ill than to world peace. Great countries like India who have passed out of that colonial stage do not conceive it possible that other countries should remain under the yoke of colonial rule.

   It may be observed that India has not been merely raising slogans against colonialism and imperialism, she has actually followed this policy. For example, when the Dutch government tried to re-establish her hold over

Indonesia. India convened a meeting of Foreign Ministers at New Delhi and made an appeal to the Security Council. As a result the Independence of Indonesia was ultimately recognized. Likewise, India supported the Independence demand to Libya and opposed the moves of the South Africa to incorporate the territories of South-West Africa into her Union. She also advocated the cause to Tunisia and Algeria.

3. **Opposed to Racial Discrimination:** The Indian government has also opposed the policy of racial discrimination, Nehru said: "We repudiate utterly the Nazi doctrine of racialism wheresover and in whatever form it may be practised. We seek no domination over other and we claim no privileged position over other people. But we do claim equal and honourable treatment of our people wherever they may go and we cannot accept any discrimination against them." India has not only condemned the policy of racial discrimination followed towards Indians in South Africa but also supported the cause of the Negroes in the United States and the black majority in Rhodesia against the white minority. India has been a strong advocate of her policy of racial equality. It was mainly due to effort of India that UN Generally Assembly condemned the Union of South Africa for its policy of Apartheid.
4. **Co-operation and Coexistence (Panchsheel):** Cooperation and coexistence has been another important principle of India's foreign policy. The idea of different systems existing side by side without clash is not new to India. This policy of coexistence is expressed in the **Panchsheel or Five Principles** of peaceful co-existence incorporated in the agreement between China and India of April, 1954. The five principles are:

- Mutual respect for each other's territorial integrity and sovereignty.
- Nonaggression.
- Non-interference in each other's internal affairs.
- Equality and mutual benefit.
- Peaceful co-existence.

5. **Faith in United Nations:** India has great faith in United Nations and stands for settlement of all disputes under the aegis of the UN through peaceful means. For that very reason the Government of India took the question of Kashmir to the United nations. The role of India in Korea and Indo-China are the outstanding examples of India's cooperation with the United Nations. However, within the United Nations India has refused to blindly follow either of the two power blocs and has determined her stand on the various world issues keeping in view the interests of world peace. When India summoned a conference of the Asian countries in New Delhi in January 1949 allegations

were levelled against her that she was trying to ignore and bypass the United Nations. Nehru at that time made it clear that "we meet to supplement the effort of the security council, not to supplant that body, we meet in no spirit of hostility to any nation or group of nations' but in an endeavour to promote peace through the extension of freedom." From time to time India has been making available to the UN the necessary men to implement its decisions. Thus she sent personnel for the observation group in Lebanon to ensure that there was no infiltration of personnel or supply of arms or other material across the Lebanese border. Similarly India contributed a contingent during the Congolese conflict.

6. **Bias in Favour of Asia:** Although India has been following a policy of friendship towards all the nations of the world, she has special interest in development the closet possible ties with other Asian and African nations which share her point of view. India has not only tried sincerely to solve the problems facing the Asian countries but has also forged them together through various conferences. The beginning in this direction was made by holding conference at New Delhi in 1947 and 1949. Even the Bandung Conference of the Afro-Asian countries was held in Asia. Profs. Palmer and Perkins describe Bandung Conference as, "the most significant international conference ever held in Asia and the fist conference of its kind in history." India has sometimes been accused of aiming at the leadership of South East Asia, but she has always disclaimed any such ambition. The fact remains that India has been a leading champion of Asia's claims to a greater place in the world affairs and she has always taken an initiative in this regard.
7. **Sympathetically Disposed towards Divided Countries:** As India had to face the bitter consequences of the partition of the country, she has always shown sympathy towards the divided countries. She opposed the partition of Palestine and suggested a Federation of the Arabs and Jews. She also opposed the division of Korea and Indo-China (Vietnam etc.). She has also been supporting the cause of German Unification to do away with the evil efforts of its partition into East and West Germany.
8. **Ties with Commonwealth:** India has also been supporter of commonwealth and joined it by a treaty. India joined the commonwealth because she could get certain economic benefits by her association with this August body. Further, on the eve of her independence India needed the shield of British navy to secure Indian ocean. But India's membership of Commonwealth has provoked lot of controversy from the very beginning. In the Indo-Pak conflict of 1965 when Great Britain sympathized with Pakistan a demand was made by many that India should quite the commonwealth. But the government

turned down this demand by pointing out that the organization was not British but mainly Afro-Asian. Majority of the members of the commonwealth belonged to Asia and Africa.

The World has witnessed unprecedented changes during the last decade. One could not have imagined that within hardly four decades of the World War-II, the controversial Berlin wall would collapse cards and the Cold War would meet an inglorious end. It was also inconceivable until a few yeas that the iron curtain over the Eastern Europe would be lifted and that the mighty Sovereignty Union would disintegrate.

Besides, until a few years ago one could not conceive of a situation where development and economics would dominate international relations and the mighty security alliances so carefully built up over the years since World War-II would lose their power and even some of them like SEATO, CENTO and Warsaw Pact would fizzle out as non-entities.

Is it not a strange irony to suggest that the billions of dollars spent on research and development (R&D) of the strategic weapon system the Strategic Defence Initiative (SDI) so assiduously built up during the Reagan years and the grand theories like zero-sum games deterrence, first strike, second strike, mutually assured destruction (MAD) are gradually becoming outdated? Similarly, is it not a fact that Third World solidarity, Non-aligned movement, the New International Economic Order, the North-South dialogues, the South-South co-operation, are gradually losing significance? Is it also unrealistic to think that the present day international politics is gradually being hijacked by the multinational, religious fundamentalists, drug barons and more recently by the cross-country terrorists?

In addition one could not conceive until a few decades ago that ethnic conflicts, and the sub-national movements would result in a dramatic redrawing of the political geography of the world. There is also no gain-saying the fact that the erstwhile non-issues like human rights, protection of global environment, the sustainable development and social issues like women, tribes, indigenous culture are gradually leaving their imprints on the restructuring of the agenda for international relations. No doubt linkage politics is going to arrive at its logical conclusion.

Right from the time of independence in 1947 when the world was ideologically divided between the two power blocs, the objectives of India's foreign policy a clearly defined by the first Prime Minister, Jawaharlal Nehru, was based on the premise of middle path which got crystallized as nonalignment.

There was obviously a clear consensus in the country for a foreign policy which revolved around an independent approach without getting entangled by either ideological or military alliances.

The major determinants for the evolution of such a foreign policy in the post-colonial phase can be identified as follows. First, India was keen to preserve its national interest by keeping away from either the Western capitalist bloc led by the United States or the socialist bloc led by the Soviet Union, Second, having emerged from the slumber of colonial exploitation, the abject poverty of the country posed a serious challenge to the evolution of a foreign policy which would substantially depend on both the blocs in order to spearhead its economic and industrial development. That's why, a mixed economy approach suited the policy planners. Third, India having emerged as a major Third World country wanted to play its role for a peaceful world order which would logically abhor violence and always support a peaceful settlement of international disputes. War was not going to be used as an instrument of its foreign policy though our foreign policy at that point of time was not passive in the sense that Nehru's India was supportive of the major UN peace keeping role in Korea, Hungary, Congo and elsewhere. The major setback to the foreign policy came at the time of Sino-Indian border conflict in 1962 when India was ignored by both the capitalist and socialist power blocs and a humiliating defeat exposed the country's earlier claim to play a global role in view of its sub-continental size and a glorious past. In spite of such a major set back, India did play a pivotal role in spearheading the Afro-Asian movement which ultimately crystallized as a Third World Solidarity at various global forums like the UN and the Commonwealth of Nations. The emergence of the Non-aligned Movement (NAM) as also a by product of that solidarity. During the 1950's and early 1960's, India also played an active role in the process of decolonization and the fight against apartheid—then prevalent in South Africa and Namibia.

Finally, although at the early stage, India wanted to improve its image in the immediate neighbourhood which was marked by some abbreviations here and there. For instance, the emphasis of Panchsheel in India's dealing with neighbours, especially China, is a case in point Signed in 1954 by Jawaharlal Nehru and Zhou Enlai, the then Prime Minister of India and China respectively.

But the Hindi-Chini bhai-bhai phase in the last stage of Nehru years soon gave way to mutual tensions over the Macmohan line and it resulted in a limited war between the two countries during 1962. India's relation with another important neighbour like Pakistan remained tense during the Nehru phase and even there after. Although India's bilateral relations with the other South Asian neighbours like Nepal, Bhutan and Sri Lanka by and large remained cordial, Nehru's spontaneous reaction to the Royal Coup in Nepal during December 1960, brought some irritants to Indo-Nepal tie. Even the issue of according citizenship to the Tamil Plantation workers in Northern Sri Lanka crâted some tensions between India and the island republic. However, it was sorted out to a certain extent during the short tenure of Lal Bahadur Shastri as India's Prime Minister (June 1964 to Jan. 1966) when the Sirimavo-Shastri Accord was signed between the two countries.

1.4 Continuity and Change

Foreign policy of any country is the product of a complex interplay of history, geography, past experience, present requirements, perceptions of the ruling elite of national interests and ideological consensus. It is also shaped and moulded by the domestic balance of forces, the regional balance of forces, the regional balance of forces, and the international balance of forces. History and geography give continuity to foreign policy, domestic and international circumstances produce changes. In the last decade of the 20th century the world is undergoing dramatic transformation. This current change in the global milieu is one of the most crucial turning points in independent India's Foreign Policy. India is now passing through a period that requires a careful assessment of opportunities and priorities, pending the making of a new foreign policy framework. Prof. Morgenthau emphasizes that national interest is the driving force behind a country's Foreign Policy.

The foreign policy of India has its origin in the past. In the very first session in 1885 the Congress denounced the annexation of Burma and objected to the military activity going on beyond the natural lines of defences of this country. At the meeting of the All India Congress Committee in Delhi in 1921 the National Congress passed its first general resolution on foreign policy, and openly declared that the present government (British) of India in no way represents Indian opinion. Another significant pronouncement about the foreign policy of India was made at the Haripura Session in 1938. The Resolution said: "The people of India desire to live in peace and friendship with their neighbours and with all other countries, and for this purpose wish to remove all cause of conflict between them. In order, therefore, to establish world peace on an enduring basis; imperialism and the exploitation of one people by another must end. Thus, the basis for the foreign policy of Free India was ready before India actually gained freedom.

1.5 Promoting National Interest

Like the foreign policies of other countries, the Indian foreign policy has also sought to promote national interest. Jawaharlal Nehru, the chief architect of India's foreign policy, said in the constituent Assembly of India on 4 December 1947 "Whatever policy we may lay down, the art of conducting the foreign affairs of a country lies in finding out what is most advantageous to the country. We may talk about peace and freedom and earnestly mean what we say. But in the ultimate analysis, a government functions for the good of the country it governs and no government dare do anything which in the short or long run is manifestly to the disadvantage of the country".

Nehru, however, did not consider the national interest of India incompatible with the interests of other nations. He said, "Some people may think of the interests of their country regardless of other consequences, or take a short-distance view. Others may think that in the long-term policy, the interest of another country is as important to them as that of their own country. The interest of peace is more important, because if war comes every one suffers, so that in the long-distance view, self-interest may itself demand a policy of cooperation with other nations, goodwill for other nations, as indeed it does demand...Therefore, we propose to look after India's interests in the context of world cooperation and world peace, in so far as world peace can be preserved".

It is evident, from the above observations of Nehru that he conceived India's national interests in the context of world co-operation and took a long term view of India's interests. However, he was not in favour of giving up India's viewpoint because other nations thoughts differently.

1.6 Indian Foreign Policy Post-1962

The year 1962 marks a watershed in the development of India's foreign policy. This change was discernible during the prime ministership of Nehru when he openly declared that India was no more no aligned so far as China was concerned. Lal Bahadur Shastri was succeeded Nehru as PM tried to cultivate friendly and intimate relations with neighbours friendly and intimate relations with neighbours like, Nepal, Burma and Sri Lanka as well as the two super powers. He succeeded in procuring military and economic assistance from both the powers and greatly strengthened India's position. What is significant that even USA despite strong protests from Pakistan continued to provide liberal military aid to India. This aid was suspended only on the outbreak of war between India and Pakistan in 1965. Professor Plamer and Perking have asserted that the Chinese attack came as a traumatic shock to India. It is true that methods of foreign policy after 1962 underwent a change, but the basic principles of India's foreign policy continued to be the same. Another outstanding feature of Indian foreign policy during the Shastri era was that the emphasis shifted to "collective decision-making".

1.6.1 Foreign Policy under Indira Gandhi: After the sudden death of Shastri, Mrs. Indira Gandhi became the P.M. The principle of "collective decision making" continued. During her period also the process of developing close relations with super powers continued. She was able to secure large financial and military assistance from USA. She also cultivated intimate relations with Soviet Union.

1.6.2 Foreign Policy under Janata Party: With the formation of Janata Government in 1977 it was expected that a drastic change in India's foreign policy would take place. It was hoped that there would be a certain amount of cooling off of relations with Soviet Union and more intimate relations with USA. The Janata Government, therefore tried to develop very intimate relations with both the super powers, and bring about greater balance and sobriety. A new chapter was opened in Indo-U.S. relations with the visit of President carter. Another outstanding feature of the Janata Party Foreign Policy was an attempt to develop more closer relations with the neighbouring countries. The Janata Government also took a number of concrete steps to improve its relations with neighbouring countries like Bangladesh, Pakistan, Nepal etc. It reached an agreement with Pakistan on the question of Salal Dam in Kashmir. The Janata Government tried to improve its relations with China for two reasons. First was heavy defence burden and second was desirable to cultivate friendly relations with Beijing on the other hand China was also eager to improve relations with India because they were so much engrossed in their domestic problems that they wanted peace on borders with India.

In addition to this, the Janata Party continued the policy of improving relations with the countries of South-East Asia and West-Asia and extended full support to the anti-racial policies and liberation movements in Africa. In short, Janata Party followed a foreign policy which was highly pragmatic and aimed at promotion of national interests.

1.6.3 Foreign Policy under Rajiv Gandhi: Rajiv Gandhi continued the foreign policy of Nehru and Indira Gandhi and reaffirmed his faith in the United nations the non-aligned movement, oppositions to colonialism. He gave importance to our economic, technological and cultural cooperation with them. Rajiv Gandhi also international economic disparities, develop closer relations with in mediate neighbours, pursue policy of non-interference and promised to pursue the concept of comma regional development of South Asia. He stood for arms race, to promote dialogue between the North and south to built a just world economic order.

1.6.4 Foreign Policy under National Front Government: The National Front Government in 1989 reiterated its determination to continue policy of non-alignment. It holds talks with the leaders of Nepal, Sri Lanka, and Pakistan to remove some of the irritants present in the relations of India with these countries.

It expressed its determination to develop more intimate relations with the U.S., without Jeopardising good relations with Soviet Union.

1.6.5 Foreign Policy under Narasimha Rao: Rao Government tried to give a new orientation to the foreign relations in the light of harsh economic realities. Greater emphasis was laid on economic diplomacy. Indian peace keeping forces took leading role in the socio-economic development of Somalia. India has moved closer to resolving boundary question with China and the two agreed to reduce their military strength on the border. With US also India improved its relations despite differences on issues like NPT, Nuclear weapons free zone in South Asia, missile programme, special 301 etc. However, American pressure on India to sign NPT and to abandon the missile programme gave set back to the process of improvement of relations with U.S.

1.6.6 Foreign Policy under United Front Government (Gujarat Doctrine): The united front Government laid great emphasis on improvement of relations with the neighbouring countries. It put forth Gujarat doctrine under which unilateral concessions were made to the neighbouring countries with regard to travel and trade, without expecting reciprocity. Effort was made to promote free trade among the SAARC countries. Another notable feature of the Gujral Doctrine was to eliminate the outside intervention in the region.

1.6.7 Foreign Policy under BJP Led Coalition Government (NDA): The BJP led coalition Government came in to power in 1998. It gave a new orientation to the foreign policy which is more realistic than moralist. It insists on reciprocity. Under the new policy, greater emphasis is being laid on security of the country. On this plea India conducted explosions at Pokhran in May 1998. Indian foreign policy under Vajpayee government laid special emphasis on:

1. Need to exercise nuclear option in the interest of national security.
2. To pursue vigorously the matter of India's permanent membership of the security council.
3. To promote closer regional relations through development of South Asian association for regional cooperation and improve bilateral relations with neighbouring countries.
4. To persuade Pakistan to abandon its policy of hostile interference in our internal affairs by supporting insurgent and terrorist groups.
5. To improve relations with China by seeking speedy resolution of the outstanding border problem.
6. To improve relations with Myanmar and promote greater cooperation in the field of defence, security, economy and culture.
7. To improve relations with Bangladesh and impress on the Bangladesh authorities the need to check illegal infiltrations into India.

1.7 Consolidation Phase: Lal Bahadur Shastri to Indira Gandhi

When Lal Bahadur Shastri took up the stewardship of the nation, the Indian image abroad was at a low key. Nehru's dream of peaceful world order with a historic role for India remained shattered. The country was facing a belligerent neighbour (Pakistan) with overt support from some external powers (China and the US) and the Soviet Russia was at best a fence-sitter. Shastri lost no time to consolidate the Indian defence force on the one hand and mend India's broken links with immediate neighbours. India during his tenure, gave a befitting reply to a belligerent neighbour like Pakistan when during the limited war in September 1965 the Indian army almost reached the outskirts of Labour before cease-fire could be declared under the auspices of the United Nations Security Council. The Tashkent Declaration which was brokered by the Soviet Union and signed between Field Marshal Ayub Khan and Lal Bahadur Shastri on 10 January 1966, provided for: (i) restoration of normal and peaceful relations between India and Pakistan; (ii) restoration of their obligations under UN charter to settle their disputes through peaceful means; (iii) agreement to base their relations on the principle of non-interference in the internal affairs of each other; and (iv) meetings at the highest and other levels on matters of direct concern to both.

In this effort to inject a dose of positive bilateralism in India's foreign policy, Shastri signed an agreement with Sirimavo Bandarnaike, the then Prime Minister of Ceylon (now Sri Lanka) in October 1964. Under the Agreement, out of the 775, 000 India Tamil settlers in Sri Lanka, 300,000 were to be granted Sri Lankan citizenship and 325,000 were to be repatriated to India within a period of 15 years. The status and future of the remaining 150,000 Tamils was to be settle later. Any assessment of Lal Bahadur's foreign policy would require a mention of his maiden broadcast to the nation on 11 June 1964, when he said: “We has all seek friendship and develop our relations with all countries irrespective of ideology or their political system... We conceive of Afro-Asian solidarity not as an end in itself but as a means for achieving certain noble objectives...The problem that mankind faces today is the achievement of peace and disarmament. Indeed what a realistic and down-to-earth statement which is even more relevant in the present global environment”.

Mrs. Indira Gandhi during her long tenure as India's Prime Minister (1966-1979) and 1980-84) further consolidated India's image as a formidable leader of the emergent Third World. When she successfully hosted the seventh non-aligned summit in New Delhi in 1983, she injected a fresh blood to a sick movement. She indeed transformed the NAM as the greatest peace movement of the world. Even if she was perceived as authoritarian by a section of the Indian elite, she emerged as a true champion of anti-imperialism, world peace and the national liberation movements the world over. She was also instrumental in correcting the coloured image of India by the Western powers, especially the United States. After the liberation of Bangladesh, in which India played a catalytic role, Richard Nixon the, then US President and his Secretary of State, Henry Kissinger, considered India to be a "new Influential".

Although India was alleged to harbour a 'pro-Soviet' title in her foreign policy, given the threats to India's security at that point of time-especially from the neo-imperialist Western powers backing the so-called "Islamabad-Beijing-Washington triangle", New Delhi had no other viable alternative.

At the thick of the civil war in Pakistan during 1970-71, the Indo-Soviet Treaty of Friendship, Peace and Co-operation was signed in 1971 and it remained valid for 20 years. It provided that the two countries (India and erstwhile Soviet Union) would keep in touch with each other on major international problems affecting the interests of both the parties. "They will not enter into or participate in military alliance which is directed against any one of them. They will obtain from providing assistance to any third party that emerged in armed conflict with one of them. If any of the two parties is attacked, both will hold mutual consultations in order to remove such a threat ad take effective measures to ensure peace and security of the countries. Neither of the parties shall enter into alliance, secret or public, which is incompatible with the treaty".

Another major landmark of Indira Gandhi era was the signing of the Shimla Agreement. Even at her moment of glory after the dismemberment of Pakistan in 1971, she proved to the rest of the world that she would not be lacking in her initiative for peace, even with a hostile neighbour. The Shimla Agreement signed between India and Pakistan in July 1972 provides as follows: (i) Both the parties would resolve their differences by peaceful means through bilateral negotiations. Both committed themselves to peaceful coexistence, respect for each other's territorial integrity, sovereignty and non-interference in each other's internal affairs. (ii) Hostile propaganda against each other would be stopped (iii) Meeting between the Heads of Governments and their representatives of the two countries would be convened to discuss future ways and means for the establishment of durable peace and normalization of relations. As the present Indian government is seized with the hostile propaganda and covert interference by Pakistan in the internal affairs of India, Shimla Agreement needs to be read between the lines in order to comprehend the double standards of Islamabad in its dealings with New Delhi.

1.8 Janata Party Government: Mending Fences with Neighbours

During the brief Janata party rule (1977 to 1979) there was a dramatic U-turn in India's neighbourhood diplomacy. The Morarji Desai government maintained a studied silence, when the military regime, headed by Zia-ul Huq, after a farcical trail by the Pakistan Supreme Court, hanged the ousted premier Zulfiqar Ali Bhutto. The Janata government's indifference to such a 'judicial murder' was calculated move to improve India's links with the immediate neighbours. Such a policy is comparable to the delayed reaction of the Deva Gowda government to the merciless public hanging of former Afghanistan President, Nazibullah, by the Taliban-led rebel government in Kabul.

The Morarji government, in order to inject a dose of positive bilateralism, signed the hitherto unthinkable Salal Agreement with Pakistan. It also signed an Agreement with Bangladesh for equitable sharing of Ganga waters between India and Bangladesh. Two separate agreements on trade and transit were signed with Nepal. Thus in all sincerity, efforts were made by the then External Affairs Minister, Atal Behari Vajpayee, to improve India's ties with the South Asian neighbours. The Janata Government's efforts to normalize relations with China, did not bring enough dividends and Vajpayee's China visit was mistimed in the sense that during that period, China launched an offensive against Vietnam.

Another novel experiment during the Janata Phase was the so-called "genuine non-alignment" or a policy of equidistance between the two super powers. But in reality, the Desai government soon realized its futility, when the Jimmy Carter government in the US refused the shipment of enriched uranium to Tarapore plant on the ground that India was non-committal to the signing of the NPT and was 'insensitive to human rights violations in Kashmir'.

1.9 Globalization Drive

The world witnessed unforeseen changes in the undercurrent of international politics since the end to 1980s, as has been discussed at the outset and accordingly leaders like Rajiv Gandhi and Narsimha Rao decided to get rid of the old dogmas. India's development strategy was radically changed. New Delhi decided to favourably respond to global market forces especially when Man Mohan Singh took charge as the Finance Minister in the Rao Cabinet. Successful techniques were evolved to get rid of so-called "Hindu rate of growth." The India economy was deregulated to the maximum possible extent, as a result of which the rate of per capita growth, which never crossed 2 percent figure in the past four decades, started showing an upward swing to the extent that many western observes started calling India as the future "Asian tiger". The spree for liberalization and globalization brought India closer to the major global economic powers like USA, Canada, Germany, France, UK, Italy and Japan. New Delhi could also improve its political and trade relations with China, another emergent Asian tiger. However, while developing India's close links with major global powers.

India's image in the Third World and in the NAM suffered a relative decline.

1.10 Gujral Doctrine

The United Front Government headed by Deva Gowda and thereafter Inder Kumar Gujral inhered a stable economy with a comfortable rate of growth. The position of foreign exchange reserve showed over the years a considerable improvement. In spite of some tensions among the coalition partners about the internal issues of political corruption, autonomy of the provinces, demand for new states, management of the public sector undertakings and allocation of resources between the Union and the States, the Government could achieve a broad consensus on foreign policy and security issues not only among the United Front partners, but also between the government and the opposition. It was clearly demonstrated when all the major political parties like the Congress and BJP unanimously supported the Indian Government's opposition to the so-called Comprehensive Test Ban Treaty (CTBT) at the negotiation stage in Geneva and at the time of voting against a resolution in the UN General Assembly.

This solid domestic, consensus and the economic improvement enabled the United Front Government to earn respect abroad. When the then Foreign Minister, I.K. Gujral, visited South-East Asia in 1996, S. Jayakumar, Foreign Minister of Singapore, while welcoming Gujral on behalf of ASEAN on 24 July said, "India stands today as a strong economy with a GNP of more than US$ 280 billion and an enormous potential for rapid growth. In terms of GNP, it (India is now ranked fifth in the world. You can provide the ASEAN with vital links to the Indian Ocean. ASEAN, on the other, hand, can be India's spring board into the Asia-Pacific. It would be hard to imagine an Asia-Pacific century without India's participation." Since 1993, India is a Full Dialogue Partner (FDP) with the ASEAN on sectoral basis. Gujral, in his replay said, "The footprints of South-East Asia are to be seen in every aspect of India's ethos". He also clearly reiterated the new Government's commitment to achieve rapid economic growth through targeted involvement of foreign capital, technology, goods and services.

As regards India's emerging links with the major global powers like the US, Germany, France, UK, Canada, China and Japan, the United Front Government practically continued the earlier policy of mutually beneficial cooperation of crucial issues like trade, FDI and technical assistance. At the same time, the Government reserved its right to take an independent stands on global and regional security matters including nuclear non-proliferation. However, at this point, several critics attacked the dismal performance of our diplomacy in a race with Japan for a non-permanent Asian seat at the UN Security Council. The very fact that New Delhi could not muster the support of more than forty member-states, showed the need for a complete reappraisal of our mission at the UN and in other global forums.

The above-mentioned diplomatic fiasco notwithstanding, the United Front Government will be remembered for its impressive record of improving relations with the neighbours. The United Front Government's Foreign Minister and thereafter its Prime Minister, I.K. Gujral, achieved this through his innovative policy known as the Gujral Doctrine. This policy was based on two basic assumptions: Firstly, India being the most powerful country in the region on, should not insist on strict and immediate reciprocation from its smaller neighbours for its goodwill gestures. Secondly, Indo-Pakistan relations being a very complex one should be regarded as a separate category and first priority be given to improving less problematic relations with neighbours like Bangladesh, Nepal and Sri Lanka. Gujral, for example concluded the Farakka Agreement with Bangladesh by agreeing to provide more Ganga water to Dhaka and thereby earned the goodwill of this neighbour. While the installation of democratic and friendly governments in Nepal. Bangladesh and Sri Lanka in the 1990s facilitated the task of Gujral, fist as Foreign Minister in the V.P. Singh Government and thereafter as the author of the Gujral doctrine in the United Front Government, his contribution in improving India's ties with these countries through his tactful and farsighted approach cannot be gainsaid.

1.11 More Continuity than Changes

1.11.1 New World Order and the Need for Foreign Policy Reorientation: The 2007 is considered as on important decade of this century for the dramatic transformation. It has brought about all over the world. The pace of change has been for too swift for any conceptual interpretations. These changes have transcended all geographical and ideological boundaries, and have put questions to long established perceptions and theories. The cold war that lasted for well over four decades between the two super powers has ended and has ushered in the so-called new world order.

1. The collapse of the Soviet Union that brought the end of cold war and the consequent end of bipolarism.
2. The emergence of a uni-cum-multipolar world where there are various new centres of power, though US still has the dominant power variables at its command.
3. The sudden emergence of geo economics as the primary factor governing politics among states, as apposed to geo-political or geo-strategy, and related to this globalisation on a truly global scale.
4. Loss of manoeuvrability for the non-aligned bloc as a consequence of fading

Pre-polarism.

The changes have been so enormous that the foreign policy and security establishments around the world are stipulating on revision. India's defence and security exports are also gearing up for addressing to new problems and issues generated by the external events. There is a need to have a fresh look at our foreign policy.

New equations, new priorities of the powers that concern India, India's interface with the global economies in its liberalization efforts all have to be taken cognizance of.

The changed international political architecture has affected India economically, geo-strategically, regionally, and from the security perspective. The macro level issues which confront India are as follows:

1. The increasing and collective pressure by great powers on non-proliferation, arms control, and disarmament issues.
2. The international trends generated by some countries to control and deny access to sophisticated technologies in the super of space exploration and satellite developments.
3. To ensure projection of India's economic potential in a manner where the necessary external contributions to Indian economy will continue.
4. Issue of more immediate concern like:

- The onslaught of world public opinion against the recent nuclear test.
- Managing the impact of sanctions in the wake of the Pokhran tests.
- Managing the persistently adversarial relationship with Pakistan.
- Pressure on human rights issue.
- Pressure on opening up of Indian economy by world bodies.
- Preparing India for the next Century.

The year 1998-2007 marked a turning point in India's foreign policy as the BJP led coalition Government of Atal Behari Vajpayee assumed power amidst apprehensions of a right-wing lurch in India's domestic and foreign policies. The conducting of vie nuclear tests by the government in May 1998 confirmed this fear and shattered domestic consensus in foreign policy. These tests also isolated India at the International front.

A careful look at the present Government's policy, however, reveals more continuity than changes. This is evident from the fact that the Vajpayee Government is not only continuing with the attempts to improve India's ties with neighbours, but it even mustered courage to talk to Pakistan on the hard core issue of Kashmir, which Gujral had avoided. At the same time, the new Government attempted to strengthen people-to-people contacts between the two estranged neighbours through opening up of the New Delhi-Lahore bus service and encouraging India-Pakistan cricket matches despite strong opposition from its partner, the Shiv Sena and by reducing visa restrictions. Even the nuclear tests were in fact, the culmination of several previous regimes' strenuous effort towards this end. Unfortunately, like previous governments, the Vajpayee government, too, could not melt the ice in India-Pakistan relations. Though India could frustrate Pakistani designs in Kargil, Islamabad's military rulers are engaged in anti-India activities.

The BJP-led Government's ambiguity towards the Non-aligned Movement (NAM) also reflects continuity than changes in India's foreign policy in the post-Cold War era. Like the Narasimha Rao and United Front Governments, the Vajpayee Government, too, is making serious efforts to improve its ties with US led Western power block without formally jettisoning the NAM. Vajpayee and his foreign Minister Jaswant Singh have thus displayed understanding of the imperatives of the post Cold War world in which NAM has lost its dynamisms and vitality even though its agenda still remains relevant.

1.12 India's Current Foreign Policy Options

The major determinants of the foreign policy of any nation are its national security interests and its economic interests. Logically, it is these two national interests around which should revolve the various formulations of the country's foreign policy. Foreign policies of nations do not function in a vacuum insulated by delusional moral and ideological obsessions. Foreign policies perforce, have to take into account the prevailing regional and international strategic realities with which a nation has to strike workable equations based on one's own existing power attributes and strategic utility to the key global powers.

India's foreign policies in the last eight years under the previous Bharatiya Janata Party (BJP) led Government can be assessed as successful when measured against the above indicators. The BJP Government's foreign policies did make India "shine" in the international arena, not by delusional rhetoric but by an initial display of power potential by carrying out the nuclear weaponisation in 1998. It was a defining moment. Initial opposition by the United States and others were soon converted into opportunities for strategic partnerships/strategic cooperation with United States, Israel, France, UK, Vietnam and Myanmar. For the first time, even joint naval exercises were held with China. India's then foreign policies were also successful in bringing significant international pressure on Pakistan to change tack.

Foreign policies of any nation need bi-partisan support, as the country's national interests do not change with a change of political power. While the economic determinant could change in terms of nuances with a change of

Government, the national security determinant cannot and should not, as the strategic perspectives that go into its formulation have to be long range.

Regrettably, the new Indian Government, led by the Congress Party and through its flip-flop and ill-considered statements has given indications, that it is all set to undo the foreign policy gains of India in the last eight years.

The Congress Party's election manifesto, formulated by its present Foreign Minister reflected the Congress Party's traditional dislike of the United States and it also reflected this Party's resentment with the gains made by the BJP Government in terms of evolving a strategic partnership with the United States. In generic terms, India's new Government has three options open in relation to giving shape to its foreign policies, and these are as under:

- Non-alignment Foreign Policy.
- Independent Foreign Policy.
- India's Inter-dependent Foreign Policy with United States Option.

1.13 India's Foreign Policy: Achievements and Failures

The foundations of India's foreign policy were laid during the freedom movement. It is the product of a complex interplay of history, geography, past experience, present requirements, perceptions of the ruling elite of national interests and ideological consensus. It is also shaped and moulded by the domestic balance of forces, the regional balance of forces. History and geography give continuity to foreign policy, domestic and international circumstances produce changes. Morgenthau is of the opinion that national interest is the driving force behind a country's foreign policy. The principles of India's foreign policy have stood the test of time a belief in friendly relations with all countries of the world, the resolution of conflicts by peaceful means, the sovereign equality of all states, independence of thought and action as manifested in the principles of non-alignment and equity in the conduct of international relations.

India's foreign policies cannot be made captive to the delusional non-alignment gladiators or India's Communist Parties who have never been known for their objectivity or to India's minority Indian Muslims vote banks where every issue is viewed in a pan-Islamic context. In today's global security environment and the international strategic realities likely to persist for the next 50 years, India neither has the luxury nor the time to find new anchors for her foreign policies from the fossilised remains of Nehruvian Non-Alignment or her "presumed power potential" not concretised so far. In the last eight years the centre-piece of India's foreign policy has been the evolution of a strong political and strategic partnership with the United States. United States and India recognized the mutual convergences and imperatives and have been engaged in establishing a substantive bi-lateral relationship. India's national security and economic interests dictate that this is India's only foreign policy option available. India's national aspirations can best be met by formulating India's foreign policy inter-dependent with United States national interests and not in opposition to it In conclusion, it may be said that though the foreign policy of India has been condemned on various grounds, it cannot be decide that in the international arena. It is the best policy of India. it has combined the twin principles of idealism and pragmatism.

1.14 Foreign Policy of UPA Government (2004 Onwards)

The UPA Government has come out with a foreign policy which is purposeful, result-oriented and pro-active. India, today, enjoys a unique profile in the international arena as a factor of stability, a model of plural and secular democracy and an economic powerhouse that is destined to play a greater role in the international affairs. India's emergence as a compulsory destination in the itineraries of leaders from all parts of the world reflects the high standing and credibility that the Government and its leadership enjoy. Amongst the earliest crisis that the Government faced was the kidnapping of three Indians for ransom in Iraq. After more than a month's long patience and delicate effort, the Government was able to ensure safe return of hostages without sacrificing any principles. The successful and mature handling this crisis set the stage for reorientation of Indian Foreign Policy in the service of the nation in a rapidly transforming and ever more challenging global environment.

1.14.1 High Priority to Relations with Neighbours: The government has re-focused India's Foreign Policy giving high priority to relations with all its neighbours. The minister for External Affairs chose Nepal for his first visit after taking over his office. A number of high level visits have been hosted from the neighbouring countries, including both the president and the Prime Minister of Sri Lanka, the Prime Minister of Pakistan, King of Bhutan, the Prime Minister of Nepal and Foreign Minister, Commerce Minister and Finance Minister of Bangladesh have been among the recent visitors.

A major landmark has been the India-Pakistan composite dialogues along with the Indo-US relations. The visit of the Head of State of Myanmar to Delhi in November 2004, the first such visit in 26 years is another landmark. This has resulted in important cross-border projects being taken up and coordinated action to deal with insurgency in border areas. Similarly the Sino-Indian relations are going through a paradigm shift.

The Government's engagement with India's neighbours has not been limited only to Government-to-Government level but has consciously encompassed different sections of society and across the political spectrum. The UPA Government believes that it is important to have frequent and regular contacts and wide-ranging discussions with the neighbouring countries at all levels to take forward and to maximize opportunities for mutually beneficial cooperation.

At the same time, the government has not hesitated to address issues where there may be differences, but has done so in a spirit of friendship and in a constructive search for practical and mutually acceptable solutions. This will be the approach to the forthcoming SAARC summit, which will be held in Dhaka in January 2005. The present government remains committed to a collective future of peace and prosperity for the entire south Asian region.

In a strong message to the world and his countrymen, Prime Minister Manmohan Singh has declared that it was not a "clash of civilizations". Their confluence will shape the destiny of the 21st century and define the role of India and Asia in the new order. His blueprint for growth and partnership between India and the world, including Pakistan and South Asia, will be based on the "idea of India" and the concept of *'Vasudhaiva Kutumbakam"*— a world view in which cultures and civilisations can co-exist.

1.15 Challenges before India's Foreign Policy

Across the world today, there are different sensitive issues standing before our foreign policy objectives. These are as follows:

1. Terrorism is now under current.
2. Environmental problem has vitiated the atmosphere of India's foreign policy.
3. Human rights violation is now at stake.
4. State sovereignty is under siege, both domestically and externally.
5. Confusion in arms control agreements. Collective pressure by great powers.
6. Volatile and uncontrollable global financial market conditions.
7. The emergence of super-national regional groupings.
8. Cross-border criminality.
9. The influence of satellite television.
10. Anarchy of the internet.

The principles and operation of India's foreign policy have been subjected to much criticism. These are as follows:

1. It has been pointed out that too much importance has been attached to idealism.
2. The policy of non-alignment pursued by India has been subjected to criticism.
3. India's membership of the commonwealth has also been a subject of much criticism. It is alleged that this has restricted the freedom of action and prevented the country from pursuing an independent foreign policy.

4. It is alleged that India has completely neglected the vital principle of power in the conduct of international relations and laid more emphasis on peaceful settlement of international disputes.
5. The foreign policy has failed to produce the desired results. India has not only failed to set the Kashmir issue resolved but also protect the people of India from policy of discrimination being pursued by South Africa.

1.15.1 Neighbourhood: The first area of focus for India's foreign policy is the neighbourhood because unless we have a peaceful and prosperous periphery we will not be able to focus on our primary tasks of socio-economic development. India must, therefore, accord the highest priority to closer political, economic and cultural ties with her neighbours and committed to building strong and enduring partnerships with all her neighbours.

Each of India's neighbours is going through accelerated internal political transformations. Bhutan is consciously introducing a form of constitutional monarchy and democracy. Recognizing changed realities, a new India-Bhutan Friendship treaty to replace the earlier one of 1949 has been signed. Both sides ratified the treaty in March. The new treaty updates the legal basis of our bilateral relations and reflects contemporary reality. Nepal is undergoing a remarkable double transition: bringing into being a new democratic order while mainstreaming the Maoists. The transition, though delicately balanced, is on course, as evidenced in last week's formation of the interim government. While the basic decisions on the direction and nature of change lie with the Nepalese people, we have given our full support to Nepal in this process and remain committed to its success. In Bangladesh too the new interim government is taking steps towards transforming the political landscape. As a friend and neighbour, India is interested in a democratic, stable and prosperous Bangladesh. While our relations with Sri Lanka continue to develop steadily, we remain concerned about continuing ethnic conflict.

It is necessary to find a negotiated political settlement to the ethnic issue within the framework of a united Sri Lanka that is acceptable to all sections of Sri Lankan society. With Pakistan, the dialogue process continues to change the relationship. The composite dialogue, the Joint Commission and the Joint Anti-terrorism Mechanism have provided a structured framework within which major issues are discussed. For India, terrorism remains a particular concern. Infiltration continues from across the border. India always has stressed to Pakistan that the success of the dialogue process is predicated on Pakistan fulfilling its commitment not to permit any territory under its control to be used to support terrorism in any manner.

The challenge for India in the neighbourhood is to build inter-dependencies which not only integrate economies but also create vested interests in each other's stability and prosperity in the subcontinent. Interestingly, today India is not the issue in any of our neighbours' political transitions; rather, the countries of the neighbourhood look to the Indian market and economy as positive factors for their own economic growth. The smooth and productive course of the 14th SAARC Summit in Delhi, free of disputes or posturing, is a reflection of changing circumstances. The hope must be that as our engagement with each of neighbours increases, the value of our bilateral linkages will outweigh the attractions of sterile confrontation.

India will continue to work with each of the neighbours, through the innovative use of development partnerships, our economic and technological capabilities, the development of cross border infrastructure projects as well as our civilisational linkages, to achieve the goal of a peaceful periphery. In this process we are ready to provide benefits to our neighbours without necessarily insisting on reciprocity.

1.15.2 SAARC and India: In addition to India's bilateral relationships, the SAARC process as contributing to the goal of building a peaceful and prosperous periphery. At the recently concluded 14th SAARC Summit in New Delhi, all the SAARC members including newly-admitted Afghanistan agreed to a vision of a South Asian community where there was a smooth flow of goods, services, peoples, technologies, knowledge, capital, culture and ideas in the region. South Asia remains one of the least integrated regions in the world. Intra-regional trade is less than 5 percent of total regional trade. In addition, cross-border investments and the flow of ideas are at rather low levels. Starting from such a low base, greater integration among South Asian countries could bring huge benefits to the people of the region.

With present high growth rates in the countries of the region, India has an opportunity to advance together through trade, open borders and economic integration, and to bring about shared prosperity between India and her neighbours. Several practical steps were agreed, such as establishing a South Asia University, a SAARC Food Bank and operationalising the SAARC Development Fund. The SAARC Summit also agreed to work together to deal with water (including flood control), environment, energy and food security, involving multilateral organizations where necessary. It will be a challenge for India's diplomacy to translate these agreements into reality. As Chair of SAARC, it will be our endeavour to usher in a new phase of effective regional cooperation, reconnecting the subcontinent to itself and the world. It is thereby hoped to create a common space of prosperity in South Asia based on enhanced economic, trade and investment linkages and sustainable social and economic development.

1.15.3 World's Major Powers: The second set of challenges is that of managing India's relationship with the world's major powers. The world today is increasingly multivalent, marked by considerable political cooperation among major powers whose economies are becoming inextricably intertwined with each other. The current global economy is increasingly defined by freer and substantial movement of capital and by the technology revolution, in particular information technology. While capital is free to roam the world, other factors of production like labour and technology are not, and access to markets remains patchy. As a result of India's development, she is on both sides of a range of issues such as IPRs–where India is both a supplier and consumer. India need to therefore use her strengths to create partnerships with major powers in a manner which would allow us political and economic space to grow. This will require the foreign policy to strengthen relations with all the major powers of the world.

India's relations with the USA have been substantially transformed in the past few years resulting in wide-ranging engagement across many fields including defence and security issues, counterterrorism, science and technology, health, trade, space, energy, agriculture, maritime cooperation and the environment. The July 18, 2005 decision to cooperate in civil nuclear energy is a major symbol of this transformed relationship. India seek to arrive at an early agreement with the US on civil nuclear energy cooperation within the parameters laid out in the July 18, 2005 India-US Joint Statement and the March 2, 2006 Separation Plan. While cooperation in nuclear energy is no doubt a very important step, India should avoid the tendency to view relations with the US only within the narrow confines of civil nuclear cooperation. There are many diverse strands to our cooperation with the US, which are progressing well, and which will impart greater resilience to the bilateral relations in the future. Relations with the US are important to India, not just because it is the superpower, but also because of the positive effect it has on the dealings with the rest of the world, and on India's access to markets, high technology and resources crucial to our future economic growth and development.

India has developed a strong partnership with the European Union covering a wide range of areas including trade and investment, culture, science and technology. Our traditional relations with Russia continue to remain strong as evidenced in the recent visit of Russia's President Vladimir Putin as the Chief Guest at our Republic Day this year. Agreements reached during the visit will significantly expand our cooperation in the fields of energy, high technology, defence and space. The strategic partnership between India and Russia is poised to deepen even further. India's relations with Japan have also developed considerably with several exchanges of high level visits. There has been a qualitative shift in India-Japan relations following our Prime Minister's visit to Japan in December 2006 and the visit of the External Affairs Minister to Japan in March 2007 and we have agreed impart a strategic and global perspective to our partnership. The visit of Chinese President Hu Jintao to India in November 2006 strengthened the process of sustained comprehensive development of India-China relations. There have been some concerns expressed about the 'peaceful rise' of China. However, as PM has said, it is our belief that there is enough space for both of us to grow. We remain hopeful about steady progress in our relations with China, and at the same time will continue to work towards a resolution of the boundary question.

1.15.4 Global Power Blocs: As we look forward to an increasing role in global affairs India need to expand its network of international relationships, political engagement and economic and technical cooperation with the world. We are looking today at expanding circles of engagement, starting with the immediate neighbourhood, West Asia, Central Asia, South-east Asia and the Indian Ocean region.

This is reflected in India's political, economic and defence engagement with these regions. The Look East policy and the consequent intensified engagement with East and South-east Asia has led to the rebuilding of India's historically benign and stabilizing role in these regions premised on the commerce of ideas and goods.

Indian companies have long had a presence in South-east Asia. Now they are venturing farther and investing in China, Japan and Australia. ASEAN and its member states are important markets for our goods and services while South Korea and Japan are important sources of investment and technology. India thus need to strengthen political, physical and economic connectivity between India and East Asia and broaden the underpinnings of our quest for peace and prosperity. We are also adding important elements to our traditional ties with countries of the Persian Gulf region by leveraging economic opportunities.

If India's politics can create an enabling environment, the focus of her economic diplomacy in coming years will be on promoting trade and investment flows especially in critical areas such as infrastructure, in assuring predictable energy supplies and in securing the widest possible access to technologies. India also hopes to work towards significantly upgrading our economic relationship with South-east Asia, East Asia, Latin America and Africa, build new investment-driven partnerships with USA and EU, and nurture a web of cooperative energy security networks in Asia and with new suppliers in West Africa, Central Asia and Latin America.

1.16 Social, Economic, and Environmental Issues

Lastly, there is a cluster of issues of the future such as food, water, energy and climate change. These are inter-linked issues, and will have critical impact as India's ability to address them successfully will greatly shape our future. All these are cross-boundary issues, which require us to work with others to solve them. Some, like water and flood control and energy have solutions in our immediate or extended neighbourhood. Hence the Delhi SAARC Summit decision to undertake regional or sub-regional projects in these areas. Others, like the environment and climate change, are global in their nature and impact and need global solutions, and will directly affect our food, water and energy security. Our participation in drawing up those solutions is essential if the outcomes are to be satisfactory and if our development is not to be affected.

Last year India was a net importer of food after many years. The size of our population, economic growth and prosperity have led to consumption and life-style changes. Assuming a 7-8 percent GDP growth rate, by 2020 India would require 340 million tonnes of food-grains. This is a challenge both for scientists as well as for the agro-management of the rain-fed and dry-land farming areas. India needs a second Green Revolution, harnessing contemporary tools like bio-technology, water conservation and rain harvesting techniques and other steps which are environmental-friendly and economically sustainable. It also need to tap into the resources of developed countries. The India-US Agriculture Knowledge Initiative announced in July 2005, is a step in this direction and aims to address new challenges and facilitate agricultural research, education, and extension.

Food security is not only about food production because in India, 2/3rd of our population is dependent on agriculture for its livelihood. It is in this sense that international trade is a vitally inter-linked component. The impasse in international trade negotiations is disappointing for us. When agriculture was brought into the multilateral trade negotiations, developing countries were given a clear understanding that trade disparities created by agricultural subsidies would be phased out in a definite time frame. Unfortunately, the developed countries, so far, are reluctant to do away with their subsidies that render the playing field quite uneven.

Ensuring adequate water supply both for drinking and for agriculture and industry will also be a critical challenge for the future. While the Indian sub-continent is fortunate to have adequate resources, India has not seen enough collaboration in its use in the past. Hence, this must be reversed. As agreed at the SAARC Summit, India will work with her neighbours in this regard.

India's continued economic growth needs increases in the supply of cheap and sustainable sources of energy. Despite our large population and GDP growth averaging over 8 percent in the last few years, our per capita electricity consumption continues to be as low as 1/6th of the world average. Presently 67 percent of its electricity comes from burning fossil fuels, and 70 percent of the oil is imported. To meet our future energy requirements we will build partnerships with other countries who have surplus energy. Additionally India will has to increase the share of non-fossil fuel based energy resources in our energy mix. The India-US civil nuclear energy cooperation is one step in this direction.

The issue of climate change and global environmental degradation is also poised as a great challenge to the foreign policy of India. India is ready to work with others on the principle of "common but differentiated responsibilities" enshrined in the UN Framework Convention on Climate Change. This issue cannot be viewed in isolation and must be seen in the context of the developmental needs of developing countries. Today India has a very low per capita level of emissions and has an energy intensity per unit of GDP which matches the best in the developed world. India looks at climate change in the context of the promises made by the international community for technology transfer and additional financing since Rio, which have remained unfulfilled. Critical technologies which can have significant impact on de-carbonization, have been out of reach of developing countries because of prohibitive costs and the existing IPR regime. A related concern for India is that trade advantages should not be sought through the instrumentality of environmental treaties. This issue will be in sharp focus at the forthcoming G8 Summit, particularly after the report of the Inter-governmental Panel on Climate Change. Addressing climate change issues in a manner that also meets our concerns will be a major preoccupation for us in the foreseeable future.

1.17 Foreign Policy Priorities, 2011

It should be clear from our discussion thus far that sustaining India's economic growth and outward orientation, and ensuring the sustainability of that process, became an important driving element shaping Indian foreign policy in recent years. The key objectives were market access, energy security and access to high technology. These objectives gained greater salience in the context of the rise of Asian economies, and the consequent competition for markets and resources. The energy security objective became even more important in the context of global fears pertaining to global warming and climate change.

Greater economic integration will be a basis for greater security, enhanced cooperative efforts and stable relations Taken together these developmental objectives shaped Indian policy towards the major powers, especially the United

States, and towards its wider neighbourhood, especially ASEAN and East Asia, the developing world and major global issues of the day, including climate change.

1.17.1 Global Environment: The most important foreign policy priority for India, from the time of our independence, has been to secure for ourselves a global environment that is conducive, and if possible supportive, of our developmental aspirations. Improving the well-being of the Indian people and modernizing India's economy are our highest national policy priorities. Jawaharlal Nehru told the Constituent Assembly in December 1947: "Talking about foreign policies, the House must remember that these are not just empty struggles on a chess board. Behind them lie all manner of things. Ultimately, foreign policy is the outcome of economic policy." Hence, the key challenge and priority will be to build relationships around the world with big and small countries that enable us to push our development process forward and sustain a higher rate of economic growth in these turbulent and difficult times.

Indeed, the salience of the economic dimension to foreign policy will be even greater in the near term as the world grapples with a global economic slow down, threats of protectionism, reduced capital flows and the challenge of environmental degradation and global warming. To sustain our growth process, we will have to ensure our energy security, food security, macro-economic and financial stability, and market access for goods and services we export. In other words, we will need to bring in new investment.

1.17.2 Relations with All Major Powers: Each of these objectives have important foreign policy implications and will shape our relations with all major powers. How we are able to tackle each of these challenges will be influenced by the rapidly changing geo-politics and geo-economics of a world gripped by an economic slowdown.

Will the United States and China arrive at a new condominium–dubbed by some as Chimerica–to deal with their respective economic problems? The lesson China has learned from the collapse of the Soviet Union is that it must not waste its resources in a confrontation with the West. Rather, it must build itself up by working with the West. China has worked with the U.S. on many fronts, reserving its anger for only key national security issues like Taiwan and Tibet. On most multilateral economic and security issues, including terrorism and climate change, and in most multilateral organizations, including the UN Security Council and the International Monetary Fund, China has been happy to work with the U.S., rather than against it.

1.17.3 Global Economic Crisis: The global economic crisis has once again made allies out of two potential adversaries. China will use the economic crisis to increase its global influence in a manner that will not threaten the U.S. in the medium term. In turn, the Bush-Rice doctrine of containing China is being replaced by the Obama-Clinton doctrine of co-opting China to deal with the economic crisis. It will always remain a love-hate relationship, but that is what most affairs are anyway!

Such a U.S.-China condominium would worry Japan, Russia, India, and even the Europeans. It would pose a major challenge for Indian foreign policy, and require creative thinking rather than retreat into old dogmas. India must continue to seek good relations with the U.S., even as it nurtures old friendships with Russia, Europe and Japan, and manage China's rise.

1.17.4 Peace and Stability in Neighbourhood: Our second foreign policy priority has been, and will remain, our need to ensure peace and stability in our neighbourhood, and meaningful relations with our neighbours. We are surrounded by countries that are at war with themselves. Internal civil conflict and terrorism plague our region. India can not sustain high and stable growth in a chronically troubled neighbourhood.

1.17.5 Terrorism and Defeating the Forces of Extremism: Winning the fight against terrorism and defeating the forces of extremism and religious fundamentalism in our region is an important foreign policy and national security priority. The conflicts in our sub-continent have drawn in all major powers, including the U.S., Russia, China, European Union, Saudi Arabia, Iran, and Japan. Fighting terrorism and extremism in the region in the context of this complex power play will remain a major challenge for Indian foreign policy.

1.17.6 Shifts in Global Dynamics: In the past two decades India has been increasingly engaged with Asia around us: Southeast, East, West, and Central Asia and the Indian Ocean region, including Africa. Both our own growth process and shifts in global dynamics will require us to nurture this new relationship we have developed with our wider Asian and African neighbourhood. Here again, dealing with China's rising influence and creating new relationships through greater economic engagement will be a key challenge.

1.17.7 New Multi-polar World: Finally, as a new multi-polar world emerges and India grows into being one of the "poles", and is expected to take up global security responsibilities, Indian foreign policy will have to grow up from its days of innocence and adolescence to adulthood. India will have to learn to take sides, offer security to others (especially in our region), and address new challenges in the field of nuclear diplomacy. As a maritime power, India will have to bring its foreign policy in line with its national security policy; winning new friends without losing old ones.

1.18 Manmohan Singh Doctrine of Foreign Policy, 2011-12

Apart from the diplomacy around the negotiation of the civil nuclear energy cooperation agreement between India, the 45-member Nuclear Suppliers Group (NSG), and the United States, the other foreign policy pre-occupations of Prime Minister Manmohan Singh have been the diplomacy associated with the building of an East Asian Community; the revitalisation of the South Asian Association for Regional Cooperation (SAARC), with a focus on normalising relations with Pakistan; and increased South-South cooperation, with a focus on development cooperation in Africa. Economic issues have been at the core of each of these initiatives. Singh's primary objective has been to improve the global and regional environment for sustaining India's growth process and overall development. In an early comment on Singh's foreign policy initiatives, C. Raja Mohan outlined four elements of what he dubbed as the Manmohan Singh Doctrine. These four elements are as follows:

1. The changing weight of India in the global economy as a factor shaping its weight in global affairs.
2. Recognition of the new opportunities available to India, as a consequence of its economic growth and openness, to improve relations with all major powers.
3. Positive impact of a new approach to the developing world, based on India's economic globalisation, on regional integration in South Asia and bilateral relations with neighbours.
4. The recognition that as an open society and an open economy India can build bridges with the world on the foundations of its democratic, liberal, plural and secular credentials.

The Manmohan Singh Doctrine is a manifestation of India's economic resurgence in an era of greater economic openness. The success of India's external liberalisation and the reintegration of the Indian economy into the growth processes of East and Southeast Asian economies have played a vital role in the popular acceptance of the validity of the many postulates of this doctrine. For this reason, the continued relevance of the doctrine will be contingent upon India's continued pursuit of high economic growth within the framework of an open and increasingly globalised economy. It is also contingent upon the process of globalisation being more inclusive. If the global economy slips into a new era of protectionism, and if the current financial crisis and the global economic slowdown, with high energy and food prices, generates a backlash against globalisation, it could strengthen the domestic critics of the Manmohan Singh Doctrine in India. Equally, the doctrine's appeal to the outside world is premised on India remaining a high growth, open economy and an open society, marked by popular commitment to the values of a liberal, plural and secular democracy. An inward-looking, internally divided, bigoted and illiberal India would have little external standing, and no external appeal.

The economic basis of Singh's foreign policy initiatives, with a focus on his ideas of:

1. Inclusive globalisation.
2. Asymmetric liberalisation.
3. And the geo-political implications of India's integration into the global economy.

The Manmohan Singh Doctrine 2011 is premised upon:

1. India's ability to sustain the recent growth momentum, of an annual average growth rate of national income of close to nine percent.
2. Assurance of energy security, food security and livelihood security.
3. Growth process being socially and regionally more inclusive and balanced.
4. Fiscal and price stability and the fiscal empowerment of the State.
5. Pursuit of employment creating industrialization and rural development.
6. Remaining a globally open economy, while pursuing closer integration with the economies of South, West, Southeast and East Asia.
7. Remaining an open and plural society, socially and politically inclusive, liberal and secular.

In a further elaboration of this "realist" and "instrumentalist" perspective on foreign policy, Nehru added, "Whatever policy we may lay down, the art of conducting the foreign affairs of a country lies in finding out what is most advantageous to the country." It is this original Nehruvian 'realist' perspective that Singh brought back to Indian thinking on foreign policy.

Several factors contributed to this shift in Indian thinking on relations with the world and the role of economics and business in international relations.

First, the collapse of the Soviet Union and the consequent disruption of an important external trade relationship. It was not just the economic and strategic fallout of this that was debilitating for India, but also the political and diplomatic fall-out. The Soviet Union was an importance "balancer" from India's point of view in its negotiations with Organisation for Economic Co-operation and Development (OECD) countries, and with multilateral financial institutions. As recently as in 1980 Indira Gandhi used the "Soviet Card", as it were, in her negotiations with the International Monetary Fund (IMF) to secure improved terms for an extended financing facility loan.

Second, the balance of payments crisis of 1990-91 and the need to adopt a stabilisation and adjustment programme to secure financial support from the IMF and the World Bank. India also reached out to Japan for bilateral assistance and found Japan unwilling to extend such support without India adopting a clear programme of reform and adjustment. Finance Minister Yashwant Sinha had to return from Tokyo empty-handed, after having been kept waiting for an appointment with his counterpart.

Third, as a consequence of the balance of payments crisis, as a result of new thinking within the policy making establishment, and thanks to new trends in remittance inflows and foreign trade, India chose to move away from external aid and debt as major sources of balance of payments support and opt for foreign trade, especially services trade, and investment, especially portfolio flows, as sources of foreign exchange.

Fourth, the 1990s saw a major change in India's approach to foreign trade in general and to a multilateral trade regime in particular. India became a founding member of the World Trade Organization (WTO) and committed itself to multilateral rules of engagement in trade. India also began to seek regional and bilateral trade agreements on a parallel track and supported the idea of a South Asian Free Trade Agreement, to begin with, and soon expressed interest in an India-ASEAN Free Trade Agreement (FTA). India's 'Look East' policy and its interest in increasing its economic interaction with the Indian Ocean Rim countries also shaped India's relations with its wider "Southern Asian" neighbourhood.

Fifth, China's rise as an open economy and a trading nation had a profound impact on political and academic thinking within India and shaped public policy both with respect to domestic and external economic policy and with respect to India's foreign and strategic policy.

Sixth, as the 1990s progressed, and more in the first few years of the new century, India discovered its global prowess in the field of information technology. The business generated by the so-called "Y2K" problem followed by the growth of Indian information technology (IT) and IT-enabled services business, the "software and outsourcing" boom, and the growth in trade in services greatly changed attitudes towards globalisation and global integration.

Seventh, in more recent years the outward-orientation of Indian business has also increased. First inspired by the experience of IT firms such as Tata Consultancy Services, Infosys and WIPRO and, subsequently, by that of pharmaceutical majors like Ranbaxy and Dr. Reddy's, Indian business groups began to move away from their earlier inward-looking "Bombay Club" mentality to a more global orientation. The recent listing of Indians among "Forbes Billionaires" is only one visible symbol of Indian business making its mark outside.

Dr. Manmohan Singh was more expansive at the subsequent Combined

Commanders in October 2011 where he summarised his approach to strategic policy, "Our strategy has to be based on three broad pillars, **first**, to strengthen ourselves economically and technologically; **second**, to acquire adequate defence capability to counter and rebut threats to our security; and **third,** to seek partnerships both on the strategic front and on the economic and technological front to widen our policy and developmental options."

An important element of the Manmohan Singh Doctrine, flowing directly from the ideas of the South Commission, is called the idea of 'Asymmetric Liberalisation'. In the South Asian context, this idea has been referred to as "non-reciprocal" liberalisation. India's smaller neighbours expected India to do more in terms of providing market access than they would be asked to do for India.

2

Major Issues in Indian Foreign Policy

2.1 Kashmir Issue

2.1.1 Kashmir Dispute: The Kashmir problem has been the most important factor which has strained the relations between two countries. Under Indian independence Act of 1947, Kashmir like other states was given the choice to join either India or Pakistan or to retain an independent status. The king of Kashmir (Hari Singh) decided not to accede to either country. Pakistan, however was not happy with this decision and started applying pressure on Kashmir to gain its accession. Failing economic pressure Pakistan, allowed armed tribes to invade Kashmir. These tribesmen were assisted by regular troops of Pakistan army. In October 1947 failing to check the raiders, the Maharaja asked for India's assistance. Government of India, however, refused to give any assistance unless Kashmir acceded to India. After the king signed the accession letters, the Indian troops were sent to Kashmir on October 27, 1947. The Indian Army drove back the raiders.

In December 1947 India took the case to the United Nations complaining against Pakistan for aiding and abetting in the raid on Kashmir. However, Pakistan took the stand that while acceding the Maharaja of Kashmir (Hari Singh) had specially promised plebiscite. According to the letter "as soon as law and order have been restored in Kashmir and its soil cleared of the invaders, the question of state's accession should be settled by a reference to the people'. This according to government of India, did not imply plebiscite. In 1951 Kashmir elected its Constituent Assembly, which confirmed the accession to India in 1954. It declared Kashmir as a self-governing state within the Republic of India.

The Security Council appointed a Commission to arrange for cease-fires in Kashmir. The commission proposed cease-fire, demilitarization and plebiscite. In February 1950 Sir Owen Dixon, an Australian, was appointed as a Mediator. But soon he admitted his failure and resigned. He was followed by Frank D. Graham of USA who also could not achieve much success. India insisted on 'vacation of aggression' by Pakistan as a pre-condition for holding of plebiscite, which was not accepted by Pakistan. In 1954 Pakistan joined the SEATO and in 1955 the Baghdad Pact. Pakistan got lot of military assistance under these pacts. During this period India made an offer of 'no war pact' with Pakistan which was rejected by her. As a result, India became suspicious of Pakistan's designs.

As a result India made slight changes in her stand on Kashmir. In March 1956 Nehru said that the first essential step was for Pakistani troops to withdraw but they are still there. Hence 'all talks of plebiscite was completely beside the point'. Secondly India could not ignore the constitutional developments and economic progress in Kashmir. Thirdly, plebiscite would mean "uprooting of things that have become fixed, legally, constitutionally and practically." This obviously meant that India was not keen to hold a plebiscite in Kashmir.

The Security Council appointed a commission to arrange for cease-fire in Kashmir. The Commission proposed cease-fire, demilitarization and plebiscite. In February, 1950 Sir Owen Dixon, an Australian, was appointed as a Mediator. But soon he admitted his failure and resigned. He was followed by Frank D. Graham of USA who also could not achieve much success. India insisted on 'vacation of aggression' by Pakistan as a precondition for holding of plebiscite, which was not accepted by Pakistan. In 1954 Pakistan joined the SEATO and in 1955 the Baghdad Pact. Pakistan got lot of military assistance under these pacts. During this period India made an officer of 'no war pact' with Pakistan which was rejected by her. As a result, India became suspicious of Pakistan's designs.

As a result India made slight changes in her stand on Kashmir. In March 1956 Nehru said that the first essential step was for Pakistani troops to withdraw but they are still there. Hence, 'all talks of plebiscite was completely beside the point'. Secondly, India could not ignore the constitutional developments and economic progress in Kashmir. Thirdly, plebiscite would mean "uprooting of things that have become fixed-legally, constitutionally and practically." This obviously meant that India was not keen to hold a plebiscite in Kashmir.

In November 1956, Kashmir constituent Assembly adopted a Constitution for the State which was modelled on the Indian Constitution. Pakistan was not at all happy with all these developments. In 1965 (August) following the Kutch dispute, Pakistan sent organized grounds of infiltrators across the cease-fire line, and later mounted large-scale attack in the Chhamb-Jaurian area, violating the international border. Thereby she threatened the communication line of India in Kashmir. The Indian troops went into action and foiled the Pakistani designs. On September 2, 1965 the UN Secretary General U Thant appealed for cease-fire. Two days later the Council met and called upon the two countries to withdraw their forces to the old cease-fire line. This appeal was again repeated on September 9. The Council authorized U Thant, the Secretary-General to visit the two countries and bring about a peaceful settlement. As a result of his efforts India agreed to an unconditional cease-fire but Pakistan wanted a 'purposeful' cease-fire based on an 'honourable settlement of the Kashmir problem'.

Subsequently the dispute was resolved through the efforts of Soviet Union, who arranged a meeting between the leaders of the two countries at Tashkent. The Tashkent declaration was signed on January 10, 1966. By this declaration the two countries agreed to settle their disputes through peaceful methods. The two countries also agreed to withdraw their forces to the position on August 5, 1965. The Tashkent declaration was a landmark in the history of Indo-Pak relations. Though the Kashmir issue was not settled, the declaration opened up the possibility of maintaining peace in the subcontinent.

After the Tashkent declaration the relations between the two countries showed a sign of improvement. On August 15, 1968, Mrs. Indira Gandhi made an offer of 'no war pact' to Pakistan to end tension between the two countries. This offer was followed by an Indian proposal of January 1, 1969 for setting up joint machinery to examine all disputes with Pakistan. This proposal for bilateral machinery was to be implemented only if Pakistan agreed to no war pact. Pakistan also showed it inclination to improve the relations, Peking was however not happy over these developments. Soon the hijacking of Indian Airlines plane to Lahore and its ultimate destruction once again created tension in the relation of the two countries. India retaliated by withdrawing permission to fly Pakistani planes over India. However, the Kashmir problem continued to strain the relations between the two countries.

2.2 Sino-Indian Border War (1962)

China and India were two great nations also as a neighbouring countries which emerged in the post-colonial phase of world politics. They are also great ancient civilisations with a history and culture dating thousands of years. India and China has had a long history of friendly and peaceful-contacts. After the establishment of the People 's Republic in China in 1949, India was one of the few first countries to extend its official diplomatic recognition. That was done in 1949.

During the Korean War, India established close contacts with China and played a positive role in the united national in defence of Chinese interest, including its right to occupy the seat of permanent member in the Security Council, occupied by Taiwan, due to US and Western Power Politics. India refused to branch China an aggressor, for its entry in support of North Korea. On 29 April, 1954, India and China signed an agreement concerning Tibet, in which India gave up its extra-territorial rights in Tibet and recognised Chinese 'Suzerainty' over Tibet and China reaffirmed the 'autonomous status' of Tibet. It was in this agreement that both the countries have developed the famous five principles of co-existence, known as the doctrine of Panchsheel.

India played a leading role in the Geneva conference on Korean place, supporting Chinese position. In the first Afro-Asian conference held at Bandung, (April 1955), India was the main proponent of China's participation. Indo-Chinese relations remained normal indeed cordial till 1957. The leaders of two countries exchanged visits and fully cooperated each.

In 1957, there was shift in China's ideological perspective. The phase of "Sweet reasonableness" and "broad agreement" with friendly countries (1949-57) was replaced since 1957-58 by a phase of rigid-dogmatism and 'ideological militancy', resulting in general stiffeners towards several countries. There was a break with Moscow and estrangement with India. Border incursion in the North Eastern Frontier Agency began in 1957 and continued till 1959. In 1959, the Chinese laid claims to about 50,000 square miles of Indian Territory in NEFA and in Aksai Chin region of Ladakh in the North West. China also refused to accept the McMohan live as Sino-Indian border. The Chinese had defiantly built the Aksai Chin-Karakpra, highway, running through Indian territory of Ladakh. Attempts at peaceful negotiations in 1958-60, did not succeed. Tibet cast a shadow an Indo-Chinese relations after the Tibetan revolt in 1959 and the flight of Dalai Lama with Tibetan refugees to India. Misgivings, distrust, stiffening of attitudes finally ended up in the Sino-Indian border war of 1962.

That completely changed the nature of the Sino-Indian relationship. It also changed India's outlook and defence and strategic problems. Indian forces more than doubled in just two years, (1962-64), new divisions were raised, re-trained and re-equipped. India emerged as a major military power in the region. This helped it to rebuff Pakistan incursion in 1965 and rout the Pakistan army in the 1971 Bangladesh war, despite China's hostile attitude towards India and its open tilt towards Pakistan. China had trained Pakistani soldiers and supplied it with weapons and military hardware. The US-China-Pakistan axis remained a major threat to Indian security in the 70s and the early 80s.

After two decades of stalemate, Sino-Indian relations were re-established with the exchange of ambassadors after 1980. New efforts are being made since 1981 to normalize relations by defusing the border dispute and concentrating on other areas of mutual interest like commerce, technology and culture in order to first build a measure of trust and confidence, and then work on a new framework of healthy bilateralism.

The border between India and China had been fixed along McMahon Line in 1914 at a Conference held at Shimla. This conference was convened to sort out border differences between Nepal, Bhutan, Sikkim and Tibet. In this conference the representatives of British India, Tibet and China took part. After detailed negotiations an agreement was concluded whereby Tibet was divided into Inner

Tibet and Outer Tibet. The boundary between Outer Tibet and India was demarcated at the high mountain peaks. This line was drawn on the suggestion of Arthur Henry McMahon, who represented British India at the Shimla Conference. This line came to be known as McMahon Line and was treated as a lawfully demarcated border between India and China. It may be noted that though the representatives of China, British India and Tibet signed the map demarcating the line between India and China, the Chinese government did not ratify it. However, the government of China did not dispute this boundary line.

2.2.1 Starting Point of Border Dispute: Differences regarding boundary between India and China first appeared in 1954 when the Maps published in China showed a large part of Indian territory as Chinese. When India brought this to the notice of the Chinese authorities they argued that these maps were the copies of the old maps and would be revised in due course. In July 1954 China sent a protest note to India alleging that the Indian troops had illegally occupied Bu-Je (Barahooti), an area within Chinese territory. India rejected this protest and asserted that this area was located within the Indian state of Uttar Pradesh and an Indian post had existed there for long. In 1956 when Chinese Prime Minister Chou En Lai visited India has attention was drawn to the fact that the Chinese maps still continue to show parts of Indian territory as part of China. He assured the Indian leaders that McMahon line was acceptable to China and necessary corrections would be carried out in the maps.

In the meanwhile the Chinese troops continued to make intrusions into Indian territory and put forth claims to more Indian territory. Nehru addressed a letter to the Chinese Prime Minister against these intrusions in December, 1958. However, the Chinese Prime Minister replied that "the Sino-India boundary has never been formally delimited", and the so called McMahon Line was the product of British policy of aggression against Tibet region of China. It may be observed that in the meanwhile the Chinese had built 110 mile long road in Aksai Chin area and fully integrated Tibet in China.

In August 1959, a strong Chinese detachment crossed into Indian territory south of Gigyitun on the NEFA borer and fired on the Indian forward picket. They arrested the entire picket comprising of 12 members, even though eight of them managed to somehow escape. Thereafter, the Chinese detachment tried to overpower the outpost at Longju, located well within the Indian territory. China, however, claimed that Longju was indisputably Chinese territory and the Indian troops had set up outpost there in grave violation of China's territorial integrity. In September, 1959 Prime Minister Cho En-lai formally laid claim to 50,000 square miles of territory. In October, 1959 the Chinese troops ambushed a party of 19 Indians in Ladakh and killed 16 of them. This evoked strong public protest in India and a demand was made in certain quarters that diplomatic relations with China be snapped.

In April 1960, the Prime Ministers of India and China met to resolve the differences. However, in view of the mounting pressure of Indian public opinion much could not be achieved. The two leaders, however, agreed that the officials of the two governments should meet and examine the relevant documents. Three rounds of talks were held between the officials of two countries in latter half of 1960, but the situation did not improve. On the country during this period, China continued to introduce into Indian territory and consolidate its hold over the already occupied territory. All this convinced the Indian leadership that the security of border with China must be strengthened and it proceeded with the building of new outposts in its territory. These moves of India were highly presented by China and the situation seemed to be heading for a direct confrontation between the two.

In the meanwhile, on 12 July 1962, the Chinese seized an Indian police post in Galban Valley of Ladakh and took four Indian Jawans as capacity. India strongly protected against this aggression but the protest was ignored by China. In fact, China had already made up its mind to launch aggression against India and had taken several preliminary steps. Thus it had fully integrated Tibet in China; it had already suspended all activities on the Taiwan issue; it had concluded an agreement with Pakistan, an enemy of India; it had already occupied about 25,000 sq. miles of Indian territory. The illegal occupation of Indian territory by China and its hostile posture greatly disturbed India. This is evident from the observation of Nehru who said on 9 December 1959 "The whole picture of the world is changing so far as India is concerned and India's borders are concerned. Here is historical change of greatest magnitude. For the first time, two major powers of Asia face each other on an armed borer. For the first time, a world power or would-be-world power sits near our borders and frontiers".

2.2.2 Chinese Invasion: In January 1962, the Chinese crossed Longju in NEFA. In June 1962 they captured the Chip-Chap and Spanggur areas of Ladakh. On 8 September 1962 the Chinese crossed the McMahon line in the Eastern sector. For the next few days there were frequent exchange of fire between the Indian and the Chinese troops. Ultimately on 20 October, 1962 China launched a big offensive both in Western and Eastern sectors of the border, overwhelming the Indian frontier posts. The attack was so sudden and massive that the Indians could not face it and were routed in NEFA. As the Indian troops were not prepared and equipped to meet such a massive threat, within three weeks China was able to above over all the mountain passes and threaten the plains of Assam. In view of this serious threat from China, India decided to seek help from friendly nations. Before this help could be procured, China announced unilateral cease-fire on 21 November, 1962 and decided to withdraw 20 kilometres behind the line of actual control existing between Indian and China on November 7, 1959. It is noteworthy that the conflict between India and China cannot be described as an area, because no formal declaration diplomatic relations and their diplomatic missions continued to work, though only with a skeleton staff.

2.2.3 Colombo Conference: Soon after the declaration of unilateral cease fire by China, the Sri Lanka Prime Minister convened a conference of the non-aligned countries at Colombo on 10 December, 1962. This conference was attended by Sri Lanka, Burma, Indonesia, Egypt Ghana and Cambodia. The conference expressed the view that the cease-fire period should be utilized to seek peaceful solution of the Sino-Indian dispute. It suggested that China should withdraw its posts in the western sector by 10 kilometres; and India should maintain its existing military position in both the sectors. The area to be vacated by China should remain demilitarized and should be managed by neutral persons to be chosen by the two countries. In NEFA the line of actual control should be accepted by both the countries and shod be treated as cease-fire line. In the middle sector the position as on September 8, 1962 should be maintained and the find solution should be found through peaceful means.

The Colombo Proposals were accepted by India, but China insisted on certain conditions which were not acceptable to India. Thus, China insisted that it alone should maintain civil posts in Western demilitarized zone and India should not have any right in the area. Likewise in the eastern section the Indian troops shall not move up to McMahon line. After sometime, President Nasser of Egypt convened second conference of the Colombo Powers but nothing came out it.

2.2.4 Impact of Sino-Indian Border War: The Chinese invasions gave a serious set back to Sino-Indian relations as well as the prestige of India. The reverses suffered by India at the hands of China greatly undermined her position in they eyes of Asian and African countries. It encouraged Pakistan to think in terms of forcing a military solution of Kashmir on India. The border war also gave a serious set back to the Indian development. As the country had to divert extra funds for the defence of the country, it was forced to abandon several development plans. Above all the war made Indians more security conscious and the people rose as one person in defending their country. T.N. Kaul has brought out the impact of 1962 war thus "The lesson of our dealing with China was that as a non-aligned country we had to depend on ourselves and make the most of our resources. We had to become self-reliant in the economic and political fields to the maximum extend possible in the minimum possible time. We had to look for reliable friends who had a mutuality of interest with us and on whom we could rely in times of difficulty. The Chinese invasion of 1962 was the first serious threat to our policy on Non-alignment. But it increased our faith in this policy as it helped us to forge better and more enduring friendship stood us in good stead in later years."

2.3 Indo-Pak War of 1971

The complexities of India-Pakistan relations have always been hard to comprehend and difficult to unravel. Mutual suspicious has been arisen out of the bitter history of partition, disparity in geographical size, population, military strength, economic resources, and technical expertise. This has been compounded by the nature and working of domestic political structures and impact of international political alignments on Indo-Pakistan relations. Professor Kalim Bahadur (Pakistan Journey to nowhere), Professor Amitabh Matoo (Vision Kashmir), Professor Ali Engineer (Pakistan's Polity and its Viability), Professor Matin Zuberi (Pakistan's Nuclear Dilemma etc.), have focused the comprehensive review of Indo-Pak relations in their respective writings in World Focus, 2001. To them, the record of conflict between India and Pakistan is long and continuous. On 4th December, 1971 Pakistan made a declaration of War against India. Even before the declaration of war against India, on 3 December 1971 the Pakistan army started aggression in the western sector. They attacked several India posts on this side of the cease in Kashmir.

The Pakistan Air Force also resorted to heavy bombardment of several Indian air force stations in November India. In the midst of these developments Indian army units based in Agarthala were directed to march into East Pakistan. The Indian Air Force also organised several air attacks on Pakistan air force bases and inflicted heavy damages. Even the Indian navy played an effective role in the conduct of war. By 15 December, 1971 the Pakistani forces in East Bengal were surrounded by the Indian troops. As there was no scope for any escape, Lt. Gen. Niazi, the commander of the Pakistani troops in East Bengal, sent a message for cease fire on 15 December, 1971 but the offer was turned down by the Indian authorities. They asked Niazi to make an unconditional surrender. After some hesitation the Pakistan forces agreed to make a surrender.

On 16 December, 1971 Ltd. Gen. Niazi signed an Instrument of Surrender which was accepted by Lt. Gen. Jagjit Singh Aurora GOC-incharge of Indian and Bangladesh Forces in the Eastern command on behalf of the Indian armed forces. This surrender included all Pakistani land, air and naval forces as also all paramilitary forces and civil armed forces. These forces agreed to lay down their arms and surrender at the place where they were currently located to the nearest regular troops in the command of Ltd. Gen Jagjit Singh Aurora. On his part Lt.

Gen. Aurora gave a solemn assurance that personnel who surrender shall be treated with dignity and respect that soldiers are entitled to an accordance with the provisions of the Geneva Convention on guaranteed the safety and well being of all Pakistan military and paramilitary forces who surrender. In all about 91 thousand Pakistani troops made a surrender before the Indian authorities. They were taken as Prisoners of War (POWs) and brought to India. The war formally came to an end on 16 December 1971 when Pakistan accepted Indian decision to observe a cease-fire with effect from the mid-night of 16 December. Thus the war listed for only 13 days.

The Indo-Pak War of 1971 proved quite decisive and left a deep impact on the power structure in South Asian Subcontinent. It led to bifurcation of Pakistan and the emergence of a new sovereign state of Bangladesh. The creation of Bangladesh gave a serious blow to the 'two nation theory' which had led to the partition of India and creation of state of Pakistan on the basis of religion.

The war, though quite disastrous for Pakistan, brought certain indirect advantages to Pakistan. In the first place it made Pakistan geographically more compact and economically more close-knit. Secondly, it led to restoration of civil government in Pakistan after a gap of almost 14 years. Thirdly, the war forced the new Pakistan leadership to concentrate on the domestic affairs and not to harp on the favourite tune of threat from India. As the people of Pakistan got thoroughly disillusioned with the military leadership due to losses suffered by the country during the 1971 war, they showed willingness to support Z.A. Bhutto. This made it easy for Bhutto to formulate and execute radical economic and military measures to get Pakistan out of mess. Fourthly, the war paved the way for Indo-Pak detente. Bhutto, quite conscious of the new realities of the situation decided to enter into direct negotiations with India to ensure durable and honourable peace in the subcontinent.

2.3.1 Indo-Pak Talks: Though India emerged victorious out of 1971 war with Pakistan, it showed no inclination to punish or humiliate Pakistan. In fact soon after the liberation of Bangladesh, India offered cease-fire to Pakistan. On 31 December, 1971 Mrs. Indira Gandhi, the Prime Minister of India announced that the existing problems between the two countries can be solved only through direct negotiations between the two countries. As Bhutto was very keen to secure the release of the Pakistan Prisoners of War at the earliest, and a number of countries had already accorded recognition to the state of Bangladesh, it seemed that he had no other choice but to hold talks with India. After several weeks of diplomatic negotiations Mrs. Gandhi announced of April 4, 1972 that India and Pakistan were in direct tough. To pave the way for final talks emissary level talks were held at Murreee in April 1972. As a result of these talks it was agreed that

Mrs. Indira Gandhi and President Bhutto would meet in June 1972 to discuss matters pertaining to mutual relations between the two countries.

2.3.2 Shimla Conference: The proposed Summit Conference was held between Prime Minister Indira Gandhi and President Z.A. Bhutto at Shimla on June 28, 1972. The high level delegates which accompanied these two leaders held extensive discussion on various issues arising our of the war as well as on general bilateral issues. After prolonged negotiations lasting for five days, the two leaders signed Shimla Agreement on July 3, 1972.

2.3.3 Shimla Agreement: The agreement stated that both governments of India and Pakistan have resolved to put an end to the confrontation and conflict which has characterized their relations and to establish durable peace in the sub-continent so that the two countries may be able to devote their energies to the pressing need of promoting welfare of their people. The two countries affirmed their faith in the principles and objectives of the UN Charter and declared that they would resolve all their differences by peaceful means through bilateral negotiations. It was further agreed that pending final settlement of any of the problems between them, neither side would unilaterally after the situation and that both the sides shall prevent and discourage all such acts as may be countries agreed to respect the territorial integrity and sovereignty of each other. They expressed their faith in the principle of peaceful co-existence, and non-interference in each other's internal affairs.

Both the sides agreed to take steps for preventing hostile propaganda against each other and exchange, such information which would promote the cause of friendly relations between the two. Both the countries agreed to withdraw their forces to their respective sides of international borer. This withdrawal was to be completed within 30 days. With regard to Jammu and Kashmir the two countries agreed to respect the line of actual control as it existed at the time of declaration of cease-fire on 17 December 1971. Both the parties agreed not to change this line of control unilaterally or by force. For further normalization of their relations the two countries agreed to resume communications, promote travel, co-operate in economic and allied matters, and have exchanges in the cultural and scientific fields.

2.4 Liberation of Bangladesh

Indo-Bangladesh Relations began on a note of high level of cordiality due to India's sympathy and support to their struggle for a new identity. In 1972, a 25 years' treaty of friendship cooperation and peace was signed, together with the Indo-Bangladesh trade pact. Both the countries pledged to strengthen world peace and security and fight against colonialism, racialism and imperialism. Two years later in 1974, the Indo-Bangladesh border agreement was signed and longstanding Farakka Barrage dispute was amicably settled. There had been considerable expansion of cooperation. There had been considerable expansion of cooperation in social, cultural and economic fields. In the field of science and technology, the two countries agreed to cooperate. The era of cordial relations between the two countries came to an end with the overthrow of Sheikh Mujibur Rehman.

Internal upheavals consequent upon the assassination of Sheikh Mujibur Rehman in 1975 changed the political situation in Bangladesh. Democratic forces suffered a set back. Indo-Bangladesh relations deteriorated. Misperceptions and misapprehensions replaced the mood of mutual trust and friendship since then Indo-Bangladesh equations have been hovering between formally correct relations to relations clouded by latent tensions and reservations. is admitted at all hands that India played a vital role in the emergence of Bangladesh as an independent state. This role continued to undergo change according to the changing conditions.

During the initial stages India decided to follow the policy of non-intervention in the affairs of Pakistan and maintained complete neutrality. However, in the wake of atrocities committed by General Tikka Khan, the Pakistan General, on men, women and children of East Bengal, India expressed concern over violation of human rights. Later on when a large number of East Bengal refugees took shelter in India and caused a serious strain on the economy of the country, India exerted pressure on Pakistan to normalise conditions in East Bengal to facilitate the return of refugees to their homes. India even tried to built up international pressure on Pakistan to take back these refugees. Prime Minister Indira Gandhi and Indian External Affairs Ministers (Swaran Singh) undertook tours to several countries to secure support for a political settlement of Each Bengal Crisis, so that the return of refugees to their homes was facilitated.

However, as these efforts failed to produce the desired result, India decided to intervene effectively to resolve the crisis. India not only provided necessary help to the refugees but also joined hands with the multi-Hani to secure their rights. This involved India in a war with Pakistan in December 1971. Indian army formed a joint command with Mukti Bahini and inflicted a defeat on Pakistan army. This paved the way for the liberation of independent Bangladesh. India other countries also granted recognition to Bangladesh and thus completed the process of liberation of Bangladesh. For the attainment of this goal India made unparalleled sacrifices both in men and material. This was naturally acknowledged by the leaders of East Bengal and they tried to cultivate most intimate relations with India.

2.5 Indian Peace Keeping Force (IPKF) in Sri Lanka

When ethnic riots broke out in August 1983 India's major concern was to prevent the crisis from escalating to a degree that might warrant the involvement of extra regional powers. Therefore the Indian Prime Minister Indira Gandhi sent her Foreign Minister Narsimha Rao, to Colombo to ascertain the facts on the spot on July 29, 1983.

On his return from Sri Lanka, Narshima Rao informed the Prime Minister that the Sri Lankan situation was serious indeed and that the government of Sri Lanka had failed to bring the ethnic violence under control. He also confirmed media report that the Sri Lankan government has sought military assistance from the United States, Britain, Pakistan and Bangladesh to meet the crisis.

In a telephone conversation with Sri Lankan President J.R. Jayawardene, while hoping for an early restoration of normalcy, the Indian Prime Minister candidly expressed disapproval of the Lankan move in seeking foreign assistance "professedly to meet a non-existent Indian intervention".

Immediately after the ethnic violence Mrs. Indira Gandhi offered India's good officers to promote a dialogue between President Jayawardene and the moderate, Tamil United Liberation Front (TULF) and she sent her special envoy G. Parthasarthy to Colombo to further advance the process of reconciliation. After intensive discussions with the President of Sri Lanka, and leaders of political parties, Parthsarathy evolved a formula which would serve as the basis for talks between the government of Sri Lanka and the TULF.

Though President of Sri Lanka accepted the good offices of India, the Lankan government was not enthusiastic about India's intervention, because Sri Lankan leaders suspected that India was giving training facilities and sanctuary to the Tamil militants who were fighting a war against Sir Lanka's armed forces.

Indian perspective was concerned more with the geopolitical fallout of the ethnic crisis and the need to prevent foreign involvement. Sri Lanka's geopolitical location was another important factor that compelled India's anxiety over any destabilizing development in the Island. India's role in Sri Lanka's ethnic conflict and Indo-Lanka relations under Indira Gandhi need to be understood in this perspective vis-a-vis changed regional policy of India.

Israel and Pakistan were the two countries that actively helped Sri Lanka in its fight against the Tamil militants. The Israeli secret service MOSSAD gave counter insurgency training to Sri Lanka's security forces and Pakistan readily responded with arms and military training for the island's army. China, South Africa, Singapore and Malaysia are the other countries which supplied arms to Sri Lanka. Under Indira Gandhi a doctrine of regional security was developed. In 1984 serious internal ethnic conflicts broke out in Sri Lanka following government's decision to settle armed Sinhalese in the Tamil majority area. This was greatly resented by the Tamils and their guerrilla organization Liberation Tigers of the Tamil Eelam (LTTE) blew up banks, mined army vehicles and cut rail and telecommunication lines.

The Sri Lankan army also retaliated and burnt down several Tamil dominated towns and villages. This resulted in the death of many innocent Tamils, and large number of them crossed over to India, to escape oppression. In Sri Lanka's foreign relations India occupies a prominent place. This is due not only to disparities between these two countries in size, population, military strength and resource potential but also to the cultural relations between these two countries. Due to the following two reasons Indo-Sri Lanka relations have undergone several phases since both countries gained independence: (1) changing security situation in the region in general and in India in particular, and (2) internal political problems faced by both India and Sri Lanka.

Jawaharlal Nehru outlined the basic principles guiding India's foreign relations in a broadcast to the nation on September 7, 1946: "End of colonialism, and racialism, independence of African and Asian countries, independence from power blocks, support for United Nations, striving for world peace and cooperation, security through commonwealth membership, friendly relations with all countries and closer links with China and Asian neighbours". These objectives were based on the role that India wanted to play in world affairs. But Nehru did not develop a regional policy for India. A combination of many factors pertaining to South Asian region finally resulted in the emergence of a dual pattern of foreign policy–a pattern that was global as well as regional." Dualism was the broad framework that was considerably discernible in India's foreign policy behaviour during Nehruvian era." Therefore it cold be argued that both globalism and regionalism have always been present in India's foreign policy. But "through the years, and under different leaders, a trends has emerged where the relative importance of globalism has slowly declined while regionalism has acquired a much larger place in India's foreign policy."

At the global level India built up her image as a non-aligned, peaceful, friendly and anti-imperialist country. Considerable efforts were made during Nehru's premiership to build up this image. It is appropriate at this juncture to evaluate India's regional policy. The military impasse in which India found herself during her first encounter with Pakistan 1948 and the humiliating defeat she suffered at the hands of Chinese in 1962 made Indian leaders to change their regional policy. The military impasse in which India found herself during her first encounter with Pakistan in 1948 and the humiliating defeat she suffered at the hands of Chinese in 1962 made Indian leaders to change their regional policy.

The broad Indian policy towards South Asia, After Nehru has revolved around the following six objectives:

1. Policies of accelerating the strategy of increasing India's military.
2. The confrontational aspect of Indo-Pakistan relations.
3. Increasingly unstable violent and guerrilla like situation that has developed within its boundaries.
4. Politics of bilateralism in her relations with her South Asian neighbours.
5. Eliminate or reduce Chinese influence in the states of the region.
6. Disallow the destabilization of any internal or external forces that are perceived inimical.

There were few such cases of destabilization for example:

1. The influx of large number of economic and political refugees from Bangladesh has seriously destabilized Assam and other areas on northeast.
2. The United Liberation Front of Assam (ULFA) a guerrilla movement operating from the area, has made Assam more unsettled an chaotic than ever.
3. The large number of Nepalese, traditionally residing in India have started a movement for the establishment of an autonomous Gorkahland.
4. The existence of a parallel government in Pakistan occupied Kashmir (POK) territory.
5. Sri Lanka's ethnic conflict and its destabilizing effect in Tamil Nadu.

Although the conflict between the Sinhalese and the Tamils in the post-independence period cold be traced to the adoption of Sinhalese as the only Official Language of the country in 1956, it reached a stage of open confrontation only in the late 1970s.

Since 1949, the Sri Lankan Tamils have been demanding regional autonomy for the Tamil dominated areas. As opportunities for public service employment dwindled as a result of economic stagnation in the 1960s and 1970s, communal antagonism between the Sinhalese and the Tamils sharpened. The leaders of the Sri Lankan Tamil community that they were discriminated against by the Sinhalese dominated government in state employment, higher education particularly at university level and in distribution of land.

In the last week of July 1983, Sri Lanka witnessed unprecedented racial riots with extensive destruction of factories, shops and houses and brutal attack and killings of defenceless Tamil people. With the July 1983 riots in Sri Lanka, a wave of spontaneous indignation swept through Tamil Nadu and life in that state came to a stand still with large number joining in public processions and meetings against the killing of Tamil in Sri Lanka. The Tamil Nadu Chief Minister M.G. Ramchandara convened an all party meeting on 28 July 1983 in Madras which condemned in no uncertain terms the killing of Tamils in Sri

Lanka. He urged the government of India to intervene to have Tamils in Sri Lanka. The Tamil United National convention held at Vaddukoddai in May 1976 decided to change its demand from that of federalism to separatism. It argued that all attempts by the Tamil political leadership to find a solution within the unitary constitution had failed. These developments provided the background for Indian involvement in the Sri Lankan ethnic conflict. Also, the Sri Lankan Tamil youths who campaigned for a separate state in the island were alleged to have had centres for training guerrillas in Tamil Nadu. This became a controversial issue between the two countries during 1983 and 1984.

The ethnic conflict in Sri Lanka became explosive in the late 1970s and in early 1980s due to the escalation of the struggle against the armed forces of Sri Lanka by Tamil militants.

2.5.1 Demand for Recall of IPKF: Despite the commendable role played by the IPKF in restoring peace in the war-torn island, President Premadasa gave a call for the recall of IPKF from Sri Lanka by 29 July 1989. India objected to the imposition of this unilateral deadline and initiated that the terms of the agreement must be fulfilled. As a protest against this stand of India, Sri Lanka refused to take part in the meeting of the SAARC Foreign Ministers at Islamabad in July 1989. Talks were initiated to defuse the situation which resulted in the conclusion of an agreement for withdrawal of IPKF. Under the agreement, a peace Committee comprising of representatives of various political and ethnic groups in north-east was set up. In the means while, though India continued with the programme of phased withdrawal of peace-keeping forces from Sri Lanka, the leaders of Sri Lanka were not happy with the pace of withdrawal.

With the assumption of power by the National Front Government in India, the relations between India and Sri Lanka showed some improvement. The new government in India expedited the process of withdrawal of IPKF from Sri Lanka. In January 1991, the two countries reached an agreement that the final solution to the vexed ethic problem of Sri Lanka could be found only through political settlement. The two countries also agreed to upgrade the existing joint trade committees. Sri Lanka on its part agreed to accept 2,00,000 Sri Lankan refugees camping in Tamil Nadu. India assured Sri Lanka that it would not be a party to any plan for political disintegration of Sri Lanka and undertook not to allow its territory to be used as base for terrorist activities against the island Republic. This undertaking of India greatly contributed to easing of tension between two countries.

After the withdrawal of Peace Keeping Forces from Sri Lanka, India tried to avoid involvement in the activities of the Tamil militants on the plea that it was an internal matter of Sri Lanka. However, the exodus of Sri Lankan Tamils in

India on account of policy of repression by Sri Lanka towards them, gave rise to problem of law and order in India. In May 1991, former Primer Minister Rajiv Gandhi was assassinated by a human bomb of LTTEE. This convinced India that the presence of LTTE refugees in India posed a serious threat to sovereignty and integrity of India. It placed an immediate ban on LTTE and announced a decision to expedite the process of repatriation of Sri Lankan refugees to their country. This hard stand of India evoked strong protests in Sri Lanka and India was accessed of making an attempt to destroy the peace process in Sri Lanka.

In the wake of SAARC Summit at Colombo in November 1991 the relations between the two countries got further strained because President Premadasa put the entire blame for the collapse of the summit on India. He even took advantage of India's absence from the summit and held informal talks with the leaders of Pakistan, Bangladesh and Maldives, where he displayed open hostility towards India. However, during the subsequent months the relations between the two countries showed an improvement. In January 1992, India and Sri Lankan reached an agreement on the repatriation of Tamil refugees to Sri Lanka. By July 1992, more than 23,000 of the officially registered 120,000 Sri Lankan Tamil refugees were flows to Sri Lanka. In October 1992 President Premadasa paid a visit to India and displayed an attitude which was at complete variance with the earlier views of Sri Lanka on questions on role of IPKF, the Indo-Sri Lankan Pact, and attitude towards LTTE.

He played down the differences over the Indo-Sri Lankan agreement and reiterated his country's commitment to devise a peaceful, negotiated and honourable settlement of the ethnic issue with the involvement of all concerned parties. Thus, the visit was quite fruitful in so far it greatly contributed to the reduction of mutual mistrust. This change in Sri Lankan attitude was evident from the fact that in December 1992, Sri Lanka turned down the demand of Pakistan to raise the Babri Masjid issue in the forthcoming SAARC meeting. In the economic field also the two countries tried to increase co-operation. As a result of this understanding trade between the two countries showed considerable increase. Thus, the hostility which characterized Indo-Sri Lanka a few years back gradually disappeared, even though the continued ethnic conflict continued to be an irritant in their relations.

The visit of President Chandrikak Kumaratunga to India in 1995 helped in re-establishing friendly and mutually beneficial ties between the two countries. During her visit to India she proposed a free-trade and investment agreement to boost economic co-operation between two countries. India also adopted a more realistic approach to the ethnic problem of Sri Lanka. In fact by now, the leaders of the two countries had come to raise that they must collaborate in fighting terrorism and improving their relations through regular contacts and consultations.

In June 1996, the Foreign Minister of Sri Lanka paid a visit to India with a view to further strengthen relations between two countries. During this visit the Indian Prime Minister (H.D. Deve Gowda) assured him that India would not extend any support to LTTE. In fact, India further extended the ban on LTTE for two yeas. In January 1997, Indian Foreign Minister (I.K. Gujral) paid a visit to Sri Lanka and announced several unilateral trade and other concessions to Sri Lanka, as a part of his good neighbourly policy. He also indicated India's desire to promote closer cultural relations with Sri Lanka and announced the decision to set up a cultural centre in Colombo. The policy of development of closer relations with Sri Lanka was also continued by BJP led coalition government of Atal Behari Vajpayee.

It is clear from the above survey of Indo-Sri Lankan relations that after some initial differences between the two countries, on account of differing foreign policy perceptions, the relations between India and Sri Lanka tended to grow along smooth lines and the leaders of two countries took similar stand's on various international issues. They also tried to develop closer economic and cultural ties. However, the issue of Tamilian minorities in Sri Lanka and denial of citizenship to them by Sri Lanka continued to train relations between the two countries. But ultimately the leaders of the two countries on account of strong historical and cultural links between the two countries, succeeded in developing close socio-economic relations. The two countries also affirmed their faith in peaceful co-existence and non-interference in each other's internal affairs. Unmindful of the Tamil problems they tried to develop friendly and co-operative relations in other spheres. The SAARC membership of the two countries also facilitated the development of closer relations.

2.6 India as Military Nuclear Power (1998)

Right from Independence, India has favoured, harnessing of nuclear energy for country's development needs. Pandit Jawaharlal Nehru, the first Prime Minister of India, from the very beginning realised the important and big role which nuclear energy could play in the socio-economic development of the country and laid emphasis on development of atomic technology for peaceful proposes. For this purpose he took steps to establish nuclear research centres, experimental nuclear reactors, nuclear reactor and nuclear power plants. In short, he did practically every thing with a view to harness the atom of peaceful purposes. This policy of peaceful use of nuclear energy was followed by Lal Bahadur Shastri as well as Mrs. Indira Gandhi. In fact under Indira Gandhi, India carried out its first underground nuclear experiment for peaceful purposes in the Pokhran range of Rajasthan desert on 18 May 1974. It may be noted that the conduct of this test by India did not in any way conflict with the commitment of the country as a signatory to the Partial Test Ban Treaty of 1963 because this treaty prohibited nuclear test only in atmosphere, including outer space or under water including territorial waters or high seas. India also did not make use of the plutonium made available for the Tarapur and Rana Pratap Sagar.

The explosion produced mixed reaction. While Pakistan felt terribly upset, the Western powers, especially USA were not exactly happy. Canada also reacted sharply and suspended all nuclear aid till the implications of the nuclear test were discussed. The western critics argued that the border line between peaceful energy and military nuclear explosions was very thin and India's peaceful nuclear explosions really constituted a step towards nuclear proliferation with strong military and non-peaceful potential. It was further argued that conduct of peaceful nuclear explosion was serious strain on India's economy and resources, and would in no way contribute to the socio-economic reconstruction of the country.

The Afro-Asian countries by the large took the things in their stride, and looked upon the experiment as a step in the search and development carried on by India in the field of atomic energy for advanced purposes. Within the country the Pokharan implosion was by and large welcome because it elevated India's status in the international community. The Jan Sangh leaders while endorsing the government stand of developing nuclear energy for peaceful purposes insisted that time had come when India's defence arrangements must also be given a nuclear dimension. L.K. Advani, in his residential address to Jan Sangh said on 3 March 1975, "The influence which China has come to wiled in global matters owns not small measures to its nuclear ability. Let us not dilly dally on this question any longer, and unmindful of the annoyance, and displeasure of Super Powers let us decide to give India's defence a nuclear dimension". However, the government did not favour abandonment of its traditional policy and continued to insist on use of nuclear energy for peaceful purposes only.

India's policy regarding peaceful use of nuclear energy underwent a change under Morarji Desai's government which took the stand that India would not conduct another peaceful nuclear explosion. Once again with the assumption of power by India Gandhi, the government reiterated that India was fully committed to pursue a peaceful nuclear policy and would not hesitate to conduct peaceful nuclear explosions for the promotion of indigenous nuclear research and technology. In view of the difficulties created by US in the supply of fuel for Tarapur plant, the government decided to step up nuclear research in nuclear fuel reprocessing technology, fast breeder reactor technology and other related areas of research with a view to attain self-reliance in nuclear technology.

However, India did not conduct another peaceful nuclear explosion. Despite Pakistan's threat to engulf the continent in nuclear warfare India has refused to deviate from the above policy and make nuclear weapons. It still holds faith in the policy of developing nuclear technology for peaceful uses and favours more and more indigenization of nuclear technology.

"The government successfully resisted the pressure from various quarters to adopt the path of nuclear weaponization, even though it asserted that it would react suitably and revise its stand if Pakistan went nuclear."

India also expressed concern over the proliferation of nuclear weapons and highlighted the dangers of proliferation. It extended support to the resolution sponsored by Ireland which demanded prevention of the dissemination of nuclear weapons and proposed restriction on the non-nuclear states regarding manufacture of nuclear weapons themselves or acquiring them for other states. However, India made it clear that the resolution should not be taken to mean that the Assembly either sanctified what had been done by the power by way of manufacture of nuclear weapons or retention of nuclear weapons by the existing nuclear weapons power.

India has been consistent opponent of the Nuclear weapons ever since there Independence. In fact, even before India gained Independence the Indian leaders expressed their shock over the dropping of the bomb at Hiroshima and Nagasaki which resulted in enormous loss of life and property. After Independence, India from every possible platform carried out a crusade against nuclear weapons and tried to wean the nations away from the path of nuclear armaments. Mr. Jawaharlal Nehru, the first Prime Minister of India and In charge of the Department of Atomic Energy stated on more than one occasions that India had nothing to do with the atom bomb and she should like to sue the nuclear energy stated on more that one occasions that India had nothing to do with the atom bomb and she should like to use the nuclear energy for peaceful purpose only.

For example while inaugurating India's Nuclear Reactor Apsara at Trombey in January 1957 he said: "No man can prophesy the future, but I should like to say on behalf of my Government of India that whatever might happen, whatever the circumstances, we shall never use this atomic energy for evil purposes. There is no condition attached to this assurance, because once a condition is attached, the value of such an assurance does not go very fat."

At the various international forums also India advocated the elimination and prohibition of the use of nuclear weapons. As early as 1948, India's representatives told the U.N. General Assembly that India stands for the exploitation of the nuclear energy only for peaceful purpose. India was willing to concede necessary powers to the international atomic development authority to ensure peaceful uses of the nuclear energy. However, India firmly opposed the idea of giving to that Authority any power which restricted the national sovereignty of a nation.

India stood for complete eliminating of the nuclear weapons and asserted that the contention of USA and USSR "that the atomic weapons would be used only to resist aggression" was not valid. Thus, Krishna Menon told the plenary meeting of the General Assembly that to talk of use of atomic weapons for limited purposes was fantastic. He said: "We shall never support in any circumstances, even if it happens to be pushed to a doctrine which says that the atomic weapons may be used as an instrument of war".

In 1961, India supported the resolution of Sweden which asked the Secretary General "to make an inquiry into the condition under which the countries not possessing nuclear weapons might be willing to give specific undertaking to refrain from manufacturing or otherwise acquiring them and to receive in future nuclear weapons in their territory on behalf of any other country." To eliminate the dangers of more countries manufacturing nuclear weapons India suggested that:

- All those nations which were as yet not manufacturing these weapons should undertake not to do so.
- The weapons already in existence should be confined to the territory of the nations which manufactured them.
- The nations possessing nuclear weapons should bind themselves by a treaty banning nuclear tests and pending such a treaty, they should refrain from such tests. In addition to this India also pleaded for the dismantlement or conversion to peaceful use of all existing nuclear weapons.

After the Sino-Indian conflict, in view of the possibility of China acquiring an atom bomb, there was a strong demand from certain quarters, that India should undertake production of nuclear weapons as a part of country's long term defence effort against China. This demand grew louder after the Chinese exploded a bomb in 1964. The then Prime Minister (Lal Bahadur Shastri) while sharing the concern of the people and Members of Parliament, reiterated the decision of his government not to produce the atom bomb for moral as well as practical considerations. He said that making of nuclear weapons would neither be in the interests of the country, nor would it benefit the mankind in any way. On practical grounds also he ruled out the bomb because it was bound to adversely affect the national economy of the country.

In the wake of Indo-Pakistan War of 1965 and the menacing postures adopted by China, a memorandum containing signatures of about 100 Members of

Parliament belonging to all parties was presented to the Prime Minister demanding an immediate decision to develop nuclear weapons. However the leadership ruled out any change in the policy and continued to express faith in the principles of utilizing the nuclear energy for peaceful purposes only.

After the explosion of the third bomb by China in May 1966, the demand for production of bomb by India grew still louder. In the election manifestoes of 1967, a number of political parties included the manufacture of nuclear weapons and missiles as their programme. They insisted on the need of harnessing of the atom bomb both for peaceful development as well as for the manufacture of nuclear weapons.

In August 1967 the two superpowers proposed a non-proliferation treaty at the Geneva Conference. India expressed its opposition to the treaty on the ground that the treaty would deprive the non nuclear countries of the benefits of the development of peaceful nuclear technology. Swaran Singh, the then India's Defence Minister told the U.N. General Assembly on 6 October 1966: "While the Government of India continue to be in favour of non-proliferation of nuclear weapons, it is equally strongly in favour of the proliferation of nuclear technology for peaceful purposes as essential means by which the developing countries can get benefit from the best advances of science and technology in this field". Similarly the Indian representative told the Eighteen-Nation Disarmament committee that "India is willing to agree to international regulation under a non-discriminatory and universal system of safeguards to ensure that no country manufactures or stockpiles nuclear weapons" while undertaking research and development of peaceful nuclear explosives.

The opposition of India to the Non-Proliferation Treaty was in the main on account of the fact that it neither assured equality to all nations, big or small, nuclear weapons states or non-nuclear weapons states, nor conceded equal rights to all countries to tame the atom. On the other hand it sought to keep the existing international power structure intact, completely disregarding the aspirations of the developing countries.

India has taken keen interest in nuclear disarmament and has been actively working with leaders of Sweden, Greece, Mexico, Argentina and Tanzania to promote nuclear disarmament. The leaders of these six countries have been meeting at regular intervals and urging the nuclear power to work for nuclear disarmament. They held such meetings at New Delhi, Ixtapa (Mexico) and Stockholm. The first meeting held at Stockholm on January 21, 1988, coming in the wake of the INF treaty between United States and Soviet, expressed satisfaction over the INF treaty but asserted that it would reduce the nuclear weapons by only four percent and called for expeditious efforts to achieve greater nuclear disarmament.

In the Special Sessions of the UN Disarmament in June 1988 Prime Minister Rajiv Gandhi proposed a three-stage time bound action plan to eliminate all nuclear weapons by 2010. He proposed that in the first stage the INF treaty should be followed by 50 percent cut in Soviet and US strategic arsenals. All production of nuclear weapons and weapon-grade fissionable material should cease immediately. To set the stage for negotiations on a comprehensive test ban treaty, moratorium on testing of nuclear weapons should be immediately imposed. He also proposed banning other weapons of mass destruction and suggested steps for precluding the development of new weapons systems based on emerging technologies.

He emphasised that negotiations must commence in the first stage itself for a new treaty to replace the NPT which was due to expire in 1995. The new treaty should give legal effect to the binding commitment of nuclear weapons states to eliminate all nuclear arms by the year 2010. The new treaty should also bind those nations which are capable of crossing the nuclear weapons threshold to undertake to restrain themselves. India also emphasised the need of restricting the development of military technology because the momentum of development of military technology was dragging the arms race out of political control. It emphasized the need of devising arrangement for controlling the continuous qualitative upgrading of nuclear verification system to ensure that no new nuclear weapons are produced any where in the world. Above all the plan emphasised the need of reducing conventional armaments and forces because without it there could be no progress in nuclear disarmament. It asserted that the key task before the international community is to ensure security at lower levels of conventional defence. Reductions must begin in areas where the bulk of the world's conventional arms and forces are concentrated.

In January 1993, India along with more than 60 nations, including five permanent members of the Security Council, signed the Paris Convention which prohibits the use of and elimination of chemical weapon within fifteen years. The convention also contains strong provisions for international inspections of suspected violations. It is noteworthy that India decided to sign the convention obligations of the member states regarding possession and elimination of weapons in a time phased manner under a stringent verification regime.

On the other hand, India refused to sign the NPT because it did not eliminate weapons discrimination in favour of nuclear powers and did not provide for an effective verification. Explaining India's stand on NPT, Prime Minister Narsimha Rao said in June 1992 "India could not sign the NPT because destruction in the world. But the fact remains that these weapons are today in the possession of some countries. There are some countries which do possess the capacity to produce weapons but have not chosen to do so. "Nuclear war would, however, affect all the countries—the haves (Nuclear haves) and have nots (Nuclear have-nots). The so called threshold states should give an undertaking that they will not cross the threshold and there could be a ban on the testing of such weapons and the production of fissile material. And at the end of the stipulated period it must be ensured that there were no nuclear weapons anywhere in the world.

In October 1993, India gave a call for an international convention on Non-Use of Nuclear Weapons and freeze on the production of such weapons and fissile material for atomic arms. It pleaded that the problem of elimination of nuclear weapons can be; resolved in the same manner in which the convention on chemical weapons had sought to eliminate the chemical weapons without any discrimination.

In May 1995 when a global conference on extension of Nuclear Non-Proliferation Treat (NPT) was held in New York and the general consensus was in favour of permanent extension of NPT, India refused to support the extension of NPT on account of its discriminatory nature, because the treaty permitted only five countries the United States, the United Kingdom, Russia, China and France, to legally possess nuclear weapon capability.

In other words, the extension of the non-proliferation treaty (NPT) was virtually a declaration by the nuclear weapon states that they have exclusive right to hold nuclear weapon in perpetuity. Further, the nuclear weapon states were not willing to accept the goal of finally moving towards 'nuclear weapon free world'.

Again in 1996 when the question of approval of Comprehensive Test Ban Treaty (CTBT) arose, India voted against it on the ground that it would sign the treaty only after the nuclear five agreed on a time-table for total removal of nuclear weapons. The treaty, according to India, was defective in so far as it does not have a fixed deadline for the elimination of all nuclear weapons. India's chief negotiator Ms. Arundhati Ghose, declared in the General Assembly that 'India world never sign this unequal treaty not now, not later until the major nuclear powers formulate a time-table for elimination of their nuclear arsenal'. The Indian external affairs minister (I.K. Gujral) however made it clear that the decision not to sign the CTBT does not mean that we are going in for new weapons, particularly nuclear weapons. It may be observed that the decision of the Government of India to oppose the CTBT was based on open and intense national debate and reflected the national consensus.

It is evident from the preceding discussion that India has followed two-fold nuclear policy. On the one hand it had tried to develop nuclear technology and capability for peaceful proposes, at the same time keeping the option open for its use for military proposes in the event of unforeseen eventuality. On the other hand India had consistently pleaded for universal nuclear disarmament.

2.6.1 Demand for Production of Nuclear Weapons: In view of the changed international environments and reported nuclear programme of Pakistan, a demand was made in certain quarters that India should go nuclear. Though Indian leaders asserted time and again that India did not want to divert its resources from socio-economic development programme to nuclear weapons programme, but in view of threat to its security on account of development of nuclear bomb by Pakistan, it had to yield to the public pressure.

2.6.2 Pokharan Test: In May 1998, India conducted five Nuclear tests at Pokhran, in order to develop a full-fledged nuclear deterrent to safeguard India's security. However, the Indian Prime Minister (Atal Bihari Vajpayee) declared that India's nuclear weapons would not be used to commit aggression or mount threat. He further assured that the country would not engage in arms race and announced a moratorium on further tests. India also indicated readiness to discuss a 'no first use' agreement with Pakistan and other countries, either bilaterally or multilaterally. India also indicated its willingness to take part in the negotiations on Fissile Material Cut Off Treaty.

The conduct of nuclear tests by India evoked strong protests from various quarters. While France merely expressed concern over Indian explosions, USA and Britain took a tough stand and favoured imposition of 'full sanctions' against India. Russia said that it 'felt let down', and China expressed 'serious concern' over the tests. Germany immediately froze fresh development aid worth 300 million D.M Japan also announced its decision to review its billion dollar aid loans to India. Both Australia and New Zealand recalled their High Commissioners as protest. European Union asserted that the explosions run counter to the treaties against nuclear testing and proliferation and would affect the peace and stability of South Asia. However, it refused to impose any sanctions against India or stop aid. US President also imposed sanctions under the 1994 Nuclear Proliferation prevention Act. This implied that 51.3 million dollar development aid to India from USA would be cut off.

China's reaction was very sharp. It accused India of 'undermining the international effort in banning nuclear tests so as to obtain hegemony in South Asia in defiance of world opinion'. It demanded that India should stop its nuclear development programme. Pakistan also severally condemned the Indian explosions. Pakistan's Foreign Minister (Gohar Ayub) said that the Indian leadership had gone berserk. Pakistan also decided to go ahead with nuclear tests and exploded six devices within 20 days of Indian explosions. This was viewed by the international community with great concern which imposed sanctions against Pakistan as well.

It is hoped, that with both India and Pakistan going overtly nuclear, that deterrence would work in South Asia (as it did work in the case of US and Soviet Union, Britain and France, and China and Russia). It is desirable that the leaders of India should adopt more conciliatory attitude towards China and Pakistan and take necessary steps for damage limitations in bilateral relations with China and Pakistan. On the other hand China must also appreciate the announcement of Indian Prime Minister Indian moratorium on further nuclear testing. The leader of India and Pakistan must also realize the importance of de-escalation of tension on both sides of the borders and conclude 'no first use of nuclear weapons' agreement. In fact, diplomacy and diplomatic negotiations alone can help promote peace and security in the subcontinent and not nuclear weapons and nuclear arms race, which would be costly and disastrous for both.

2.6.3 India's Nuclear Doctrine: In 1998, PM Atal Behari Vajpayee propounded a nuclear doctrine for India. The doctrine is based on three principles. These are as follows:

1. Minimum Nuclear Deterrence.
2. No first use.
3. No use against non-nuclear tests.

To ensure the independence and integrity of the country, the country would maintain a minimum but credible nuclear deterrent. The PM clarified that India can maintain credibility of nuclear deterrent in future without testing. He said that India and already announced a voluntary 'moratorium' and expressed willingness to move towards its dejure formalisation. The PM said that the only purpose of India's nuclear arsenal was to prevent blackmail from other nuclear powers. India had no interest in engaging other states in the arms race and would keep its arsenal at the lowest possible level required for credible deterrence. It may be noted that the minimum deterrence refers to a level of nuclear capability which will deter aggression and coercive diplomacy.

PM Vajpayee preferred to make a unilateral commitment and announced no first use doctrine. This implies India is not to first use nuclear weapons against unclear weapon states. To effectively deal with the nuclear adversaries India must be able to weapons deploy and deliver a second strike within 24 hours and capable of inflicting unacceptable damage on the adversary.

India has committed not to use nuclear weapons against non-nuclear weapons states.

2.6.4 National Convention for Nuclear Disarmament: The convention was held at the New Delhi in November 2000 and adopted a Charter for nuclear disarmament and peace. It identified the agenda for India as well as nuclear weapon countries and those on the nuclear threshold. The Agenda with regard to India stated that there should be no assembly of nuclear weapons, no induction and development of nuclear weapons and no acquisition and development of advanced research into nuclear weapons. The convention demanded similar measures of nuclear restraint from Pakistan. The Convention urged the five nuclear powers to immediately de-alert their nuclear weapons systems; stop further research into advanced nuclear weapons; and to take pledge of 'no first use'.

2.7 War against Terrorism

International terrorism has emerged as a global problem affecting countries in all regions. This is a particularly grave problem in situations, where terrorism is sponsored by States across national frontiers against other countries in quest for territorial expansion. The resolution adopted by the Sixth Committee on "Measures to Eliminate International Terrorism" underlines growing international consensus to prevent and combat terrorism. India has contributed to strengthening this consensus. India is party to major international conventions against terrorism. India has also proposed a Comprehensive Convention against International Terrorism. The 53rd UNGA gave legislative mandate to negotiate this convention on a priority basis, after discussions on the draft conventions against nuclear terrorism and financing of terrorist activities have been completed. As a country deeply affected by the menace of terrorism, India stands ready to extend cooperation to UN's efforts to curb this problem.

2.7.1 Global Nature of the Problem: Threat of terrorism is no longer limited to a particular country or region. It transcends international boundaries. Advance in technology and communications has extended the reach of groups and States sponsoring terrorism. Sarin gas attack in Tokyo some years ago has raised the danger of weapons of mass destruction falling into the hands of terrorists. Terrorists use electronic media to organise their subversive activities. They have access to flow of funds from abroad, including money raised through so called charitable organisations. They enjoy foreign sanctuaries. They are answerable to none. They violate international standards of human rights, and humanitarian law, with impunity.

2.7.2 International Terrorism as an Instrument of State Policy: Organised terrorism as an instrument of policy by certain states is very different in scale, nature and consequences than actions of stray individuals and groups. Sustained campaign of terrorist violence is not possible without sanctuaries, training, financing, encouragement and assistance by States. Government patronage gives terrorist groups and individuals enormous resources and safe haven. As the object of terrorism sponsored by States is to destabilise other countries and governments, it poses a threat to international peace and security.

The Declaration on "Measures to Eliminate International Terrorism" enjoins a positive obligation on Member States to ensure that not only the government organs do not sponsor terrorism, but their territory is not used by terrorist groups and individuals. The argument that a given State was not responsible for actions of terrorist groups based on its territory, is not tenable. The Declaration also clearly lays down that acts of terrorism are criminal acts, whatever the underlying considerations. Support to terrorism in any form - political, diplomatic, moral or material must be condemned. Nexus between terrorism, fundamentalism and drug trafficking pose a threat to civil society, democratic pluralism and human rights.

2.7.3 Need for Strengthening Legal Framework: The problem of international terrorism has to be addressed by strengthening international legal regime as well as domestic legislation and implementation. The UNGA resolution "Measures to Eliminate International Terrorism" has urged the Member States to ensure that the jurisdiction of their courts enables them to bring to trial the perpetrators of terrorist acts and to cooperate with and provide assistance to other states and relevant international and regional organisations. The success of this effort requires political will on part of the Member States.

2.7.4 Comprehensive Convention against International Terrorism: Existing international conventions against terrorism do not adequately address the issue of State responsibility to prevent and refrain from acts of terrorism. This concept is reflected in the Security Council resolutions imposing sanctions on States accused of sponsoring terrorism. A legal convention adopted by the UN General Assembly would provide a more broad-based basis for combating international terrorism and avoid controversies arising from unilateral action. India has therefore, proposed adoption of a comprehensive convention against international terrorism. A draft has already been circulated. During 53rd UNGA session, the Sixth Committee also gave legislative mandate to negotiate the proposed Convention on priority basis after conclusion of discussions on draft conventions currently under consideration.

2.7.5 India's Contribution to Preventing and Combating Terrorism: India has played a major part in strengthening international consensus against terrorism in UN, NAM and SAARC fora. India is party to major international conventions against terrorism, and has also incorporated them in domestic legislation:

1. Convention on Offences and certain other Acts committed on Board Aircraft, signed at Tokyo on 14th September, 1963. This Convention has been given effect to in India by the Tokyo Convention Act, 1975 (20 of 1975).
2. Convention for the Suppression of Unlawful Seizure of Aircraft, signed at the Hague on 16th September, 1973. This Convention is implemented

through the Anti-Hijacking Act, 1982 (Act No. 65) of 1982).

3. Convention for the Suppression of Unlawful Acts against the Safety of Civil Aviation, concluded at Montreal on 23rd September, 1971 and the 1988 Protocol for the Suppression of Unlawful Acts of Violence at Airports serving International Civil Aviation Suppression of Unlawful Acts against Safety of Civil Aviation Act, 1982 (66 of 1982). This Convention is implemented through the Suppression of Unlawful Acts Against Safety of Civil Aviation Act, 1982 (66 of 1982).
4. Convention on the Prevention and Punishment. of Crimes against Internationally Protected Persons, including Diplomatic Agents, adopted in New York on 14th December, 1973. This Convention is implemented through the provisions of the Indian Penal Code, 1960.
5. International Convention against the taking of hostages, adopted in New York on 7th December, 1979. This is given effect in India under section 364 A of the Indian Penal Code, 1960.
6. UN Convention against Illicit Traffic in Narcotic Drugs and Psychotropic Substances, 1988. This is implemented in India by the Narcotic Drug and Psychotropic Substances (amendment) Act, 1989 which amended the Narcotic Drugs and Psychotropic Substances Act, 1985.
7. International Conventions against the taking of hostages, adopted in New York on 7th December, 1979.

The Government has signed and ratified the International Convention for the Suppression of Terrorism.

India is party to the following regional conventions:

- SAARC Convention on the Suppression of Terrorism, 1987 This is implemented in India by SAARC Convention (Suppression of Terrorism) Act, 1993 (36 of 1993).
- SAARC Convention on Narcotic Drugs and Psychotropic Substances, 1990.

Since the provisions are basically based on the UN 1988 Convention, the provisions of the SAARC Convention on the Suppression of Terrorism are implementable under the Narcotic Drugs and Psychotropic Substances Act, 1985 as amended in 1989.

India has also played a role in evolving NAM consensus against terrorism. NAM has unequivocally affirmed that criminal acts intended or calculated to provoke a state of terror in the general public, a group of persons or particular persons, for whatever purposes, are unjustifiable. XII NAM Summit at Durban in 1998 has also re-affirmed that all Member States have an obligation to refrain from organising, assisting or participating in terrorist acts in the territories of other States. The Summit unequivocally condemned any political, diplomatic, moral or material support to terrorism. The NAM Summit also called for early adoption and implementation of a comprehensive convention against international terrorism.

2.7.6 Impact of International Terrorism in India: Since 1988, India has suffered total of 45,182 terrorist incidents in J&K alone. Though in many incidents security forces were targeted but majority involved attacks on civilians.

Pakistan supported terrorists are also responsible for 2,466 kidnappings and 791 cases of extortion since 1989. Pakistan supported terrorism also resulted in extensive destruction of property in J&K. There were targeted attacks on educational institutions (780) in a bid to destroy the modem education system, which the fundamentalist ideology of the terrorists did not approve.

Since 1988, security forces have recovered very large number of weapons from terrorists in J&K. This included 889 rocket launchers, 347 rockets, 1525 rocket boosters, 1124 machine guns, 20,193 AK series rifles, 34,141 grenades, 21,332 kilograms of explosives and 1970 bombs. The range and sophistication of weapons show the intensity of terrorist campaign, which cannot be sustained without the support of Pakistan (or neighbouring country) in violation of all bilateral and international commitments.

Pakistan has also supported terrorism in other parts of India. On March 12, 1993, serial blasts in Mumbai resulted in killings of around 260 persons and injury to 700 others. The loss of property was estimated at ₹ 270 million. According to some of the culprits arrested, 22 persons involved in the blasts had received training in handling arms/explosives in Pakistan in February 1993. The weapons and explosives used in the blast were brought to India by boats which picked up their consignments from a Pakistan Marine Agency vessel near the Karachi coast.

During the period 4-10 July, 1995 member of the terrorist group 'AL FARAN' kidnapped 4 British citizens, 3 US citizens, One German and one Norwegian to use as hostages in their demand for the release of 3 important HUA (Harkatul Ansar) of Pakistani nationality and some other militants.

There were six incidents of hijacking of Indian Airlines aircraft since the eruption of terrorist activities in Punjab. Attempts were made in all these cases to take the aircrafts to Pakistan. The hijackers succeeded in hijacking the aircrafts to Pakistan in two cases. In September 1981, a Delhi-Amritsar-Srinagar flight was hijacked to Lahore by Dal Khalsa commandos who demanded the release of Bhindranwale. In August 1982, two flights—one from Delhi to Srinagar and the other from Jodhpur were diverted to Amritsar. Two planes hijacked in July and August 1984 ended up on Lahore and Dubai respectively.

A human bomb attack was made on Beant Singh, Chief Minister of Punjab on

August 31, 1995. The attack resulted in assassination of Punjab Chief Minister, killing of 17 others and injury to many more. The attack was carried out by a hardcore terrorist group based in Pakistan, where they were given sanctuary and assistance by the ISI.

Terrorist's trained in Pakistan carried out a series of explosions in India during 1997. This included 26 explosions in Delhi killing 11 persons and injuring 241, 5 explosions in Haryana during 1996/97 killing 1 and injuring 39 and 3 explosions in UP during October 1997 killing 2 and injuring 19 persons. The culprits arrested revealed that they received training in Pakistan Occupied Kashmir.

According to well documented reports from international sources, Pakistan continues to provide sanctuary to terrorist groups like former Harkat-ul-Ansar and current Harkat-ul-Mujahidin and Lashkar-e-Taiba, which have threatened not only targets in India, but also in many other countries. These organisations enjoy safe haven in Pakistan, openly raise funds and recruit new cadres. Pakistan has also used Afghan territory and nationals to foment terrorist activities in India as well as other parts of the world. The UNGA Declaration "Measures to Eliminate International Terrorism" states that acts of terrorism are criminal acts and unjustifiable whatever the considerations of a political, philosophical, ideological, racial, ethnic, religious or any other nature that may be invoked to justify them.

Pakistan's actions are not only violative of the basic norms relating to conduct of inter-state relations, but also of the bilateral treaty obligations flowing out of the Shimla Agreement and Lahore Declaration. Under the Lahore Declaration, the two countries have reaffirmed their condemnation of terrorism and their determination to combat this menace.

2.8 India's Approach to Human Rights

In 1947, India emerged from the dark shadow of colonial rule through a historic non-violent struggle for independence led by Mahatma Gandhi. The people of India, across the length and breadth of the country and encompassing every segment of our society, exercised their right to self-determination. In their hour of triumph, they recognised the cardinal importance of efforts to universalise the enjoyment of this basic right of all peoples still struggling under colonial rule. It has been India's privilege to play a leading role in the historic struggle for de-colonisation. The right of peoples under alien subjugation, domination and exploitation, to freely determine their political status and freely pursue their economic, social and cultural development was recognised as a result of initiatives in which India, as a founder member of the Non-aligned Movement, was at the forefront. Today, the majority of the membership of the UN comprises former colonies; this is clearly a measure of the success of the historic struggle for self-determination.

One glaring and unfortunate exception is Palestine. India remains steadfast in its support for and solidarity with the people of Palestine, as they struggle to realise the inalienable right of self-determination, and achieve their goal of a sovereign, independent State of Palestine with well-defined and secured borders, living at peace with the State of Israel.

India's consistent view is that self-determination is a right applicable to the people of non-self-governing colonies and trust territories. The Declaration on Principles of International Law concerning Friendly Relations and Cooperation Among States adopted in 1970, and subsequently the Vienna Declaration and Programme for Action adopted at the World Conference on Human Rights in 1993 in particular addressed themselves to the question of self-determination. They asserted that the right of self determination shall not be construed as authorising or encouraging any action which would dismember or impair, totally or in part, the territorial integrity or political unity of sovereign and independent States conducting themselves in compliance with the principle of equal rights and self determination of peoples and thus possessed of a Government representing the whole people belonging to the territory without discrimination of any kind. It has also been recognized that any attempt aimed at the partial or total disruption of the national unity and territorial integrity of a State or country or at its political independence is incompatible with the purposes and principles of the UN Charter. The principle of equal rights and self-determination of peoples enjoins that every State shall refrain from any action aimed at the partial or total disruption of the national unity and territorial integrity of any other State or country.

In the international arena, India played an active part in the drafting of the International Convention on the Elimination of all forms of Racial Discrimination and was among its early signatories. It is therefore a matter of deep concern to India that there has been a recrudescence of racism, xenophobia, exclusivism and racial profiling in many parts of the world, including in those countries which are signatories to the Convention. These trends pose a serious challenge to the attainment of internationally accepted human rights standards and laws. The first and foremost priority therefore has to be the display of political will by states to implement the commitments they have assumed, and to abide by their international obligations. Secondly, there is need for countries which have not done so to immediately ratify the Convention.

3

India and the Non-aligned Movement (NAM)

3.1 Non-aligned Movement: An Introduction

Whatever be the claims of the leading players of the *Non-aligned Movement* (NAM) on its relevance in the present day changed context, there is no denying to the widespread cynicism about its role and its capacity to live up to its professions. The talk of its relevance would carry conviction only if it is seen as producing results and what is equally important could command the attention of the industrialized nations as represented by the G-8.Assuming that it is able to carve out a place for itself in the international field, the movement would remain vulnerable on many counts. Beginning with a grouping of about 50 nations, it is now more than 185 strong and as such, unwieldy to be able to evolve a unified approach to the diverse challenges facing their people. While recognising the inevitability of honest differences of opinion, it would be hard to dispel the suspicion that some member states allow themselves to be used as the tools of big powers, outside the movement only to wreck it from within. This may be too uncharitable a characterisation of the strong convictions of some of them but, given the realities of global politics, it needs to be mentioned because of the severe blows received by NAM. The NAM would be operating in an inhabitable climate needs to be recognised.

This is a strange irony that the NAM consists of the majority of the nations, but it is susceptible to the pressures of the powerful minority. The industrialized few have just to show indifference in order to convey a message to the developing world. That is what happened when the Indonesian president and chairman of NAM was able to obtain a grudging admission in the Parlour of the Halifax Summit of the G-8, but there was nothing to suggest that he could convey the concerns of the movement to the club of the rich. The NAM needs to hammer out concrete plans of action to deal with the arrogance of the industrialized nations.

The developing world is not that powerless. It has some effective leverages. The real problem is whether it is in a position to mobilise the support of the mass of its members to activate its strength. It has the advantage of numbers barring the universal organisations like the UN, no other grouping has so many nations in its fold. It has a vast spread, covering all the continents and geographical regions.

It is at the receiving end of social injustice, economic imbalances and all of its nations share the pinch. In some cases, the conditions are distressing what with about one billion of their inhabitants living in extreme poverty, 500 millions suffering from hunger and unemployment growing at an alarming rate. This shared misery should create a joint stake in united, ameliorative actions. That is the first strong point of the NAM.

Their second strength is the sum total of their markets. The developing world provides the bulk of the consumers for the products manufactured by the rich nations. Now that the era of state controlled economics is a thing of the past and the market forces are at work. It is possible for the NAM nations to change the unfavourable terms of trade and on the one hand, get remunerative prices for the primary goods supplied by them and thus prevent their exploitation and on the other, ensure through well-planned strategies that they do not to pay exorbitant prices for the products manufactured by the industrialised nations. The size of the market commanded by the developing world places it in a commanding position.

The advantage is opting to be lost by the uncontrolled display of divisions in the non-aligned ranks. The trouble arises when it causes permanent divisions, bitterness and acrimony. One has not to go far to be clear about the potential of such a danger. Pakistan could be depended upon to strike discordant notes and thus distract the attention of the NAM from its cherished objective. It would be a pleasant surprise if the Pakistan PM resists the temptations of raising Kashmir at the NAM forum.

In the case of SAARC, Pakistan has been campaigning feverishly to amend the charter, especially the provision which bars the discussion of contentions problems and bilateral disputes. Of course, it has not had its way. In the case of NAM, it has succeeded in so far its proposal for establishing a mechanism for setting bilateral disputes remains on the table. It found a place in the Jakarta Declaration and may be reiterated at the meeting. But Pakistan would have to reckon with the situation whereby the international community's bored to death due to the recurring references to Kashmir in world fora.

Whatever its strength or weaknesses, the NAM is set to address issues the relevance of which to its member-nations could not be underestimated. The Jakarta meeting was the first to be held well after the end of the cold war and as such sought to reassess its relevance and to charter a new course. This process will continue. It will mean addressing the unfinished agenda covering major areas such as:

- Disarmament.
- North-South Dialogue.
- South-South Cooperation.

- Reform of UN.
- Expansion of the Security Council.
- Human Rights.
- Peacekeeping.
- Environment etc.

The summit document reaffirms the continued validity and relevance of the principles and objectives of the movement. These include the safeguarding of the independence, territorial integrity and sovereignty of states, the attainment of general and complete disarmament under effective international control self-determination of peoples under domination and colonial or foreign occupation, equality among nations, full respect for international law, the democratisation, international relations, economic and social development, equitable international economic order, the development of human resources, the protection and promotion of all human rights and fundamental freedoms, including the right to development and the coexistence of different systems, cultures and societies.

The movement should continue to play an active and effective role in laying down the base and defining the characteristics of a new era in international relations.

The NAM stands both on the unfinished agenda of the past as also on new emerging issues, on which the big powers and the industrialized world have taken a different, high-prosite stand. The NAM documents do not fulfil the goal on a nuclear free world through the elimination of weapons according to a time bound schedule. In actual practice, the NAM members find it hard to live up to their professions, as was evident during the NPT review conference which decided on the indefinite extension of the treaty.

The factors contributing to its relevance are as follows:

1. The paradigm shift of power from military to economic, Globalization of economy, external debt problems, North-South cooperation and South-South solidarity are the order of the day. The Acra foreign minister meeting gave a clear indication to the movement.
2. The end of bi-polarism and the characterized unipolar world gives relevance to non-alignment.
3. The present nature of international situation gives more room for strengthening and restructuring the UN so as to render it more democratic and effective with the support of NAM.
4. The new focus of NAM should be towards eradicating poverty, hunger famine, malnutrition, illiteracy and called upon the international community to render necessary help in this regard.
5. There is also a perceptible change in the nature of the security problems

facing the international community especially developing nations.

In the era of globalization, the NAM is trying hard to prove its worth by striving to work for the following contemporary issues.

- Combating international terrorism,
- Setting up a new international order through the UN, and
- Fighting poverty, drug trafficking and environmental degradation etc.

It is said that the cold war did influence the shaping of nonalignment as a foreign policy, but it is certainly wrong to assume that nonalignment is a mere response to cold war. In fact, nonalignment as a foreign policy is committed to universal problems of peace and freedom and hence has relevance both in the cold war period as well as non-cold war periods. All the changes indicate the vindication of the stand of NAM.

Non-alignment is one of those phenomena of international politics which appeared on the international scene after the Second World War and which represent an important force in the shaping of the nature of international relations. Indeed, the origin and development of non-alignment has been the most popular and influential development of our times. It is presently being followed by nearly 2/3rd of the several states which constitute the world community and has been one of the most spectacular and influential developments of the post-war international relations.

Emerging as a principle of the foreign policies of a small number of newly emerged sovereign independent states like India, non-alignment has come to develop into the most influential and popular movement of our times. It has come to be regarded by many scholars of international relations as the best concept for a future world order. Non-alignment, together with its off schools-panchashilla and beneficial bilateralism or multilateralism constitutes a model for a future world order.

The origin and development of non-alignment can be legitimately described as an outstanding and one of the most influential developments of the contemporary era of international relations. Non-alignment as the principle of foreign policy stands for the policy of keeping away from power politics, super-power rivalry, cold war and the alliance systems of the two hostile blocs. It stands for independent actions on the part of the non-aligned states in international relations.

It seeks to prevent the spread of the hegemonious control which each of the two super power tries to exercise over their respective camp followers. In other words, we can say that non-alignment as a principle of the foreign policy of newly emerged sovereign independent states of our times has been the direct product of the determination of these states to remain away from the military alliances of the two super powers, and to fight the systematic and subtle attempts made by the competing rival power blocs to suck in the new states into their own global strategies and thereby to use them as pawns on the chess board of international relations. Out of this determination of the new states there emerged and developed the non-aligned movement—a big third world movement against the continued attempts which were being made by the two super powers and their bloc actors for maintaining their neo-colonialistic control over the new states.

Non-alignment has come to be the most popular term in the dictionary of international relations there continues to be divergent interpretations of this term, particularly by the Western scholars. Initially, it was described with the help of such terms as "Neutrality" or "Neutralism", or, Neutralisation" etc.

George Schwarzenberger refers to six terms:

1. Isolationism.
2. Non-commitment.
3. Neutrality.
4. Neutralisation.
5. Unilateralism.
6. Non-involvement.

Isolationism stands for policy of aloofness, but non-alignment refers to aloofness from military alliances and cold war and not from international relations. Likewise, non-commitment refers to the politics of detachment from other power in multi-corner relationship; neutrality describes the political and legal status of a state which decides to remain neutral in war between the belligerents; neutralisation means the permanent legal status of neutrality conferred on a stage e.g. Switzerland; unilateralism involves the policy of taking calculated unilateral risk and decisions; and non-involvement stands for keeping away from the struggle between the different ideologies and powers. These terms are nowhere near to the meaning of non-alignment.

Non-alignment is neither a legal status nor a diplomatic means, nor even a principle of aloofness and infection. On the other hand, it means a fundamental principle of foreign policy under which a nation, while keeping herself free from cold war and military alliances, actively participates in international relations on the basis of both, its prudent national interests and the demands of international objectives of peace and security. It is the principle of foreign policy which stands for keeping out of alliances in general and military pacts in particular. The term is commonly used to describe the foreign policies of those nations which are not in alliance with either the communist or the anti-communist bloc.

The credit for using for the first time, the term 'non-alignment' belongs to George Liska who used it to describe the policies of the states which decided not to join either of the two blocs in world politics of post-War years. It was after him that the term non-alignment came to be adopted for describing the policy of keeping aloof from alliances, cold war and power-politics among the two super powers and their blocs.

In simple words, non-alignment stands for keeping away from the cold war and military alliances and yet participating actively in the international relations through independent decision-making based upon the world view and the national interests of the nation. In an era when the world stood virtually divided into two blocs, with cold war in between them, policy makers of several states, like India thought it well to keep away from the cold war and to concentrate upon the securing of the security and other national interests.

Non-alignment regards military alliances as the instruments of cold war and tensions and as such dangerous for world peace and security. These are the means by which the super power can infiltrate into the security and independence of the member nations. These, therefore, constitute a source of limitation both on world peace and upon the freedom of nations. Consequently, non-alignment stands for anti-alliance and anti-cold war principles. As the architect of attempt by a nation to keep itself aloof from military blocs, it means, trying to view the things as far as possible, not from military point of view though that has to come in sometimes, but we must have independent view point and must have friendly relations with all countries. Nehru also termed non-alignment as Independent Foreign Policy. M.S. Rajan, while defining non-alignment writer, "specifically and negatively non-alignment meant the rejection of military or political alliances. Positively, it meant taking of ad-hoc decisions on international problems, as and when they came up according to the merits of each case".

Non-alignment as a fundamental principle of a foreign policy stands for: opposition to cold war; non-membership of military and political alliances, keeping away from power blocs: and the policy to act independently in international relations i.e. taking all decisions on the basis of national interests and independent assessment of the world view. It stands for full participation in international relations and does not admit either isolationism or involvement based upon prior commitments. It is a principle which fully supports and upholds the cause of international peace and security and for this advocates non-involvement in cold war and alliances.

3.2 Facial Appearance of Non-aligned Movement

Since Non-alignment has now come to be a fully developed and comprehensive concept, it becomes difficult to construct a single conceptualisation encompassing all its characteristics. The only alternative course for understanding it lies in analysing its main features. Its chief features can be briefly explained as under:

3.2.1 Peaceful Co-existence and Non-interference: Peaceful co-existence and non-interference are two main principles of the concept of Panchshilla. Non-alignment too stands for these two. Non-alignment believes that cold war and its attempts to maintain peace through preparation for war are unjust and harmful concepts. These should be replaced by the faith in peaceful coexistence and non-interference. Non-alignment accepts that nations with different political systems can peacefully co-exist and co-operate and work for mutual benefits, world peace and prosperity. That it is possible to maintain and develop friendship between communist and non-communist countries. Non-alignment, as such is the principle of friendship and cooperation with all without any discrimination. Peaceful coexistence and beneficial bilateralism are two vitally important off-shoots of non-alignment has always stood for peaceful coexistence, non-interference, mutual friendship and cooperation with all other nations. Through it, non-aligned states have been successful in developing friendly and co-operative relations with both communist and non-communist nations.

3.2.2 Keeping Away from Power Politics: Non-alignment is an anti-power-politics concept. It rejects the struggle to be more powerful than others. It accepts the right of the nation to be powerful, but only for satisfying the goals of its national interest. It rejects unhealthy struggle for local, regional, continental or world domination. It opposes the concept of power for the sake of power or status-making or for dominating others. It opposes the power-struggle aimed at imposing one's desires and objectives upon others. It regards power-struggle as a step towards the violation of international peace and security. Describing this aspect of non-alignment, as practised by India, PM Nehru observed, "India should keep away from the power politics of groups aligned against one another, which has led in the past to two world wars and which may again lead to disasters on even vaster scales". Against cold war and power politics, non-alignment supports peaceful co-existence and mutual development through cooperation, friendship and peace.

3.2.3 Opposition to Cold War: The origin of non-alignment came at a time when the war-time cooperation between America and Russia had been forgotten in favour of Cold War—the war of nerves, the propaganda war, the ideological war and the war in which instead of bullets, accusations, charges and counter charges were levelled against each other by the two super powers and attempts were made by each to isolate the other. The peace after the war came to be a tense peace and the cold war between USA and USSR kept the world at the brink of war. Each of the two tried to win other states, particularly the newly emerged sovereign states, like India. International peace was preached and toasted but cold war was practised. The new states, like India considered Cold War to be totally harmful for international peace as well as for the peace and security of the nations. As such, opposition to cold war was adopted by them as a fundamental principle of their foreign policies. Non-alignment opposes cold war as an abnormal and dangerous policy and seeks to keep away from the tensions and ill practices that it generates. It rejects cold war and upholds peaceful co-existence and co-operation among nations.

3.2.4 Non-alignment is Neither a Diplomatic Means nor a Legal Status: Non-alignment is very different from diplomatic neutrality which a nation may practise at times of an international crisis. Diplomatic neutrality involves the policy of no action even when the facts of the crisis are known i.e. it is known who is wrong and who is right and yet no decision or action is taken. As against this, George Liska says, "Non-alignment stands for distinguishing between right and wrong and supporting the right". It is also not the war-time neutrality by which a nation acquires the neutral status and remains away from the war. Non-alignment is the principle of keeping away from cold war and military alliances. It involves independent and full action based upon self-judgement and national interest. It does not mean sitting on fence or refusal to examine. It is not a negative or opportunistic policy of exploiting the war. It is dynamic and positive policy of action. It is not a legal status of involving permanently neutralized position as is enjoyed by Switzerland. It is that principle or that policy which the government adopts and which guides the foreign relations of the nation. That is why with every change of government, faith in non-alignment has to be restated. For example non-alignment is not a legal status of India, it is just one, though fundamental, principle of Indian foreign policy.

3.2.5 Opposition to Military/Political Alliances: To quote Nehru, "When we say our policy is one of non-alignment, obviously we mean non-alignment with military blocs". Non-alignment opposes all type of military/political/security alliances which are nothing but means of tension and power politics. It opposes, tooth and nail, the security alliances like NATO, SEATO and WARSAW Pact etc. as the instruments of cold war. These alliances constitute a source of pressure and the means used by its superpowers for maintaining their hegemony or control over the members of their respective alliances. In the words of Nehru, "In the last few year, the spread of this policy (military alliances) to Asia has not added to world's security, or to any country's security...it has really come in the way of a country's progress." The alliance is regarded by politics and for perpetuating the control over other nations…these to act independently and to make them act with prior commitments and subjective values. Non-alignment as such stands for keeping away from instruments of cold war. Non-alignment holds that the alliances are the biggest dangers to world peace because each alliance has a counter alliance and hence it generates fear, suspicion, hatred, distrust in the international environmental and consequently, sets the stage for a possible violation of peace in the name of security. Non-alignment regards alliances as instruments of war, imperialism and neo-colonialism, and hence opposes them.

3.2.6 Support for Independent Foreign Policy: In fact, the origin of non-alignment was, to a large extent also due to the desire of new states to keep their foreign policies independent from the possible pressures from the super powers and the developed nations. It was felt that alignment with any one bloc or super power would limit the freedom of action. It would lead to camp-following and biased decision-making. Further, alignment would prevent the basing of foreign policy decisions and options upon national interest and their view of the world situation.

3.2.7 A Policy of Action, not Isolationism: Sometimes, non-alignment is either confused with isolationism or denounced as a policy of inaction. Non-alignment rejects isolationism i.e. the practice of keeping away from international relations. It accepts the right and the obligation to participate fully in international relations. It rejects the policy of being a helpless spectator. It stands for full and bold participation in world politics and for freely expressing one's views on all international issues and problems. It stands for full co-operation for the securing of international peace, security and development. Non-aligned countries have been fully and actively involved in the process of international relations. They have been always vocal in expressing their opinions, and taking decisions and actions in respect of various international issues and problems. They have never lagged behind in discharging their international obligations. India as a non-aligned nation is most enthusiastic member of the U.N. and other international organizations. She acts and react to every change in international relations.

As such non-alignment is neither a principle of inaction nor pacifism nor of even isolationism. It is non-involvement in cold war, military alliances and power-politics. It is a policy of action based upon national interests of the nation and upon the international milieu. Speaking before the American Congress, in 1949, Nehru explained this vital aspect of non-alignment: "When freedom would be threatened and justice would be in peril, when the security of states would be jeopardized, we cannot remain indifferent and we will not remain indifferent, our policy is not one of indifference. Our policy is that there should be active efforts for world peace and it should be given a firm foundation."

3.2.8 Non-alignment is not Alignment with the Non-aligned: Another vital feature of non-alignment is that it is opposed not only to the existing two blocs of powers but also to the creation of a third bloc—the block of the non-aligned nations. This policy is not based on the desire to build up "a third force" or "a third bloc". There is nothing like India's Monroe Doctrine and there was nothing like 'Nehru Doctrine' behind Indian non-alignment. The aim of non-alignment is alliances and supports peace in a positive way and believes in cooperation non-aligned states have always opposed, and very successfully, the attempts to transform the group of the non-aligned into a bloc. Non-alignment is a movement but is not backed by any formal organizational structure or constitution.

3.2.9 Non-alignment is a Policy of Peace: Non-alignment stands for peace through peaceful co-existence and cooperation among nations. It rejects cold war and alliances as the instruments of war instead of peace. It means a policy of peace, a policy of "talking in a quite voice and not shouting" or "a policy converting strong feelings into strength and not into bad temper". It is based on the premise that war is not inevitable and that it can be avoided. Cold war, military alliances and power politics are based upon the concept of inevitability of war, particularly war between the opposing blocs. Non-alignment rejects war and therefore military alliances and power politics. It supports peace through peaceful means. It supports peaceful settlement of all disputes and peaceful adjustment as the best means for resolution of conflict among nations. The development of non-alignment as an international movement has for its basis such a logic.

As a principle of foreign policy, it stands for freedom from commitment to any power bloc and the independence of choice and action in external affairs. It is not a negative principle of inaction or neutralism or isolationism. On the contrary, it is a principle of action, it is a dynamic concept and regards independence of foreign policy as the fundamental and most vital element. In 1961, Nehru, Nasser and Tito accepted the following five essentials or tests of Non-alignments.

1. Non-membership of any military alliance or bloc.
2. Absence of bilateral military alliance with any big power.
3. Independent Foreign Policy based upon non-alignment and peaceful co-existence.
4. Absence of foreign military base/bases on the territory of the state.
5. Each nation that wishes to be accepted as a non-aligned nation must satisfy all these five conditions.
6. Opposition to colonialism and support for liberation movements.

3.3 Evolutions and Contemporary Relevance of NAM

The history of the evolution of non-aligned movement can be traced into three parts:

In its present stage of its evolution, Non-alignment has been developing into a very popular, rather most popular, and an influential movement in international relations. Its strength has been rapidly increasing both in respect of the number of the non-aligned countries as well as the effect that its voice has started exercising upon the world community. The process by which the non-aligned movements have been developing can be studied through a review of seven summit conferences of the non-aligned nations that have been held so far.

Side by side with the first stage of its evolution, the second stage started developing when some of the leaders of the non-aligned countries decided to establish and develop contacts and cooperation among the new states. The lead that India took in holding the Asian Relations conference in New Delhi in 1947 and the success with which the prominent leaders of Asia and Africa could organise the Bandung Conference in New Delhi in 1947 and the success with which the prominent leaders of Asia and Africa could organise the Bandung Conference in April 1955, went a long way in preparing the ground work for the emergence of the movement of the non-aligned in international relations. The Bandung spirit and the ten principles which were adopted by this historic conference provided the much needed solid ground to non-aligned movement.

The Bandung Conference made several other nations realise the importance of non-alignment as a policy of keeping away from Cold War and Military alliances, and as a policy of independence in foreign relations, peaceful co-existence, and friendship and cooperation with all without any discrimination on the basis of ideological differences among various political systems. Many countries came forward to realise the justness and soundness of the concept. They adopt it and started taking keen interest in spreading and strengthening it. Nehru, Nasser and Tito emerged as the three strong stalwarts of non-alignment developed into an international movement and stared conducting a crusade against power-politics, cold war, imperialism, colonialism, neo-colonialism, apartheid, armament race and nuclear proliferation. It started working for enlarging the area of peace, freedom, prosperity and mutual cooperation. By 1961, Non-alignment became ready for being launched as an international movement for peace, freedom cooperation and property. The initiation came in the form of the First Summit of the Non-aligned countries and this event marked the entry of non-alignment into the third stage of its evolution.

As a preparatory step to the First Summit, the diplomats of the non-aligned states met at Cairo and laid down five general principles which constituted the test for judging as to whether a country was non-aligned or not. These are as follows:

1. A country should follow an independent policy based upon the principle of

peaceful coexistence and not aligning with power blocs or a trend in favour of such a policy.
2. It should consistently have supported movements for national independence.
3. It should not be a member of multilateral military alliances concluded in the context of great power conflict.
4. In case of bilateral military agreement with a great power, or membership of a regional defence pact, the agreement or pact should not be one deliberately concluded in the context of great power conflicts.
5. In case of lease of military basis to a foreign power, the concession should not have been made in the context great power conflicts.

With the adoption of non-alignment as a fundamental principle of their foreign policies by several states, particularly by India, Burma, Indonesia, Egypt, Yugoslavia and Ghana, these countries became the torch bearers of non-alignment. Their successful and fruitful adherence to non-alignment, despite stiff opposition from both the super power and their camp followers, gave a tremendous popularity to non-alignment as an ideal and pragmatic principle of foreign policy. The success which these countries achieved in establishing even relations with the members of both the two blocs of cold war era and the material and prestige gains which they could secure through independence in the conduct of their foreign relations, made the new states realise fully the utility and necessity of adopting non-alignment. Thus, in the first stage of its evolution, non-alignment became a popular principle of the foreign policies of a large number of new states which emerged on the world map as result of their successful fight against imperialism and colonialism.

The rise and development of non-aligned movement can be described as a key development in post-War era, which has changed the nature and character of contemporary international relations in many spheres and in many ways. It has come to be regarded as the most effective answer to the power game and cold war politics that the two super powers, through their respective blocs, have been playing in international relations. Nearly 2/3rd of the total members of the international community regard non-alignment as the fundamental principle of their foreign policies, which has helped them in the past to maintain their freedom of action and to secure the goals of their national interests. Presently, it stands recognized as one of the best approaches to peace and security which can be adopted as the basis of a future world order.

The non-aligned movement has been instrumental in transforming nationalism into internationalism and bipolarity into polycentrism. It has done a yeoman's service to the cause of international peace and security by refusing to have faith in orthodox bipolarity between democracy and communism, between the West and the East, and between the United States and the Soviet Union. It has successfully asserted that the needs of humankind go beyond the ideological conflict between capitalism and socialism to the need for friendship, cooperation, peace and universal brotherhood. It has drawn attention, to a universal concept of order and has played a key role in reducing the role of concept of order and has played a key role in reducing the role of cold war in international relations. Non-alignment has indeed helped the new states to sustain their independence and to concentrate upon the new states to sustain their independence and to concentrate upon the task of internal socio-economic reconstruction. By helping the new states to pursue independence in foreign relations it has behaved as an instrument of their sovereignty. It has encouraged the process of international conflict resolution through pacific means and beneficial bilateralism.

A review of the development of NAM as made above amply demonstrates the fact that ever since its origin it has been steadily growing in size, and after 25 years of its operationalisation it has come to be a forceful factor of contemporary international relations. Beginning as a group of like minded nations which were opposed to cold war, power politics and military alliances, it has come to be a strong anti-colonialism, anti-neo-colonialism, antiapartheid third world movement which is committed to secure for all the nations an equitable and just international economic order, stable peace and security in the world and an honourable, dignified and full participation in international intercourse.

In the words of Dr. Shri Ram Sharma, "The scope and horizon of non-alignment have greatly expanded over the years. From a concept of non-involvement or non partisanship with either of the power blocs in the context of a bipolar world, non-alignment has now become synonymous with real national independence. From the stage when it was taken as a kind of neutrality or fence sitting, it has assumed the positive character of dynamic involvement in world affairs, judging every issue on merit, taking a principled stand without fear or favour, relentlessly and consistently pursuing follow-up action and finally acting as the prompter of peace and equitable prosperity in a world of acquisitive and exploitative process. The time is not far off when non-alignment would be taken as the normal and natural attribute of sovereignty and independence."

Today outside the UN General Assembly, there is no international organization as largely representative as the Non-aligned community. There is scarcely a third world country which does not subscribe to non-alignment as its credo indeed it has registered a phenomenal growth from 25 members in 1961 to 96 members in 1985. Modelled on unity in diversity, nationalism with internationalism, independence with collective enterprises, the NAM represents a key factor in contemporary international relations. The criticism that NAM is an unobjective and biased view of the pro-power-polite supporters—NAM represents the unity of the Third World. In its developed form, it continues to be a fully relevant movement designed to secure the due political and economic rights of Third World countries i.e. the rights that stand denied to them by the big and dominant powers of our times.

Some critics have alleged that in the present context of international developments—the end of cold war, dismantling of blocs, collapse of Soviet Union and erosion of its super power status—non-alignment has lost all relevance and the non-aligned developing countries should redefine their international position in the new world setting. This view largely rests on the assumption that non-alignments was mainly the product of the cold war. It is true that the Cold War did influence the shaping of non-alignment as a foreign policy, but it is certainly wrong to assume that non-alignment is a mere response to Cold War. Cold War was by no means the cause of emergence of non-alignment. In fact non-alignment as a foreign policy is committed to universal problems of peace and freedom and hence has relevance both in the Cold War period as well as non-Cold War periods.

It is true that non-alignment emerged at a time when Cold War and bloc politics, they are confronted with several other challenges like proliferation of weapons of mass destruction, cross border terrorism, natural disasters and environment degradation. All these factors pose a serious threat to peace and democracy. Hence, at present non-alignment is confronted with the problem of creation of new world based on rational, democratic, equitable and non-exploitative inter-state relations.

Non-alignment shall continue to be relevant as long a there is exploitation, war, destruction, hunger, poverty and disease on the earth. It remains relevant to the changing world scenario, irrespective of the fact whether there is cold war or detente whether the world is unipolar, bipolar or multipolar. It can help in promoting greater economic and political cooperation between the developing and developed countries on fair and equitable basis and ensure respect for political independence of the developing third world countries. But probably the most important role which non-alignment can play in the changing context is to protect the economic interests of the third world countries by acting against discriminatory trade compacts like Multifibre Agreements, and work for creation of more favourable new order.

In short, it can be said that the philosophy of the movement is as relevant as ever and its underlying tenets remain unchanged. As the aspirations of NAM countries for true equality, genuine independence and unfettered development remain unfulfilled, the movement can play a dynamic role towards the attainment of these objectives. The other important issues on the agenda of the NAM are democratization of the United Nations and economic development. In short, the movement still has a vital role to play.

3.4 Socio-political Basis of Non-alignment: Domestic and Global

In the origin and development of non-alignment as a principle of foreign policy, a number of factors have played an important role. There was indeed a number of reasons which justified the adoption of non-alignment as the policy of keeping away from Cold War and alliances. The emergence of Cold War, military political alliances, headed by a super power, gave rise to the need for keeping away from these developments.

The newly emerged sovereign states regarded these developments as unfruitful and harmful both for international peace as well as for the security of new nations. In the words of T.N. Kaul, "Nehru believed peace was the most urgent need of the world in general and of newly independent countries in particular. He felt that if these latter countries kept out of the two rival, hostile military blocs, they would increase the chances of peace. If they lined up with one bloc or the other, they would play into the hands of the great powers and thereby increase tension and the danger building, the necessity to fight under-development and poverty and the love for maintaining freedom of action also provided the ground for the adoption of non-alignment.

Thus, both negative and positive, external and internal factors influenced the formulation and adoption of the principle of non-alignment. In the words of K.P. Mishra, "The concept of non-alignment may be said to attempt a harmonious blend of negative which have helped the formulation and development of the concept of non-alignment".

In the era of Cold War, both super powers worked hard to consolidate their respective power positions. For this purpose they adopted the system of entering into military and political alliances with their respective supporters, rather camp followers. America through a number of such alliances, like NATO, SEATO, Anzus, etc. was in a position to organise its friends and supporters into the American bloc. Russia countered the American move by entering into Warsaw Pact with communist countries who owed allegiance and support to it. The system of alliances and counter alliances created highly tense situation in which the members of one alliances were regarded as the enemies of the other alliances. These alliances, as the instruments of cold war, were responsible for the spread of mutual fear and distrust among the nations. These made the environment highly tense. The new nations like India were greatly disturbed because they regarded these alliances as dangerous instruments.

They, therefore, wanted to keep away from these alliances. India regarded these alliances as very harmful agencies working against the regarded these alliances as very harmful agencies working against the interest of international peace and security. "The formation of these alliances," believed Nehru, "increased the chances of Third World War". India, as such, chose to keep aloof from these alliances. Outlining this policy, Nehru said "India proposed, as far as possible, to keep away from the politics of groups aligned against one another, which have led in the past to world wars and which may again lead to disasters on an even vaster scale". These alliances were opposed by the non-aligned states as dangerous both for world peace and the peace, security and freedom of the nations. Establishment of military alliances was an important feature of Cold War era but the non-aligned felt that these alliances were unfruitful for world peace as well as for the defence for the parties to these alliances.

As such the best possible way was to keep out of the alliances. Further, joining of any one alliance would have given rise to enmity with the members of the opposite alliance and this was what many countries never wanted. Hence they decided to remain out of alliances and the power politics of the super powers. This aspect, combined with opposition to cold war provided a formidable basis for the origin of non-alignment.

The end of the Second World War was accompanied by the emergence of cold war between the two super powers-America and Russia. The war-time cooperation was forgotten and the attempts were made to dominate the world scene. The power vacuum that developed as a result of the wakened position of the formerly powerful states made America and Russia competitors for securing a dominant position in world politics. Both became increasingly critical towards each other and each came out with the policy aimed at isolating the other. Both got engaged in race for armaments. America wanted to maintain her superior power position, having monopoly over atomic weapons, and superior power position, having monopoly over atomic weapons, and using its position for increasing her influence over other nations, particularly upon the newly emerging sovereign states. It started strongly opposing monopoly over atomic weapons, and using its position for increasing her influence over other nations, particularly upon the newly emerging sovereign states.

It started particularly upon the newly emerging sovereign states. It started strongly opposing and challenging the growing power of Soviet Russia. Such American moves at the increase of Russian power and influence in world politics. It started working hard for the spread of communism and was successful in securing the establishment of communist systems in many states of Eastern Europe. In 1949, the emergence of China as a communist state gave a big boost to its spread communism and to oppose and challenge America capitalism. The net result came to be the emergence of Cold war between USA and USSR.

The new states were keen to avoid the Cold War as it was considered to be highly dangerous for international peace and security. They felt that Cold War can lead to a new war and hence seriously limit rather virtually end their independence of action.

After having suffered long under the yoke of British imperialism, the new states developed a strong opposition to the practices of imperialism and colonialism. Each such state was keen and determined to preserve her independence. As such new independence states did not want to directly, nor even remotely, help or tolerate any condition of outside control over their policies and decisions. They felt certain that involvement in any alliance would not only thrust them into cold war but also it would give rise to the chances of super power control over their policies. It would lead to a new form of imperialism. Formation of military alliances was interpreted as an attempt at repeating the old colonial process. It was felt that through these alliances the developed and powerful nations would again endanger the freedom of the Asian countries. The leaders of the new states believed, as Nehru has observed: "Alliances seek to extension of cold war to areas which attempt to be the masters of their own destiny and escape neo-colonialism'. Hence they decided to oppose strongly the alliances of both the colonialism, as such, gave further support to the adoption of the principle of non-alignment.

The new states wanted peace. They wanted it more than others because they, after centuries of sufferings, wanted to work for their development into a developed and welfare state. Their leaders believed that involvement in cold war and power politics on the side of any one super power would involve the risk of war and aggression from the opposite side. It was therefore necessary in the interest of peace that they should remain non-aligned and work—for securing peace through peaceful co-operation and friendship with other nations.

The fundamental problem facing the states after their independence was internal and not external. They were poor, economically backward and dependent. Though they possessed adequate natural resources and vast man power, exploitation of these resources was not an easy task. It not only required resource mobilization, development of indigenous technology and import of technical know-how till the development of technology at home, but also a favourable global environment conducive to the pursuit of this goal, for its economic development needed foreign help - economic as well as technological, from all the developed countries.

After having achieved its independence, each new state was committed to uphold its national interest which included freedom of action in foreign relations. Alignment with any bloc as super power would have limited the freedom to formulate and follow independent foreign policy decision. A new state, therefore, adopted the policy of non-alignment because it meant independence of policy and action.

It was after independence that the new states like India got the opportunity to base their foreign policy on their national interests. The policy before independence was always governed by the imperial interests of the imperial powers. After independence, each new state was totally committed to the task of independence, each new state was totally committed to the task of shaping her economy, polity and even society in accordance with her own outlook and way of life.

Another positive reason which led to the adoption of non-alignment was the acceptance of peace and peaceful means as the fundamental values. The struggle for independence that took place in most of the states was governed by the values of peace and prosperity. After becoming independent, they were naturally committed to peace.

Another important reason for the adoption of non-alignment was the desire of new states to play an active role in world politics, of course, without involving themselves in cold war and without jeopardising their national interests. After independence, they realized their international obligations, particularly towards the support for world peace and security; the liquidation of imperialism, colonialism and racialism; the support for the national liberation movements; the support for UNO etc. They wanted to play a positive role in the comity of nations and did not wish to shirk their responsibilities or to practise isolationism. This naturally required freedom of action and keeping out of the alliances and power blocs. They were not prepared to be camp-followers. Hence, they opted for the policy of non-alignment.

Thus, non-alignment was adopted by a number of newly emerged independence states as the fundamental principle of their foreign policies for a variety of reasons. Many factors played a role in its conceptualisation and formulation. It was adopted after a careful and through examination of various issues and alternatives.

At the Bandung Conference of the Afro-Asia countries held in 1955 they laid emphasis on the need of diversification of the export of the non-aligned countries. However, at this stage as the non-aligned movement was chiefly occupied with political aspects of decolonisation and preservation of peace, independence and national sovereignty etc.

The Second Non-aligned Summit at its Cairo meet in October 1964 laid emphasis on economic development and cooperation and urged "all the countries to contribute to the rapid evolution of a new and just economic order under which all nations can live without fear or want or despair and rise to their full stature in the family of nations (because) the structure of world economy and the existing international institutions of international trade and development have failed either to reduce the disparity or to rectify serious and growing imbalances between developing countries".

After the Cairo Conference the non-aligned countries played a leading role in the evolution of the new International Economic Order and adopted a number of resolutions and declarations. The important steps take in this regard include the Algiers Charter (1967) and the Second UNCTAD Resolution and Declaration (New Delhi, 1968).

It was only in 1970s that the non-aligned movement made a determined bid to establish NIEO. A blueprint for the NIEO was prepared at the Lusaka meet and specific guidelines for policies and action programme for economic development were prepared.

The Lusaka Declaration held the structural weakness of the present world order responsible for the distressing economic condition of developing countries and asserted that the "rapid transformation of the world economic system requires achieving implementation of concerned and coordinated policies and the measures so as to build a partnership between the developing and developed countries on the foundations of equal and mutual advantages and for the common goals of peace, development and prosperity."

The Algiers Conference made more forceful plea for fundamental changes in the existing inequitable international economic relations and the need for a new international economic order. The Conference emphasised that self-reliance and collective reliance were prerequisites for the attainment of international economic development goals. Above all, it asked the UN General Assembly "to draw up a charter on economic rights and duties of states."

The idea was developed further at the non-aligned meet held at Colombo (1976) and Havana (1979). The Colombo Summit paid special attention to the Economic Action Programme. It expressed regret that the capitalist countries were not responding to and implementing the decisions of the UN and suggested an Action programme to achieve New International Economic Order. One of the outstanding feature of this action programme was emphasis on a new universal and equitable monetary order. The Havana Conference in its Declaration also asserted that "the establishment of the New International Economic Order is one of the most important and most urgent tasks facing the non-aligned movements and the democratization of international economic relations constitute its political substance."

The Seventh Non-aligned Conference (New Delhi, 1983) again emphasised the need of establishing a New International Economic Order and emphasised that "the prevailing, international system which runs counter to the basic interests of the developing countries was profoundly unjust and incompatible with the accelerated development of the non-aligned and other developing countries and warned that failure to establish the NIEO based on equality and justice would have serious adverse economic and political consequences for all."

Thus, we can say that the non-aligned and developing countries have been consistently working for the evolution of a New International Economic Order with a view to gain greater share in the world economy for the developing countries of the Third World. The development was jeopardized because of the unhelpful attitude of the affluent countries. However, due to persistent efforts of the non-aligned countries the attitude of the affluent countries has somewhat softened and an atmosphere has been created in which we can expected that the developing countries may get sufficient quantity of assistance from the developed countries. But it would certainly be too much to expect that the advanced countries, who are facing the problem of energy, inflation and recession, would be willing to make any major concessions of the developing countries.

Fully conscious of this fact, the non-aligned countries at the Havana summit held in September 1979 recommended promotion of collective self-reliance among the non-aligned and other developing countries. It urged coordinated action in the field of raw materials, trade, transport, industrialisation, food and agriculture, fisheries, insurance, health, tourism, sports, telecommunication, currency and finance and other areas. It also called on richer non-aligned member countries to increase financial assistance to the poorer non-aligned countries and make more foreign investments in other non-aligned countries. This clearly shows that the non-developed countries have now come to realize that the major responsibility for their development lies with themselves and they must try to achieve development through mutual cooperation.

The 12th Non-aligned summit was held at Durban (South Africa) in September 1998. It discussed the issues of Cross-border terrorism, global disarmament and relevance of non-aligned movement in the era of economic globalization. The summit called for an international summit to tackle the problem of terrorism. It gave a call for universal non-discriminatory nuclear regime and adopted a proposal for an international conference in 1999 to work for complete elimination of weapons of mass destruction. It stressed the significance of universal adherence to the Comprehensive Test Ban Treaty (CTBT) by nuclear weapon states. The summit highlighted the need for a constructive dialogue between the developed and developing countries to ensure better trade co-operation and establishment of an equitable international economic order. It also called for a dialogue to review the role of the existing financial bodies like the IMF, World Bank and WTO in the developing countries. Above all, the summit emphasized the relevance of the NAM in the present context and urged the non-aligned countries not to allow foreign troops on their soil.

A perusal of the development of non-aligned movement as outlined above, shows that the movement has steadily grown in size as well as contents. Whereas at the first conference of the non-aligned at Belgrade, the members made general appeal to United States and Soviet Union to refrain from nuclear tests in the interest of world peace, in subsequent meeting it tried to extend the sphere of its interest. At the Cairo meeting the principle of peaceful co-existence was emphasized. At the Lusaka meeting the movement criticized military alliances and condemned the practice of leasing out bases to the foreign powers. It also, emphasized the need of economic co-operation. The Algiers Summit laid emphasis on elimination of tension and creation of climate of peace.

The Colombo meet went a step further and laid emphasis on economic emancipation of the developing countries and creation of a new international economic order. The scope of the movement was further widened in the Havana and New Delhi Summits and it laid emphasis on the end of South-South co-operation. It also pleaded for greater cooperation in the field of sports. In the Harare Summit it decided to setup Africa fund to help the border line states to frustrate the design of Pretoria regime. The Belgrade Summit of 1989 emphasized the need of tackling the problem of external debts facing the Third World countries and took the stand that world peace and security greatly depended on development. It also urged the international community to set aside financial resources for environmental cooperation.

The Jakarta Summit of 1992 called for shaping a new International order in which UN would play more important role. It also set up a high level working group to consider proposals for restructuring and democratization of the UN system. It impressed on the developing countries to ensure balanced and equitable conclusion of Uruguay Round of talks so that interests of all parties were protected. It called for acceleration of efforts for elimination of all weapons of mass destruction. The Cartagena Summit of 1995 called for establishment of nuclear weapon-free zones as a first step towards elimination of weapon of mass destruction. It called for reform of the World Bank and IMF and pledged to step up South-South Cooperation. It also put forth demand for writing off of the debts of low-income developing countries.

In short, the scope of the non-aligned movement has greatly grown over the years and it has become a strong constructive moral force in the international politics. It has greatly contributed to international understanding and promotion of world peace. It has enabled the non-aligned countries to interstate their fragile states into a volatile international system dominated by the two major powers. It has promoted collective self-reliance among the non-aligned countries and helped them to retain their sovereignty and authenticity in a predominantly bipolar international system.

Durban Summit of 1998 discussed the issues of cross-border terrorism, global disarmament and relevance of non-aligned movement in the present context. It called for joint global response to terrorism; universal, non-discriminatory, nuclear regime; constructive dialogue between the developed and developing countries to ensure better trade cooperation. It also insisted on review of the role of the global financial bodies like IMF, World Bank and WTO. The Summit also urged the non-aligned countries not to allow foreign troops on their soil.

The 13th summit of the Foreign Ministers of the Non-aligned Movement was held at Cartegena (Colombia) in April 2000. Fifty Foreign Ministers from 115-members countries deliberated on three main issues viz., peace, disarmaments and development. At this Summit, India proposed a comprehensive international convention against terrorism and demanded an immediate end to foreign military support to Taliban ruled Afghanistan. Another notable proposal mooted by India related to withdrawal of military ruled member states from NAM. This proposal was accepted and it was agreed that the final declaration will call for adoption of this clause during the next summit in Dhaka. It may be observed that at present only three members of NAM viz., Pakistan, Myanmar and Ivory Coast, are under military rule.

Critics have alleged that the Non-Aligned Movement has not been able to live up to the expectations of the founding fathers. Various countries adopted policy of non-alignment with a view to protect and promote their national interests. Objectively speaking the movement has failed to preserve peace and some of its members have been involved in disputes such as Afghanistan, Iran-Iraq, Cambodia, Namibia, Western Sahahra etc. The members of non-aligned movement have not been able to play any effective role in resolving these disputes. Similarly the Non-Aligned Movement has failed to keep the arms race under check.

In fact, most of the non-aligned countries themselves are spending huge amounts on defence preparations. Non-aligned movement has also failed to resolve some of the ongoing problems like Apartheid etc. No doubt, policy of Apartheid has considerably weakened, but this has become possible due to increasing economic pressure from the West European powers and America, rather than pressure from non-aligned movement. In fact some of the black African states, which are members of NAM, are active partners of South Africa. Another major shortcoming of the non-aligned Movement emphasized by the critics is that there is dichotomy between what the NAM leaders preach and what they actually practice. Often the NAM leaders have taken stand on various issues in United Nations which is at variance with the consensus evolved at the meetings of NAM.

The above criticism is, however, not wholly correct. The non-alignment has consistently grown in popularity. This is evident from the fact that in comparison to 1961 when 25 states participated in the Non-aligned conference at Jakarta, the number of non-aligned countries has increased to 113. Despite minor differences among members of Non-aligned Movement, it has played important role in favour of world peace, disarmament, development and decolonisation. It is well known that the non-aligned countries have played an active role at the United Nations and have refused to deviate from their chosen path despite all pressures.

3.5 Contributions of NAM

The main contributions of the non-aligned countries are outlined below:

1. Non-aligned countries have promoted the ideology of co-existence or 'live and let live' by keeping themselves away from the two blocs into which the world had got divided in the post-World War II period.
2. Though initially the two super powers were sceptical about the non-aligned countries, but in course of time they thought it desirable to win their favour. This naturally enabled the non-aligned nations to play a more effective role in international politics.
3. Non-alignment countries have played a major role in the process of decolonisation and freedom of the slave countries. This was quite natural in view of the fact that most of the non-aligned countries were themselves colonies of the western powers and were subjected to economic, social and political exploitation.
4. The enormous growth in the number of the Non-aligned countries greatly contributed to the easing of cold war and encouraged the newly independent countries to keep away from power blocs.
5. Non-alignment has discouraged the armament race and thereby contributed to the promotion of world peace. It is well known that the Moscow Test Ban Treaty of 1963 was made possible largely due to the efforts of the non-aligned states.
6. Non-aligned nations paid great attention to the problem of economic

development and played a vital role in the formation of the UNCTAD. They were also instrumental in the formation of the Group of 77.

7. Non-aligned Movement also tried to resolve differences and conflicts among various members states although its efforts did not meet with much success.
8. It greatly transformed the nature of the United Nations and acted as a check on the arbitrary powers of the permanent members of the Security Council because by virtue of their overwhelming strength in the General Assembly the non-aligned countries were able to impose some moral check on the big powers.
9. Non-aligned countries have vehemently criticized policy of racial discrimination and pleaded for equality among people of all races.
10. Finally, non-aligned movement has contributed to the end of game of power politics by keeping aloof from power blocks.

3.6 Continuity and Change in NAM

Non-aligned movement is that at present is led by a new generation of leaders. This point was highlighted by India's Foreign Minister P.V. Narsimha Rao at symposium organized at the Jawaharlal Nehru University, New Delhi. He said: "The first generation of leaders who founded and nurtured the non-aligned movements were influenced by their respective struggles for freedom in the anti-colonial and anti-imperialist tradition. However, the movement is led by a new generation of leaders, who though steeped in their respective national and political traditions are tempered by the real politics of international relations of the decades of the 1960s and 1970s." Above all, the non-aligned movement has greatly expanded and at present 113 sovereign states are members of this movement. These states professing and practicing different ideologies have by and large preserved the unit of the movement by observing the basic principles of the movement steadfastly.

The non-aligned movement has undergone considerable changes since its origin. It is faced with an international situation which is far more complex. Numerous power centres have appeared which have deep inter-relationship with various non-aligned and developing countries.

There is a greater political consciousness amongst the people of poorer countries and they have come to insist on removal of inequality and disequilibriums in the social and economic spheres. Further, majority of the resources have been monopolized by the developed counties and the gap between the developed and developing countries is getting wider day by day. Seventy percent of the people who live in the developing and undeveloped countries get only 15 percent of the world production. Even the traditional colonialism which has virtually reached a point of extinction has been replaced by a neo-colonialism and capitalist imperialism.

Though the Non-Aligned Movement has enormously grown it is also confronted with serious problems. Firstly, some of the members of non-aligned movement, though committed to solve their problems; through peaceful methods, are involved in open conflicts which has tended to render the movement weak. Secondly, some of the non-aligned countries are spending enormous amounts on their defence which has contributed to their slow development due to diversion of their limited resources to military preparations. If the non-aligned movement is to be effective and pose a serious challenge to the anti-imperialist forces, the member states must avoid policy of confrontation and concentrate on their development.

B.K. Kaul in his book 'New Horizons of Non-Alignments' suggested following measures for the strengthening of the non-aligned movement. First, the non-aligned nations and other states sympathetic to the non-aligned nations should try to solve their mutual disputes by peaceful means only, avoid arms race, should not have any direct or indirect military connection with any power bloc, and eliminate all kinds of strategic bases on their soil.

All this would reduce the burden of their defence budgets. All the Non-aligned nations should declare that an aggression of any one of them would be treated as aggression against all—and they should promise to give every possible moral and material support, including military help, till aggressions is defeated. Such a declaration would act as a deterrent to future aggression. The non-aligned nations should try to bring about a real and effective disarmament among the big powers. This is vital to effect saving in expenditure on armament which can be fruitfully diverted for the development purposes and elimination of poverty. Fourthly, the non-aligned nations should fight against the exploitative and restrictive practices of the advanced countries and try to reduce their dependence on aid from these countries. They should try to develop and cultivate mutually beneficial economic and trade relations with the advanced countries as well as among themselves. Insistence should be laid on equitable exchange of manufactured goods and payments of adequate prices for the primary products exported by the countries of the Third World.

Some critics have alleged that in the present context of international developments-the end of cold war, dismantling of blocs, collapse of Soviet Union and erosion of its super power status. Non-alignments has lost all relevance and the non-aligned developing countries should redefine their international position in the new world setting. This view largely rests on the assumption that non-alignments was mainly the product of the Cold War. It is true that the Cold War did influence the shaping of non-alignments—is a mere response to Cold War. Cold War was by no means the cause of emergence of non-alignment. In fact non-alignments as a foreign policy is committed to universal problems of peace and freedom and hence has relevance both in the Cold War period as well as non-cold war periods, It is true that non-alignment emerged at a time when cold war and bloc politics were dominant feature of international politics, but its main objectives to project and preserve the newly attained independence of the members states and promote their economic and political development.

Though the countries of the third world at present do not face the challenges of bloc politics, they are confronted present do not face the challenge was of bloc politics, they are confronted with several other challenges like proliferation of weapons of mass destruction, cross border terrorism, natural disasters and environmental degradation. All these factors pose a serious threat to peace and democracy. Hence, at present non-alignment is confronted with the problem of creation of a new world based on rational, democratic, equitable and non-exploitative inter state relations. Non-alignments shall continue to be relevant as long as there is exploitation, war, destruction, hunger, poverty and disease on the earth. It remains relevant to the changing world scenario, irrespective of the fact whether there is Cold War or detente whether the world is unipolar, bipolar or multipolar. It can help in promoting greater economic and political co-operation between the developing and developed countries on fair and equitable basis and ensure respect for political independence of the developing third world countries. But probably the most important role which nonalignment can play in the changing context is to protect the economic interests of the third world countries by acting against discriminatory trade compacts like Multifibre Agreements, and work for creation of more favourable new order.

In short, it can be aid that the philosophy of the movement is as relevant as ever and its underlying tents remain unchanged. As the aspirations of NAM countries for true equality, genuine independence and unfettered development remain unfulfilled, the movement can play a dynamic role towards the attainment of these objectives. The other important issues on the agenda of the NAM are democratization of the United Nations and economic development. In short, the movement still has a vital role to play.

During the initial stages the non-aligned countries worked through the United Nations to get the principle of state sovereignty over natural resources accepted. At the Bandung Conference of the Afro-Asian countries held in 1955 they laid emphasis on the need of diversification of the export of the non-aligned countries. However, at this stage as the non-aligned movement was chiefly occupied with political aspects of decolonation and preservation of peace, independence and national sovereignty etc. It did not lay much emphasis on the economic issues. It was only in the 1960s that the non-aligned movement started thinking in term of the NIEO because by this time the process of decolonisation had made further development and it began to be emphasized that economic emancipation was an essential ingredient of the political decolonisation.

3.7 Critical Evaluation of NAM

Ever since its origin, non-alignment has been the object of severe criticism. The critics have criticized it as a policy based upon idealism and have expressed doubt about its operational ability as a principle of foreign policy. Many critics have not hesitated to denounce it as a policy of passivity and inaction, and to level the charge that in the name of non-alignment the new states have been keen to remain away from international relations. Further where as some of its many western critics still describe it as a policy of undesirable neutrality, others criticise it as a policy of double-alignment.

Even after nearly 40 years of its operation in international relations, the critics still keep on finding faults with the concept of non-alignment. They quote the failure of the non-aligned countries like India, both in developing the desired friendly and cooperative relations with other nations and in achieving certain vital goals of their national interests, and as such they advocate against the continuance of non-alignment.

The critics raise the following arguments against non-alignment:

Non-alignment is a Principle of Inaction and Pacifism-The critics of non-alignment further criticise it as a policy of helplessness, weakness and inaction in the name of neutrality in Cold War. Through Non-alignment the new states have been refraining from taking strong policy decisions. Their decisions have been attempts to follow the middle path and to play safe.

1. Non-alignment is on unrealistic and idealistic principle: The critics of non-alignment, particularly the western and American critics, reject non-alignment as an idealistic and utopian principle which can not be operationalised. Keeping away from the cold war and maintaining equidistant from the two super powers can be talked and theoretically justified but can't be practised effectively. The critics argue that since time immemorial, alignment has been the principle of international living and it continues to be a valid principle even in the post-war period. No nation, particularly a poor and under-developed nation can develop without securing real and effective help from other nations and for this, alignment with some happens to be the only just choice.
2. Non-alignment is really double alignment: Many American critics of non-

alignment strongly denounce non-alignment as a policy of double alignment. They argue that through it the new state have been trying to practice double standards for securing aid and help from both the Western and the communist nations.

3. Non-alignment has been a source of friendliness: The critics hold that non-alignment has been responsible for the lack of sincere and real friends of a non-aligned country in foreign relations. They quote the example of India. India's strong criticism of Americana foreign policy as the policy of Cold War and alliances and its decisions in Korean, Vietnamese issues, etc. denied for her the real and strong friendship of America.
4. Non-alignment has ceased to be a relevant principle: Another line of argument against non-alignment has been that though it was quite justified for the new states to follow non-alignment in the era of Cold War and power politics among the two super powers, it no longer suits them to keep up non-alignment in the changed international environment. It has been on all these grounds that critics reject non-alignment. It has, according to them, earned almost negligible gains for the non-aligned countries. However, all these arguments against Indian non-alignment appear to be subjective and governed by the individual prejudices of the critics.
5. Non-alignment is a realistic and pragmatic concept: It is indeed fundamentally wrong to describe non-alignment as unrealistic and idealistic. The success with which the non-aligned countries have practised nonalignment in the course of their relations with the super powers as well as with other like indeed countries of the Third World bears ample proof of the realistic and pragmatic nature of non-alignment. Today both the super powers realise the importance of non-alignment.
6. Non-alignment involves full action and participation in international relations: A correct assessment and evaluation of non-alignment can be possible only by freeing oneself from prejudices. It is wrong to call this policy as a policy of neutralism, passivity and inaction. Such a view would mean ignoring the real nature of non-alignment.
7. Non-alignment has helped the new states to act out their desired roles in international relations: The principle of non-alignment has helped the new states to play an active part in world politics of post-War era. In spite of their weak power-position due to poverty, economic and industrial backwardness and very limited military power, they have been in a position to maintain their individuality and play an active role in world politics in the era of Cold War.
8. Non-alignment has been a source of influence on the politics of the two super powers: The commitment of the new states following non-alignment to

follow independent foreign policy and to take decisions based on individual judgement has been a source of strength. Both USA and USSR are now prepared to share their views with them and have been very keen to secure their support. Non-aligned countries have been successful in influencing the policies of great powers on many international issues and problems.

9. Non-alignment is not double alignment: Further non-alignment is not double alignment. It does not stand for military or political alignment with any state. It has no faith in non-alignment, nevertheless it stands for friendship and cooperation based upon equality and mutual respect with all. It is indeed lack of objective judgement that makers some people call it double alignment.
10. Positive role of non-alignment in weakening Cold War: Non-alignment has definitely played a role in the weakening the Cold War. The decision of some states, like India, to follow nonalignment was a source of weakness for the cold war. In 1950s, had India joined any one bloc, it would have further invigorated the cold war.
11. Non-alignment is better than alignment: The success of the non-alignment can be further explained by conducting a comparative study of the working of the policies of alignment and non-alignment. Presently, non-alignment has come to be an international movement.
12. Specific Merits secured through non-alignment: Non-alignment has been a source of big advantages both for the states which have followed it as well as for the world community at large. For the non-aligned nations, it has helped them: (a) to maintain their independence of action; (b) to secure economic aid; (c) to concentrate upon the task of internal reconstruction and development; and (d) to play an active role in international relations.

4

India and the Nuclear Issues

4.1 Nuclear Doctrine of India

In view of the persistent demand from various quarters that India should clearly state its strategic policy, Prime Minister Atal Behari Vajpayee propounded a Nuclear Doctrine for India in his statement before the Lok Sabha on August 4, 1998. The doctrine, though still in the stage of evolution, is based on following three principles:

1. **Minimum Nuclear Deterrence:** To ensure that the independence and integrity of the country is not jeopardised, the country would maintain a minimum but credible nuclear deterrent. The Prime Minister clarified that India can maintain credibility of nuclear deterrent in future without testing. He said that India had already announced a voluntary 'moratorium' and expressed willingness to move towards its dejure formalisation. However, the Prime Minister asserted that India reserved the right to review this decision if in its judgement extraordinary events take place which jeopardise India's supreme national interests. The Prime Minister said that the only purpose of India's nuclear arsenal was to prevent blackmail from other nuclear powers. India had no interest in engaging other states in an arms race and would keep its arsenal at the lowest possible level required for credible deterrence. It may be noted that the minimum deterrence refers to a level of nuclear capability which will better aggression and coercive diplomacy. But if this deterrence fails, the country has the political will and capacity to retaliate with nuclear weapons, after abroading the first strike. It is the possibility of damage due to second strike which will deter the fist use of nuclear weapons.
2. **No First Use:** Though India in the past has said on several occasions that it is willing to negotiate 'nuclear no-first-use' arrangements with other nuclear powers either bilaterally or multilaterally, but Prime Minister Vajpayee preferred to make a unilateral commitment and announced no first use-doctrine. This implies that India is not to first use nuclear weapons against nuclear weapons states. To effectively deal with the nuclear adversaries India must be able to weaponries, deploy and deliver a second strike within 24 hours and capable of inflicting unacceptable damage on the adversary.
3. **No Use against Non-Nuclear States:** Having stated that India shall not be

the first to use nuclear weapons, there hardly exists any basis for their use against countries which do not possess nuclear weapons. Therefore, India has committed not to use nuclear weapons against non-nuclear weapons states.

According to the critics the Indian nuclear doctrine suffers from several short-comings. In the first place, India's offer of no first use to China seems illogical in view of the fact that India justified its policy of going nuclear on the plea that Chinahad gone nuclear. Secondly, China's conventional forces are far superior to India and hence it looks a weakening deterrence. Thirdly, it is desirable in the interest of India that Pakistan and ensure that nuclear weapons are never used. Despite the above shortcomings it cannot be denied that the low intensity nuclear deterrence between India and Pakistan has been in operation since 1990, and despite low intensity conflict in Jammu and Kashmir for the last ten years, it has not blown up into a full scale war.

4.1.1 Criticism of the Nuclear Doctrine: The Indian Nuclear Doctrine suffers from several short comings.

- **In the first place** India's offer of no first use' to China seems illogical. The fact that India justified its policy of giving nuclear on the plea that China had gone nuclear.
- **Secondly,** China's conventional forces are far superior to India. Hence it looks a weakening deterrence.
- **Thirdly,** it is desirable in the interest of India that it should enter into bilateral "no first use" agreement with China and Pakistan and ensure that nuclear weapons are never used.
- **Fourthly,** India must enter into an agreement with China and Pakistan for non-targeting each other.

4.2 Objectives of India's Nuclear Programme

There are many objectives of India before nuclear programme. These are as follows:

1. India wants to use the latest technology for the development of nuclear power.
2. India wants to ensure nuclear power generation amidst global economic competition.
3. India wants to establish nuclear power reactors and safe use of radioactive substances.
4. India wants to understand role of nuclear power in economic development

4.3 India and Nuclear Weapons

India has been a consistent opponent of the nuclear weapons since her independence. In fact, even before India gained Independence the Indian leaders expressed their shock over the dropping of the bomb at Hiroshima and Nagasaki. It resulted in enormous loss of life and property. After Independence, India from every possible platform, carried out a crusade against nuclear weapons. Mr. Jawaharlal Nehru, the first PM of India, said that India had nothing to do with the atom bomb and she should like to use the nuclear energy for peaceful purpose only. For example while inaugurating India's Nuclear Reactor Apsara at Trombay in January 1957, he said "I can say with some assurance on behalf of my future government India that whatever might happen, whatever the circumstances, we shall never use this atomic energy for evil purposes".

The main questions of India with nuclear weapons are:

1. Use of nuclear energy for peaceful purposes.
2. Not to use the atomic energy for evil purposes.
3. Elimination and prohibition of the use of nuclear weapons.
4. Proliferation of nuclear weapons and dangers of proliferation.

At the various international forums India advocated the elimination and prohibition of the use of nuclear weapons. In 1948, India's representative told the UN General Assembly that India stands for the exploitation of the nuclear energy only for peaceful purposes.

The second argument was that India stood for complete elimination of the nuclear weapons and asserted that the contention of USA and USSR "that the atomic weapons would be used, only to resist aggression", was not valid.

India also expressed concern over the proliferation of nuclear weapons and highlighted the dangers of proliferation.

In 1961, India suggested to eliminate the dangers of more countries manufacturing nuclear weapons. The main suggestions behind India are:

1. All those nations which were as yet not manufacturing these weapons should undertake not to do so.
2. Secondly, the weapons already in existence should be confined to the territory of nations which manufactured them.
3. The nations possessing nuclear weapons should bind themselves by a treaty banning nuclear tests and pending such a treaty, they should retain from such tests.

In addition to, India also pleaded for the dismantlement or conversion to peaceful use of all existing nuclear weapons.

The demand for bomb gains strength issue was being raised in the following grounds:

1. Sino-Indian conflict
2. Indo-Pak War of 1965.

3. Super powers demand for non-proliferation.

There was a strong demand for bomb during the time of China-India conflict. The issue behind India was that India should undertake production of nuclear weapons as part of country's long term defence effort against china. This demand grew when China exploded a bomb in 1964. That time Lal Bahadur Shastri was the PM. He reiterated the decision of his government not to produce the atom bomb for moral as well as practical considerations. On practical grounds he ruled out the bomb because it was bound to adversely affect the national economy of the country.

In the second phase, during the time of Indo-Pak war of 1965, a memorandum containing signatures of about 100 members of parliament demanded an immediate decision to develop nuclear weapons. But the attempt was in vain, the same thing continued. After the explosion of third bomb by China in 1966, the demand for production of bomb by India grew still louder.

In Aug, 1967, the two superpowers proposed a non-proliferation treaty at the Geneva conference. India also expressed its opposition to the treaty. Because of following:

1. It would deprive the non-nuclear countries.
2. It found that the treaty is discriminatory.
3. Indian objection was that it was mainly against the unequal nature of the treaty and misuse of international public opinion to over-serve a policy of vertical proliferation.
4. India's objection was that the nuclear powers were interested in freezing the status quo for power distribution than in nuclear disarmament.

Right from Independence, India has favoured elimination of nuclear energy for country's development needs. Jawaharlal Nehru realized the important and big role of nuclear energy, outlined as follows:

1. It laid emphasis on development of atomic technology for peaceful purposes.
2. It could play for socio-economic development of the country.
3. For this purpose, Nehru took steps to establish nuclear research centres, experimental nuclear reactors, and nuclear power plants.

This policy of peaceful use of nuclear energy was followed by Lal Bahadur Shastri as well as Mrs. Indira Gandhi. Under the leadership of Mrs. Gandhi, the ground nuclear experiment for peaceful purposes in the Pokhran was discussed. It may be noted that the conduct of this test by India did not in any conflict with the commitment of the country as a signatory to the partial test ban treaty of 1963. The explosion produced mixed reaction. The superpowers were not exactly happy.

India's policy regarding peaceful use of nuclear energy underwent a change under Morarji Desai's government. It took the stand that it would not conduct another peaceful nuclear explosions.

4.4 Pokharan Test and Nuclear Empowerment of India

In May 1998, India conducted five nuclear tests at Pokhran in order to develop a full fledged nuclear deterrent to safeguard India's security. India also indicated readiness to discuss a 'no first use' agreement with Pakistan and other countries, either bilaterally or multilaterally. India also indicated its willingness to take part in the negotiations on fissile material cut off treaty.

These tests established that "India has a proven capability for a weaponised nuclear programme". The main reasons behind the conduct of the test are as follows:

1. There has been a gradual deterioration in the security environment in the 1980's and 1990's due to nuclear and missile proliferation. India has been the victim of externally aided and abetted terrorism, military and clandestine war.
2. The NPT, which was discriminatory in nature, sought to perpetuate the existence of nuclear weapons in the hands of five nuclear countries. These nuclear power countries were not willing to move towards a nuclear weapons free world.
3. India's nuclear weapons are "weapons of self-defence". It would ensure that India is not subjected to nuclear threats or coercion. He clarified that India does not want to engage in arms race.
4. The PM stated, that India was willing to observe a voluntary moratorium and refrain from conducting underground nuclear test explosions. He indicated India's willingness to more towards dejure formalisation of this declaration.

The conduct of nuclear test by India evoked strong protests from various quarters. USA and Britain, took a tough stand and favoured imposition of 'full sanctions' against India. Russia said it "felt let down' and China expressed 'serious concern' over the tests. China's reaction was very sharp. It demanded that India should stop its nuclear development programme. Pakistan also seriously condemned the Indian explosions.

On account of changed international environments and Pakistan's nuclear programme, a demand was made in certain quarters that India should go nuclear. In view of the growing public pressure and other considerations, the government was obliged to give a rethinking to its nuclear programme.

Public opinion was sharply divided on the issue whether India should produce nuclear weapons or not. Those who favoured India gang nuclear, argued that:

1. Since Pakistan was close to having on atom bomb, India could not afford to remain non-nuclear state.

2. The production of nuclear bomb would lead to reduction in India's spending of defence.
3. With Pakistan's GNP being only a fraction of India's GNP, there was no chance of Pakistan joining nuclear arms race with India.
4. Even in the interest of its international prestige India must go nuclear.

On the other hand those who were opposed to production of nuclear weapons by India put forth the following arguments. These are as under:

1. It would seriously hamper the socio-economic development of the country by diverting the much needed finances to development of bomb.
2. It would give rise to nuclear arms race in the sub-continent and pose a serious threat to the peace in the region.
3. It would give a serious set block to the movement for disarmament and arms control and encourage nuclear arms race in the subcontinent.
4. The production of nuclear weapons would compel India to bring about for reaching changes in its defence and security set-up.
5. It would give a serious setback to India's image as a peace loving and non-aligned country and undermine his position.
6. Finally it would greatly contribute to tension and lead to the deterioration of existing environments in South Asia.

It is evident from the preceding discussion that India has followed two fold nuclear policy. On the one hand it had tried to develop nuclear technology and capability for peaceful purposes, at the some time keeping the option open for its use for military purposes.

On the other hand, India has consistently pleaded for universal nuclear disarmament.

The period since 1945, when, the first atom bomb was exploded, is popularly known as nuclear age. Nuclear age has positively influenced the concepts and actual operations of international relations in a number of ways.

1. Impact on the traditional basis of state power.
2. Impact on concepts of national state sovereignty.
3. Breakdown of traditional theory of balance of power.
4. It has given setback to alliance system.
5. Preservation of status quo.
6. Less importance of force in settlement of disputes.
7. Has forced powers to act with restraint.
8. Deterrent effect of nuclear weapons.
9. Strengthened effect of nuclear weapons.
10. Encouraged closer contacts between adversaries.
11. Encouraged serious efforts at disarmament and world peace.

12. It has undermined importance of war as an instrument for settlement of disputes.

The nuclear weapons have diffused and diluted the importance of the traditional basis of state power. The traditional factors like population, territory, industrial capacity etc. are no more considered as the chief components of national power. In pre-nuclear era, the traditional factors greatly contributed towards the power of a state. At present, the nuclear energy has come to be considered as the chief factor of national power.

The concepts of national state and state sovereignty have been greatly affected by the nuclear age. In the nuclear age the security of the citizens depends more on the adversaries of the state.

In the pre-nuclear age, there were a number of independent centres of power. In the nuclear age, with the emergence of two superpowers and the other states, engaging oneself was a much inferior position. It is no more possible to operate the theory of balance of power in the traditional fashion. The traditional theory of power is now in operation.

Now the traditional balance of power has become balance of terror. Technological superiority has been in the nuclear age.

The nuclear weapons have also given serious setback to the system of alliances, which was prominent feature of international relations. In the pre-nuclear age the states frequently concluded alliances, to protect their interests and offered protection to smaller states. These alliances have become irrelevant in the nuclear age.

The nuclear age has also given less importance of force in settlement of disputes, for example, the Hague Convention of 1899 and 1907, the Convention of League of Nations etc.

4.5 India and Disarmament

Since Independence, India has consistently pursued the objective of global disarmament based on the principles of universality, non-discrimination and effective compliance. Given the horrific destructive capacity of nuclear weapons, India has always believed that a world free of nuclear weapons would enhance both global security and India's own national security. Thus India has always advocated that the highest priority be given to nuclear disarmament as a first step towards general and complete disarmament.

As early as 1948, India called for limiting the use of atomic energy for peaceful purposes only, and the elimination of atomic weapons from national armaments. India was the first country to call to an end to all nuclear testing in 1954. This was followed up in subsequent decades by many other initiatives, for example, on the Partial Test Ban Treaty, and the call for international negotiations on nuclear non-proliferation. In 1978, India proposed negotiations for an international convention that would prohibit the use of threat of use of nuclear weapons. This was followed by another initiative in 1982 calling for a "nuclear freeze", i.e. prohibition on the production of fissile material for weapons, on production of nuclear weapons, and related delivery systems. At the special sessions of the United Nations General Assembly on disarmament, India put forward a number of serious proposals including the 1988 Comprehensive Plan for total elimination of weapons of mass destruction in a phased manner. It was a matter of regret that the proposals made by India along with several other countries did not receive a positive responsive and instead, a limited and distorted non-proliferation agenda, meant above all to perpetuate nuclear weapons was shaped.

India was compelled by considerations of national security to establish and adopt a policy of keeping its nuclear option open while it continued to work for global nuclear disarmament. India's nuclear capability was demonstrated in 1974. India exercised an unparalleled restraint in not weaponising its nuclear capability. It is relevant to recall, that during this period, when we voluntarily and totally desisted from testing, over 35,000 nuclear weapons were developed through a series of tests by states possessing nuclear weapons. This was happened even as Article VI of the Non-Proliferation Treaty committed the Nuclear Weapons States, party to the NPT, to take steps in good faith for nuclear disarmament. India was obliged to stand apart on the CTBT in 1996 after having been actively engaged in the negotiations for two and a half years precisely because the issues of non-proliferation, global disarmament and India's concerns about her security and strategic autonomy were ignored.

India's continued commitment to nuclear disarmament and non-proliferation is clear from the voluntary measures announced by India after undertaking a limited series of underground nuclear tests last year. India remains committed to converting its voluntary moratorium into a de jure obligation in accordance with our long held positions on disarmament, and in response to the desire of the international community that the CTBT should come into effect in September 1999. India has declared that it will maintain a minimum credible nuclear deterrent and will not engage in an arms race. India has declared a no-first-use doctrine. We are willing to strengthen this commitment by undertaking bilateral agreements as well as engaging in discussions for a global no-first-use agreement. India believes that a global no-first-use agreement would be the first step towards the delegitimization of nuclear weapons. India remains the only state possessing nuclear weapons to unambiguously call for a Nuclear Weapons

Convention to ban and eliminate nuclear weapons just as the Biological Weapons Convention (BWC) and the Chemical Weapons Convention (CWC) have banned the other two categories of weapons of mass destruction.

4.5.1 Nuclear Disarmament and Non-proliferation: In 1996, India, along with the members of the Group of 21 countries, put forward a proposal, submitted to the Conference on Disarmament (CD), of a Programme of Action calling for a phased elimination of nuclear weapons (1996-2020). India has also unambiguously indicated its commitment to the establishment of an ad hoc committee in the Conference on Disarmament in Geneva to negotiate global nuclear disarmament. India is also the only state with nuclear weapons, which responded positively to certain aspects of the 8-Nation initiative on disarmament, entitled "Towards a Nuclear-Weapon Free World", put forward in June 1998 by Brazil, Egypt, Ireland, Mexico, New Zealand, South Africa and Sweden. At the NAM Summit in Durban, at India's initiative, NAM agreed that an international conference be held, preferably in 1999, with the objective of arriving at an agreement, before the end of this millennium, on a phased programme for the complete elimination of all nuclear weapons. The call for the elimination of nuclear weapons has been reiterated once again by Prime Minister in his address to the UN General Assembly. India remains committed to cooperation with like minded states to attain this goal. India also introduced a resolution in the 53rd General Assembly calling for reducing nuclear danger by de-alerting nuclear weapons.

India is fully committed to the goal of curbing nuclear proliferation in all its aspects. It was at India's initiative that the item "non-proliferation of nuclear weapons" was included in the agenda of the UN in 1964. In 1965, India along with other like-minded countries submitted a joint memorandum towards achieving a solution to the problem or proliferation; it included the conclusion of an international nuclear non-proliferation treaty. However, the NPT as it emerged from these negotiations, was flawed and discriminatory, seeking to create a permanent division between the nuclear 'haves' and 'have-nots'. India believes that the indefinite and unconditional extension of the NPT in May 1995 has only served to legitimize nuclear arsenals of the NPT states possessing nuclear weapons into perpetuity, thus posing a major obstacle to the goal of global nuclear disarmament. The NPT Preparatory Commission (PrepCom) meetings held in 1997 and 1998 have also clearly demonstrated this reluctance on the part of the five NPT states possessing nuclear weapons to take steps towards a speedy process of global nuclear disarmament.

India has developed wide-ranging expertise in nuclear technology but has ensured through a stringent and effective system of export controls that there is no proliferation of these technologies for weapons purposes. India's record in this matter is, in fact, better than some of the NPT signatories. At the same time, we are against ad hoc regimes or cartels which attempt to restrict high technology in an arbitrary, unequal and patently discriminatory manner. They need to be universalised, made transparent and equitable.

4.6 Non-proliferation Treaty (NPT)

The NPT is a landmark international treaty whose objective is to prevent the spread of nuclear weapons and weapons technology, to promote co-operation in the peaceful uses of nuclear energy and to further the goal of achieving nuclear disarmament and general and complete disarmament. The Treaty represents the only binding commitment in a multilateral treaty to the goal of disarmament by the nuclear-weapon States. Opened for signature in 1968, the Treaty entered into force in 1970. A total of 187 parties have joined the Treaty, including the five nuclear-weapon States. More countries have ratified the NPT than any other arms limitation and disarmament agreement, a testament to the Treaty's significance.

To further the goal of non-proliferation and as a confidence-building measure between States parties, the Treaty establishes a safeguards system under the responsibility of the International Atomic Energy Agency (IAEA). Safeguards are used to verify compliance with the Treaty through inspections conducted by the IAEA. The Treaty promotes co-operation in the field of peaceful nuclear technology and equal access to this technology for all States parties, while safeguards prevent the diversion of fissile material for weapons use.

The provisions of the Treaty, particularly article VIII, paragraph 3, envisage a review of the operation of the Treaty every five years, a provision which was reaffirmed by the States parties at the 1995 NPT Review and Extension Conference.

The 2000 Review Conference of the Parties to the Treaty on the Non-Proliferation of Nuclear Weapons (NPT) met at the United Nations in New York from 24 April to 19 May 2000. The Conference was the first to meet following the Treaty's indefinite extension at the 1995 Conference. States parties examined the implementation of the Treaty's provisions since 1995, taking into account the decisions on the principles and objectives for nuclear non-proliferation and disarmament and the strengthening of the review process for the Treaty as well as the resolution on the Middle East adopted at the 1995 Conference.

The Treaty on the Non-Proliferation of Nuclear Weapons (NPT) is one of the great success stories of arms control. It has made major contributions to global security and economic well being. It has been remarkably successful in achieving its main goals and with nearly 190 parties—has become the most widely-adhered to arms control treaty in history. The NPT is an indispensable tool in preventing the spread of nuclear weapons.

The need to prevent the spread of nuclear weapons was evident from the first days of the nuclear era. By 1964, there were five declared nuclear weapon states-the United States, the former Soviet Union, the United Kingdom, France and China. Many predicted that the nuclear club could grow to 20-30 countries within two decades. It rapidly became clear that if the many peaceful uses of nuclear technology were to be developed, states needed credible assurances that nuclear programs would not be diverted to military applications.

In 1961, the United Nations General Assembly approved a resolution sponsored by Ireland calling on all states to conclude an international agreement that would ban the acquisition and transfer of nuclear weapons. In 1965, the Geneva disarmament conference began consideration of a draft non-proliferation treaty. Negotiations were completed in 1968 and, on July 1 of that year, the NPT was opened for signature. On March 5, 1970, the NPT entered into force. The United States, United Kingdom, and the former Soviet Union were among the 43 original parties.

Important members of the international community did not embrace the NPT in 1970. There were many questions. Would its terms be honoured? Would the inspections of civil nuclear facilities lead to commercial espionage? Would others join the Treaty? Would it provide real benefits?

Over time, the many benefits of the NPT became clear. The NPT establishes a political and legal barrier to the spread of nuclear weapons. That fact alone offered to many states a compelling rationale for joining. The growth in Treaty membership toward universality has been steady over the years. From 43 original parties in 1970 the number grew to 96 in 1975, 132 in 1985, 177 in 1995, and stands at nearly 190 today. Israel, India and Pakistan remain outside the Treaty. North Korea joined the NPT in 1985, but in January 2003 announced its intention to withdraw from the Treaty.

In 1995, the parties faced the critical decision of whether to extend the NPT indefinitely or for a fixed period or periods. A majority decision was necessary. There was some speculation that the international community was not ready to make the NPT a permanent fixture of global security. However, at the Conference called to consider this issue, it was decided by consensus on May 11, 1995, that a majority of parties supported the indefinite extension of the Treaty.

There is a strong international consensus that the further spread of nuclear weapons would endanger the security of all countries, threaten global and regional stability, and undermine efforts to achieve peaceful solutions to existing problems among states. The NPT, and the norm of non-proliferation that it supports, are the primary reasons why the proliferation of nuclear weapons has been far slower than predicted in the 1960s.

The security benefits of the NPT are evident in every region of the world. South Africa's accession to the NPT in 1991 enhanced the security of all African states and opened the way for the negotiation of a treaty to make Africa a nuclear-weapon-free zone. Widespread acceptance of the NPT in Latin America and Southeast Asia has reinforced the desire of nations in these regions to ensure that nuclear weapons do not undermine their security.

There have been challenges to the NPT. Iraq was found to be in violation of the NPT in 1991. Its nuclear program was neutralized through action by coalition military forces in the spring of 2003 following 12 years of Iraqi non-compliance. In Asia, North Korea's failure to meet its NPT obligations, and its action to withdraw from the Treaty, undermine regional and global security. Iran failed to fulfil its obligations under Iran's NPT safeguards agreement according to reports issued in 2003 by the International Atomic Energy Agency. In November 2003, the IAEA Board of Governors deplored Iran's breaches of its obligations and urged compliance. In the last days of 2003, Libya announced its intention to abandon its efforts to acquire weapons of mass destruction. Carrying out this pledge will require Libya to demonstrate full compliance with the NPT and Libya's safeguards agreement with the IAEA. In all four cases, the international community responded strongly, insisting on full compliance with the NPT. The NPT is a critical tool in efforts to restrain the nuclear programs of these countries.

Nuclear proliferation in South Asia in 1998 poses a continuing challenge. But the tests by India and Pakistan that year also reinforced the NPT, as nations around the world condemned these actions and reaffirmed the critical importance of the Treaty.

In Europe and Central Asia, great political and economic changes have occurred over the last 15 years as a result of the dissolution of the former Soviet Union and the Warsaw Pact. In the midst of these massive changes, the NPT has provided stability. All of the newly independent states of the former Soviet Union transferred nuclear weapons deployed on their territories to Russia and joined the NPT as non-nuclear-weapon states.

4.6.1 Safeguards and Security: The International Atomic Energy Agency (IAEA), founded in 1957, is the primary mechanism for verifying that parties to the NPT are complying with its terms. The implementation of IAEA safeguards is further evidence of the way in which the NPT strengthens international security. Safeguards under the Treaty, including international inspections, help to deter the use of nuclear material for nuclear explosive purposes, and thus are an important confidence-building measure.

In light of the lessons learned from Iraq in the early 1990s, the members of the IAEA have taken measures to strengthen the Agency's safeguards system. These include a reaffirmation of the IAEA's right to conduct special inspections and the use of new tools for the detection of clandestine nuclear facilities. In 1997, the IAEA adopted a model protocol for existing safeguards agreements under the NPT that is designed to give the IAEA a stronger role and more effective tools for conducting worldwide inspections.

4.6.2 Nuclear Arms Control and Reduction: The NPT's role in checking nuclear proliferation also is critical to reducing existing nuclear arsenals. A vast array of actions has been taken in recent years that meet the objectives of NPT Article VI, which calls for effective measures relating to nuclear disarmament. Since the fall of the Berlin wall, the United States and the former Soviet Union (now the Russian Federation) have taken many dramatic steps to reduce Cold War stockpiles of nuclear weapons. The U.S. alone has dismantled approximately 13,000 nuclear weapons over this period.

Today, the nuclear arms race between the United States and Russia is over. They have agreed on further reductions in nuclear weapons and their delivery systems, and on taking other steps to reduce their nuclear weapon infrastructures.

The START I Treaty has significantly cut the number of strategic nuclear warheads deployed by the United States and the former Soviet Union. The U.S.-Russia Moscow Treaty, which entered into force in 2003, calls for reductions in the number of deployed strategic nuclear warheads to the lowest levels in decades.

Dramatic reductions have also been made in stockpiles and deployments of shorter-range nuclear weapons. Over 85 percent of tactical nuclear weapons dedicated to the NATO alliance have been withdrawn over the past decade and the United States has removed nuclear weapons from all surface naval ships and naval aircraft. In effect, these actions have de-nuclearized the U.S. Army, the U.S. Marine Corps, and the surface and air components of the U.S. Navy.

The United States halted production of fissile material for nuclear weapons many years ago. More than 200 tons of fissile material have been removed from the U.S. military stockpile and will be placed under IAEA safeguards as soon as practical. The United States and Russia support bilateral and multilateral measures to establish a legally binding halt in the production of fissile material for nuclear weapons. For example, both countries support in principle the negotiation of a multilateral Fissile Material Cut-off Treaty. They also are obligated under a 1997 bilateral agreement not to restart any shutdown plutonium production reactors and not to produce plutonium for nuclear weapons in any such reactors still in operation. They are also working on ways to store safely and to dispose of stocks of fissile material no longer needed for defence purposes.

The United States has not conducted a nuclear test explosion since 1992, and senior U.S. officials have noted there is no foreseeable need to change that policy. The United States is not producing or developing any new nuclear weapons. Policies are in place designed to reduce U.S. reliance on nuclear weapons through enhancing the role of advanced conventional weapons and developing missile defences.

The NPT creates a vital and irreplaceable framework for peaceful nuclear cooperation by providing assurances that non-nuclear-weapon state NPT parties will devote their nuclear programs exclusively to peaceful purposes. However, it is important that this Article IV benefit not be abused by NPT parties and that any peaceful nuclear program fully conform with the NPT's non-proliferation principles. Some NPT parties have violated the Treaty and in doing so should not, in the view of the United States, remain eligible for Article IV benefits. Consistent with its NPT Article IV obligations, the United States has for many years granted preference to NPT parties with exemplary commitments to nuclear non-proliferation when considering U.S. assistance to foreign nuclear programs.

The United States aids nuclear programs through the IAEA by providing a voluntary financial contribution and certain "in-kind" assistance. This assistance supports many IAEA programs that benefit developing countries, which comprise the majority of NPT parties. Among such projects are nuclear applications in the fields of water resources and environmental pollution, nutrition and agriculture, and human health. The U.S. cash contribution for IAEA technical assistance projects from 2000 through 2003 totalled over US$ 85 million, providing approximately 1/3rd of the total available resources.

The primary legal vehicle for bilateral U.S. assistance is an agreement concluded under Section 123 of the Atomic Energy Act. There are more than 25 such agreements in force. Hundreds of millions of dollars of fuel, nuclear equipment, and other commodities are exported from the United States to NPT Parties pursuant to these agreements each year. Also, U.S. Department of Energy laboratories have signed bilateral agreements with scientific institutions in several NPT developing countries to promote collaboration on various nuclear technology applications.

The world is emerging from the Cold War, a period marked by costly and spiralling nuclear competition. As the international community moves into a new era, the NPT will remain critical in a world where security is defined increasingly by the absence of nuclear weapons programs, rather than by their presence, and by the sharp reduction, not expansion, of existing nuclear arsenals.

The NPT is vital for security, arms control and disarmament, and economic and social development throughout the world. By rededicating themselves to the NPT, its parties can ensure that this Treaty will play an even more vital role in the new millennium.

4.6.3 ABC of NPT:

1. **Signed on:** July 1, 1968 at New York, United States.
2. **Became Effective from:** March 5, 1970.
3. **Ratification by:** The United Kingdom, the Soviet Union, the United States, and 40 other signatory states.
4. **Major Countries not Signatory:** India, Israel, Pakistan, North Korea.
5. **Three Pillars of NPT:** Non-Proliferation, Disarmament and Peaceful use of nuclear energy.

4.6.4 Key Provisions of the NPT: Under Article I, the nuclear weapon states undertake not to transfer to any recipient whatsoever nuclear weapons or other nuclear explosive devices, and not to assist encourage or induce any non-nuclear-weapon state to manufacture or otherwise acquire nuclear weapons or other nuclear explosive devices.

Under Article II, each non-nuclear-weapon state pledges not to receive, manufacture, or otherwise acquire nuclear weapons or other nuclear explosive devices; and not to seek or receive assistance in their manufacture.

Article III obliges each non-nuclear-weapon state to accept comprehensive international safeguards through agreements negotiated with the International Atomic Energy Agency (IAEA). The intent of these safeguards is to deter and detect the diversion of nuclear material for nuclear explosive purposes.

Under Article IV, parties may engage in peaceful nuclear programs in a manner consistent with Articles I and II and are expected to assist the nuclear programs of other parties, with special attention to the needs of developing countries.

Article VI obligates all parties to pursue good-faith negotiations on effective measures relating to ending the nuclear arms race at an early date, to nuclear disarmament, and to achieving a treaty on general and complete disarmament under strict and effective international control.

Article VII recognizes the right of any group of states to conclude regional treaties ensuring the total absence of nuclear weapons in their respective territories.

Considering the devastation that would be visited upon all mankind by a nuclear war and the consequent need to make every effort to avert the danger of such a war and to take measures to safeguard the security of peoples, Believing that the proliferation of nuclear weapons would seriously enhance the danger of nuclear war, In conformity with resolutions of the United Nations General

Assembly calling for the conclusion of an agreement on the prevention of wider dissemination of nuclear weapons, Undertaking to cooperate in facilitating the application of International Atomic Energy Agency safeguards on peaceful nuclear activities;

Expressing their support for research, development and other efforts to further the application, within the framework of the International Atomic Energy Agency safeguards system, of the principle of safeguarding effectively the flow of source and special fissionable materials by use of instruments and other techniques at certain strategic points;

Affirming the principle that the benefits of peaceful applications of nuclear technology, including any technological by-products which may be derived by nuclear-weapon States from the development of nuclear explosive devices, should be available for peaceful purposes to all Parties of the Treaty, whether nuclear-weapon or non-nuclear weapon States;

Convinced that, in furtherance of this principle, all Parties to the Treaty are entitled to participate in the fullest possible exchange of scientific information for, and to contribute alone or in cooperation with other States to, the further development of the applications of atomic energy for peaceful purposes;

Declaring their intention to achieve at the earliest possible date the cessation of the nuclear arms race and to undertake effective measures in the direction of nuclear disarmament;

Urging the cooperation of all States in the attainment of this objective;

Recalling the determination expressed by the Parties to the 1963 Treaty banning nuclear weapon tests in the atmosphere, in outer space and under water in its Preamble to seek to achieve the discontinuance of all test explosions of nuclear weapons for all time and to continue negotiations to this end;

Desiring to further the easing of international tension and the strengthening of trust between States in order to facilitate the cessation of the manufacture of nuclear weapons, the liquidation of all their existing stockpiles, and the elimination from national arsenals of nuclear weapons and the means of their delivery pursuant to a Treaty on general and complete disarmament under strict and effective international control.

4.6.5 Reaction to Treaty: The non-proliferation treaty (NPT) produced a mixed reaction. While some considered it is a great landmark which could prove to be turning point in human history, the others looked at the treaty as an attempt on the part of the United States and Soviet Union to establish their nuclear hegemony over the entire world. For example, President Johnson of USA described the treaty as "the most important international agreement in the field of disarmament since the nuclear Age began." He described it as the first step towards the ending of the peril of nuclear war. Similarly, Soviet Foreign Minister Gromyko said that the treaty constituted "one of the most important steps ever undertaken to restrain the nuclear arms race in the name of the lasting interests of peace.

On the other hand, the Chinese Government strongly denounced the NPT. It described the treaty as "a big plot and a big fraud of the US imperialists and Soviet revisionists." They alleged that through this treaty the United States and the Soviet Union wished to deprive the non-nuclear nations under US-Soviet Nuclear threat. It bound the non nuclear states and deprived them of their right to develop nuclear nations' weapons for self-defence and even restricted their freedom to use the atomic energy for peaceful purposes.

Similarly India also highlighted numerous loopholes in the treaty. It found the treaty discriminatory in so far it avoided equal and mutual obligations of nuclear weapon and non-nuclear weapon states. The treaty while denying nuclear weapons to the non-nuclear weapon states, did not prohibit the nuclear weapon states to proliferate their nuclear weapons. The other shortcomings of the treaty which were highlighted by India included absence of equal rights to all the countries to tame the atom to solve their socio-economic problems and failure to guarantee security to all the states.

The Indian attitude towards the treaty was best summed up by K. Subramanyam: "The Indian objection was mainly against the unequal nature of the treaty and the misuse of international public opinion to observe a policy of vertical proliferation by a few powers and the dangers of first nuclear use. In India's view this was not a non-proliferation treaty but a measured design to disarm the unarmed."

The nuclear powers were interested in freezing the status quo in regard to the current international powers distribution than in nuclear disarmament. No wonder, on account of its opposition to the Non-Proliferation Treaty, India refused to accede to it on the ground that the NPT in its present form was designed mainly as a political instrument of the two superpowers to divide nations into the nuclear have and the nuclear have-nots. It asserted that a non-proliferation agreement which ignores the present proliferation and preoccupies itself with the future proliferation is naturally unrealistic and ineffective. It confers all the benefits on the nuclear weapon powers and the burdens on the non-nuclear nations. India not only refused to join the NPT but also conducted a nuclear explosion. It declined to submit its nuclear activities to comprehensive international safeguards and consistently rejected the proposals for the setting up of a nuclear weapon free zone in South Asia.

It may be noted that India is not the only country which has refused to ratify the NPT. A number of other countries also refused to do so. These include Pakistan, Israel, Egypt (which signed the treaty but announced that it would ratify the same only if Israel did), South Africa, Spain, Argentina, Brazil etc. Even the then two nuclear powers China and France refused to sign the treaty. The main ground on which most of these states refused to sign the treaty was that it was discriminatory in nature and sought to perpetuate a discriminatory nuclear world order for the benefit of the nuclear states. Further, they demanded that the advantages of the peaceful uses of nuclear technology should not be denied to the developing nations. India went to the extent of proposing at the UN that since the existing Nuclear Non-Proliferation Treaty was discriminatory and places the developing countries at a disadvantage a new Treaty.

4.6.6 Indefinite Extension of NPT: In May 1995, Nuclear Non-Proliferation treaty Review and Extension Conference was held at New York which decided to extend the treaty indefinitely. It may be noted that USA and her Western allies were in favour of unlimited extension of the treaty, while the non-nuclear weapons states opposed its indefinite extension. The decision of the Conference to extend it indefinitely was diplomatic victory for United States. The permanent extension of the NPT means that only five countries. The United States, the United Kingdom, Russia, China and France can now legally possess nuclear weapons capability. In short, the NPT in its present form has put the 'nuclear haves' in a privileged position by permitting them to keep nuclear weapons, while the other states shall not be permitted to acquire them. To placate the non-weapon states, a list of disarmament goals was attached to the extension decision. One of the objectives outlined in the goals is completion of a comprehensive nuclear test ban treaty by next year. India opposed the permanent extension of the treaty on the two places. First, it does not adequately reflect India's place for equitable, global nuclear disarmament and divides the world into nuclear haves and have-notes. Secondly, the signing of the NPT as a non-nuclear weapon state is not warranted due to consideration of security of India because the country is flanked by a declared nuclear power.

4.7 Comprehensive Nuclear Test Ban Treaty (CTBT)

India's commitment to a comprehensive ban on nuclear testing dates back to 1954 when Jawaharlal Nehru called for a "standstill agreement" whereby testing of all nuclear weapons was to be immediately suspended, pending an agreement on their complete prohibition. It was again at India's initiative that the item "Suspension of Nuclear and Thermo-Nuclear Tests" was included in the agenda of the UN in 1959.

During the course of the negotiations in the Conference on Disarmament

(CD) Geneva on the CTBT, India put forward a number of proposals consistent with the mandate adopted by the CD in 1994. These proposals were aimed at ensuring that the CTBT would be truly comprehensive and would be part of the step-by-step process of eliminating all nuclear weapons. However, these proposals were regrettably ignored and instead, Article XIV on Entry. Into Force requiring India to join the treaty before it became operational was adopted in violation of basic treaty law. India was thus forced to declare its opposition to the CTBT as it emerged.

After concluding a series of tests on May 13, 1998, India immediately announced a voluntary moratorium on further underground nuclear test explosions. In announcing this moratorium, India accepted the core obligation of a test ban and also addressed the general wish of the international community. India also announced its willingness to move towards a de jure formalization of the voluntary undertaking. India is now engaged in discussions with key interlocutors on a range of issues, including the CTBT. India is prepared to bring these discussions to a successful conclusion, so that the entry into force of the CTBT is not delayed beyond September 1999. For the successful conclusion of talks, creation of a positive environment by India's interlocutors is a necessary ingredient. India expects that other countries, as indicated in Article XIV of the CTBT, will adhere to this Treaty without conditions.

The Comprehensive Test Ban Treaty (CTBT)—described as the "longest sought and hardest fought for arms control treaty in history"—was opened for signature in September 1996. The CTBT obligates countries that sign and ratify "not to carry out any nuclear weapon test explosion or any other nuclear explosion." It provides for an extensive verification regime including an International Monitoring System (IMS) to detect nuclear explosions, a global infrastructure for satellite communications from IMS stations to an International Data Centre (IDC) that processes and distributes data to State Parties, and for on-site inspections, which may be requested by any State Party to determine whether suspected cheating has occurred. To implement these verification arrangements, the treaty establishes a Comprehensive Test Ban Organization (CTBTO) located in Vienna.

To enter into force, the 44 countries that in 1996 possessed nuclear research or power reactors must ratify the CTBT. At present, 41 of these 44 countries have signed the treaty but only 31 have ratified. Non-signatories include India, North Korea, and Pakistan. The United States, which led the effort to conclude a CTBT and was the first to sign the treaty and China was among those who have signed but not ratified. In 1999, the U.S. Senate, whose advice and consent is required for international treaties to become valid and binding, voted not to give its consent to ratify. Beside partisan considerations, this was prompted by concerns with the ability of the United States to maintain the safety, security, and reliability of the U.S. nuclear weapons stockpile, and with the adequacy of the treaty's verification provisions to detect low-yield tests. The current administration, which in general is sceptical of the value of arms control treaties as a means of enhancing U.S. national security has said that it will not seek Senate reconsideration of the treaty. However, it supports the continuation by all states of the voluntary testing moratorium that is in place, as well as maintaining and completing the IMS, which is seen as value added to U.S. national technical means of detection. But the administration does not support funding for or participation in on-site inspection related activities that would be used as part of challenge inspections after the treaty entered into force.

4.7.1 Comprehensive Nuclear Test Ban Treaty:

1. **Opened for Signature:** September 10, 1996 in New York.
2. **Entered into Force:** Not yet in force.
3. **Conditions for Entry into Force:** The treaty will enter into force 180 days after it is ratified by all of the following 44 countries: Algeria, Argentina, Australia, Austria, Bangladesh, Belgium, Brazil, Bulgaria, Canada, Chile, People's Republic of China, Colombia, Democratic People's Republic of Korea, Democratic Republic of the Congo, Egypt, Finland, France, Germany, Hungary, India, Indonesia, Iran (Islamic Republic of), Israel, Italy, Japan, Mexico, Netherlands, Norway, Pakistan, Peru, Poland, Romania, Republic of Korea, Russian Federation, Slovakia, South Africa, Spain, Sweden, Switzerland, Turkey, Ukraine, United Kingdom of Great Britain and Northern Ireland, United States of America, Vietnam.
4. **Parties:** 144, including 35 of the 44 countries (as of 1 February 2008).

4.7.2 Why is the Comprehensive Test Ban Treaty important? The CTBT has been seen as an essential step toward nuclear disarmament for over four decades. It bans all nuclear tests, anytime, anywhere and comprehensively. Without the CTBT, the United States, Russia, China, France the United Kingdom, India and Pakistan are not prohibited from conducting further underground test explosions. The effort to establish an international norm against nuclear testing must not be abandoned after the enormous effort on the part of governments and NGOs, especially when the ratifications of only thirteen states is required for Entry Into Force.

The Treaty is intended to stop the qualitative nuclear arms race. The CTBT does not prohibit research on nuclear weapons, including sub critical tests. But it is very difficult, if not impossible, to develop new nuclear weapons without nuclear test explosions. This explains why all Nuclear Weapons States have resisted such a treaty for over four decades. Now that an agreement on the test ban has been reached and Entry Into Force is within reach, the effort to establish an international norm against nuclear testing must be actively pursued. Should the CTBT not enter into force, all the enormous effort on the part of governments and NGOs would be lost.

The CTBT will prevent further horrendous health and environmental damage caused by nuclear test explosions once and for all.

The CTBTO (the organization of the CTBT and the Secretariat of the Conferences) is already making great strides to establish a wide-ranging monitoring and verification system, including an International Monitoring System and an International Data Centre, which together with national technical means and ten of thousands of civilian monitoring stations, will detect and deter would-be testers, and therefore, will build confidence between all nations that nuclear testing has stopped.

The Entry Into Force (EIF) Conference is expected to be an opportunity for:

1. Announcing ratifications and signatures.
2. Calling on those states that have not yet signed or ratified the CTBT to join the international consensus to end nuclear testing.
3. Urging states with active nuclear weapon research programmes and test sites to take actions that would reinforce the CTBT and support its goals, such as refraining from activities at test sites that might be construed as CTBT violations, halting research, development and production of nuclear warheads based on modifications of existing designs, that give them new military capabilities.
4. Examining ways and means of removing obstacles which delay Entry Into Force.
5. Discussing and agreeing on specific measures to convince the last holdout states to support the test ban.
6. Support for the Comprehensive Test Ban Treaty Organisation in Vienna that has made significant progress in setting up the International Monitoring System and International Data Centre, so that the CTBT's verification system is ready by the time the treaty enters into force.
7. Condemning any future testing.
8. Calling upon governments, businesses and peoples to take decisive action in reaction to any future testing.

4.8 Fissile Material Cut-off Treaty (FMCT)

India supports the ban on production of fissile material for nuclear weapons purposes. This demand has been articulated by India in the UN through concrete proposals like the Action Plan which it presented in 1988. India also co-sponsored a UN General Assembly resolution (48/75 L) in 1993, which called for an early commencement of negotiations for the prohibition of the production of fissile material for nuclear weapons or other nuclear explosive devices. India has joined the consensus in the Conference on Disarmament on establishing an ad hoc committee to negotiate an FMCT. India believes that this is an integral part of the nuclear disarmament process. It would also go a long way in arresting problems of illegal transfers of nuclear material. India supports efforts for negotiations on a universal, non-discriminatory and verifiable fissile material cut-off treaty that would prohibit the future production of fissile material for weapons purposes but would permit such production for civilian uses.

Negative Security Assurances (NSAs) and Nuclear Weapon Free Zones (NWFZs): India has always maintained that NSAs provide illusory benefits, and that the real security assurance is complete elimination of nuclear weapons, and also that in the interim, if NSAs are to be given, they should be provided through an international, comprehensive, legally-binding and irreversible agreement. Similarly, consideration of security assurances in the narrow strait-jacket of Nuclear Weapon Free Zones (NWFZs) cannot do justice to the wide variety of concerns that emanate from the global nature of the threat posed by nuclear weapons.

As a responsible state possessing nuclear weapons, India has stated that it does not intend to use nuclear weapons to commit aggression or for mounting threats against any country. India respects the sovereign choice exercised by states not possessing nuclear weapons in establishing NWFZs on the basis of agreements freely arrived at among the states of the region concerned. At the fifth session of the ASEAN Regional Forum in Manila, India stated that it fully respects the status of the Nuclear Weapon Free Zone in South East Asia and is ready to convert this commitment into a legal obligation.

India will remain responsive to the expressed need for commitments to other nuclear weapon free zones as well.

4.9 Chemical Weapons Convention (CWC)

India is an original signatory to the Chemical Weapons Convention, having signed it on 14 January 1993, and was among the first 65 countries to have ratified the Treaty. The universal and non-discriminatory character of the CWC are primarily responsible for the large number of signatories and the equally large numbers of ratifications. The implementation of the CWC involves a combination of voluntary declarations and mandatory verification arrangements aimed at ensuring compliance in a transparent and universal manner. A National Authority

(NA) has been set up to oversee implementation of the Convention in India. As the first Chairperson of the Executive Council of the Organization for Chemical Weapons (OPCW), India guided the deliberations of the organization during its crucial first year. Implementation of all obligations assumed by India to the Convention and related activities have proceeded satisfactorily. India believes that the provisions of the Convention require to be implemented in a non-discriminatory manner. National implementing legislations containing provisions which undermine the Convention hold out the prospect of leading to matching responses by other states parties thereby leading to an unnecessary dilution of the spirit and the confidence reposed in the CWC by a great majority of countries party to the CWC. Similarly, the existence of technology denial regimes such as the Australia Group remains an aberration when seen against the large number of ratifications the Convention has enjoyed so far.

4.10 Biological and Toxin Weapons Convention (BTWC)

India ratified the Biological Weapons Convention in 1974. India has participated in all four Review Conferences of the Biological and Toxin Weapons Convention (BTWC) and in the meetings of the Group of Governmental Experts. India is currently participating in the negotiations of the Ad hoc Group of the States Parties of the BTWC with the aim to strengthen the convention by a protocol, including possible verification measures. India maintains that these measures should be non-discriminatory and avoid any negative impact on scientific research, international cooperation and industrial development.

4.11 Anti-Personnel Landmines (APLs)

India is fully committed to the eventual elimination of anti-personnel landmines and achievement of the objective of a non-discriminatory and universal ban on APLs. A beginning can be made with a ban on export and transfer of APLs, that would enjoy an international consensus, and by addressing humanitarian concerns and legitimate defence requirements of states. India is sensitive to the humanitarian aspects of the landmine crisis and the need for a strong international response. Aware that APLs have been used indiscriminately in conflicts not of an international nature, India has called for a ban on their use in all internal conflicts. India follows a conscious policy of not exporting APLs. India has also been contributing to UN de-mining efforts since the Congo peacekeeping operations in 1963. An officer of the Indian Army is presently deployed with the UN Mine Action Centre in Bosnia. India is presently in the process of ratifying amended Protocol II of the 1980 Inhumane Weapons Convention, which deals with anti-personnel landmines. India stands ready to negotiate a ban on the export and transfer of landmines in the Conference on Disarmament.

4.12 Transparency in Conventional Weapons Transfers and Small Arms

India is committed to strengthening the norm of transparency in conventional armaments in general, and greater participation in the UN Register of Conventional Arms in particular. India has reported to the Register annually since 1994. The issue of proliferation of, and illicit trafficking in, small arms has moved up the agenda of the international community on disarmament issues. India is acutely aware of this problem and intends to participate actively in international search for effective solutions, including a proposed international conference to discuss the issue of illicit trafficking in small arms in all its aspects.

4.13 India's Efforts at Total Nuclear Disarmament

India has taken keen interest in nuclear disarmament. It has been actively working with leaders of Sweden, Greece, Mexico, Argentina and Tanzania to promote nuclear disarmament. Under INF treaty, it asserted that it would reduce the nuclear weapons. This treaty also demanded the suspension of all nuclear testing by all states.

In a special session of the UN on Disarmament in June 1988 PM Rajiv Gandhi proposed a three-stage time bound action plan. These are as follows:

1. To eliminate all nuclear weapons by 2010.
2. INF treaty should be followed by 50 percent cut in Soviet and US strategic arsenals.
3. All production of nuclear weapons and weapon grade fissionable material should cease immediately.
4. There should be negotiations for comprehensive test ban treaty.
5. Moratorium on testing of nuclear weapons should be immediately imposed.
6. We also proposed banning other weapons of mass destruction and suggested steps for development of new weapons system based on emerging technologies.

The Prime Minister, Dr. Manmohan Singh, inaugurated the International Conference on "Towards A World Free of Nuclear Weapons" in New Delhi in May 2008. The Prime Minister reiterated that India has no intention to engage in an arms race with anyone and said that India is fully committed to nuclear disarmament that is global, universal and non-discriminatory in nature. The prime Minister introduced an Action Plan calling on the international community to negotiate a binding agreement on general and complete disarmament. At the heart of the Action Plan was a commitment to eliminate all nuclear weapons in three stages by 2010.

The Rajiv Gandhi Action Plan was a comprehensive exposition of India's approach towards global disarmament and continuity in our thinking. It symbolized the continuity in our thinking since 1954, when India pioneered the call for a complete ban on nuclear testing. The essential features of the Action Plan continue to remain valid even today.

A review of developments since 1988 presents a mixed picture on how far the world has moved to realise the vision of Rajiv Gandhi. On the one hand, the end of the Cold War has created an opportunity for the world to move away from the dangerous doctrines that were based on the precept of Mutually Assured Destruction. Greater engagement and realization of the inter-dependent nature of global security among major powers has created new space for action on disarmament. In 1993, the Conference on Disarmament was able to finalise the Chemical Weapons Convention, a multilateral, non-discriminatory and internationally verifiable treaty aimed at eliminating an entire category of weapons of mass destruction by a fixed date, namely 2012.

On the other hand, the painful reality is that the goal of global disarmament, based on the principles of universality, non-discrimination and effective compliance, still remains a distant one.

Even more disturbing, however, is the emergence of new threats and challenges to global security. I refer to the growing risk that nuclear weapons may be acquired by terrorists or those driven by extreme ideologies; the increasing danger of non-state actors, accessing nuclear materials and devices; the development of new weapon systems based on emerging technologies which pose challenges to space security and provide new roles for nuclear weapons; and the weakening of multilateralism even as bilateral arms control processes falter in shifting strategic landscapes.

India, which has witnessed rapid economic growth in the last few years, and is poised for even higher growth rates in the future, needs a peaceful international environment so that we can focus our resources on improving the lives of our people. the energy needs will continue to rise in the foreseeable future. We do not have the luxury of limiting our options of energy sources. We therefore wish to create an international environment in which nuclear technology is used not for destructive purposes but for helping us meet our national development goals and our energy security.

India is fully aware of its responsibilities as a nuclear weapon state. We have a declared doctrine of no first-use that is based on credible minimum deterrence. We have in place strict controls on export of nuclear and fissile related materials and technology. India has no intention to engage in an arms race with anyone.

Above all, India is fully committed to nuclear disarmament that is global, universal and non-discriminatory in nature. The pursuit of this goal will enhance not only our security but the security of all other countries.

These objectives cannot be achieved through partial methods and approaches. The only effective form of nuclear disarmament and elimination of nuclear weapons is global disarmament. Nuclear weapons know no boundaries. Even today the nuclear arsenals in possession of the major powers are enough to destroy the world many times over. In this scenario it is not possible to "regionalize" nuclear disarmament.

It is in keeping with this approach that India has recently submitted a Working Paper on Nuclear Disarmament to the UN General Assembly, containing initiatives on nuclear disarmament. We hope to stimulate a debate and promote consensus on the way forward. These proposals have also been submitted before the Conference on Disarmament in Geneva. They are a set of practical measures for working towards the goal of a nuclear weapons free world. We do not wish to exclude other measures that may contribute to achieving this goal nor do we hold that there is a rigid hierarchy among these steps and a specific sequencing for their implementation. The measures suggested by India included:

1. Reaffirmation of the unequivocal commitment of all nuclear weapon States to the goal of complete elimination of nuclear weapons.
2. Reduction of the salience of nuclear weapons in security doctrines.
3. Adoption of measures by nuclear weapon States to reduce nuclear danger, including the risks of accidental use of nuclear weapons.
4. Negotiation of a global agreement among nuclear weapon States on 'no-first-use' of nuclear weapons.
5. Negotiation of a universal and legally-binding agreement on non-use of nuclear weapons against non-nuclear weapon States.
6. Negotiation of a Convention on the complete prohibition of the use or threat of use of nuclear weapons.
7. Negotiation of a Nuclear Weapons Convention prohibiting the development, production, stockpiling and use of nuclear weapons and on their destruction, leading to the global, non-discriminatory and verifiable elimination of nuclear weapons with a specified timeframe.

These proposals retain the spirit and substance of the Rajiv Gandhi Action Plan.

4.14 India after the Indo-US Nuclear Deal

Ever since prime Minister Manmohan Singh and US President George W. Bush has signed on the historic Indo-US Civil Nuclear Deal, there has been a huge public debate on it. Meanwhile, Americans who till now could not locate India on the map, started wondering about the threats to the world peace and US supremacy. In India too, the deal faced severe criticism from different sections.

But contrary to the fears on both sides, this deal will change the existing world order for our good. India, hopefully, will become a superpower and one of the strongest allies of the US. The US considers China to be a serious threat as the country continues to march on with its nuclear and space programs. To top it all, China doest not follow democracy. Although the country has embraced capitalism in a certain way, the decisions that rule the country are largely autocratic. Not only this, the country's support to Pakistan's nuclear program and indiscriminate arms' sale to various other countries is considered as a serious threats to world peace.

Although Pakistan has been trying to gratify US whenever it can, the fact remains that it is one of the largest breeding grounds for Islamic terrorists who are a constant threat to the US and the western world along with India. And the US knows this too well. In a power equation so skewed, India, as a good friend will be of great use to negate the Chinese threat and gain supremacy over the Indian Ocean and South East Asia.

It's for those in the opposition to know that India, the largest democracy in the world, has never been led by selfish interests. The Kashmir issue may well be something that the world can point out. But even with their point of view, if a country can leave Tibet in Chinese hands and have a sound sleep, then Kashmir was always an integral part of India. India had always showed restraint to go the nuclear way, with not even threatening to employ its nuke capabilities during the Kargil war.

Another point in the argument against the deal is that it will solely benefit the US. But, nobody is willing to understand that not only US, India too has a lot to gain from this pact. Through the deal, the US, strategically, accepts India's nuclear prowess, thus strengthening India's geopolitical position. Not only this, the deal is also bound to boost India's chances to make it to the United Nations Security Council. Although the deal does not embody such expectations, it can become an issue to discuss at a later date, of course. The catch is if you trust someone with nuclear weapons then trust them on everything. India will also gain leverage while discussing border issues with its neighbours, especially China.

Apart from these strategic advantages, the deal will help India to reap a lot of economic benefits. India's power need depends highly on conventional sources like coal. India has two advantages: first, sub-standard coal which creates huge pollution and which will eventually get used up and second, imports of high quality coal, which comes at a high price. None of them are viable as a long-term plan. According to the Planning Commission, India needs to increase its power supply five to seven times to sustain a steady growth of eight percent per annum till 2031. It is reasonably unlikely that the options available will see India through. The nuclear deal that will help India import Uranium ore and civilian nuclear technology from the developed countries, including the US, can just solve the puzzle of "How to meet India's growing power needs?"

Once the power infrastructure of the country is firmly in place, there will be no looking back for India on the economic front.

Now the question is: If everything is so nice about the nuclear deal then why are the opposition parties so worried? Apparently, the Opposition is not clear about its duties in the running of the country. The Opposition has misunderstood that its prime duty is to oppose anything that the government does or undertakes to do. If we closely examine the foreign policies of the erstwhile BJP government, it would be hard to imagine that the same party is opposing the nuclear deal. Mr. Jaswant Singh was ready to sign the Comprehensive Test Ban Treaty (CTBT) and Mr. Brajesh Mishra used to preach that India could do well if it puts nuclear facilities under safeguard (subject to inspection from International Atomic Energy Agency (IAEA), the UN nuclear watchdog) in return of Uranium ores. The present deal puts 16 of India's 22 nuclear facilities under the IAEA safeguard and an unprecedented pledge to let India import uranium and state-of-the-art nuclear technology for civilian uses. Undeniably, Mr Manmohan Singh has clinched a better Deal. Is it realiy a matter of distress?

Even the Left, prime ally at the Centre, is up in arms against the deal. For the Left, it seems more of its long-time political line of an undying opposition for anything that is American. As Communists in a democratic set-up they attach scepticism to all things American. Recently in a press conference, Mr. Jyoti Basu, the octogenarian leader and member of the CPM politburo, said that US is a "killer state". If the war in Iraq led him to make that comment, then definitely Mr Basu and his comrades missed out on Russia (then Soviet Union) when it occupied Afghanistan or was fighting a bloody battle in Chechnya. Pakistan, with all its terrorist activities failed to gain the 'title'. The time is ripe for India to come to the forefront of the world political order and raise the bar for economic independence. It will be for their own good if all major political parties overcome their narrow political motivations and come together to create an environment that will make the nation's future perfect.

Following are the key aspects of the Indo-US civil nuclear deal:

1. The agreement not to hinder or interfere with India's nuclear programme for military purposes.
2. US will help India negotiate with the IAEA for an India-specific fuel supply

agreement.

3. Washington will support New Delhi develop strategic reserves of nuclear fuel to guard against future disruption of supply.
4. In case of disruption, US and India will jointly convene a group of friendly supplier countries to include nations like Russia, France and the UK to pursue such measures to restore fuel supply.
5. Both the countries agree to facilitate nuclear trade between themselves in the interest of respective industries and consumers.
6. India and the US agree to transfer nuclear material, non-nuclear material, equipment and components.
7. Any special fissionable material transferred under the agreement shall be low enriched uranium.
8. Low enriched uranium can be transferred for use as fuel in reactor experiments and in reactors for conversion or fabrication.
9. The ambit of the deal include research, development, design, construction, operation, maintenance and use of nuclear reactors, reactor experiments and decommissioning.
10. The US will have the right to seek return of nuclear fuel and technology but it will compensate for the costs incurred as a consequence of such removal.
11. India can develop strategic reserve of nuclear fuel to guard against any disruption of supply over the lifetime of its reactors.
12. Agreement provides for consultations on the circumstances, including changed security environment, before termination of the nuclear cooperation.
13. Provision for one-year notice period before termination of the agreement.
14. The US to engage Nuclear Suppliers Group to help India obtain full access to the international fuel market, including reliable, uninterrupted and continual access to fuel supplies from firms in several nations.
15. The US will have the right to seek return of nuclear fuel and technology.
16. In case of return, Washington will compensate New Delhi promptly for the "fair market value thereof" and the costs incurred as a consequence of such removal.
17. Both the countries to set up a Joint Committee for implementation of the civil nuclear agreement and development of further cooperation in this field.
18. The agreement grants prior consent to reprocess spent fuel.
19. Sensitive nuclear technology, nuclear facilities and major critical components can be transferred after amendment to the agreement.
20. India will establish a new national facility dedicated to reprocessing safeguarded nuclear material under IAEA safeguards.
21. Nuclear material and equipment transferred to India by the US.

4.14.1 What does Indo-US nuclear deal mean? The US House of Representatives voted on July 26 2006 to approve a landmark deal that will allow the United States to sell civilian nuclear technology to India.

4.14.2 What is the Pact?

1. The legislation amends Section 123 of the Atomic Energy Act of 1954. It lets the US make a one-time exception for India to keep its nuclear weapons without signing the Nuclear Non-Proliferation Treaty (NPT).
2. The amendment overturns a 30-year-old US ban on supplying India with nuclear fuel and technology, implemented after India's first nuclear test in 1974.
3. Under the amendment, India must separate its civilian and military nuclear facilities, and submit civilian facilities to inspections by the International Atomic Energy Agency (IAEA).

4.14.3 Why is it Controversial?

1. Critics say it undermines the NPT, which holds that only countries which renounce nuclear weapons qualify for civilian nuclear assistance.
2. The accord sends the wrong message: it could undercut a US-led campaign to curtail Iran's nuclear program, and open the way for a potential arms race in South Asia.
3. India says 14 of its 22 nuclear facilities are civilian. Critics say the pact could make bomb making at the other eight easier, as civilian nuclear fuel needs will be met by the US.

4.14.4 What do the Deal's Supporters Say?

1. US President George Bush calls the deal necessary to reflect the countries' improved relations. It strengthens international security by tightening US ties to ally India, the world's biggest democracy. It also ensures some of its nuclear industry will undergo international inspection.
2. New Delhi, which relies on imported oil for some 70 percent of its energy needs, says nuclear power will help feed its rapidly expanding economy.
3. France, which signed a similar deal with India in February 2006, says the move will help fight climate change and aid non-proliferation efforts.

4.14.5 How is Pakistan Involved?

1. Pakistan sought a similar civilian technology deal with the US but was refused last in March. It is the only other confirmed nuclear power not to have signed the NPT - saying it will join after India does.
2. Pakistan's own expanding nuclear program could fan the rivalry between India and Pakistan.

4.14.6 International Rivalries?

1. China is said to have supported Pakistan's nuclear weapons program since the

1980s. Some analysts see the Indo-US deal as part of attempts by larger powers, the US and China, to shore up influence in South Asia by building up rival arsenals.

2. The IAEA said in 2004 that Libya and Iran's nuclear programs were based on Chinese technology provided by Pakistan.

4.14.7 Impact on India's Foreign Policy

1. India's policy towards Iran has already undergone a sea change even before the Indo-US nuclear deal comes into existence. Our vote against Iran at IAEA was the litmus test. While India, for obvious reasons, would not welcome a new entrant in the Nuclear Club, this factor alone should not have swung our vote. Iran has not violated the NPT in any major way while Pakistan, China and N. Korea have clandestinely and openly violated major provisions of NPT. Action taken by IAEA against Pakistan could not come to fruition due to Pakistan's intransigent stand that A.R. Khan, the thief in charge of the Pakistan's nuclear programme, would not be made available for questioning by IAEA. Pakistan has been allowed to go scot-free and unpunished due to backing by US and the inability of IAEA to proceed against Pakistan.
2. Pakistan's doctrine of 'first use of nuclear weapons', as against ours of 'non-first use', and Pakistan's repeated threats to use nuclear weapons against India are a threat to India's existence.
3. This is in stark contrast to Iran's putative intention. By our vote at IAEA we have gravely damaged our burgeoning and mutually beneficial economic matrix of deals, especially in the hydro-carbons sector, in which India remains and will remain for the near future a big importer. The fact that India did not energetically and implacably oppose clandestine selling of nuclear equipment by Pakistan has weakened India's position and diminished her stature within the global nuclear community, especially IAEA. This has put India in a bind where we are not even seen as a country capable of defending its strategic allies. We are already being dubbed as a US stooge. How does all this square up in our long term quest for membership of the UN Security Council?
4. There has been a great deal of heat and dissonance generated over the Indo-US Nuclear Deal. A certain amount of dissonance would be expected in a fractious democracy, especially when the Government is one of coalition, that too with the intransigent and rather opportunistic communists. But the heat has been unbearable and the dissonance deafening. For the first time since Independence, not only there is no political consensus across the political spectrum, rather there is wide chasm and discord.
5. Since 1947, our foreign policy has been defined and enunciated into a form

and with such contents that it has enjoyed multi-partisan support of a preponderant majority far exceeding Congress party's strength in the Parliament. The nuclear component of our foreign policy has evolved from the need for autonomy in our defence and security framework. That was the reason behind Pt. Nehru's endorsement of the nuclear policy formulated by late Dr. H. Bhabha.

6. India has also worked very hard for peaceful development of nuclear energy. We were able to withstand the political after-effect generated by 1973 and 1998 explosions. Even though 1998 explosions should have been made before the conclusion of CTBT, as done by France and China, our stature actually grew and the Great Powers that condemned us for our nuclear tests came back unconditionally, not only to normalize their relations but also to enter into strategic dialogue with us. This was helped, undoubtedly, by the opening up of our economy in 1991 leading to vigorous economic growth over the last 15 years.
7. Late Rajiv Gandhi had the vision to foresee the problem of scarcity of energy in India and under his leadership, the Ministry of External Affairs (I was the Joint Secretary dealing with the USSR) was able to achieve a strategic breakthrough in persuading the then USSR to put up 10 x 1000 Mw Nuclear Power Plants. Nuclear fuel was to be supplied by the USSR. As we did not wish to have the spent fuel with its con-commitant safeguards and disposal problems, we persuaded the USSR to take it back. The Soviet export of plant/machinery was on standard soft terms (48 percent grant element), but it increased to 52 percent on my persuasion. Soviet Union also agreed to provide nuclear fuel on concessional terms. There was no unilateral, bilateral or multilateral condition imposed by the USSR, except that these power plants would be under project specific safeguards and not full-scale safeguards of IAEA, which was entirely un-objectionable.
8. India has the agreement and the format for unlimited development of nuclear energy in cooperation with Russia. Why go for a deal, specially with the US, that it would come under severe, unreasonable, stringent and totally gratuitous conditions.
9. India has declared a unilateral voluntary moratorium on nuclear explosions, meaning clearly that if our security and circumstances so demanded in future, we could and would undertake Nuclear Tests. Being bound by the putative agreement with US, we would not be able to do so without violating the entire agreement. Our agreements with Nuclear Supplier Group et al and US would be revoked, even though the IAEA safeguards would continue.
10. India is not going to get any special treatment from IAEA for safeguards.

IAEA has only two kinds of safeguards: one for non-nuclear NPT signatory states and the other for 5 NWS (Nuclear Weapon States: USA, USSR, China, UK, and France). In fact, when we are a declared Nuclear Weapons Power, for us to sign safeguards akin to those applicable to non-nuclear weapon NPT countries would be politically humiliating and strategically disastrous, cancelling in one swoop all our cumulative and hard fought gains over the past forty years in attacking the unjust and discriminatory NPT and our carving out a highly respectable place in the global nuclear community.

4.15 Nuclear Liability Bill, 2010

The Civil Liability for Nuclear Damage Bill, 2010 or Nuclear Liability Bill is a highly debated and controversial bill which was passed by both houses of Indian parliament. The Bill aims to provide a civil liability for nuclear damage and prompt compensation to the victims of a nuclear incident through a no-fault liability to the operator, appointment of Claims Commissioner, establishment of Nuclear Damage Claims Commission and for matters connected therewith or incidental thereto. This is one of the last steps needed to activate the 2008 Indo-U.S. civilian nuclear agreement as the United state nuclear reactor manufacturing companies will require the liability bill to get insurance in their home state. After this bill becomes an act, India will become a member of the international convention on liability in the civil nuclear arena. The government has encountered fierce opposition when trying to push this bill through parliament on several occasions. This is because it contains several controversial clauses that the opposition parties claim to be 'unconstitutional'. The opposition believes the bill is being pushed through due to US pressure though this is denied by the government.

The bill effectively caps the maximum amount of liability in case of each nuclear accident at ₹ 1,500 crore (US$ 304.2 million) to be paid by the operator of the nuclear plant.

The bill will require amendments in the Atomic Energy Act 1962 allowing private investment in the Indian nuclear power program. The issue of an accident is sensitive in India, where a gas leak in a Union Carbide factory in Bhopal city killed about 3,800 people in 1984 in one of the world's worst industrial disasters.

India has an ambitious goal to increase 5-fold the amount of electricity produced from nuclear power plants to 20,000 MWe by 2020. This will be further increased to 63,000 MWe by 2032. In this way, India will produce 25 percent of its electricity from nuclear power plants by 2050. India's present production of electricity through nuclear power is 4780 MWe. To increase the share of nuclear power, foreign companies would need to be involved in the manufacture and supply of nuclear reactors. Although there is no international obligation for such a bill, in order to attract the US companies involved in nuclear commerce such as General Electric and Westinghouse, it is necessary to introduce a liability bill which would help these private companies in getting insurance cover in their home state. Thus, the Bill will help in the realization of the Indo-U.S. Nuclear deal

The Lok Sabha passed the civil nuclear liability bill after government dropped the contentious provision of "intent" in the case of accident adopting a BJP amendment, paving the way for nuclear commerce with the world. The Civil Liability for the Nuclear Damages Bill, 2010 was adopted by the House by a voice vote after it rejected a CPM amendment that sought to fix the liability cap on suppliers in case of accidents at ₹ 10,000 crore instead of the ₹ 1,500 crore proposed in the measure. The amended Clause 17(B) now does not have the word "intent" with regard to suppliers or their employees in causing an accident in a nuclear plant, a provision that was strongly objected to by BJP and Left parties which felt it was aimed at diluting the suppliers' liability.

5

Conflict and Co-operation in South Asia

India's foreign relations reflect a traditional policy of non-alignment the exigencies of domestic economic reform and development, and the changing post-Cold War international environment. India's relations with the world have evolved considerably since the British colonial period (1757-1947), when a foreign power monopolized external relations and defence relations. On attaining Independence in 1947, few Indians had experience in making or conducting foreign policy. However, the country's oldest political party, the Indian National Congress, had established a small foreign department in 1925 to make overseas contacts and to publicize its freedom struggle. From the late 1920s on, Jawaharlal Nehru, who had the most long-standing interest in world affairs among independence leaders, formulated the Congress stance on international issues. As a member of the interim government in 1946, Nehru articulated India's approach to the world.

During Nehru's tenure as Prime Minister (1947-64), he achieved a domestic consensus on the definition of Indian national interests and foreign policy goals—building a unified and integrated nation-state based on secular, democratic principles; defending Indian territory and protecting its security interests; guaranteeing India's independence internationally through nonalignment; and promoting national economic development unencumbered by over reliance on any country or group of countries. These objectives were closely related to the determinants of India's foreign relations: the historical legacy of South Asia; India's geo-political position and security requirements; and India's economic needs as a large developing nation. From 1947 until the late 1980s, New Delhi's foreign policy goals enabled it to achieve some successes in carving out an independent international role. Regionally, India was the predominant power because of its size, its population (the world's second-largest after China), and its growing military strength. However, relations with its neighbours, Pakistan in particular, were often tense and fraught with conflict. In addition, globally India's non-aligned stance was not a viable substitute for the political and economic role it wished to play.

India's international influence varied over the years after independence. Indian prestige and moral authority were high in the 1950s and facilitated the acquisition of developmental assistance from both East and West. Although the prestige stemmed from India's non-aligned stance, the nation was unable to prevent Cold War politics from becoming intertwined with interstate relations in South Asia. In the 1960s and 1970s, New Delhi's international position among developed and developing countries faded in the course of wars with China and Pakistan, disputes with other countries in South Asia, and India's attempt to balance Pakistan's support from the United States and China by signing the Treaty of Peace, Friendship, and Cooperation with the Soviet Union in August 1971. Although India obtained substantial Soviet military and economic aid, which helped to strengthen the nation, India's influence was undercut regionally and internationally by the perception that its friendship with the Soviet Union prevented a more forthright condemnation of the Soviet presence in Afghanistan. In the 1980s, New Delhi improved relations with the United States, other developed countries, and China while continuing close ties with the Soviet Union. Relations with its South Asian neighbours, especially Pakistan, Sri Lanka, and Nepal, occupied much of the energies of the Ministry of External Affairs.

In the 1990s, India's economic problems and the demise of the bipolar world political system have forced New Delhi to reassess its foreign policy and to adjust its foreign relations. Previous policies proved inadequate to cope with the serious domestic and international problems facing India. The end of the Cold War gutted the core meaning of nonalignment and left Indian foreign policy without significant direction. The hard, pragmatic considerations of the early 1990s were still viewed within the non-aligned framework of the past, but the disintegration of the Soviet Union removed much of India's international leverage, for which relations with Russia and the other post-Soviet states could not compensate.

Pragmatic security, economic considerations, and domestic political influences have reinforced New Delhi's reliance on the United States and other developed countries; caused New Delhi to abandon its anti-Israeli policy in the Middle East; and resulted in the courtship of the Central Asian republics and the newly industrializing economies of East and Southeast Asia. Although India shares the concerns of Russia, China, and many members of the Non-aligned Movement (see Glossary) about the pre-eminent position of the United States and other developed countries, different national interests and perceptions make it improbable that India can turn cooperation with these countries to its advantage on most international issues. Furthermore, although Cold War politics have ceased to be a factor in South Asia, the most intractable problems in India's relations with Pakistan—conflict over Kashmir, support for separatists, and nuclear and ballistic missile programs—still face the two countries.

5.1 Toward Co-operative Security in South Asia

The notion of collective security has always been attractive for students of international affairs. Yet, it has also been the most elusive in practice. Throughout the evolution of Westphalia system of international relations, many saw that the concept of collective security was the only alternative to perpetual war and conflict. Rooted in the principle of "all for one and one for all", the idea of collective security posits that peace cannot be secured in an environment of self-help and balance of power. This notion is contested by realists who insist that pursuit of power, conflict and hegemony are natural conditions of international system and that it is not possible for states to put collective interest above that of the national interest. The context of this age-old argument, however, has been transformed in recent decades amidst the rise of a number of new concepts such as common security, comprehensive security, cooperative security, and human security. Common security emphasizes the reality of interdependence among adversarial states and the importance of developing shared perspectives. Comprehensive security brings into consideration many traditional non-military challenges. The proponents of human security challenge the traditional state-centric model of security and demand that peace and well being of the individual receive the primary focus.

It is easy to argue from the traditional perspective that given the deep divisions and security problems within the Subcontinent, the idea of collective security is an unattainable in the foreseeable future. Could "collective self-defence", a lesser form than collective security be considered an appropriate model for South Asia? Different regions in recent history—most notably Europe and South East Asia—have put in place varying forms of collective self-defence arrangements. Collective self-defence was successful in Europe given the common threat faced by the West European nations during the Cold War from the Soviet Union. Under the leadership of the United States, the West European states found it necessary to bury their past differences which led to a series of wars and face the perceived all-encompassing threat from the Soviet Union in a united manner. In South East Asia, too, shared internal and external threats allowed security cooperation among the regional states.

South Asia, however, has found it hard to emulate either West Europe which had alliance-based collective defence arrangements or South East Asia with is looser forms of regional cooperation. While the Cold War dynamics forced stronger forms of cooperation in West Europe and South East Asia, they sharpened the intra-regional security problems in the Subcontinent. The problems between India and Pakistan that arose out of the Partition got accentuated by the impact of the Cold War. India and Pakistan joined the opposing coalitions of the global Cold War. While the alliances they formed—Pakistan with U.S. and China and India with the Soviet Union—seemed to provide stability at one level, they also created the conditions for long-term instability in the region. The combination of regional and global dynamics meant that let alone collective security or collective self-defence the states of South Asia found it impossible to have even normal neighbourly relations. While South Asia is a long way from implementing either collective security or collective self-defence, the traditional debate on security in the region has been altered by the impulses of globalization as well as regional developments.

While collective security and collective self-defence will remain unrealisable goals, the changed global and regional context allows the nations of the Subcontinent to pursue cooperative security. Unlike "collective security", cooperative security is not rooted in idealist notions of how the world ought to be. Cooperative security also accepts the reality on the ground that an alliance like relationship between India and all her neighbours is not possible in the foreseeable future. But the idea of cooperative security recognises the reality of profound interdependence among the South Asian nations in both economic and security realms. The imperatives of this new interdependence range from common steps to avoid a nuclear war between India and Pakistan to the implementation of a free trade area in the Subcontinent. It could indeed be argued that the outlines of such a cooperative security regime in South Asia have begun to emerge. The challenge now is to lend political energy to the processes of problem-solving and accelerate wide ranging regional cooperation.

The Twelfth SAARC summit has helped lift the profound veil of pessimism that had engulfed the prospects for SAARC. The signing of a framework free trade agreement has launched a new era of cooperation in hard areas of commerce and trade. While many elements of detail need to be sorted out, the agreement to create SAFTA is indeed a turning point in the evolution of South Asian regionalism and has restored the intuitional credibility of SAARC. The Twelfth SAARC Summit has also opened the doors for thinking about trans-border energy cooperation and even bolder concepts such as common currency. It has also talked about engaging other regional groupings and nations to widen the ambit of regional and trans-regional economic integration. While much hard work remains to be done, it has created the basis for optimism about future direction of regionalism in the subcontinent.

Cooperative security is premised on the assumption that states will act in their own self-interest. That self-interest is evident in the case for regional free trade and trans-border energy cooperation. Yet, states in the region have been unable to act even when it serves their own national interest. While Sri Lanka has shown a forward-looking vision for economic cooperation, the same cannot be said about others. Bangladesh seems reluctant to follow the logic of regional integration despite being increasingly tied to the Indian economy. Pakistan too holds back on beneficial economic regionalism, citing the importance of settling the question of Jammu and Kashmir first. Negative thinking is also pervasive in New Delhi, where the tunnel vision and tight-fistedness of its economic bureaucracy is constraining rather than facilitating the integration of the Subcontinent. Despite the dramatic surge in its exports to its South Asian neighbours and much slower rise in imports from the neighbours during the 1990s, India has been niggardly in opening its market.

South Asians nations have wallowed in poverty for so long and marketed it abroad for aid—that they find it hard to conceive of shared prosperity through greater economic integration. Breaking out of this cycle is possible only if South Asian states move towards depoliticise issues of economic cooperation and build the habits of cooperative security. Depoliticisation of economic cooperation need not mean avoiding the negotiation on long-standing political disputes. Finding final settlements to difficult issues, completing the negotiations on delineation of boundaries, respecting the security concerns of others are all in the self-interest of individual nations of South Asia. The temptation to put either one—conflict resolution and normalisation of bilateral relations—ahead of the other has resulted in lack of movement on both fronts. Cooperative security demands walking on both legs—expanding economic cooperation wherever possible and making sustained efforts to resolve political disputes.

5.2 South Asian Security after the Cold War

The end of the Cold War at the global level did not match any of the expectations for a peace dividend in South Asia. At first cut, the 1990s seemed a depressing decade for the Subcontinent in terms of peace and development. The early hopeful signs of democratization at the turn of the decade vanished into thin air by the time the new millennium arrived. The Army returned to the centre-stage in Pakistan amidst the incompetence of its political class. Democratic politics in Nepal failed to deliver, and the parliamentary system in Bangladesh degenerated into a war of bandhs. The rapid dissipation of the hopes for more representative and effective governance in the Subcontinent during the 1990s was accompanied by the rise of religious extremism and anti-modernism in the region, exemplified most significantly by the Taliban in Afghanistan.

The north-western parts of the Subcontinent became the epicentre of terrorism in the world with an impact that ranged from Tanzania to Tajikistan and Manhattan to Mindanao. In India, the destructive trail of the Hindutva ideology moved from the demolition of the Babri Masjid to the gruesome communal riots during early 2002 in Gujarat. Civil wars from Kashmir to Jaffna meanwhile raged on, with victims countless for any one to enumerate. The introduction of nuclear weapons, covertly at the turn of the 1990s and overtly at the end of the decade, combined the weapons of mass destruction with violence, terrorism, jihad and inter-state conflict. All optimism for the future of the Subcontinent—either in terms of internal security or inter-state security—appeared to have been smothered.

Yet the very negative developments in the Subcontinent carried within them the seeds of a radical transformation of the region. The international impact of the extremist forces—dramatised on September 11 2001—inevitably drew retribution from the sole super power of the international system. Never mind the irony that it was the U.S. policy of pitting jihadis against godless Soviet Communists in Afghanistan in the 1980s that produced Osama bin Laden and his jihadi allies. The American War on terrorism has had its intended and unintended consequences. The Taliban was ousted, and the Army in Pakistan has become the instrument to clean up the jihadi mess that was nurtured by it in the 1980s and 1990s. Equally important, it has focused international attention on the Subcontinent and its intra-state and inter-state wars. Never in the past has the international system paid so much attention to the problems of regional security in South Asia. During the Cold War the external environment complicated the security politics of South Asia. Now an external environment may be emerging that is favourable to a reasonable resolution of South Asia's security challenges.

The accumulated impact of globalization on the politics and economics of the Subcontinent over the last decade has begun to reveal a radical transformation. The Indo-Pak military confrontation since the attack on Parliament on December 13 has brought the Anglo-American powers into play in a manner that has not been seen since the early 1960s. The prospect, however remote, of a war between India and Pakistan escalating into a nuclear exchange has forced the international community to explore a final resolution of the underlying political conflict between the Sub-continental rivals. The Kashmir question is not the only one among the regional conflicts that is on the Anglo-American radar. The expansive American war on terrorism has brought the United States, with Britain in tow, and the European Union into a political effort to deal with the other security challenges in South Asia—the tragic war in Sri Lanka and the Maoist insurgency in Nepal. The world has begun to impinge on the Subcontinent. Along with the global war on terror that is focused on Afghanistan, there have been Anglo-American efforts to defuse the Indo-Pak tensions, the Norwegian mediation between the Singhalese and Tamils in Sri Lanka, and the international initiative on Nepal led by Britain. The security dynamics of the Subcontinent are being altered irreversibly.

But external environment alone is not enough to resolve regional security problems. It needs political courage and statesmanship within the region to grasp the new challenges as well as opportunities for peace and development in the subcontinent. To some extent the pressures from below are already forcing states in the region to act more purposefully. After a series of military crises and real wars, India and Pakistan have finally recognised the importance of a sustained bilateral engagement that would involve both bilateral cooperation and conflict resolution. There is also recognition throughout South Asia that the time has come deal with the civil wars within the region in a more innovative and political manner rather than trying to deal with them as law and order problems. The current efforts at peace within the region can at best be characterised as "work in progress" with no guaranteed prospect of success. But there is no denying the fact that the assumptions and premises on how to end conflict have begun to be questioned and revised in a fundamental manner. That is a reason for hope.

More subtle, but even more significant, has been the consequences of economic globalization in the 1990s. Under pressure from the "Washington Consensus", all nations of the Subcontinent have adopted liberal economic policies. As they open up their markets to the world, the South Asian states are discovering that they cannot keep them closed to their own neighbour, India. While Islamabad continues to resist normal trade relations with New Delhi, some of the smaller countries of the region have begun to acknowledge that their economic future is now intertwined with that of India. There is no escape from the logic of globalisation that demands deeper trade relations and economic integration with India. Meanwhile, proposals for mega-projects for pipelines and transportation corridors, straddling across borders in South Asia, promise to further deepen economic integration in the Subcontinent.

Whatever might be its other negative consequences, the relentless pressures of globalization are helping to break down the economic walls within the Subcontinent. Trade volumes within South Asia have begun to surge, although entirely in India's favour at the moment. Bangladesh and Sri Lanka are among the top ten export destinations for Indian goods. Nothing less than a reversal of the economic Partition of the Subcontinent is now on the cards. After the Partition divided British India into separate states, insular economic policies and political differences had made borders into high-security barriers. Now globalization offers the prospect of transforming these borders into zones of economic cooperation and reconnect regions that were once part of the same economic and cultural space.

5.3 Towards Positive Unilateralism

For all its own internal difficulties, the task of leading the region towards economic modernization, political moderation, and social development inevitably falls on New Delhi. One of the most significant developments in India since 1991 has been radical rethinking about the relevance of a more effective regionalism in the subcontinent and a sea change in the Indian policy towards her smaller neighbours. This was based on the recognition of the acute crisis that had enveloped India's relations with her neighbours at the turn of the 1990s. At the heart of the changing Indian policy towards the neighbours is the so-called "Gujral doctrine", named after Inder Kumar Gujral who served as the external affairs minister during 1996-97 and as prime minister during 1997-98.

Mr. Gujral's willingness to go more than half the distance in resolving the long-standing problems of the Subcontinent was followed by his successors. Although the doctrine was named after Mr. Gujral, given his enthusiastic articulation of it, the broad lines of it were followed by the government of P.V. Narasimha Rao, (1991-96) and that of Vajpayee, who followed Gujral. Yashwant Sinha, foreign minister under the BJP led coalition explicitly acknowledged the debt to his predecessors and the Vajpayee government's commitment to take it forward. He has coined a new expression for the core of "Gujral Doctrine", namely to "institutionalizing positive asymmetry in favour of our neighbours".

No state bases its policy on altruism. India's new regional policy has been guided by three imperatives. First is the recognition that India cannot fulfil its aspirations for a larger international profile without addressing its problems in the neighbourhood. The real tensions in India's relations with all its neighbours will act as a huge fetter on its attempts to become a major power on the global scene. India cannot run away from its neighbourhood. However frustrating it might be, there is no alternative available for Indian diplomacy other than a substantive and patient engagement of its neighbours.

Second, as it coped with the emerging globalisation of regional security, India had to discard much of its traditional baggage about the role of other major powers in the subcontinent. Shedding the past suspicion of the major powers has become necessary. In the past, New Delhi had sought to keep the other powers out of the region, claiming some kind of an exclusive mandate as a regional power to manage the affairs of the Subcontinent. That approach has been neither credible nor effective. New Delhi does not have the luxury of pursuing a kind of Monroe doctrine for the region. Instead of trying to keep other powers out of the region, India must work with them to promote economic modernization, social harmony, and political moderation. The old way of looking at the internationalisation of South Asian security is to define it as a set back. The other is to take advantage of the trend to achieve India's interests. India's focus is slowly shifting away from mechanics to political outcomes.

Third, India has begun to recognise that it has a huge stake in the rapid economic development of its neighbourhood. The economic performance of India has been the best in South Asia during the decade of 1990s. But that rapid development is no guarantor of stability in South Asia. Without all boats rising in South Asia at the same time, India can neither prosper nor be secure. While globalisation is chipping away at the notion of South Asia as an exclusive sphere of influence of India, it is reinforcing the primacy of the Indian market in the long-term evolution of the South Asian economies. The integration of the markets of the Subcontinent over the coming decades is inevitable. This has opened the doors for unilateral Indian initiatives to promote economic integration and political stability in South Asia.

Globalization is beckoning India with the prospect of resolving long-standing conflicts in the region and re-integrating the South Asian market. If India can think big and act bold, a prosperous Subcontinent is within the realm of political imagination. An Indian strategy to shape such a future would involve shedding excessive suspicion of other great powers, finding ways to act in cooperation with them, and discarding the old slogans on "internationalisation", 'bilateralism' and 'reciprocity'. Such a strategy must consider unilateral economic actions that will accelerate integration of the region. Instead embarking on tortuous bilateral negotiations on trade with the smaller neighbours, India can alter the economic dynamics of the region through unilateral actions. Security multilateralism and positive economic unilateralism from India are the keys to a different future in the Subcontinent.

5.4 SAFTA and Economic Cooperation

International trade helps in improving welfare by allowing higher levels of consumption and investment than otherwise possible. In a labour surplus country like Pakistan it also helps in generating higher employment and higher wage rates with positive implications for income distribution and poverty, thus further raising the level of social welfare.

While the promotion of multilateral trade, mandate of WTO, promises higher rate of economic growth across the globe, the spread of regional blocs denies the advantages of free trade to the countries that are not part of the group. Therefore, for enjoying benefits of higher trade, including improved resource allocation, higher level of technical and X-efficiency and wider options for consumers and exposure to new ideas, technologies and products, the South Asian countries must ensure trade facilitation, higher investment and economic cooperation in other areas of economic development for the countries of the region.

Although the South Asian Association for Regional Cooperation (SAARC) has been in existence for about 20 years, intra-regional trade is still around 4 percent of their total trade [See IRS (2004)]. The South Asian Preferential Trade Agreement (SAPTA) signed in the mid-90s has helped little in promoting the intra-regional trade because most of the products of export interest to the regional countries were excluded from the preferential treatment. It reflects mistrust and unwillingness of the South Asian countries to increase their interdependence, that augurs well for political and economic cohesion.

The SAARC summit declaration of Islamabad promises a South Asian Free Trade Area (SAFTA). It calls for reduction in import duties to 20 percent by 2006 and between 0-5 percent by 2013 but allows the less developed economies to reduce the rate of duties to 0-5 percent by the year 2016. SAFTA allows the countries to notify the negative list which will not enjoy concessional import duties. Obviously, if the negative list is quite large, the impact of the agreements will be little. Considering the significance of trade to welfare, it is hoped that the South Asian countries will keep the negative list small.

5.5 Intra-regional Trade and SAPTA

For promoting intra-regional trade, a preferential treaty (SAPTA) was signed in 1994 and in the first round that came into effect in 1995. Concessions were granted on 226 products in 1995 after the first round. It took four rounds to agree on 4700 products out of 6000 by the year 2000, with India leading the list, Maldives being the last in the list.

Despite the concessions to a large number of products, there has hardly been any increase in intra-regional trade in the total international trade of the region. This is because of the following:

1. Firstly, negotiations under SAPTA have been conducted mainly on a product-by-product basis, which allows some flexibility to each member country, but takes a lot of time.
2. Second, the tariff cuts offered under SAPTA have not been enough. For example, India has offered the preferences on many products and the margins have been maximum, but its MFN rates are typically higher than those of its partners, and as such concessions had very little impact.
3. Third, most of the products to which were given concessions are not widely traded in the region. Confining solely to the tariffs and leaving para-tariff and non-tariff measures out of the negotiations has limited the growth of intra-regional trade as has high local content criterion. The countries have comparative advantage in similar products which also tends to reduce the

trade potential.

5.6 SAFTA Agreements and Possibilities of Intra-regional Trade

SAARC's Islamabad declaration in 1994 promises South Asian Free Trade Area SAFTA) which would come into force on January 1, 2006, to be fully implemented by the end of 2015. Under the agreement, tariff reductions, rules of origin, safeguards, institutional structures, and dispute settlement will be sorted out by various committees.

It also calls for harmonisation of standards and customs procedures, mutual recognition of test results and transport infrastructure cooperation. These measures would hopefully help in promoting the intra-regional trade.

SAFTA's tariff reduction program calls upon India, Pakistan, and Sri Lanka, to reduce tariffs to 20 percent by 2006. While Nepal, Bhutan, Bangladesh and Maldives, less developed countries, are required to reduce tariffs to 30 percent by 2006. Following that Pakistan and India in five years, Sri Lanka in six years and other SAARC countries in 8 years shall have to reduce their tariffs to 0-5 percent. Moreover, India, Pakistan, and Sri Lanka will reduce their tariffs on imports from the relatively less developed countries to 0-5 percent by January 1, 2009.

The agreement calls for elimination of all quantitative restrictions for products on the tariff liberalisation list. The agreement allows a negative list, but it provides for reviewing the number of products on the sensitive list at four-year intervals to reduce the list and expand the free trade coverage of the Agreement.

Regional groupings have proliferated around the globe. While some have been successful, others have not. World Bank (2004) reviews the regional experiences around the world and points out six broad conclusions for the success of such groupings of free trade.

Firstly, a regional trade agreement does not automatically result in increased trade and growth. Whereas the intention at the time of formation of the group is always to promote intra-regional trade and economic cooperation in all the fields, a large number of interest groups emerge who on the grounds of injury to their industry, call for exemption of reduction in the import duties.

The experience with SAPTA has been disappointing for this reason. SAFTA allows a sensitive list and if the list is large, then it may not see higher intra-regional trade.

Whenever trade would be promoted, the industries in which the country does not have comparative advantage will close down. Moreover, agreements that kept in place high external border barriers, protect inefficient activities and undermine the competitiveness of all countries.

Second, the trading arrangements with unilateral efforts among members to reduce external protection have been more successful. Reducing trade barriers vis-à-vis the rest of the world creates an incentive for all members to export. It augments competition that drives domestic productivity. When external protection is generally low, trade creation usually dominates trade diversion, and so the risk that regional agreements will be a drag on growth is substantially reduced. Indeed regional agreements where members have had low external protection have enjoyed greatest success.

Third, the agreements between the countries with different factor endowments have shown more consistent success because of the opportunities to exploit different comparative wage rates, capital availability, technological levels that give rise to differing factor proportions in production. However, this conclusion runs contrary to the success of EU. The promotion of intra-industry trade would result in higher growth even if factor endowments are similar.

Fourth, a regional integration framework that helps in trade creation and competition amongst regional countries would help in lowering domestic prices and providing new technology. It is impossible to have the benefits of a regional agreement without exposing the member economies to new competition.

Fifth, competition in services also results in successful integration. Lowering the cost of telecommunications, finance, business services, and retail and wholesale commerce would result in productivity gains. Finally, there is a need to streamline borders transactions through trade facilitation. Increase in efficiency within the region often spills over into trade outside the region as well, because improving customs or improving efficiency of ports helps both intraregional trade and international trade.

To ensure the success of SAFTA, the member countries have to take a number of initiatives. Firstly, all countries must have very small negative list. If the list is large, the SAFTA would become redundant. There should be a firm basis to exclude products and ground rules should be laid down and be transparent. Second, keeping rules of origin simple and transparent and they must not become devices of protection and impediments to trade. The SAPTA rules, which are quite stringent, need to be revised. Third, ambitious agreements to establish detailed investors' protections and separate dispute panel resolution systems should be left for the future, because it could delay the progress unnecessarily. Fourth, since some of the SAARC members may dump and some may provide subsidies to exports and hence unfair competition, the transparent anti-dumping and countervailing methods may be necessary. However, anti-dumping actions and countervailing duties against regional partners can bring back the protectionist tendencies; anti-dumping mechanisms can stifle the benefits for SAFTA arrangements.

What would be the impact of SAFTA? RIS (2004) reports results of studies conducted in the framework of gravity model. It suggests that complete elimination of tariffs under SAFTA may increase the intra-regional trade by 1.6 times. It further suggests that in the dynamic framework the gains from liberalisation are at least 25 percent higher than the static gains. However, these gains are grossly in view of SAARC's large trade potential; it exists both in trade diversion from traditional sources towards SAARC countries by removing the constraints and trade creation and expansion by easing import restrictions on products which SAARC countries are not trading in but are their major exports. While more than half the exports of manufactured goods from South Asia consist of textiles and leather products, they are subject to very high rates of import duties and/or quantitative restrictions and even outright bans in South Asia.

Similarly, rather limited trade in engineering goods is owing to a number of factors including reliance on foreign aid to finance the import of capital goods, poor quality of goods and heavy import duties on capital goods even by the countries who are themselves exporters of capital goods.

Intra-industry trade can play an important role in bolstering economic and trade relations within the region. This is because intra-industry trade can take place even in situations where the trade and production structures of the trading partners lack strong complementarities, as observed in South Asian countries. Whereas the intensity of intra-industry trade is low, the potential for widening the scope of this type of trade within the region is rather large. However, that can only be realised if the import duties are low. Intra-industry trade is largely driven by product differentiation and increasing returns to scale. Therefore, an increased level of intra-industry trade in the region can only be achieved if the regional countries develop the technological capacity to produce different product varieties at declining average cost.

Lack of trade complementarities causes weak trade linkages in South Asia. However, trade complementarities can be developed within the region if countries achieve vertical specialisation through production sharing arrangements. The manufacturing of components for automobile and engineering industries would be quite helpful. Similarly, in chemical industries the possibilities exist. Vertical specialisation would not only allow the regional trading partners to strengthen their trade ties, but also enable them to reap economies of scale by concentrating on a specific production process in the value-addition chain. Therefore, as in the case of various regional trading groups around the world, the South Asian countries can boost economic cooperation by developing vertically integrated production structures, thereby attaining vertical specialisation.

Joint ventures can pool regional resources to promote industrialisation and economic growth in South Asia. Since the South Asian countries have collectively gained substantial experience in agro-based industries, textiles and clothing, paper and pulp, and light engineering, there seems to be scope for joint ventures in these areas. The establishment of joint ventures will particularly benefit the small South Asian countries because they lack the resources to undertake industrial investment efficiently.

The signing of SAFTA has created euphoria in the South Asian countries. However, there are, at least, two possibilities which may make the agreement redundant. Firstly, all the countries are members of WTO and would reduce the tariff levels. If their MFN tariffs are close to preferential tariffs under SAFTA, intra-regional trade may not grow rapidly. Though one could argue that at lower rate of import duty, with or without SAFTA, the intra-regional and trade outside the region would flourish. Second and more importantly, if the negative list is large and includes most of the products of export interest of South Asian countries, trade would not flourish. The SAARC countries must make an effort to make SAFTA a success to expedite economic development, mainly because of the problems in global market access and the higher transaction costs of producing for the world market. The expansion of regional trade yields gains in production specialisation, efficiency and improved quality of exports, which benefit the countries participating in the regional co-operation effort.

5.7 India and SAARC

South Asia has been recognised as a distinct region in the world. There are commonalities in the region in the field of socio-economic and cultural advancement. The history of International relations in this region has been marked more by conflict than cooperation. Now it is a matter of satisfaction that regional cooperation has acquired a firm institutional base through different Summit.

To face the challenges of globalisation and reap its benefits, what is called for is regional co-operation among the South Asian nations. India being the biggest and the most powerful state in the region has to take the responsibility by striking a balance.

Indeed such ties could be plausibly built on co-operative footings if India and its neighbours are individually as well as collectively able to relate themselves to two dominant trends in post cold war world, globalisation and regional co-operation.

In its broad sense, the term globalisation involves shrinking of distances between peoples, societies, states and continents and consequent emergence of consciousness of the world as a whole. The unprecedented movement of goods, services, capital, finances, technologies, arms, drugs, crime and information are in turn constantly facilitating shrinking of distances across the world. In the process, states as well as civil societies across the world are engaged in negotiating with the challenges of globalisation with a great vigour. India and other South Asian nations are no exception to this rule. For instance, like most other states these states are working through international regimes like WTO while dealing with trade issues under globalisation. Also, these civil societies are operating through diverse international networks of inter-societal movements dealing with the problems of human right and environment. Briefly, the phase of globalisation has changed the dimension of inter-state and inter-societal conflicts as well as cooperation.

The second dominant trend in contemporary international relation has been proliferation of organisations that promote regional co-operation. In a way this trend in the current content, could as well be construed as a response to globalisation. Thus old and established organisations like European Community (EC) or South African Development Co-ordination Council (SADCC) are being recast to form more expansive or inclusive unit like the European Union or South African Development Community (SADC) respectively. Also new regional organisations are created like the North American Free Trade Agreement (NAFTA). By and large the effective functioning of such organisations, particularly in the third world, depends on the role played by regionally dominant states. For instance regionally dominant states like South Africa, Nigeria, Brazil, Indonesia, Iran and India have been playing an important role in promoting the projects of regional co-operation in their respective regions.

In view of these dominant trends in international relations, it would be worthwhile to place the relationship between India and South Asia in the changing context. In fact India's strength in the world affairs and capacity to negotiate with the phase of globalisation greatly depends upon the prospects of harmony and co-operation among the South-Asian states. Evidently, the promotion of regional organisations such as South Asian Association for Regional Co-operation (SAARC) would enjoy added significance in this context. Hence, at this juncture it would be essential to reflect on a few pertinent questions that have no impact on India's ties with its South Asian neighbours as well as prospects of regional co-operation in South Asia.

South Asia is often described as Indo-centric region owing to two dominant reasons. First there is an evident asymmetry in distribution of power within the region between India, on the one hand and the rest of states in South Asia on the other. India is incontestably the most powerful state of South Asia. Certain obvious elements of state power such as India's size, location, natural and mineral resources, substantial trained man power, level of industrialisation, military might including nuclear capabilities and stable democratic polity offer an obvious evidence of India's overwhelming advantage over its neighbours.

This asymmetry in power between India and its immediate neighbours have often made the latter state apprehensive of India's hegemonistic ambition in the region. Important developments such as the war of 1971 and the birth of Bangladesh as also India's military intervention in Sri Lanka and Maldives during the late 1980s have reinforced such-apprehensions, second in linguistic cultural and social terms, India is the hub of the South Asia where all the predominant social and cultural streams can converge.

To put it sharply, India has several commonalities with all its neighbours. For instance, there are people of Tamil ethnic origin in Sri Lanka and Tamil Nadu is a Tamil speaking state within the Indian union. Bengali, Punjabi and Urdu languages bind the people of Bangladesh, Pakistan and India. The existence of major religious groups belonging to Hindu, Buddhist and Islamic faith binds Nepal, Sri Lanka, Pakistan, Bangladesh and India together. To put it sharply, unlike all other South-Asian states, the multi-cultural society of India provides far more diverse ranges of bridges to link the heterogeneous peoples of South Asia. Considering the centrality of its position, India, under normal circumstances, has to be a leader to steer through the projects of regional co-operation in South Asia in a globalising world.

India has made its own contribution in building the projects of regional co-operation in South Asia. For instance, India has stressed on regional cooperation and non-reciprocity of relationship between India and its smaller neighbours did usher in a new phase of co-operation. Thus, India chooses to promote trade with Sri Lanka and Bangladesh by lifting tariffs and trade barriers performing to a variety of primary products. Similarly, India and Bangladesh signed an agreement on sharing of Ganga water and efforts were made to execute the agreement on Mahakali river between India and Nepal. Indeed, promoting ties among the competitive economies such as those of South Asian countries is an uphill task. However, several developmental problems such as poverty, unemployment, illiteracy, AIDS and health care, gender discrimination, child labour and depleting water resources have been staring at the South-Asian states. India plausibly can negotiate and build a notion of a region and projects of regional co-operation. So far as Indo-Pak relations are concerned, if India and Pakistan fail to recognise the significance of regional co-operation, the on-going tension between these states, would continue to scuttle any substantive modes of building regional co-operation that promote developmental objectives.

In fact the best way to promote regional co-operation would be to keep the Kashmir issue in the background for the time being and concentrate on more pressing development requirements of the region as a whole. The Kashmir issue essentially has to be construed in bilateral terms, but the deadlock between India and Pakistan in the process of negotiations over Kashmir has made its resolution difficult; as a result, the issue is increasingly getting internationalised.

Owing to the lack of substantial co-operation among the South Asian states, the negative offshoots of the conflict such as traffic in arms and drugs, cross border terrorism, terrorism stemming from religious fanaticism of any kind has begun to capture the foreground of social space. In order to reverse this trend, people-to-people contact and constant emphasis on co-operation as well as promotion of development related issues have become a necessity. In substance, only creative politicians and intellectuals with a constructive and tolerant mindset can steer the South-Asian region to face the challenges of globalisation. In this major endeavour India will have to share the responsibility.

Ten summit level meetings of the SAARC have been held since the Association has been established. A wide ranging programme for co-operation in areas like agriculture and rural development, social development, environment, meteorology, and forestry, science and technology, human resource, energy etc. has been developed since its inception in 1985. SAARC members have also co-operated extensively in the forums like the WTO and on environment related issues. NGO's, cultural organisations, human right groups, journalism and academic institutions and the member countries have come closer leading to the evolution of a distinctly South Asian identity and fostering a feeling of togetherness.

While regional economic co-operation has grown in 'soft' areas in SAARC, the countries of South Asia have to vastly expand their co-operation in core areas like trade, industry and investment. If the organisation is to make a meaningful contribution towards enhancing regional progress and prosperity, the Ninth SAARC summit in Maldives set up a 'Group of eminent persons', to identify measures to enhance the effectiveness of the Association. The group that included the former foreign secretary Muchkund Dubey and Dr. V.A. Panandiker from India, came out with a report entitled 'SAARC Vision Beyond the year 2000'.

The core recommendation of this group was that negotiations should be concluded by 2001 for South Asia to become a free trade Area by 2008, with least developed countries joining it by 2010. Investments are to be promoted by finalising a regional investment agreement and custom procedure, custom infrastructure and standards simultaneously harmonised.

The ultimate aim is to make SAARC a customs union by 2015 and an Economic community by 2020. If implemented the committee's recommendations could well lead to South Asia becoming a region where there would be virtually free movement of people, goods, services and investments across national boundaries.

Our economic relations with our neighbours in South Asia are forced to expand rapidly. Exports from Nepal and Bhutan already enjoy duty free access to our markets. We have recently concluded a free trade agreement with Sri Lanka. Indian companies are increasing their investments and collaboration there. We have removed all quantitative restrictions for SAARC countries in 1998 during the course of negotiations for South Asian preferential trading agreement.

A sub-regional 'Growth Quadrangle' comprising-Nepal, Bhutan, Bangladesh and India was set up in 1996. This grouping needs to be activated for the development and optimum utilisation of river water and other resources and to tackle issues like flood control – all areas where functional co-operation can be of immense benefit.

Set up in 1997, BIMSTEC group, bringing together the littoral states of the Bay of Bengal–Bangladesh, Myanmar, Sri Lanka and Thailand has an immense potential. It focuses on enhancing cooperation in crucial areas like transportation links trade, investment, tourism, fisheries and agriculture. It is committed to consultation on developing the Asian Highway Network. It should bring India and other participating SAARC members together with Myanmar and Thailand– both members of ASEAN – in a free trade agreement. Such co-operation will give a boost to property in our north-eastern states. Our co-operation with the countries of the economically dynamic South-East Asian region is now re-inforced by our interaction with them in groupings like the ASEAN regional forum and BIMSTEC. The initiative on the 'Ganga Mekong Swarna Bhoomi Project' taken at the recent ARF meeting will develop our transportation and communication links and economic co-operation not only with Myanmar and Thailand but also with Vietnam, Laos and Cambodia. It would also enhance our participation in the development of the Mekong basin.

The forums like Indian Ocean Rim Association for Regional Co-operation need to be activated with measures for expansion of trade, investment and communication ties in Indian Ocean region.

5.8 SAARC Summits

It is observed that regional cooperation is a means for the fuller realization of the national goals and objectives set by each member country. Its primary purpose is to strengthen the opportunity for the progress of each country within the region. This organization has also emphasized the role of academics, researchers, non-governmental organizations, and other in promoting SAARC spirit. United effort is needed to solve these problems. Thus the main objectives for which SAARC stands, are:

1. Greater interchange of experience in various fields of development.
2. Cultural exchange and cooperation.
3. Cooperation in the application of science and technology.
4. Expansion of economic relationship.

SAARC is a well defined entity in political and geographical terms. It is also a region having common problems like under development, poverty and population growth. The success of SAARC in the field of transfer of technology development of Himalayas resources and environmental protection is inspiring. The goal of a federation of cultures on the basis of prosperity has also materialized.

SAARC operates through the meetings of the Heads of State of Government, Council of Ministers, Standing Committee of Foreign Secretaries, Technical Committees, Action Committees and the Secretariat. The meeting of Heads of State consists of all members states and is the highest authority of the Association. It is held annually.

The council of ministers comprises the foreign ministers of the member states and formulates policies, review the progress of cooperation, decision of new areas of cooperation and the mechanism necessary for those purpose. The standing committee is responsible for overall monitoring and coordination of programme of action. The technical committees comprising representatives of members states are responsible for the implementation, coordination and monitoring of programmes in their respective areas of cooperation. At present there are 11 technical committees.

5.8.1 12th SAARC Summit: The 12th SAARC Summit held in Islamabad from January 4-6 2004, focussed on the scourge of terrorism in the region. This summit was preceded by the most unprecedented events in its history. In spite of all difficulties, the Summit took place very peacefully. The main agenda before the 12th SAARC Summit could be analysed in the following ways.

- Poverty alleviation.
- Curbing women and child trafficking.
- Suppression of Terrorism.
- Enhancement of economic cooperation.

The 12th South Asian Association for Regional Cooperation Summit will be remembered as path-breaking. The Joint statement setting the stage for peace, the signing of the South Asian Free Trade Area agreement establishing a free trade zone in South Asia by 2006 and moving towards an economic union and the signing of the additional protocol on terrorism are all major heralders of change. The Joint statement was also a victory for common sense and for moderation.

SAARC countries also decided to work towards the creation of a South Asian economic union and the establishment of a regional food bank as part of a plan to tackle poverty in the region. They also focussed to examine the feasibility of a South Asian development Bank. Last but not least, the seven page 43 point declaration envisioned South Asia to be a peaceful and stable region where each nation was at place with itself and its neighbours and their conflicts, differences and disputes were addressed through peaceful means and dialogue. The declaration also reaffirmed its pledge to promote good neighbourly relations on the basis of the principles of sovereign equality, territorial integrity, and national independence, non-used of force, non-intervention and non-interference and peaceful settlement of disputes.

5.8.2 13th SAARC Summit: The 13th Summit of the seven-member regional forum, South Asian Association of Regional Cooperation (SAARC) was held with the leaders agreeing to realise the vision of the South Asian Economic Union in a phased and planned manner. They agreed to draw a road map for enhanced cooperation. In the 8-page "Dhaka Declaration," the leaders directed all SAARC institutions and mechanisms to work collectively towards a decade dedicated to the implementation of the plans.

While this would enable SAARC to realise its basic objective of improving the quality of life of South Asian people, it would also create an enabling environment for the establishment of a South Asian Economic Union. They directed the standing committee to formulate its recommendations at its next special session, on a Vision for SAARC's Third Decade and the course of action.

Bangladesh capital Dhaka played host to the conference of the SAARC leaders for the third time, having the unique honour of being the launching pad for the first summit in 1985 and then again in the seventh summit in 1993.

This time, fittingly, the new "Dhaka Declaration" has been adopted by the summit at a crucially important juncture as the forum enters the third decade amid growing needs and priorities to make the SAARC more action-oriented. The Declaration envisages manifold activities for rejuvenating the SAARC programmes in the days ahead with the emphasis on poverty alleviation, increasing economic activities among the members and combating terrorism.

The new chairperson of the SAARC, host nation Bangladesh's Prime Minister Begum Khaleda Zia, presided over the concluding session held in the International Conference Centre (ICC) at the Prime Minister's office. Bhutan's Prime Minister Lyonpo Sangay Ngedup, Indian Prime Minister Dr. Manmohan

Singh, Maldives President Maumoon Abdul Gayoom, Nepalese King Gyanendra Bir Bikram Shah Dev and Pakistan Prime Minister Shawkat Aziz were present. Sri Lankan President Chandrika Kumaratunga earlier left for home owing to her preoccupation with the presidential elections on November 17.The summit decided that the 14th SAARC Summit will take place in India in 2007.

5.8.3 14th SAARC Summit: India hosted the 14th SAARC Summit in New Delhi on April 3-4, 2007 thereby assuming the Chairmanship of SAARC. For the first time in its history, SAARC expanded its membership at the 14th Summit to include Afghanistan as the eighth member. This year, for the first time, five outside observers, China, Japan, United States, South Korea, and the European Union attended the SAARC summit. Iran has also been welcomed as an Observer in SAARC. The 29th Council of Ministers Meeting (7-8 December, 2007) approved the request of Mauritius to be associated as Observer to SAARC.

The two-day Summit with eight nations including Afghanistan as a new member by adopting a 30-point Declaration gave a wider mandate to promote peace and development in the region through greater connectivity in trade, movement of people and through flow of ideas. The immediate objective of the Summit was the formation of a modality to fight against terrorism in the South Asian region. The SAARC members also expressed satisfaction at the launching of 2007 as the 'Year of Green South Asia. The leaders of the SAARC nations also expressed positive reception over the offer of the Maldives to host the 15th Summit Meeting of the Heads of States or Governments of the South Asian Association for the Regional Cooperation (SAARC). The declaration also welcomed Iran's association with the SAARC as an observer status.

During the Summit all the leaders agreed to improve intra-regional connectivity through physical, economic and people to people connectivity. In case of physical connectivity, an important decision was to extend the SAARC Regional Multimodal Transport Study to Afghanistan. For economic connectivity, SAARC countries committed themselves to early operationalization of the SAARC Development Fund (SDF) and implementing trade facilitation measures. The Heads of Government agreed to strengthen the security network by sharing of information, increased frequency of meetings between security chiefs and consider India's proposal to work towards finalizing an Agreement on Mutual Legal Assistance in Criminal Matters.

5.8.4 15th SAARC Summit: The Fifteenth Summit of SAARC was held in Colombo, Sri Lanka on August 1-3, 2008. The issues discussed were regional cooperation, partnership for growth for the peoples of South Asia, connectivity, energy, the environment, water resources, poverty alleviation, the SAARC Development Fund, transport, information and communications technology development, science and technology, tourism, culture, the South Asian Free Trade Area, the SAARC Social Charter, women and children, education, combating terrorism, and the admission of Australia and Myanamar as observers.

At the Summit, one of the major points of discussion was the global food crisis. The SAARC heads of government made a statement saying "in view of the emerging global situation of reduced food availability and worldwide rise in food prices, we direct that an extra-ordinary meeting of the Agriculture Ministers of the SAARC Member States be convened in New Delhi, India in November 2008, to evolve and implement people-centred short to medium term regional strategy and collaborative projects." They also acknowledged the need to forge greater cooperation with the international community to ensure the food availability and nutrition security.

5.8.5 16th SAARC Summit: The Sixteenth Summit was held in Thimpu, Bhutan on April 28-29, 2010. Bhutan hosted the SAARC summit for the first time. This was marked the silver jubilee celebration of SAARC that was formed in Bangladesh in December 1985. Climate change was the central issue of the summit with summit's theme "Towards a Green and Happy South Asia". Outcome of Thimpu Summit regarding climate change issue:

1. SAARC leaders signed a SAARC Convention on Cooperation on Environment to tackle the problem of climate change.
2. The SAARC nations also pledged to plant 10 million trees over the next 5 years.
3. India proposed setting up of climate innovation centres in South Asia to develop sustainable energy technologies.
4. India offered services of India's mission on sustaining the Himalayan Ecosystem to the SAARC member states saying that the initiative could serve as a nucleus for regional cooperation in this vital area.
5. India announced "India endowment for climate change" in South Asia to help member states meet their urgent adaption and capacity building needs posed by the climate change.
6. The seven-page 'Thimphu Silver Jubilee Declaration-Towards a Green and Happy South Asia' emphasised the importance of reducing dependence on high-carbon technologies for economic growth and hoped promotion of climate resilience will promote both development and poverty eradication in a sustainable manner.

5.8.6 17th SAARC Summit: The Seventeenth Summit was held from November 10-11, 2011 in Addu City, Maldives. The Meeting, which was held at the Equatorial Convention Centre, Addu City was opened by the outgoing Chair of SAARC, Prime Minister of the Royal Government of Bhutan, H.E. Lyonchhen

Jigmi Yoezer Thinley.

H.E. Mohamed Nasheed was elected as the Chairperson of the 17th SAARC Summit. In his inaugural address President Nasheed highlighted three areas of cooperation in which progress should be made; trade, transport and economic integration; security issues such piracy and climate change; and good governance. President also called on the Member States to establish a commission to address issues of gender inequalities in South Asia. The Head of States of all the SAARC Member States addressed the Meeting. The inaugural meeting was attended by Foreign/External Ministers of SAARC Member States, the Secretary General of SAARC, the Heads of Observer Delegation, Cabinet Ministers of the Maldives, Ministers in the visiting delegations and other state dignitaries. In her address Secretary General stated that the Summit being held under the theme of "Building Bridges" provides further impetus and momentum to build the many bridges that needs to be built: from bridging the gaps created by uneven economic development and income distribution, the gaps in recognizing and respecting the equality of men and women, the closing of space between intent and implementation. In this Meeting, the Foreign Ministers of the respective Member States signed four agreements.

SAARC Agreement on Rapid Response to Natural Disasters SAARC Agreement on Multilateral Arrangement on Recognition of Conformity Assessment SAARC Agreement on Implementation of Regional Standards SAARC Seed Bank Agreement In addition, the Addu Declaration of the Seventeenth SAARC Summit was also adopted.

6

India's Relations with Neighbours

6.1 India and Pakistan

Relations with Pakistan have demanded a high proportion of India's international energies and undoubtedly will continue to do so. India and Pakistan have divergent national ideologies and have been unable to establish a mutually acceptable power equation in South Asia. The national ideologies of pluralism, democracy, and secularism for India and of Islam for Pakistan grew out of the pre-Independence struggle between the Congress and the All-India Muslim League, and in the early 1990s the line between domestic and foreign politics in India's relations with Pakistan remained blurred. Because great-power competition—between the United States and the Soviet Union and between the Soviet Union and China—became intertwined with the conflicts between India and Pakistan, India was unable to attain its goal of insulating South Asia from global rivalries. This superpower involvement enabled Pakistan to use external force in the face of India's superior endowments of population and resources.

The most difficult problem in relations between India and Pakistan since partition in August 1947 has been their dispute over Kashmir. Pakistan's leaders did not accept the legality of the Instrument of Accession of Kashmir to India, and undeclared war broke out in October 1947. It was the first of three conflicts between the two countries. Pakistan's representatives ever since have argued that the people of Kashmir should be allowed to exercise their right to self-determination through a plebiscite, as promised by Nehru and required by UN Security Council resolutions in 1948 and 1949. The inconclusive fighting led to an UN-arranged cease-fire starting on January 1, 1949.

On July 18, 1949, the two sides signed the Karachi Agreement establishing a cease-fire line that was to be supervised by the UN. The demarcation left Srinagar and almost 139,000 square kilometres under Indian control and 83,807 square kilometres under Pakistani control. Of these two areas, China occupied 37,555 square kilometres in India's Ladakh District (part of which is known as Aksai Chin) in 1962 and Pakistan ceded, in effect, 5,180 square kilometres in the Karakoram area to China when the two countries demarcated their common border in 1961-65, leaving India with 101,387 square kilometres and Pakistan with 78,387 square kilometres. Starting in January 1949, and still in place in

1995, the UN Military Observer Group in India and Pakistan was tasked with supervising the cease-fire in Kashmir. The group comprises thirty-eight observers—from Belgium, Chile, Denmark, Finland, Italy, Norway, Sweden, and Uruguay—who rotate their headquarters every six months between Srinagar (summer) and Rawalpindi, Pakistan (winter).

In 1952, the elected and overwhelmingly Muslim Constituent Assembly of Jammu and Kashmir, led by the popular Sheikh Mohammed Abdullah, voted in favour of confirming accession to India. Thereafter, India regarded this vote as an adequate expression of popular will and demurred on holding a plebiscite. After 1953 Jammu and Kashmir was identified as standing for the secular, pluralistic, and democratic principles of the Indian polity. Nehru refused to discuss the subject bilaterally until 1963, when India, under pressure from the United States and Britain, engaged in six rounds of secret talks with Pakistan on "Kashmir and other related issues." These negotiations failed, as did the 1964 attempt at mediation made by Abdullah, who recently had been released from a long detention by the Indian government because of his objections to Indian control.

Armed infiltrators from Pakistan crossed the cease-fire line, and the number of skirmishes between Indian and Pakistani troops increased in the summer of 1965. Starting on August 5, 1965, India alleged, Pakistani forces began to infiltrate the Indian-controlled portion of Jammu and Kashmir. India made a countermove in late August, and by September 1, 1965, the second conflict had fully erupted as Pakistan launched an attack across the international line of control in southwest Jammu and Kashmir. Indian forces retaliated on September 6 in Pakistan's Punjab Province and prevailed over Pakistan's apparent superiority in tanks and aircraft. A cease-fire called by the UN Security Council on September 23 was observed by both sides. At Tashkent, Uzbekistan, in January 1966, the belligerents agreed to restore the status quo ante and to resolve outstanding issues by negotiation.

The third war between India and Pakistan, in December 1971, cantered in the east over the secession of East Pakistan (which became Bangladesh), but it also included engagements in Kashmir and elsewhere on the India-West Pakistan front. India's military victory was complete. The independence of Bangladesh was widely interpreted in India—but not in Pakistan—as an ideological victory disproving the "Two Nations Theory" pushed by the Muslim League and that led to partition in 1947. At Shimla, Himachal Pradesh, on July 2, 1972, Indira Gandhi and Pakistan's President Zulfikar Ali Bhutto signed the Shimla Accord by which India would return all personnel and captured territory in the west and the two countries would "settle their differences by peaceful means through bilateral negotiations." External bodies, including the UN, were excluded from the process. The fighting had resulted in the capture of each other's territory at various points along the cease-fire line, but the Shimla Accord defined a new line of control that deviated in only minor ways from the 1949 cease-fire line. The two sides agreed not to alter the actual line of control unilaterally and promised to respect it "without prejudice to the recognized position of either side." Both sides further undertook to "refrain from the threat or use of force in violation of the line."

During the late 1970s and early 1980s, Jammu and Kashmir prospered under a virtually autonomous government led first by Sheikh Abdullah and then by his son Farooq Abdullah. In the summer of 1984, differences between Srinagar and New Delhi led to the dismissal of Farooq's government by highly questionable means. Kashmir once again became an irritant in bilateral relations. Indian diplomats consistently accused Pakistan of trying to "internationalize" the Kashmir dispute in violation of the Shimla Accord.

In the mid to late 1980s, the political situation in Kashmir became increasingly unstable. In March 1986, New Delhi invoked President's Rule to remove Farooq's successor, Ghulam Mohammed Shah, as chief minister, and replace his rule with that of Governor Jagmohan, who had been appointed by the central government in 1984. In state elections held in 1987, Farooq's political party, the National Conference, forged an alliance with Rajiv Gandhi's Congress (I), which won a majority in the state elections. Farooq's government failed to deal with Kashmir's economic problems and the endemic corruption of its public institutions, providing fertile ground for militant Kashmiris who demanded either independence or association with Pakistan.

A rising spiral of unrest, demonstrations, armed attacks by Kashmiri separatists, and armed suppression by Indian security forces started in 1988 and was still occurring in the mid-1990s. New Delhi charged Islamabad (Pakistan's capital) with assisting insurgents in Jammu and Kashmir, and Prime Minister V.P. Singh warned that India should be psychologically prepared for war. In Pakistan Prime Minister Benazir Bhutto stated that Pakistan was willing to fight a "thousand-year war" for control of Kashmir. Under pressure from the United States, the Soviet Union, and China to avoid a military conflict and solve their dispute under the terms of the Shimla Accord, India and Pakistan backed off in May 1990 and engaged in a series of talks on confidence-building measures for the rest of the year. Tensions reached new heights in the early and mid-1990s with increasing internal unrest in Jammu and Kashmir, charges of human rights abuses, and repeated clashes between Indian paramilitary forces and Kashmiri militants, allegedly armed with Pakistani-supplied weapons.

A concurrent irritant related to the Kashmir dispute was the confrontation over the Siachen Glacier near the Karakoram Pass, which is located in northeast Jammu and Kashmir. In 1984, Indian officials, citing Pakistan's "cartographic aggression" extending the line of control northeast toward the Karakoram Pass, contended that Pakistan intended to occupy the Siachen Glacier in order to stage an attack into Indian-controlled Kashmir. After New Delhi airlifted troops into the western parts of the Saltoro Mountains, Islamabad deployed troops opposite them. Both sides maintained 5,000 troops in temperatures averaging -40°C. The estimated cost for India was about 10 percent of the annual defence budget for FY 1992. After several skirmishes between the opposing troops, negotiations to resolve this confrontation began with five rounds of talks between 1986 and 1989. After a three-year hiatus because of tensions caused by the other Kashmir conflict, a sixth round of talks was held in November 1992. Some progress was made on the details of an agreement. In March 1994, Indian diplomats garnered enough support at the UN Human Rights Commission to force Pakistan to withdraw a resolution charging India with human rights violations in Jammu and Kashmir. The two sides were encouraged to resolve their dispute through bilateral talks.

After the Soviet Union invaded Afghanistan in December 1979 and Indira Gandhi returned to power in 1980, she quickly dispatched a special emissary to assure Pakistani president General Mohammad Zia-ul-Haq that he could remove as many divisions as he wished from the Indian border without fear of any advantage being taken by India and suggested talks on reduction of force levels. Indian officials worked hard to prevent Zia from using the Afghan crisis as an opportunity to alter the regional balance of power by acquiring advanced weapons from the United States. In addition, Indira Gandhi attempted to avoid antagonizing the Soviet Union, democratic elements in Pakistan, and the substantial anti-Pakistan lobby within India. These largely secret efforts culminated in the visit of Minister of External Affairs P.V. Narasimha Rao to Pakistan in June 1981, during which time he declared publicly that India was "unequivocally committed to respect Pakistan's national unity, territorial integrity, and sovereign equality" as well as its right to obtain arms for self-defence.

Despite the setback suffered when the United States and Pakistan announced a new security and military assistance program, regular meetings took place between high Indian and Pakistani officials. These meetings were institutionalized in late 1982 in the Indo-Pakistan Joint Commission, which included sub-commissions for trade, economics, information, and travel. Indira Gandhi also received Zia on November 1, 1982, in New Delhi, and during their meeting they authorized their foreign ministers and foreign secretaries to proceed with talks leading to the establishment of the South Asian Association for Regional Cooperation.

In the mid and late 1980s, India-Pakistan relations settled into a pattern of ups and downs. Despite the signing of an economic and trade agreement, little progress was made in concluding a comprehensive, long-term economic agreement to have non-discriminatory bilateral trade. In addition, New Delhi charged Islamabad with arming and training Sikh terrorists in Punjab. The government's 1984 *White Paper on the Punjab Agitation* stated that India's strength, unity, and secularism were targets of attack. The December 1985 visit of Zia to India, during which both sides agreed not to attack each other's nuclear facilities, ushered in a brief phase of cordiality, in which another agreement expanding trade was signed. The cordiality evaporated in early 1986, with further Indian unhappiness over Pakistan's alleged interference in Punjab and the bungled Pakistani handling of the terrorist seizure of a Pan American airliner in which many Indians died. For its part, Pakistan was disturbed by anti-Muslim riots in India, and Zia accused India of assisting the political campaign of Benazir Bhutto.

Between November 1986 and February 1987, first India, then Pakistan, conducted provocative military manoeuvres along their border that raised tensions considerably. India's "Operation Brass Tacks" took place in Rajasthan, across from Pakistan's troubled Sindh Province, and Pakistan's manoeuvres were located close to India's state of Punjab. The crisis atmosphere was heightened when Pakistan's premier nuclear scientist Abdul Qadir Khan revealed in a March 1987 interview that Pakistan had manufactured a nuclear bomb. Although Khan later retracted his statement, India stated that the disclosure was "forcing us to review our option." The tensions created by the military exercises and the nuclear issue were defused following talks at the foreign secretary level in New Delhi (January 31-February 4) and Islamabad (February 27-March 2), during which the two sides agreed to a phased troop withdrawal to peacetime positions.

The sudden death of Zia in an air crash in August 1988 and the assumption of the prime ministership by Benazir Bhutto in December 1988 after democratic elections provided the two countries with an unexpected opportunity to improve relations. Rajiv Gandhi's attendance at the SAARC summit in Islamabad in December 1988 permitted the two prime ministers to establish a personal rapport and to sign three bilateral agreements, including one proscribing attacks on each other's nuclear facilities. Despite the personal sympathy between the two leaders and Bhutto's initial emphasis on the 1972 Shimla Accord as the basis for warmer bilateral ties, domestic political pressures, particularly relating to unrest in Sindh, Punjab, and Kashmir effectively destroyed the chances for improved relations in

1989 and 1990. For her part, Bhutto backed away from her comments on the Shimla Accord by continuing to press the Kashmir issue internationally, and Indian public opinion forced Rajiv Gandhi and his successor, V.P. Singh, to take a hard line on events relating to Kashmir.

In the early 1990s, Indian-Pakistani relations remained troubled despite bilateral efforts and changes in the international environment. High-level dialogue on a range of bilateral issues took place between foreign ministers and prime ministers at the UN and at other international meetings. However, discussions over confidence-building measures, begun in the summer of 1990 as a response to the Kashmir confrontation, were cancelled in June 1992 following mutual expulsions of diplomats for alleged espionage activities. In June 1991, Pakistani prime minister Mian Nawaz Sharif proposed talks by India, Pakistan, the United States, the Soviet Union, and China to consider making South Asia a nuclear-free zone, but the minority governments of Chandra Shekhar and subsequently that of Narasimha Rao declined to participate. Nevertheless, negotiations concerning the Siachen Glacier resumed in November 1992 after a hiatus of three years. By the mid-1990s, little had occurred to improve bilateral relations as unrest in Jammu and Kashmir accelerated and domestic politics in both nations were unsettled.

6.2 India and Bangladesh

Although India played a major role in the establishment of an independent Bangladesh on April 17, 1971, New Delhi's relations with Dhaka, the capital of Bangladesh, were neither close nor free from dispute. In 1975 Bangladesh began to move away from the linguistic nationalism that had marked its liberation struggle and linked it to India's West Bengal state. Instead, Dhaka stressed Islam as the binding force in Bangladeshi nationalism. The new emphasis on Islam, combined with Bangladeshi concern over India's military build-up and bilateral disputes over riparian borders, shared water resources, and illegal immigration of Bangladeshis into West Bengal, made for fluctuations in India-Bangladesh relations.

Relations are generally good, nevertheless; the two countries have maintained a dialogue on a variety of issues and initiated a modest program of joint economic cooperation. In 1977 New Delhi and Dhaka signed an agreement—that is renewed annually on sharing the waters of the Ganga (Ganges) River during the dry season, but the two sides made little progress in achieving a permanent solution to their other problems. The main item of contention is the Farakka Barrage, where the Ganga divides into two branches and India has built a feeder canal that controls the flow by rechanneling water on the Indian side of the river.

The two nations were still at odds, despite high-level talks, in the mid-1990s.

In the mid and late 1980s, India's plan to erect a fence to prevent cross-border migration from Bangladesh and Bangladesh's desire that Chakma insurgents not receive Indian covert assistance and refuge in India were major irritants in bilateral relations. As agreed eighteen years earlier, in June 1992 India granted a perpetual lease to Bangladesh for the narrow, 1.5-hectare Tin Bigha corridor in the Ganga's delta that had long separated an enclave of Bangladeshis from their homeland. The two countries signed new agreements to enhance economic cooperation. Bangladesh also received Indian developmental assistance, but that aid was minor compared with the amounts India granted to Nepal, Bhutan, Sri Lanka, and Maldives. The year 1991 also witnessed the first-ever visit of an Indian army chief of staff to Dhaka.

Relations between India and Bangladesh are at a palpable low and the immigration issue has contributed towards this in a great measure. While the Awami League government had been keen on continuing friendly ties with India, however, the Bangladesh National Party (BNP), formed with the help of religious extremist groups, has never been sympathetic towards India. With BNP coming to power the influence of ISI and anti-India activities across the border have increased many fold. With the changing strategic environment in the subcontinent, Bangladesh has assumed a new geo-political significance for India to:

- Contain anti-Indian activities in the North-eastern states.
- Plug a permeable border which is all of 4,000 km. long.
- Check the strategic ambitions of China.
- Restrict the entry of any major powers in the South Asian region etc.

India was the first country to recognise Bangladesh as a separate state. It supported Bangladesh in its war of Independence in 1971. Soon after its independence from Pakistan, India provided it all the help for its reconstruction.
Bangladesh acknowledged the Indian help with gratitude and indicated its desire to work in close cooperation with India. In 1972, India and Bangladesh signed a treaty of friendship, co-operation and peace for 25 years on the pattern of Indo-Soviet treaty of 1971. Both the countries pledged to strengthen world peace and security and fight against colonialism, racism and imperialism.

During the regime of Mujibur Rehman, the relationship between the two countries was most friendly and cordial. It was during this period that the Border Agreement of 1974 was reached and implemented. After the assassination of Mujibur Rehman, Gen. Ziaur Rehman brought anti-India stance, calling India's role as that of Big brother. The Farakka Dam issue and the Joint-River Commission were the bones of contention between the two countries. After the assassination of Ziaur Rehman, Gen. Ershad took over the reigns of the government in Bangladesh.

During this period the leasing of Tin Bigha corridor was agreed upon which removed some of the irritants in the Indo-Bangladesh border dispute. Broadly speaking, though the subsequent leaders after the Mujibur Rehman indicated their desire to develop friendly relationship with India, but certain differences marred this cordial relationship.

There are several broad issues viz., migration, insurgency, border disputes, anti-Hindu attacks and dispute over Moore island etc. that have been major irritants in the Indo-Bangladesh bonhomie. On each of these areas both sides adopt conflicting positions or minimise their relative importance to the bilateral relations.

If migration, insurgency and communal tensions are prime Indian concerns, Bangladesh tend to highlight disputes over border demarcation, the Ganga water sharing and trade liberalisation.

6.3 India and Sri Lanka

The two major factors influencing India's relations with Sri Lanka have been security and the shared ethnicity of Tamils living in southern India and in northern and eastern Sri Lanka. Before 1980 common security perceptions and New Delhi's reluctance to intervene in internal affairs in Sri Lanka's capital of Colombo made for relatively close ties between the two countries' governments. Beginning in the mid-1950s, and coinciding with the withdrawal of Britain's military presence in the Indian Ocean, India and Sri Lanka increasingly came to share regional security interests. In the 1970s, New Delhi and Colombo enjoyed close ties on the strength of the relationship between Indira Gandhi and Sri Lanka's prime minister, Mrs. Sirimavo Ratwatte Dias (S.R.D.) Bandaranaike. India fully approved Sri Lanka's desire to replace the British security umbrella with an Indian one, and both sides pursued a policy of nonalignment and cooperated to minimize Western influence in the Indian Ocean.

In the 1980s, ethnic conflict between Sri Lankan Sinhalese in the south and Sri Lankan Tamils in the north escalated, and Tamil separatists established bases and received funding, weapons, and, reportedly, training in India. The clandestine assistance came from private sources and, according to some observers, the state government of Tamil Nadu, and was tolerated by the central government until 1987. Anti-Tamil violence in Colombo in July 1983 prompted India to intervene in the Tamil-Sinhalese conflict, but mediatory efforts failed to prevent the deterioration of the situation. In May 1987, after the Sri Lankan government attempted to regain control of the Jaffna region, in the extreme northern area of the island, by means of an economic blockade and military action, India supplied food and medicine by air and sea to the region.

On July 29, 1987, Indian prime minister Rajiv Gandhi and Sri Lankan president Junius Richard (J.R.) Jayawardene signed an accord designed to settle the conflict by sending the Indian Peace Keeping Force (IPKF) to establish order and disarm Tamil separatists, to establish new administrative bodies and hold elections to accommodate Tamil demands for autonomy, and to repatriate Tamil refugees in India and Sri Lanka. The accord also forbade the military use of Sri Lankan ports or broadcasting facilities by outside powers. The Liberation Tigers of Tamil Eelam (LTTE), the most militant separatist group, refused to disarm, and Indian troops sustained heavy casualties while failing to destroy the LTTE. In June 1989, newly elected Sri Lankan president Ranasinghe Premadasa demanded the withdrawal of the IPKF. Despite the tensions between the two countries created by this request, New Delhi completed the withdrawal in March 1990.

Bilateral relations improved somewhat in the early 1990s, as the government attempted to expand economic, scientific, and cultural cooperation. India continued to take an interest in the status of Sri Lankan Tamils, but without the direct intervention that characterized the 1980s. The May 1991 assassination of Rajiv Gandhi, allegedly by the LTTE, forced New Delhi to crack down on the LTTE presence in Tamil Nadu and to institute naval patrols in the Palk Strait to interdict LTTE movements to India. In January 1992, repatriation of Tamil refugees to Sri Lanka commenced and was still underway in 1994.

Communal tensions and rivalry have marked the politics of Sri-Lanka since 1950 and the ethnic problem has been gradually brewing. By 1970, the demand for separate Tamil States was raised and the terrorist activities attributed to Tamil separatists stated in the North. Communal riots in1977, 1981 and 1983 widened the gulf of mistrust between the communities and Tamil sense of grievances and victimization were increased. Tamils sought the support of their ancestral Indian Tamils living in South India. Eventually, the separatist guerrilla bases started increasing in the South Indian State of Tamil Nadu.

The institutional framework for the relationship is provided by frequent contact at political level, including the highest one. President Mahinda Rajapaksa made his first visit abroad after his victory at the November 2005 elections to India on December 27-30, 2005. His second visit to India was on November 25-29, 2006. On April 1-4, 2007 he visited India for the 14th SAARC Summit. His last visit to India was on October 12-14, 2007. Prime Minister Ratnasiri Wickremanayake visited India on January 28-30, 2007. Foreign Minister Rohitha Bogollagama visited India on a number of occasions, on December 7-8, 2007 for the SAARC Council of Ministers Meeting. Leader of Opposition Ranil

Wickremesinghe also visited India on a number of occasions, the last one on on December 28, 2007. From our side, our external affairs minister (EAM) visited Sri Lanka on January 9-10, 2007. The 6th meeting of the Joint Commission, co-chaired by EAM, took place in Colombo on June 10, 2005. A Parliamentary delegation headed by Lok Sabha Deputy Speaker Charanjit Singh Atwal visited Sri Lanka on March 28-April 3, 2006 to participate in the 4th Conference of the Association of SAARC Speakers and Parliamentarians.

There is regular contact at the official level including Foreign Secretary led Foreign Office Consultations (last held in Colombo in May 2005) [*Last FS level visit to Sri Lanka was on November 23-24, 2006*], Commerce Secretary level talks (last held in Delhi in January 2006), talks between Customs authorities, fisheries officials, the Navy/Coast Guards etc.

A large number of Sri Lankan Tamils have taken shelter in India because of disturbed conditions in the island. While there is no record of the number of Sri Lankans who came and went illegally, a total of 2,78,549 are recognised as official refugees. These persons came in three phases; 134,053 between 1983 and 1989, 122,078 between 1989 and 1991 and 22,418 from 1996 until today. The influx of refugees has substantially reduced in the recent past and no refugee has arrived in 2004. A large number of these refugees have returned to Sri Lanka or have assimilated into Tamil Nadu society. At present there are 55,000 refugees in 102 camps in Tamil Nadu. The policy of the Government of India towards the refugees, as laid down by the Committee of Secretaries in September, 1983, has been to discourage their coming to India. However, in case they do arrive, they are to be accommodated in relief camps with the ultimate objective of arranging for their early repatriation. An interministerial committee chaired by the Ministry of Home Affairs has been constituted to look into the modalities of repatriation.

Pending their repatriation, various relief facilities are provided to them such as shelter, cash doles, clothing, subsidized rations, utensils and medical care. The entire expenditure on relief to these refugees is borne by the Government of India. An amount of approximately ₹ 328 crore has been spent on this purpose by the Government of India up to May, 2004 and an outlay of ₹ 27 crore was further provided. The Sri Lankan government's policy gives priority to internally displaced persons in Sri Lanka and Sri Lankans in Europe as compared to refugees returning from India. The UNHCR has a limited role in facilitating the repatriation of refugees. It ascertains willingness of refugees to return and has also financed the return of 3000 refugees.

6.4 India and Nepal

Relations between India and Nepal are close yet fraught with difficulties stemming from geography, economics, the problems inherent in big power-small power relations, and common ethnic and linguistic identities that overlap the two countries' borders. In 1950 New Delhi and Kathmandu initiated their intertwined relationship with the Treaty of Peace and Friendship and accompanying letters that defined security relations between the two countries, and an agreement governing both bilateral trade and trade transiting Indian soil. The 1950 treaty and letters stated that "neither government shall tolerate any threat to the security of the other by a foreign aggressor" and obligated both sides "to inform each other of any serious friction or misunderstanding with any neighbouring state likely to cause any breach in the friendly relations subsisting between the two governments." These accords cemented a "special relationship" between India and Nepal that granted Nepal preferential economic treatment and provided Nepalese in India the same economic and educational opportunities as Indian citizens.

In the 1950s, Nepal welcomed close relations with India, but as the number of Nepalese living and working in India increased and the involvement of India in Nepal's economy deepened in the 1960s and after, so too did Nepalese discomfort with the special relationship. Tensions came to a head in the mid-1970s, when Nepal pressed for substantial amendments in its favour in the trade and transit treaty and openly criticized India's 1975 annexation of Sikkim as an Indian state. In 1975 King Birendra Bir Bikram Shah Dev proposed that Nepal be recognized internationally as a zone of peace; he received support from China and Pakistan. In New Delhi's view, if the king's proposal did not contradict the 1950 treaty and was merely an extension of nonalignment, it was unnecessary; if it was a repudiation of the special relationship, it represented a possible threat to India's security and could not be endorsed. In 1984, Nepal repeated the proposal, but there was no reaction from India. Nepal continually promoted the proposal in international forums, with Chinese support; by 1990 it had won the support of 112 countries.

In 1978 India agreed to separate trade and transit treaties, satisfying a long-term Nepalese demand. In 1988, when the two treaties were up for renewal, Nepal's refusal to accommodate India's wishes on the transit treaty caused India to call for a single trade and transit treaty. Thereafter, Nepal took a hard-line position that led to a serious crisis in India-Nepal relations. After two extensions, the two treaties expired on March 23, 1989, resulting in a virtual Indian economic blockade of Nepal that lasted until late April 1990. Although economic issues were a major factor in the two countries' confrontation, Indian dissatisfaction with Nepal's 1988 acquisition of Chinese weaponry played an important role. New Delhi perceived the arms purchase as an indication of Kathmandu's intent to build a military relationship with Beijing, in violation of the 1950 treaty and letters exchanged in 1959 and 1965, which included Nepal in India's security zone and precluded arms purchases without India's approval. India linked security with economic relations and insisted on reviewing India-Nepal relations as a whole. Nepal had to back down after worsening economic conditions led to a change in Nepal's political system, in which the king was forced to institute a parliamentary democracy. The new government sought quick restoration of amicable relations with India.

The special security relationship between New Delhi and Kathmandu was re-established during the June 1990 New Delhi meeting of Nepal's Prime Minister Krishna Prasad Bhattarai and Indian Prime Minister V.P. Singh. During the December 1991 visit to India by Nepalese Prime Minister Girija Prasad Koirala, the two countries signed new, separate trade and transit treaties and other economic agreements designed to accord Nepal additional economic benefits.

Indian-Nepali relations appeared to be undergoing still more reassessment when Nepal's prime minister Man Mohan Adhikary visited New Delhi in April 1995 and insisted on a major review of the 1950 peace and friendship treaty. In the face of benign statements by his Indian hosts relating to the treaty, Adhikary sought greater economic independence for his landlocked nation while simultaneously striving to improve ties with China.

Indo-Nepalese trade relations can be traced back to ancient times. Kautilya (400 B.C.), great economist of that time, mentions Nepal as the principal exporter of woollen goods. Increased trade activities were seen between northern India and Nepal during the golden age of Guptas (beginning in 320 A.D.). During the Nepal-Tibet war of 1791, the East India Company proposed a 7-clause treaty under which imports and exports of goods between India and British India would be subject to 2.25 percent customs duty. A peace treaty of Sugauli in 1816 enabled the British to enter the Nepalese markets. In the early days, foreign trade of Nepal was limited mainly with India and Tibet. The only trade route in between India and Tibet was through Nepal. It had helped very much in developing trade of Nepal.

The importance of economic and trade relation with India is to remain as same as it was in the past from the Nepalese perspective. Its significance may further be high in years to come. Trade relationship between Nepal and India, by and large, is being considered to be smooth. In the realm of global trade integration the trade relation between these two countries needs to improve further. On the other hand, in the present era of trade specialization both the countries need to develop their own specific trade activities based on the scale of economies, value addition and competition. This study aims to explore the scope for trade improvement between Nepal and India. Thus, the study pertains an immense scope in this direction. The author further traces the existing security relations and strategic perceptions of India and Nepal and attempts to identify the common and divergent perceptions existing, if any with special reference to Natwar's visit to Nepal. It tries to understand the reasons *for the erosion of mutuality and its impact on Indo-Nepal relationship in the present scenario.*

However, major proportion of the Nepalese trade was with India. Trade with Tibet was focused for meeting the basic requirements in the Himalayan and hilly region, whereas trade with India consisted of export and import of several agricultural, mineral and forest products. Before the nineteenth century, imports from India consisted of a few items of which scrap metals, precious stones, spices, tobacco etc. were among them. Whereas Nepal exported most of her primary products like timber, rice, ghee etc. Nepal's trade with India continued till 1923 without having a trade agreement with British India. Prior to the signing of this trade agreement, British East India Company was interested to have trade relations with Nepal, for expansion of its own exports. The opening of direct India-Tibet route via Gyantse routes further promoted Nepal to develop trade with India. Moreover, the development of good transportation system and the creation of many trade centres in the northern India further helped to enhance the trade turnover between Nepal and India.

Economic relationship between Nepal and India is unique. There are historical, geographical, cultural, linguistic, ethnic, social and family links between people living in India and Nepal. Institutions relating to government and the economic activities are also more or less similar. Therefore, the trade and other related relationship between Nepal and India has its own significance.

Trade relationship between these two countries often goes beyond the economic reason significantly influenced by the social-ethical norms and values. Research and studies reveal that both the countries have comparative cost advantages in trading amongst themselves for several reasons. Historic trade relation, geographical proximity, identical culture, similar agriculture productions are cited few examples quite repeatedly.

Economical transport cost is seen as another important factor determining the volume of trade between these countries. In view of the rising energy costs, it often considered that the transport costs are likely to rise so that the transport cost advantage to both these countries trading with each other is likely to increase in future. This would further increase the potential for trade between these countries. Timilsina (2000), on the other hand, notes that the economic cooperation between Nepal and India is based on the movements of goods and services across Nepal-India border of about 1,600 km. The movement is free and spontaneous.

This movement further accelerated by the movement of people for economic pursuits, social and marriage relations. The cultural ties and non-existence of visa system have created better environment for the conduction of free trade between the two countries. Indo-Nepal trade has its own importance for the economic development of both these countries.

Both the countries have realized the significance of bilateral trade. Trade with India is likely to play further a key role in trade and industrial fronts in the future as well. Trade and transit treaties held between the two countries are continuously reflecting the fact. And, these treaties have increasingly guided the trade direction, more specifically in the case of Nepal. Taking into account these factors, this study has made an attempt to analyze some of the key issues related with Indo-Nepal trade relation and scope for improving trade relationship between these countries in the future.

The conventional economic wisdom holds that trade is beneficial to growth of a country. Although one country may have a higher productivity in the production of all goods compared to another country, the relative productivities in producing different goods will differ. Trade is based on the relative comparative advantage and increases welfare in both countries. It has been increasingly stressed in recent years that welfare would only come from increased exports. Trade liberalization, in this direction, paints a picture suitable for export promotion.

It is noteworthy to note that the South Asian economies (SAEs) launched comprehensive reform programs at the beginning of the 1990s. However, some attempts were made towards the opening up of trade and investment regimes in the 1980s. The reform initiatives included, among other things, reducing the level and dispersion of tariffs and quantitative restrictions and improving regulations on domestic and improving regulations on domestic and foreign investments. Nepal and India also stepped towards economic reform process during this period. The new economic thinking involving speedy economic liberalization oriented toward free and competitive market in Nepal and India has, by and large, contributed in changing the scenario of Indo-Nepal trade relation.

India is extending economic and technical support to Nepal for almost for decades since 1951. India was the most important donor to Nepal in the early decades after the independence of India. The signing of the India-Nepal Treaty of Peace and Friendship in 1950 established the framework for the unique ties between the two countries. Since the early fifties, India has contributed significantly to the economic development of Nepal. Beginning with major irrigation projects such as the Koshi and Gandak barrages, Indian assistance has significantly contributed to the development of the economic structure in Nepal. Areas of economic relation were mainly confined to the basic infrastructure which covers; airports, irrigation, agriculture, supply of drinking water, roads, bridges, power projects, heath, industrial estates, communication, surveys, education, forestry, building construction, ex-servicemen welfare etc.

Indian assistance to Nepal has increased over the years. From the assistance of an average of ₹ 150 million in the mid-1980s, it reached to ₹ 750 million in 1999/2000. So far over 120 agreements and letters of exchange have been concluded for Indian aided projects in Nepal totalling over ₹ 4000 million. These figures do not include the supply of subsidized commodities such as rice, sugar, cement, fertilizers, petrochemical etc., refund of excise duty levied on items exported from India, ₹ 500 million stand-by credit facility etc. During the year 2000-2001, the utilization was approximately ₹ 450 million. A High Level Task Force (HLTF) has also been formed to oversee the progress in Indian-assisted Projects to Nepal.

6.5 India and Maldives

India and Maldives share ethnic, linguistic, cultural, religious and commercial links steeped in antiquity and enjoy close, cordial and multi-dimensional relations. India was among the first to recognise Maldives after its Independence in 1965 and to establish diplomatic relations. India established its mission at the level of CDA in 1972 and resident High Commissioner in 1980. Maldives opened a full-fledged resident High Commission in New Delhi in November 2004.

The bilateral relations have been nurtured and strengthened by regular contacts at the highest levels. Since establishment of diplomatic relations, almost all the Prime Ministers of India visited the Maldives. President Gayoom's last official visit was in March/April 2005. Dr. Ahmed Shaheed, Foreign Minister of Maldives paid an official visit to India from August 11-14, 2005. Besides holding talks with the External Affairs Minister, he also called on the PM and Shri L.K. Advani, Leader of Opposition in the Lok Sabha during the NDA government.

On international issues, Maldives has traditionally been supportive of India and broadly coordinated its position with that of India in multilateral fora, such as the UN, the Commonwealth, the NAM and the SAARC. During his recent visit to India in March 2005, President Gayoom expressed full support for India's candidature for a permanent seat in the UN Security Council. Maldives has also decided to co sponsor the G-4 framework resolution.

Two main concerns of Maldives in the international fora include its status as an LDC country and the threat posed to the low-lying islands by global warming. India has been supportive of Maldives on both issues.

Since 1988, defence has been a major area of cooperation between India and Maldives. India has adopted a very flexible and accommodating approach to meet Maldivian requirements of defence training and equipment. With the establishment of a separate police organization in September 2004, India has also agreed to meet the training needs of this force.

Under the Economic and Technical Cooperation Agreement, signed in February, 1986, a Joint Commission for Economic and Technical Cooperation was set up between India and the Maldives. Co-chaired by External Affairs Minister and Maldivian Foreign Minister, the Joint Commission meetings took place in 1990, 1992, 1995 and 2000. The meeting identified areas for strengthening bilateral economic cooperation. India has been offering assistance in Maldives' developmental process. The major projects executed by India are:

- Indira Gandhi Memorial Hospital.
- Maldives' Institute of Technical Education (MITE).
- Faculty of Hospitality and Tourism Studies.
- Male International Airport.
- As agreed during the 4th session of the India-Maldives Joint Commission for Economic and Technical Cooperation, India gifted equipment for road construction/maintenance worth ₹ 3.5 crore to Maldives in October 3, 2001.
- Human Resource Development.

India and Maldives signed a trade agreement in 1981. Growing from modest beginnings, India-Maldives bilateral trade is now heavily in favour of India. While Indian exports to the Maldives during 2010-11 were worth ₹ 485 crore, imports were worth only ₹ 145 crore. Indian exports to the Maldives were 9 percent of the total imports of the country in 2010. After Singapore and UAE, India is now the third largest exporter to Maldives.

Indian imports from the Maldives primarily comprise cowrie shells and red corals, Indian exports to the Maldives include agriculture and poultry produce, sugar, fruits, vegetables, spices, rice, atta, textiles, drugs and medicines, a variety of engineering and industrial products, sand and aggregate, cement for building etc. Tuticorin Port in Tamil Nadu is mostly used for the Indian exports.

The State Bank of India has been playing a vital role in economic development of the Maldives since February, 1974 through promotion of island resorts, export of marine products and business enterprises.

Three historical mosques have been successfully restored by Indian experts. The projects are Friday Mosque, Male' (1988), Fenfushi Mosque in South Ari Atoll (July, 2001) and the Dharumavantha Rasgefaanu Mosquein Male' (December, 2004).

6.6 India-Bhutan Relations

Bhutan, also referred to as Druk Yul (The land of the Thunder Dragon) is one of India's closest neighbours. It has an area of 46,500 square kilometres and houses a population of 7,00,000. It shares its border with the Tibet autonomous region of the People's Republic of China in the north and a 700 km. long border with the Indian States of Sikkim, Arunachal Pradesh, West Bengal and Assam to the south.

India and Bhutan have traditionally enjoyed a warm and cordial relationship. This traditional relationship has undergone some structural changes in recent times. Bhutan as the closest ally of India in South Asia, always supported India in the SAARC forums and toed Indian line at the United Nations and International forums. A new "strategic partnership" has emerged out of the ashes of the "Operation All Clear". India and Bhutan enjoy a close relationship based on trust and mutual understanding. Over the years, our economies have increasingly developed interlinkages, particularly in the mutually beneficial sector of hydroelectric power.

This special relationship is further sustained by the tradition of regular visits and extensive exchange of views at the highest levels between the two countries. His Majesty the King of Bhutan was the Chief Guest at the Republic Day celebrations in 2005. The Royal Bhutan Army undertook successful operations in December 2003-January 2004 to evict the Indian Insurgent Groups based in Bhutan. This unprecedented gesture of Bhutan has been widely acknowledged and appreciated, including in the Parliament.

India's bilateral political relations with Bhutan have matured over the years and are characterised by close trust and understanding and extensive cooperation in the field of economic development.

Bhutan consults India on all matters pertaining to its security and foreign policy. Bhutan has perfected the art of living comfortably with its giant neighbour India and has been successful in manipulating India's magnanimity for Bhutan's own overall development. At least three elements of mutual security concerns have prompted king's unscheduled visit to India in 2005. The King's visit's aim was to firm up an 'institutionalized mechanism' to deal with trans-border insurgency and other security matters of mutual interests.

First, Bhutan has become concerned of China's road building ventures on its immediate northern borders in recent times. In November, 2004, it reportedly lodged a formal protest to Beijing stating that some of China's road programme violated the Bhutan-China Agreement on Peace and Tranquillity on Borders, 1998. The agreement stipulates that China and Bhutan will maintain peace and tranquillity on the borders, uphold status quo of the boundary prior to March

1959 and not resort to unilateral action to alter the status quo of the border. China purportedly agreed to suspend the construction work till next border talk in 2005.

Secondly, in November Pakistani Prime Minister Shaukat Aziz visited Bhutan as SAARC chairman. He led a large size of Pakistani delegation that filled in three air force planes. The Pakistani leader reportedly lobbied with Bhutanese leaders to allow Pakistan open an embassy in Bhutan. India, is highly sensitive about Pakistan's 'growing' engagement in the region as such it was a matter of serious concerns. King's visit to India was purportedly to assuage the Indian concerns and consult India on this sensitive matter.

Thirdly, Bhutan army aided by Indian army launched the "Operation All Clear" to flush out India's northeast militants form Bhutanese territories on December 15, 2003. This could be the dawn of the new Indo-Bhutan 'strategic partnership'. The northeast militants were provided official sanctuary in Bhutan since 1991 in return for their support in terrorizing the Nepali-speaking southern Bhutanese to leave Bhutan. Bhutan finally launched joint military operations, but after securing Indian assurances that the 'operation once launched should not be abandoned for political dialogue with militants and Bhutanese territory should be totally sanitized of the Indian militants. Bhutan was concerned of backlash from the militants. The militants had long warned the King of dire consequences of military operations against them. Such threats are believed to be greater now. Despite the official "mission accomplished' announcement made on January 15 2004, the ULFA militants reportedly hoisted its flag and celebrated the 25th Raising Day at their camp in eastern Bhutan in April, 2004, sending clear message that the militants are still strong inside Bhutan.

There is cooperation between the Indian Army and the Royal Bhutan Army. There is an Indian Military Training Team (IMTRAT), which assists the RBA in areas largely relating to Training.

In return for Bhutan's military offensive, India assured Bhutan of its continued support for military and development projects. India is preparing a comprehensive modernization package for the Bhutanese army. It has agreed to sell low-tech arms to Bhutan -5.56-mm INSAS assault rifles, 51 mm or 81-mm mortars, night-vision devices, winter clothing to the Bhutanese army and military vehicles. It has also agreed to increase the military training of Bhutanese army officers in India. India will also establish a joint military grid to patrol against the Indian militants.

Mutually beneficial economic inter-linkages between India and Bhutan have been an important element in our bilateral relations. Planned development efforts in Bhutan began in the early 1960s. The First Five Year Plan (FYP) of Bhutan was launched in 1961. Since then, India has been extending financial assistance to Bhutan's FYPs. India continues to be the principal donor for the economic development of Bhutan. So far, nine Five Year Plans of Bhutan have been completed, two of which were totally financed by India. India has also contributed to Bhutan's development outside the scope of the Five Year Plans. Since the 4th FYP, Bhutan has started availing financial assistance from sources other than India including from multilateral agencies.

India is the single largest donor to Bhutan, in fact, it has flooded Bhutan with enormous economic aid. The Government of India committed assistance worth ₹ 3400 crores during the Tenth Five Year Plan. Indian Government's assistance during the Ninth Five Year Plan (2002-08) of Bhutan was ₹ 2610.14 crore. Government of India also extended a standby credit facility of ₹ 300 crores to Bhutan in March 2009 to help Bhutan overcome rupee liquidity crunch.

Bhutan also enjoys complete free trade with India. Bhutan's import from India increased from ₹ 189 crore in 2002-03 to ₹ 801 crore in 2010-11, registering a growth of 423 percent. Its export to India in 2010-11 increased to ₹ 917 crore from ₹ 155 crore in 2002-03, an increase of over 591 percent over the previous year, according to Ministry of Commerce and Industry, Government of India.

Some of the major projects in Bhutan carried out with Indian assistance were Paro Airport, Bhutan Broadcasting Station, Major Highways, Electricity Distribution System for Thimphu and Paro; Indo-Bhutan Microwave Link, Exploration of Mineral Resources, and Survey and Mapping and Chukha and Kurichu Hydropower Projects, Penden Cement Plant. Some of the important projects envisaged in future include establishment of railway linkages between border towns of India and Bhutan, cooperation in agriculture and allied sectors and construction of 2 major hospitals in Bhutan.

India has taken up some major projects in Bhutan under our Plan assistance. These include the 1020 MW Tala Project, likely to be completed in 2006. In addition DPR for the Punatsangchu mega hydel project is under preparation. GOI is also committed to the establishment of a 0.5 million tonne cement project, Dungsum Cement Plant. Government of India has also made commitment to assist Bhutan to prepare DPRs in respect of two major Hydro Projects viz. Punatsangchhu–II and Mangdechu.

A free trade regime exists between India and Bhutan. The India-Bhutan Trade and Commerce Agreement which expired in March 2005 has been renewed for another 10 years. The agreement will continue until proposed amendments by the two sides are agreed.

The Agreement on Trade and Commerce also provides for duty free transit of Bhutanese merchandise for trade with third countries. India is not only Bhutan's main development partner but also its largest trade partner. During 2009, imports from India were of the order of ₹ 23.3 billion and constituted 80 percent of Bhutan's total imports. Bhutan's exports to India in 2009 amounted to ₹ 20.5 billion and constituted 94 percent of its total exports.

Mineral products, rice, machinery and mechanical appliances, base metal and base metal products, cereals, fruits, nuts, coffee, prepared food stuffs, transport equipment, chemical products, animal products, vegetable oil, plastic and rubber products, textiles, wood and wood products are India's main exports to Bhutan. Besides electricity, calcium carbide, gypsum, ferro-silicon, particle board and Portland cement are the main imports from Bhutan. Indian vehicles dominate the automobile market and have captured more than 80 percent of the market. Government of India funded projects have also contributed to increasing imports from India. Although Bhutan's economy is inextricably linked with India, efforts towards diversification of markets and products are actively pursued. Imports from Singapore have picked up in electronics and from Bangladesh and Thailand for consumer goods.

There is close bilateral cooperation in the educational and cultural fields between India and Bhutan. India provides technical expertise and services of specialists to Bhutan in various fields. Government of India's scholarships are granted to about 50 Bhutanese students every year in Indian Institutions of higher learning. These GOI Scholarships are in addition to the ITEC/TCS of Colombo Plan schemes. A six month long event called Festival of India was organised from June to November 2003 with the theme "Eternal Friendship and Cooperation". An India-Bhutan Foundation has also been established to promote people-to-people contacts.

Bhutan is bounded on three sides by India. From east to west, the Indian states of Sikkim, West Bengal, Assam, and Arunachal Pradesh (formerly the North-East Frontier Agency) border Bhutan. In view of the long-standing political disputes and border confrontations between India and China, Bhutan has long been part of India's strategic defence plan. In the view of some Indian strategists, Bhutan was a weak link in India's defence against China.

The key document guiding relations with India is the Treaty of Friendship between the Government of India and the Government of Bhutan of 1949. The ten-article treaty, in force in perpetuity, calls for peace between the two countries and assures Indian non-interference in Bhutan's internal affairs in return for Bhutan's agreeing "to be guided by the advice of the Government of India in regard to its external relations" (Article 2). The treaty provides for compensation by India at a higher rate than provided in the 1865 and 1910 British treaties, and it returned Bhutan's Dewangiri territory seized by Britain in the Duar War. It also guarantees free trade between the countries and duty-free transit across India of Bhutan's imports. Furthermore, the treaty assures the rights of citizens of each country and the extradition of criminals seeking refuge in either country.

Events in Tibet have had causal effects on Bhutan-Indian relations. When the Chinese communists took over Tibet in 1951, Bhutan braced itself against a renewed external threat with a modernization program and a new defence posture. In his first visit to Bhutan in 1958, Indian Prime Minister Jawaharlal Nehru reiterated India's wish that Bhutan remain an independent country. Following precedent, Bhutan sided with India when the Chinese army occupied Tibet in 1959 and a border dispute emerged between China and India. A de facto alliance developed between Bhutan and India by 1960, and Indian aid increasingly bolstered Bhutan's strategic infrastructure development. In times of crisis between India and China or between Bhutan and China, India was quick to assure Bhutan of military assistance. Concerns were raised by Bhutan, however, during the 1971 Indo-Pakistani War when there were doubts about India's ability to protect Bhutan against China (which sided with Pakistan) while fighting a two-front war.

In 1960, Druk Gyalpo had said that Bhutan was not 100 percent independent because of the 1949 treaty, and until Bhutan emerged into the world of international diplomacy by joining the UN in 1971, Article 2 of the treaty seemed intact. Admission to the UN, however, changed Bhutan's perspective on the world beyond India and Thimphu's traditional dependence on New Delhi. Two years later, Bhutan and Bangladesh exchanged diplomatic recognition, hinting further at Thimphu's independent attitude. A new interpretation of the relationship emerged in 1974 when Bhutan's minister of foreign affairs said that whether or not Bhutan followed India's advice and guidance on foreign policy matters was optional. Bhutan had raised its representation in India to the ambassadorial level in 1971 and in 1978 changed the name of its diplomatic office in New Delhi from the Royal Bhutan Mission to the Royal Bhutan Embassy to further reflect its sovereign status. A new trade agreement between Bhutan and India in 1972 provided an exemption from export duties for goods from Bhutan to third countries.

The Druk Gyalpo's statement in 1979 that the 1949 treaty needed to be "updated" was still another move asserting independence. Members of the National Assembly speaking just before the Druk Gyalpo's "update" announcement made the interpretation that Article 2 only required Bhutan to seek India's advice and guidance on matters of external affairs. Bhutan exerted its independent stance at the Non-Aligned Movement summit conference in Havana, also in 1979, by voting with China and some Southeast Asian countries rather than with India on the issue of allowing Cambodia's Khmer Rouge to be seated at the conference. Bhutan's votes in the UN on such issues as the status of landlocked nations also did not follow India's leads.

Despite a history of good relations between Bhutan and India, bilateral border issues went long unresolved. Indo-Bhutanese borders had been delineated in the Treaty of Peace of 1865 between Bhutan and Britain, but it was not until the period between 1973 and 1984 that a detailed delineation and demarcation was made. Border demarcation talks with India generally resolved disagreements except for several small sectors, including the middle zone between Sarbhang and Geylegphug and the eastern frontier with Arunachal Pradesh.

India and Bhutan reached another milestone in their age-old friendship. When the two countries signed a landmark agreement for establishing rail links between bordering towns. The two sides also decided to step up cooperation on agriculture and power sectors. Bhutan has also supported India's Candidature as a Permanent members of the UN Security Council, while acknowledging India's International stature and its ability to contribute towards enhancing the effectiveness of the UN under the memorandum of understanding. The two sides have agreed to conduct feasibility studies for extension of the Indian railway network from West Bengal and Assam to nearest border towns of Bhutan. The agreement is part of the overall strategy of upgrading borders infrastructure and connectivity with Bhutan. It will examine links between Hasimara (West Bengal) and Phuemtscholing (approximately 18 km. with a bifurcation to Rasakha); the 70 km. stretch between Kokrajhar (Assam) and Gelephu; 940 km. distance between Patusala (Assam) and Nanglam; Rangla (Assam) and samdrupjongkhar via Darranga (about 60 km.); and Bamarhat (West Bengal) and Samtse (approximately 16 km.). Bhutan also strongly supports India's induction as a permanent member of the Security Council.

With the successful elections for the 47-members National Assembly on 24 March 2008, the Himalayan kingdom of Bhutan has emerged as a parliamentary democracy, paving way for an elected Prime Minister for the first time in the country's history. Democratic transition in Bhutan is a healthy sign of people's participation in governance. India has hailed the first ever elections in Bhutan as a "great moment" in the history of Bhutan. Indeed, India-Bhutan relations are set to reach a new height of mutual cooperation, as India, the world largest democracy will find it more convenient in dealing with a democratic (though not multi-party) Bhutan. The elections will not only further boost bilateral relations but will also strengthen trade, military, and culture ties between the two countries. Bhutan's foreign policy is guided by India, which also contributes substantially to its development budget. On 8 February 2007, India and Bhutan signed the India-Bhutan Friendship Treaty, which updates the Treaty signed in Darjeeling on 8 August 1949, and sets forth the framework for bilateral relations. The updated Treaty reiterates that there shall be perpetual peace and friendship between India and Bhutan. It includes fresh provisions for consolidating and expanding economic cooperation for mutual and long-term benefit, and cooperation in the fields of culture, education, health, sports, and science and technology. The signing of the India-Bhutan Friendship Treaty signals the further deepening and strengthening of this unique and special relationship, and a democratic Bhutan will prove to be a trusted ally of India in pursuit of its Look East Policy.

7

India and South East Asia

During the pre-Independence era, India's Foreign Policy was largely Euro-centric. East Asia figured nowhere in the foreign policy of British India. The South East Asia was theatre of major power rivalry in the cold war era. During those days India refused a close interaction with the region because of its non-aligned policy. But during Rajiv Gandhi's tenure India conveyed its willingness to be associated with the region. The initial response of the ASEAN countries was not warm due to India's adherence to socialist-oriented economic arrangements and also due to Indo-Pak tensions. India's relations with South-East Asia entered a new phase after the Indo-Pak war of 1965.

In the wake of Cultural Revolution of China, there was an increase in the activities of the communists in the countries of South East Asia. This encouraged non-communists countries to come closer. This also paved ways for improvement of India's relations with these countries. The confliot between USSR and China, the partial withdrawal of the Americans from Vietnam and normalization of relations between China and USA also had its impact on the policy of the countries of South-east Asia. This provided a good opportunity to India to cultivate better relations with countries of South-east Asia. The politics of Indian Ocean also influenced India's relations with the countries of South East Asia.

It cannot be denied that India's Pro-Soviet till in the foreign policy greatly hampered the development of friendly and cooperative relations with the countries of South East Asia. However, with the disintegration of the Soviet Union towards the end of 1991 the Pro-Soviet tilt of India automatically disappeared. This removed one of the hurdles for India to improve relations with the countries of South-East Asia. In Jan 1992 the ASEAN at its Summit held in Singapore accepted India as a sectoral partner in specific areas like trade, investment science and technology and training, in the hope that it would help the process of global economic integration.

In the 1970s and 1980s, India's close ties with the Soviet Union and its pro-Soviet, pro-Vietnamese policies toward Cambodia precluded development of any constructive relations between India on the one hand and the countries of the Association of Southeast Asian Nations on the other. Furthermore, India's military build-up, particularly of its naval capabilities and naval installations in the Andaman and Nicobar Islands, worried ASEAN policy makers, who saw India as a potential threat to regional security. Indian-ASEAN relations improved in the 1990s as the result of the end of the bipolar world system, the UN-brokered peace settlement in Cambodia, and the break-up of the Soviet Union. For its part, New Delhi sought to boost economic and trade ties with the region and to establish closer political and defence ties in order to counteract China's growing influence in Southeast Asia. ASEAN countries grew less concerned with India's regional ambitions after New Delhi's decision to curtail its naval build-up because of financial restraints. In January 1992, ASEAN accepted India's proposal to become a "sectoral dialogue partner" in the areas of trade, technical and labour development, technology, and tourism. India's new role was expected to facilitate economic cooperation. In January 1993, India and Malaysia signed a memorandum of understanding on defence cooperation.

India has had close ties with Cambodia, Laos, and Vietnam as a result of its 1954-73 chairmanship of the International Commissions of Control and Supervision established by the 1954 Geneva Accords on Indochina. These relations were enhanced by India's friendship with the Soviet Union, particularly after 1971 and, in the case of Vietnam, shared perceptions of the threat from China. With regard to Cambodia, India recognized the Vietnamese-installed regime in 1980 and worked to avert censure of the regime in the annual UN General Assembly and triennial Non-aligned Movement summit meetings. In the late 1980s, Indian diplomats attempted to facilitate the search for peace in Cambodia, and India participated in the 1989 Paris Peace Conference on Cambodia and in subsequent efforts to find a solution to the Cambodian situation. New Delhi played a minor but nevertheless constructive role before and after the Agreement on a Comprehensive Political Settlement of the Cambodia Conflict and three other documents were signed in Paris on October 23, 1991. India contributed more than 1,700 civilian, military, and police personnel to the United Nations Advanced Mission in Cambodia and the United Nations Transitional Authority in Cambodia.

During 1996-97, India's relations with the countries of the South East Asian region and the South Pacific continued to improve. As a validation of a conscious adoption of a "Look East" Policy, India became a full Dialogue Partner of the Association of South East Asian Nations (ASEAN) and participated for the first time at the Post Ministerial Conference (PMC) of ASEAN in Jakarta in July 1996. India also participated for the first time in the meeting of the ASEAN Regional Forum (ARF) which deliberates on the security and political concerns of the Asia Pacific region.

7.1 India's Look East Policy: An Overview

India's foreign policy has cast a relook at 'look east policy'. There are many reasons why India has chosen this at its new thrust area. India today has a very legitimate and intense interest in South-East Asia. Myanmar, Malaysia, Vietnam, Singapore and Indonesia and other SEA and East Asian Countries have become integral to India's new look East Policy which was initiated by Mr. Narsimha Rao Government in the early 90s. India has given paramount importance to its economic interest, national security and strategic imperatives in these countries. There are different factors standing behind India's interest in 'Look East Policy'. These are as follows:

1. It is the economic interest that is compelling India to exploit this region. With an exclusive economic zone of two million kilometres, India needs to exploit this region. India is currently collaborating with the South-East Asian Countries in trade and investment. From US$ 2.9 billion of exports in 1996-97, India's exports to ASEAN surged to US$ 27.2 billion in 2010-11. India's trade with Australia, Japan and Korea has also increased manifold.
2. From the strategic and security point of view, the region is important for India. It has forged defence links with many countries of this region as a means to strengthen political understanding. India has entered the ASEAN regional forum which is perhaps the only system where security issues of the region could be talked about.
3. Energy security is also key issue of India in ASEAN. Since central and West Asia is a politically volatile area, India needs to tap petroleum and energy needs from other areas.
4. Extradition is also a priority areas between India and Look-East Policy.
5. Mutual legal assistance on the criminal matters.
6. Joint work on security issues with or without an international strategic content.
7. Crime against narcotics was also the area of interest.
8. Counter Terrorism was also the identified as an integral aspect of co-operation.
9. Both the sides exchanged views and assessments on other areas such as money laundering, currency and document counter feiting, trafficking in arms and human beings.

India is poised to make itself a significant player in the emerging Asian balance of power. The first phase of the Look East policy launched by the Narasimha Rao Government in the early 1990s focussed on renewing contact with a region that India had drifted away from, thanks to the logic of the Cold War and its own insular economic policies. India's de facto alliance with the

Soviet Union had left its ties with the other major Asian powers—China, Japan—and the United States terribly stunted. New Delhi's tailing of Moscow on regional security issues also left it in a politically antagonistic mode with key regional groupings such as the Association of South East Asian Nations (ASEAN). India's inward-looking orientation disconnected it from the neighbourhood to the East, kept it apart from the economic dynamism of East Asia. By the turn of the 1990s, India had marginalised itself comprehensively in Asia.

As India launched itself on the course of globalisation in 1991, East and South East Asia began to loom large in its national economic strategy. The first years of the Look East policy saw a steady expansion of trade and investment links with the region. The pace of integration with the East slowed somewhat after the economic crisis that affected the region in the late 1990s. But as East Asia comes out of the crisis, the centrality of the economic imperative remains undiminished. Without a quicker pace of economic reforms and better integration of its foreign and trade policies, India will not be able to effectively sustain its Look East strategy.

The first phase of the Look East policy saw India establish institutional linkages with the regional organisations. Although New Delhi could not become a member of the larger Asia Pacific Economic Cooperation (APEC) forum and the ASEM—the Asia Europe consultative mechanism—it joined the ASEAN as a full dialogue partner and a member of its political and security wing, the ASEAN Regional Forum (ARF). The ASEAN plus one summit later this year will cap India's successful political engagement of South East Asia during the 1990s.

Clouding India's political prospects in Asia during the 1990s were its uncertain relationships with the two great powers—the U.S. and China—and the key regional actors such as Japan and Australia. Although the end of the Cold War opened the door for a new engagement with all these players, the nuclear issue tended to complicate ties. But India's post-Pokhran political isolation did not last too long. Its successful resolution of the nuclear tensions with the U.S. paved the way for a return to the region with an enhanced political standing. Nothing has elevated India's strategic profile in the region more than the new relationship it has built with the U.S., which will remain the dominant power in Asia for a long time to come. In the Cold War, India ended more often than not opposing the U.S. on regional security issues. After the Cold War, the first phase of India's Look East policy was accompanied by an expanding but tentative political engagement with the U.S.

The second phase of the Look East policy is likely to be underscored by the emerging security partnership between New Delhi and Washington.

The Prime Minister, Atal Behari Vajpayee's visit to Singapore and Cambodia and the earlier swing through Asia by the External Affairs Minister, Jaswant Singh, mark the launch of the second phase in India's Look East policy. With a productive engagement of all the great powers and an intensified interaction with the sub-regions of the great continent in place, India is poised to make itself a significant player in the emerging Asian balance of power.

The second phase in India's Look East policy has a new dimension—the development of India's remote northeast. India's search for a new economic relationship with South East Asia is no longer driven by considerations of globalisation, but by the domestic imperative of developing the Northeast by increasing its connectivity to the outside world. Instead of consciously trying to isolate the Northeast from external influences, as it had done in the past, New Delhi is now recognising the importance of opening it up for commercial linkages with South East Asia.

Mr. Singh's visit to Thailand and Myanmar brought into focus this new element in the strategy. By taking advantage of Myanmar as a land bridge to South East Asia, India hopes to transform the Northeast from a security burden into a land of economic opportunity. While the success of this strategy will depend a lot on the ability of the Central Government and the North-eastern States to put adequate infrastructure in place and clean up the political act, the external conditions for a viable strategy towards the development of the Northeast are being realised.

The first phase of the Look East policy saw India establish institutional linkages with the regional organisations. Although New Delhi could not become a member of the larger Asia Pacific Economic Cooperation (APEC) forum and the ASEM—the Asia Europe consultative mechanism—it joined the ASEAN as a full dialogue partner and a member of its political and security wing, the ASEAN Regional Forum (ARF). The ASEAN plus one summit later this year will cap India's successful political engagement of South East Asia during the 1990s. Clouding India's political prospects in Asia during the 1990s were its uncertain relationships with the two great powers—the U.S. and China—and the key regional actors such as Japan and Australia.

Although the end of the Cold War opened the door for a new engagement with all these players, the nuclear issue tended to complicate ties. But India's post-Pokhran political isolation did not last too long. Its successful resolution of the nuclear tensions with the U.S. paved the way for a return to the region with an enhanced political standing. Nothing has elevated India's strategic profile in the region more than the new relationship it has built with the U.S., which will remain the dominant power in Asia for a long time to come. In the Cold War, India ended more often than not opposing the U.S. on regional security issues.

After the Cold War, the first phase of India's Look East policy was accompanied by an expanding but tentative political engagement with the U.S.

The second phase of the Look East policy is likely to be underscored by the emerging security partnership between New Delhi and Washington. The advent of the Bush administration, its decision to lift the nuclear sanctions against India and the unfolding regional scenario after September 11 has helped cement the notion of a "natural alliance" between New Delhi and Washington. And at the heart of the new security convergence between the two is the prospective cooperation in maintaining a stable balance of power in the Indian Ocean/Pacific regions.

India's new dalliance with the U.S. has, not surprisingly, eased the path for building more intensive security links with the American allies in the ASEAN—Australia, South Korea and Japan.

Somewhat counter-intuitively, India's improved ties with the U.S. have also created the space for a more self-confident and mature engagement with China. Mr. Singh's four-day visit to China earlier this month reflected the Indian determination to take advantage of the changed Asian context to move the relationship towards problem-solving and mutually beneficial cooperation. In the first phase of the Look East policy, the prospect for Sino-Indian political cooperation was premised on resisting "hegemonism"—a Chinese code word for American dominance. But it saw very little movement in resolving intractable bilateral disputes over boundary, Sikkim, and Pakistan. The second phase of the Look East policy, premised unambiguously on New Delhi drawing closer to Washington, has ironically created the basis for addressing issues that have divided India and China for long.

It is in the context of a rapidly expanding Indo-U.S. cooperation, greater uncertainty in Sino-U.S. ties, and the profound impact of the American war against terrorism in the region that New Delhi and Beijing have agreed to refashion their wary relationship. They have unveiled the framework for a broad-based dialogue on all issues of mutual concern and accelerate the clarification of the Line of Actual Control, resolve the dispute over Sikkim and liberate their relationship from Pakistan. Add to it the decision to aggressively pursue the huge prospects for bilateral economic cooperation and a new recipe has been created for transforming Sino-Indian relations.

Bilateral relations with Thailand were further strengthened. Princess Dr. Chulabhorn Mahidol, the youngest daughter of the King of Thailand, visited India from 19 November-1 December 1996 in connection with the United Nations Environment Program (UNEP) Award Ceremony. Another Royal guest from Thailand was the second daughter of the King, Princess Maha Chakri

Sirindhorn, who visited Andaman and Nicobar Islands from 21-26 December 1996. The Festival of Thailand in India timed to coincide with 50th Anniversary of Indian independence was inaugurated by Princess Maha Chakri Sirindhorn. Vice-president Shri K. R. Narayanan transited through Bangkok on his way to Mongolia.

The Singapore government took the initiative in holding the first-ever-Global Indian Entrepreneurs Conference (GIEC) in June 1996 bringing together Indian and Indian origin businessmen from around the globe. Finance Minister Shri P Chidambaram was the keynote speaker at the Conference. India and Singapore held week long Anti Submarine Warfare Exercises off Visakhapatnam from 3-13 March 1996. Chief of Naval Staff of Singapore participated in the concluding function of the Exercises. Bilateral trade and investment relations with Singapore continued to grow.

Malaysian Prime Minister Dr. Mahathir bin Mohamad paid a state visit to India from 19-22 December 1996 to receive the 1994 Jawaharlal Nehru Award for International Understanding. Dr. Mahathir also delivered the First India-ASEAN Lecture instituted under the Full Dialogue Partnership with ASEAN. During the official visit of the Minister of External Affairs to Malaysia on 18 and 19 August 1996 ports, power and highways were identified as three areas where Malaysian expertise can be beneficial to India.

The Second Meeting of the Indo-Brunei joint Committee was held. Though bilateral trade between the two countries is limited, the two countries are seeking ways to expand it.

President of Philippines Fidel V. Ramos paid a State visit to India from 3-5 March 1997. He was accompanied by leaders of the business community in Philippines. To further acquaint Philippines' commerce and industry with reforms in India, the Indian Embassy organized two Business Seminars on the emerging opportunities in India in the new economic environment. The second Meeting of the India-Philippines Joint Business Council was held in New Delhi in September 1996.

India continued to have friendly and close relations with Indonesia. Minister of External Affairs visited Indonesia in July 1996 to attend the ASEAN Regional Forum (ARF) and ASEAN-PMC meetings in Jakarta where India was formally admitted as member of the ARF and Full Dialogue Partner of ASEAN. Chief of Naval Staff attended the inauguration of the Indonesia Air Show held in Jakarta on 20 June 1996. During the World Food Summit held in Rome, Prime Minister had a meeting with the Indonesian President on November 16, 1996. The two leaders discussed means to build and expand bilateral relations and the need to strengthen India's relations with ASEAN countries in general. Indonesia agreed to

India's proposal for setting up a Telemetry Tracking ground station at Biak (Kalimantan) for continuous monitoring of the Indian Space Research Organization's (ISRO) Geosynchronous Satellite Launch Vehicle (GSLV). An agreement for cooperation in the field of space science is in the final stages of negotiation. In December 1996, India and Indonesia signed a Cultural Exchange Program for the year 1997-1999 under the aegis of the India-Indonesia Cultural Agreement with a view to promoting further understanding and closer cooperation in the field of culture and education. The holding of an exclusive Indian Trade Exhibition in Jakarta in March 1996 coincided with the meeting of the Joint Business Council. FICCI opened an office in Jakarta.

India maintained very close and friendly relations with Vietnam. Prime Minister of Vietnam paid an official visit to India in March 1997. The Third Meeting of the India-Vietnam Joint Working Group (JWG) was held in New Delhi on 16 and 17 January 1997 to review progress on various bilateral cooperation programs and a Work Plan for Agricultural Cooperation was signed during the JWG meeting. Chief of Naval Staff visited Vietnam in May 1996. Another Rupee credit of ₹ 90 crore on soft terms was extended to Vietnam for capital goods imports from India.

India continued to have very close and warm relations with Laos. An MOU for cooperation in the field of agriculture was negotiated. Government of India pledged to provide medicines worth ₹ 15 lakh to Laos as flood relief.

Relations with Cambodia remained very friendly and warm. An agreement to set up an India-Cambodia Joint Commission on Trade, Economic, Scientific and Technological Cooperation was finalized. First Prime Minister of Cambodia Prince Norodom Ranariddh visited Bodh Gaya, Patna on 16 December 1996 on a pilgrimage.

7.2 India and ASEAN

The Association of South East Asian Nations (ASEAN) came into existence in 1967. It was brought up with the objective of bringing together the countries of South East Asia to cooperate in maintaining regional security, peace, stability and development. ASEAN is a regional organisation was initially formed by the govt of Indonesia, Malaysia, Philippines, Singapore, Thailand when their foreign ministers signed to Bangkok declaration on 8th Aug, 1967. Its aim is to accelerate economic stability of South-east Asia. After conclusion of its 34th annual foreign ministers meet ASEAN has come a long way. It is considered to be one of the most influential associations in the World. Presently ASEAN association has 10 members along with Brunei, Vietnam, Laos, Myanmar and Cambodia joining respectively in 1984, 1995, 1997 and 1999. Their mutual interests are (a) strategic and (b) economic.

However, gradually India made a bid to cultivate closer relations with ASEAN and ultimately succeeded in joining the ASEAN regional forum (ARF) on 23 July 1996 as full dialogue partner. This would enable India to take a closer look at many issues which are in dispute among the countries of the region. India's entry as a full dialogue partner into the ASEAN reflects India's growing interest in this port of the world which has gained considerable economic prominence.

It thus, took nine years from 1987 to 1996 for India to become a stable participant in the first ASEAN-India Summit that was also held in Phnom Pehn. Secondly, a major paradigm shift also occurred in India's Foreign Policy. The shift was evident in to form of India's Look East Policy. Looking east is also significant in view of the factual India shares a close cultural legacy with the East Asian Countries. This policy has evidently adopted a three pronged approach.

1. To renew political contacts with the ASEAN Countries.
2. To increase economic interaction with the region.
3. To forge defence links with many countries of the region.

Two windows are available through which India can further look east one is the 19-strong 10R-ARC or Indian Ocean Rim Association for Regional cooperation and BIMST-EC or Bangladesh, India, Myanmar, Sri Lanka, and Thailand Economic cooperation, both of which India is a part. The Mekanganga project is yet another evidence of the emerging relations between the two sides. The Indian president and PM have visited the region several times to accelerate the pace of the emerging relations. A joint statement issued after summit mentioned the setting up of an India-ASEAN Regional Trade and Investment Area as a "long-term objective". The draft framework agreement was readied for discussion by the economic ministers when they met in Phnom Penn in October 2003. In 2010-11, Indian exports to ASEAN were worth US$ 27.27 billion and imports from the ASEAN region were worth US$ 30.60 billion.

Realizing the scope for greater cooperation in the economic field, the two sides agreed to work towards an ASEAN-India Free Trade Area over a period of 10 years. Till then, the two sides have agreed to explore possibilities into broad-based bilateral agreement in areas are as under:

- Science and technology.
- Information technology (IT).
- Biotechnology.
- Space technology application.
- Financial services.
- Human resource development.
- Education and so on.

The positive aspect of the business involvement is that there have been investments from ASEAN to India as also from India to ASEAN members. To balance the trade, it is imperative to encourage trade, joint ventures, and technology transfers. In this connection, the first Indo-ASEAN business summit in New Delhi and Hyderabad on October 17 and 18, 2003 provided the necessary backdrop. The 6 main agendas of the business meet were on:

- Infrastructure.
- IT.
- Biotechnology.
- Tourism.

Sixthly, the continuing India-ASEAN dialogue at the highest would also boost India's efforts in sub-regional economic cooperation namely, BIMSTEC, Mekang Ganga Project in which India is associated with the five ASEAN countries Cambodia, Laos, Myanmar, Vietnam and Thailand. Another effort to build a road linking Thailand to India through Myanmar would go a long way in facilitating free trade.

7.3 19th ASEAN Summit in Bali, Indonesia, November 2011

The Sixth East Asia Summit (EAS), chaired by H.E. Dr. H. Susilo Bambang Yudhoyono, President of the Republic of Indonesia, was held on 19 November 2011 in Bali, Indonesia. The Summit was attended by the Heads of State/Government of ASEAN Member States, Australia, the People's Republic of China, the Republic of India, Japan, the Republic of Korea, the United States of America. The Foreign Minister of the Russian Federation and the Minister of Foreign Affairs of New Zealand attended the Summit on behalf of their respective Leaders. Declaring that India's partnership with the Association of South East Asian Nations (ASEAN) is the foundation of its 'Look East Policy,' Prime Minister Manmohan Singh has said that greater physical connectivity between India and the 10-member grouping remains New Delhi's "strategic objective."

In his statement at the ninth ASEAN-India Summit here on Saturday, Dr. Singh listed proposals, among others, for an India-Myanmar-Thailand highway and its extension to Laos and Cambodia, and the development of a new highway also linking Vietnam. He also referred to a study on a Mekong-India economic corridor, which proposes to link corridors in the peninsular, and possibly the north-eastern, regions of India with the East Asian region.

With ratification of the India-ASEAN Free Trade Agreement (FTA) for Trade in Goods in August this year, the ideas to push for greater physical connectivity could be expected to gather pace. In his concluding remarks, Dr. Singh appreciated the "widespread" support from every ASEAN leader for early conclusion of the India-ASEAN FTA on Services and Investment and hoped that the agreement would be concluded by March 2012. "I would suggest that all these different proposals [for enhanced physical connectivity] should be studied in an integrated manner by our officials so that we take considered decisions to optimise our resources and efforts,"

He described as "growing" India's cooperation with the ASEAN in maritime security, counter-terrorism, training, exercises and disaster management. Dr. Singh said India's trade with ASEAN had increased by 30 percent in 2010-2011, crossing the US$ 50-billion mark, and with such a rate of growth, the target of US$ 70 billion by 2012 would be feasible. He also extended a personal invitation to the ASEAN heads of state to participate in the special ASEAN-India Commemorative Summit scheduled in New Delhi for the third week of December. Later in the day, in his statement at the sixth East Asia Summit Plenary Session, Dr. Singh underscored that India fully subscribed to the view that the East Asia Summit process must be centred on the ASEAN, and the ASEAN should be its driving force. He later left for Singapore on a two-day visit. Strengthening of economic ties would top the agenda of his interaction with Singapore leaders.

One of the highlights of the Summit was the exchange of views on the dispute in the South China Sea that involves several ASEAN countries and China. China and the U.S. showed diverging perspectives on finding a solution to these disputes, with the former favouring bilateral negotiations between the parties involved and the latter supporting a multilateral approach.

At the sixth East Asia Summit, held on the November 19, 2011, the U.S. and Russia were welcomed as the new official members of the EAS group. President Obama's participation to this summit, at a time of internal turmoil, was interpreted as a powerful symbol of the U.S. shift towards Asia. Scholars underlined that the U.S. might see the EAS as a useful tool to counter China's influence and introduce new issues on the EAS agenda. This summit is the first summit-level regional grouping to gather all of Asia's great powers.

Obama's strategy of re-engaging in Asia has a clear economic interest behind it, as the single most prominent message during his Asia trip was that expanded economic ties with Asia would lead to the creation of jobs in the U.S. However, in order to pursue successfully an economic agenda in the Asia-Pacific, the US will need to find a way to peacefully cooperate with China.

7.4 India and Myanmar

The close interaction with Myanmar has shown substantive benefits in promoting our security and regional interests. Confidence was soon promoted to such an extent that in 1995, the Indian and Myanmar armed forces launched a coordinated operation against well armed groups of insurgents from the NSCN (IM), the PLA, and ULFA amongst others in a cooperation code named 'Golden Bird'. Such cooperation has continued, with the Myanmar forces launching operation in close consultation with us against the NSCN (Khaplang), (the insurgent group has not joined the NSCN (IM) in ending its military operations.)

There also has been expanding co-operation in dealing with the menace of narcotics trafficking. Contacts between the military authorities and the home ministries of the two countries have led to growing co-operation in transforming the Indo-Myanmar border into border of peace, tranquillity and co-operation. Representatives of state governments bordering Myanmar actively participate in discussions on these issues.

Our relations with Myanmar are now looking at a new horizon with the passage of time. As our interaction with the economies of the ASEAN countries seeks to attain new dimensions, Myanmar gathers increasing importance in our "Look East" policies as our only land bridge to South-east Asia and Indo-China.

Engineers of the Border Road Organisation have completed the work on construction of a highway linking Tamu on the Manipur border with the rail head to Mandalay at Kalemyo. This highway will be a part of the larger Asian highway network traversing across the Asian land mass. It will be an integral part of our efforts to build new bridges of bilateral and regional economic co-operation with the entire economically vibrant east and south-east Asian regions.

There is a need for introducing a number of trade facilitation measures to promote border trade with Myanmar and Bangladesh, including transportation system that allow cross-border movements of vehicles and the provisions of auxiliaries like weight bridges and cold storages. It is also sensible and economically more viable if India gets into counter-trade agreements with Myanmar. It will be economical for Myanmar to provide agricultural commodities like rice and dal to our north-eastern states in exchange for other Indian products rather than pay huge subsidies for the supply.

Given the high level of literacy and prevalent use of English in some of our north-eastern states like Mizoram, the IT industry must be persuaded to move into software parks in the region. These parks will serve to attract business with our eastern neighbours. While moves are under way to construct an international airport at Guwahati, there is need to take measures to promote foreign investment by attracting tourists from ASEAN and other East Asian countries, including China towards the north-eastern states. The land routes in Myanmar bordering Manipur and Mizoram should be opened for travel and tourism and pilgrimage.

China and Myanmar are now not only opening out their economies to foreign investments but also endeavouring to become major tourism destinations. While India attracts barely 2.5 million tourist annually, the estimated number of tourists who visited China in 1990 is 72 million. There might be big discussions in India on China posing strategic threats to us, but the fact that unless we set our house in order and shed our policies regarded as sacred cows, like reservations for the small scale sector and treating tourism policies as highly taxed luxury industries, we will find ourselves increasingly marginalised by China and other east Asian countries, both industrially and in spheres like tourism.

While much has been spoken over providing movement to our Look East Policy, these policies will serve our national interest best only if they are integrally linked to promotion of the economic progress and welfare of the people of our north-eastern states.

India-Myanmar relations are rooted in shared historical, ethnic, cultural and religious ties. As the land of Lord Buddha, India is a country of pilgrimage for the people of Myanmar. India and Myanmar share a long land of over 1600 km. and a maritime boundary in the Bay of Bengal. A large population of Indian origin (according to some estimates about 2.5 million) lives in Myanmar.

India and Myanmar signed a Treaty of Friendship in 1951. Bilateral relations were close during the period U Nu was Prime Minister (1948-62). During the years Myanmar was ruled by Gen. Ne Win (1962-1988), bilateral relations were static but cordial. During the preceding decade, India-Myanmar relations have developed and diversified satisfactorily. A number of agreements, including the Tripartite Maritime Agreement between India, Myanmar and Thailand determining the tri-junction point in the Andaman Sea, Border Trade Agreement, MoU on Cooperation between the Civilian Border Authorities have been signed. Institutional mechanisms for facilitating regular dialogue on a range of issues of bilateral interest have also been established.

In 2002, our Consulate General in Mandalay was re-opened and the Consulate General of Myanmar was set up in Kolkata. The close interaction with Myanmar has shown substantive benefits in promoting our security and regional interests. Confidence was soon promoted to such an extent that in 1995, the Indian and Myanmar armed forces launched a coordinated operation against well armed groups of insurgents from the NSCN (IM), the PLA, and ULFA amongst others in a cooperation code named 'Golden Bird'. Such cooperation has continued, with the Myanmar forces launching operation in close consultation with us against the NSCN (Khaplang), (the insurgent group has not joined the NSCN (IM) in ending its military operations.)

There also has been expanding co-operation in dealing with the menace of narcotics trafficking. Contacts between the military authorities and the home ministries of the two countries have led to growing co-operation in transforming the Indo-Myanmar border into border of peace, tranquillity and co-operation. Representatives of state governments bordering Myanmar actively participate in discussions on these issues.

Our relations with Myanmar are now looking at a new horizon with the passage of time. As our interaction with the economies of the ASEAN countries seeks to attain new dimensions, Myanmar gathers increasing importance in our "Look East" policies as our only land bridge to South-east Asia and Indo-China.

In the Joint Statement released at the end of the visit, the Myanmar government expressed full support for India's bid for permanent membership of the UN Security Council. Meetings also took place at the ministerial level between the visiting ministers and their Indian counterparts. Apart from New Delhi, the delegation visited Agra, Bangalore, Sarnath, Bodh Gaya and Kolkata.

In 2005, the Minister of Petroleum and Natural Gas paid a visit to Myanmar from 11-14 January 2005 during which a bilateral MoU on Cooperation in the Hydrocarbon Sector was signed. In addition, in-principle agreement was reached between the Petroleum/Energy Ministers of India, Myanmar and Bangladesh on construction of a gas pipeline from Myanmar to India via Bangladesh. This was followed by EAM's visit to Myanmar from 24-27 March 2005. Myanmar Deputy Foreign Minister U. Kyaw Thu was in New Delhi in October 2005 for the Foreign Office Consultations and called on EAM and Minister of State, Shri E. Ahamed during his visit. The last high-level visit in 2005 was by the Chief of Army Staff General J.J. Singh to Myanmar from October 29 to November 2, 2005, which was very well received. The first high-level visit to Myanmar in 2006 was that of Chief of Naval Staff Admiral Arun Prakash in January. The Myanmar Commerce Minister visited Kolkata in January 2006 for the Partnership Summit.

India and Myanmar on 27 September 2011 agreed to set a 3 billion US dollars as trade target. The trade target will be achieved by 2015. At present, the bilateral trade between India and Myanmar is 1.5 billion US dollars. This was decided at a fourth meeting of joint trade commission which was attended by the Union Commerce Minister, Anand Sharma and the Myanmar's Minister of Commerce, U. Win Myint. India and Myanmar also agreed to build a Land Custom Station at India-Myanmar Border (Mizoram) to facilitate the movement of vehicles and goods entering and leaving Mizoram. Both nations noted that the border trade point at Moreh on the Indian side and Tamu on the Myanmar side had huge potential for normal trade.

It should be noted that one third of India's imports of pulses and one-fifth of

India's imports of timber are from Myanmar. At present, pulses and wood products accounts for 97.5 percent of Myanmar's total exports to India while pharmaceuticals and buffalo meat accounted for 45 percent of India's total exports to Myanmar. India and Myanmar implemented the India-ASEAN (Association of Southeast Asian Nations) Free Trade Agreement (FTA) on 1 September 2010. India had also implemented the Duty Free Tariff Preference (DFTP) scheme for Myanmar in January 2009, under which Myanmar would gain market access for 94 percent of India's products at zero duty. India and Myanmar have also increased the list of items for border trade from 22 to 40.

7.5 India and Vietnam

India provided full support to Vietnamese struggle against the imperialist forces of France and later on Japan. India had been concerned with the plight of the Viet Minh and the conflict between the two Vietnams–North Vietnam (under Ho-Chi-Minh) and South Vietnam (Ngo Dinh Diem). India wanted to work for peace and development in the region.

But the non-cooperation of Ngo Diem regime in South Vietnam which was under American influence, came in the way. Ho-Chi Minh and the liberation struggle in Vietnam received tremendous support from the Indian people. The then Prime-Minister Mrs. Indira Gandhi called American intervention in Vietnam's imperialist aggression and called for America's immediate withdrawal from the region.

After unification, Vietnam maintained good relations with India but it was only in 1990s that India stressed on forging extensive ties with Vietnam in relation to its Look East Policy.

The Vietnamese President Mr. Tran Du Luong became the first president of United Vietnam after Ho-chi-Minh in 1958 to visit India in December 1999 and stressed on extensive bilateral relation between the two countries. The visit was reciprocated by Indian Prime-Minister Mr. Atal Bihari Vajpayee, who visited Vietnam on January 7, 2001. The two countries signed a memorandum of understanding which declared that both the countries will work for strengthening cultural ties, tourism and goodwill in bilateral relation.

The major points of agreements related to Information technology, (India can develop software parts in Vietnam and thus help in growth of IT in Vietnam), Science and technology and peaceful use of nuclear technology co-operation (India promised to provide technology for peaceful use as well as training to Vietnamese scientists).

The Vietnamese leaders supported India's claim for entry into United Nations Security Council as well as member status in ASEAN. Reciprocating it, India assured Vietnamese leaders of its support to Vietnamese effort to enter W.T.O.

Vietnam also stressed on increased Indian investment for various infrastructural projects in Vietnam and applauded efforts of players like Ranbaxy, ONGC etc. which have led initiative in investing in Vietnam.

Vietnam is the fourth largest producer of oil and gas in South-East Asia. Also, it is the major earner of foreign exchange for Vietnam. Thus Vietnam will emerge as another destination of crude oil research for India. It will be a major boost to bilateral ties and will reduce India's dependence on gulf countries for the crude oil.

India provided full support to Vietnamese struggle against the imperialist forces of France and later on Japan. India had been concerned with the plight of the Viet Minh and the conflict between the two Vietnams–North Vietnam (under Ho-Chi-Minh) and South Vietnam (Ngo Dinh Diem). India wanted to work for peace and development in the region.

But the non-cooperation of Ngo Diem regime in South Vietnam which was under American influence, came in the way. Ho-Chi Minh and the liberation struggle in Vietnam received tremendous support from the Indian people. The then Prime-Minister Mrs. Indira Gandhi called American intervention in Vietnam's imperialist aggression and called for America's immediate withdrawal from the region.

After unification, Vietnam maintained good relations with India but it was only in 1990s that India stressed on forging extensive ties with Vietnam in relation to its Look East Policy.

The Vietnamese President Mr. Tran Du Luong became the first president of United Vietnam after Ho-chi-Minh in 1958 to visit India in December 1999 and stressed on extensive bilateral relation between the two countries. The visit was reciprocated by Indian Prime Minister Mr. Atal Bihari Vajpayee, who visited Vietnam on January 7, 2001. The two countries signed a memorandum of understanding which declared that both the countries will work for strengthening cultural ties, tourism and goodwill in bilateral relation.

The Vietnamese leaders supported India's claim for entry into United Nations Security Council as well as member status in ASEAN. Reciprocating it India assured Vietnamese leaders of its support to Vietnamese effort to enter W.T.O.

The traditionally close and cordial relations between India and Vietnam have their historical roots in the common struggle for liberation from foreign rule and the national struggle for independence. The father of Vietnam's freedom struggle, the late President Ho Chi Minh, is known to have had contacts with Indian freedom fighters including Jawaharlal Nehru whom he had reportedly met at a Conference on anti-colonialism at Brussels in 1927. Pandit Jawaharlal Nehru was one of the first visitors to Vietnam after its glorious victory against the French at Dien Bien Phu in 1954. President Ho Chi Minh went to India in February, 1958. President Rajendra Prasad visited Vietnam in 1959.

India has a number of ongoing cooperation programmes with Vietnam. The progress of these programmes is reviewed during meeting of India-Vietnam Joint Commission for Economic, Scientific and Technical Cooperation which was established on 18th December, 1982. The Foreign Ministers of the two countries are the joint co-chairmen. So far 12 meetings of the Joint Commission have taken place, alternatively in New Delhi and Hanoi.

The 12th Meeting of the Joint Commission under the Co-Chairmanship of EAM Shri K. Natwar Singh and Vietnamese Foreign Minister Mr. Nguyen Dy Nien was held in Hanoi on October 18, 2004 during which the leaders of the two delegations reaffirmed the close, cordial and mutually beneficial relations that exist between India and Vietnam. The JCM discussed the entire range of India-Vietnam interaction in the economic, commercial, industrial, scientific and technological, information technology, health, education and HRD assistance, cultural fields etc. A Plan of Action for 2004-2006 for implementing the Joint Declaration on Comprehensive Cooperation Framework between Vietnam and India, signed in May 2003 during the visit to India of the General Secretary of the Communist Party of Vietnam, Mr. Nong Duc Manh, was also signed during the Meeting.

An agreement on bilateral cooperation in Science and Technology was first concluded in 1976, and renewed in February 1996 with provision for joint research and exchange of scientists in various areas. Under the Agreement, a Joint Committee on Science and Technology was constituted in 1997 to oversee implementation and report progress to the Indo-Vietnam Joint Commission on biotechnology, infrastructure, mining, etc. RITES Ltd. has supplied 20 electric diesel electric locomotives to Vietnam Railways under lines of credit extended by the Government of India. Antrix has bid for construction and launch of Vietnam's first telecommunication satellite VINASAT. A decision on the award of the contract is pending.

In August 1999, the First India-Vietnam Protocol on Information Technology was signed, which details types of possible cooperation in the field of information technology. The Government of Vietnam has identified India as a strategic partner in this field. India is helping Vietnam in setting up of an Advanced Resources Centre in IT in Hanoi. It is also assisting in human resources development in IT in the country. Both these projects are being funded by the Government of India. Indian companies Aptech, NIIT and Tata Infotech have franchised setting up of 40 training centres in IT in Vietnam. ONGC Videsh Ltd.

has invested US$ 162 million in Vietnam in a major joint venture in offshore oil natural gas exploration in Nam Con Son basin in southern Vietnam.

The major points of agreements related to Information technology, (India can develop software parts in Vietnam and thus help in growth of IT in Vietnam), Science and technology and peaceful use of nuclear technology co-operation (India promised to provide technology for peaceful use as well as training to Vietnamese scientists).

7.6 India and Indonesia

Indonesia is the largest country in the south-east Asian region. The leader of Indonesia's Independence movement, Sukarno, was friendly with Nehru. India and Indonesia signed a treaty of friendship in March 1951 to promote "perpetual peace and unalterable friendship".

Indonesia initially supported India to forge Afro-Asian unity to accelerate the pace of decolonisation. It hosted the Afro-Asian conference at Bandung in 1955. But Indonesia under Sukarno began to advocate the concept of New Emerging Forces (NEFOS) against the old established forces. It started a record against colonialism, neo-colonialism and imperialism. India did not share these militant ideas in international relations. India's refusal to join NEFOS offended Indonesia.

When China invaded India, Indonesia gave a very cool response and even showed a strand of support to China. In September 1964 the Ayub-Sukarno communique, supported Pakistan's stand on Kashmir and in the following year Indonesia urged NEFOS to help Pakistan in its war against India. However, the diplomatic, cultural and economic relations between the two countries continued. However, after Sukarno the relation became cordial.

Recently Indonesian president Abdur-Rahman Wahid visited India and the visit was reciprocated by the then Prime Minister A.B. Vajpayee in January 2001. Both the countries showed their commitment towards each other for bilateral trade relation and territorial integrity, security concerns and developing commercial ties and raising issues for developing countries at various world fora.

The strategic and defence partnership between India and Indonesia has received impetus from two different sources of commitment–commitment emanating from the improved bilateral relationship and India's commitment to its growing strategic engagement with the ASEAN. Apart from bilateral defence cooperation, the two countries have engaged bilaterally in addressing non-traditional security challenges facing the region such as terrorism, maritime piracy and so on. India and Indonesia signed a Bilateral Agreement on Cooperative Activities in the Field of Defence in 2001. India has been supplying defence equipment, especially for the Indonesian navy and the two countries are exploring other areas for defence cooperation.

Indonesia has shown its keen interest in importing items such as batteries for torpedoes, engines for Parchim-class corvettes, repair facilities for Type 209 submarines and so on. India had proposed a draft Memorandum of Understanding on Defence Cooperation in 1995 with the focus on supplies, technologies, joint production and joint projects. Although the MoU has been signed by both the countries, it is yet to be ratified by the Indonesian Parliament.

During the visit of the Indonesian President, Mr. Susilo Bambang Yudhoyono in November 2005, the two countries agreed to hold an annual "strategic dialogue" at the level of senior officials, with the first meeting to be held in the first half of 2006. An MoU on cooperation between the countries' diplomatic training institutes has been signed.

India has been providing training to Indonesian military officers under the ITEC-I program. India and Indonesia signed a Memorandum of Understanding on Combating International Terrorism in July 2004, which provided for the formation of a Joint Working Group (JWG) on Counter Terrorism. The JWG held its first meeting in New Delhi in February 2005 and agreed to strengthen bilateral cooperation in combating terrorism and other transnational crimes and in maritime security through exchange of information and intelligence, capacity building and legal cooperation. During the Regional Meeting of the Ad Hoc Group of Law Enforcement Practitioners, held in Bali in August 2004, India stressed devising institutional mechanisms for sharing of information relevant to each country and speedy extradition of persons involved in terrorist activities.

An important area of bilateral cooperation is the issue of maritime terrorism and piracy in and around the Malacca Strait. The key components of cooperation have been visits of Indian navies to Indonesian ports and vice-versa, conducting joint naval exercises, escorts of Indonesian ships in the Andaman Sea and so on. Since 1995, Indonesia, along with Singapore, Thailand and Malaysia has been taking part in the biennial gathering of ships known as MILAN hosted by India.

India has also been conducting bilateral Search and Rescue Operations with Indonesia named Indopura SAREX. Since 1997, bilateral SAREX has been converted into a multilateral maritime operation comprising of India, Indonesia, Malaysia and Singapore. Indian naval ships have been paying goodwill visits to Indonesian ports. India has also proposed joint patrol in and around the Malacca Strait, but Indonesia has shown its reluctance in allowing extra-regional navies in the Strait. In the aftermath of Tsunami, India launched the Operation Ghambir in January 2005 and sent food and medical supplies to Indonesia through its hospital ship INS Nirupak and a corvette INS Khukri. President Yudhoyono during his visit to India in November 2005 and the Indonesian Vice President Dr. Jusuf

Kalla, during his visit in January 2007, expressed their country's gratitude for India's assistance in Tsunami relief operations.

The centuries old economic relationship between India and Indonesia have been formalized and firmly established through a number of agreements, declarations and MoUs. The first trading agreement was signed in January 1953, further extended in June 1978, when the two countries agreed to develop mechanisms in order to strengthen and diversify trade and commercial links. Both the countries signed a bilateral Agreement on Avoidance of Double Taxation in January, 1986.

The two countries also signed an Agreement for the Promotion and Protection of Investments, during the G-15 meeting in Jamaica in February 1999 and which came into force in January 2004. An India-Indonesia Joint Commission Meeting (JCM) was held in Yogyakarta in September 2003, which mandated the promotion of bilateral economic and commercial relations and the setting up of an "India-Indonesia Expert Working Group."

The expert working group is expected to recommend directly to the JCM on finding out ways and mechanisms to further expand their economic cooperation. During the 2005 visit of the Indonesian President, the two countries also signed a Memorandum of Understanding on setting up of a Joint Study Group to examine the feasibility of entering into a Comprehensive Economic Cooperation Agreement.

The total value of bilateral trade has gone up from US$ 1.12 billion in 1995-96 to US$ 16.16 billion in 2010-11. India imports palm/vegetable oil–crude and processed–coal, petroleum and paper products, and spices whereas major Indonesian imports are textile yarn, chemicals, electric power machinery and parts, refined petroleum products, iron and steel goods, wheat, rice and sugar.

India is the largest importer of crude palm oil and Indonesia has become India's second largest trading partner in ASEAN after Singapore. Energy forms another important area in which the two countries are exploring the possibility of cooperation. During her visit to India in 2002, then Indonesian President, Sukarnoputri, addressing a joint meeting sponsored by the FICCI and the CII in 2002, had expressed her country's willingness to supply oil and gas to India. India is now studying the possibility of procuring natural gas from Indonesia through an undersea pipeline from Aceh to the Nicobar Islands. The bilateral trade has gone further up with Indonesia's economic recovery and a growing realization between the two countries about the strategic necessity of strong economic bilateral relations.

Although the two countries signed an agreement on Technical and Scientific Cooperation as early as 1982, their cooperation on the ground began to take place only after India's active participation in ASEAN affairs, the success stories of India's Information and Technology revolution and the economic crisis in Indonesia. During the last ten years, the two countries have opened up new areas for scientific and technological cooperation, including areas such as remote sensing, satellite launching, and space technologies, thereby, further strengthening and diversifying their bilateral engagement. The Indian Space Research Organisation (ISRO) and the National Institute of Aeronautics and Space of Indonesia (LAPAN) signed a MoU on cooperation in 2002 in space application, capacity building, remote sensing and space technologies.

The LAPAN has provided logistical and technical support to the ISRO for the setting up of its second Telemetry, Tracking and Command Centre at Biak in West Papua, the easternmost province of Indonesia. On 10th January 2007, ISRO successfully launched Indonesia's micro-satellite LAPAN TUBSAT piggyback on its Polar Satellite Launch Vehicle. India and Indonesia have agreed to establish a Joint Committee with equal representatives from both sides to negotiate and agree on a MoU for a Programme of Cooperation, as proposed under the Agreement on Technical and Scientific Cooperation. During his visit, President Yudhoyono called for more scientific development oriented cooperation such as the development of rockets for scientific purposes and satellite technologies; the utilization of Indian remote sensing satellites, tele-education and tele-health.

The two countries have also been deliberating both on bilateral and regional cooperation in developing early warning systems against natural disasters such as the early Tsunami Warning Systems and disaster management. India has also agreed to assist Indonesia in setting up of a vocational training centre in Aceh, the Tsunami-devastated province of Indonesia. Apart from the bilateral collaboration in the space technology and disaster management, the two countries have also engaged in cooperation in the field of bio-technology, pharmaceutical industries and information and technology.

Cultural linkages between India and Indonesia date back to the early centuries of the Christian era. Signifying their ancient cultural relations, the two countries signed a Cultural Agreement as early as 1955, which has acted as the central guideline for bilateral cultural interaction. The cultural agreement has been updated regularly through the Cultural Exchange Programme (CEP), which has facilitated inter-institutional linkages and collaborative research programmes between the two countries. Much of the cultural activities are either sponsored or undertaken by the Indian Council of Cultural Relations (ICCR), which oversees India's cultural relations with other countries.

The Indian government set up the Jawaharlal Nehru Indian Culture Centre

(JNICC) in Jakarta in 1989 to conduct cultural activities in Indonesia. Indian films have a large viewership in Indonesia and they are regularly telecast, dubbed in Bahasa Indonesia. During Yudhoyono's visit, the two countries agreed to establish an Indonesia-India Friendship Association (IIFA), based in New Delhi and Jakarta. Comprising of community leaders from the two countries, the IIFA will aim to forge greater people-to-people cultural linkages. ICCR through its education programmes and scholarships provide an institutional support system for cooperation in human resources development. While experts and officials have received training and scholarship under ITEC programmes and the Colombo Plan, Indonesian students have received scholarships to study in India under the General Cultural Scholarship Scheme and Hindi Scholarship programmes.

While the 'China threat' theory has helped India gain Indonesia's cooperation in regional strategic deliberations and entry into forums such as ASEAN, ARF and the East Asian Summit, the Pakistan factor has limited their bilateral cooperation. Although India and Indonesia have worked together in international forums such as WTO, they have adopted competitive approaches on certain issues such as the issue of Asian candidature in an expanded UN Security Council. The existing visa regime has also been a matter of unease between the two countries. In the economic sector, issues of comprehensive trade agreement or preferential trade agreement have been delayed due to difference over the listing of protected goods. While Indonesia wants palm oil in the free trade list, India has kept it in the list of protected items to provide security to palm oil producers in its south.

The limited nature of international transportation between the two countries has been another matter of concern in the area of bilateral economic and trade links. While Air India flies only once a week to Indonesia, Air Garuda, Indonesia's national carrier does not have any flight to India. Nevertheless, over the years the two countries have moved closer to each other and engaged in cooperative initiatives on bilateral and multilateral issues. Despite challenges, the two countries have reassured each other of continued cooperation in different sectors without letting divergences hinder their bilateral engagement. For example, during his visit to India in 2000, the then Indonesian President, Abdurrahman Wahid, decided not to go to Pakistan as a major political gesture to Indian establishment. India's rising profile in the ASEAN region has come about not only because of its great power projection but also because of the acceptance of that stature by the major ASEAN countries such as Indonesia.

7.7 India and Malaysia

Malaysia inhabited by Malays, Chinese and the Indian communities, has had a democratic political setup. It supported India to strengthen Afro-Asian solidarity. Malaysia supported India at various international fora and forged closer economic ties.

Malaysia welcomed the largest number of Indian joint ventures. Thus the relation after independence was forged on a sound footing of mutual trust and cooperation. Malaysia supported India's stand of non-alignment against hegemonistic designs of power blocs and neo-colonialism.

After the 1990s with India laying stress on developing close relations with south-east neighbours, relation with Malaysia has got an spurt. Prime Minister Atal Bihari Vajpayee visited Malaysia to intensify economic and political cooperation between the two countries. President Mahathir Mohammad reiterated his country's commitment towards Indian stand against terrorism and multi-polar world.

He also stressed on the relevance of NAM and forging of an alliance of developing countries with India as a core partner. Both the countries signed a memorandum of understanding which declares the two country's co-operation in the field of science and technology, joint ventures, information technology, tourism and cultural exchange and infrastructural development. Malaysia also became the first country to which India offered the use of Global Satellite Launch Vehicle (GSLV) to launch its own satellite.

India and Malaysia have age-old political and cultural ties dating to the pre-Christian era. The strong influence of India permeates the social mores of Malaysia, the etymology of its language, common family traditions and the rituals of the royalty. The bilateral relationship embraces all aspects: political, economic, education, defence and cultural, with recent focus on economic and commercial relations.

7.8 India and Thailand

Diplomatic relations between India and Thailand were established soon after India gained independence. However, till a few years ago, there was no real meaningful content in our bilateral relations. The end of the Cold War has led to a significant improvement in our bilateral relations. This has been reinforced by increasing economic and commercial links, exchanges of high level visits on both sides and India's dialogue partnership with ASEAN and the resultant membership of ASEAN Regional Forum (ARF) and with the formation of the sub-regional grouping BIMSTEC and launching of Mekong-Ganga Cooperation in November 2000. Thailand's 'Look West' policy complements India's 'Look East' policy.

The mistrust of the Cold War years began to dissipate with the landmark exchange of visits by India's Prime Minister Mr. Rajiv Gandhi in 1986 and Thai Prime Minister Gen Chatichai Choonhavan in 1989. Other highlights were Royal visits to India–HRH Crown Prince Maha Vajiralongkorn's visit in April 1992 and December, 1998 and HRH Princess Maha Chakri Sirindhorn's visit in March 1987.

Mr. Yashwant Sinha, the then Finance Minister attended the First Meeting of the Asian Cooperation Dialogue (ACD) hosted by Thailand in the resort town of Cha-am/Hua Hin on June 18-19, 2002. Discussions included Asian Bond and an Asian credit rating agency. On bilateral issues, bilateral Free Trade Area agreement and speeding up of trilateral initiative of Thailand, Myanmar and India for transport network linking India's North East with South East Asia, were discussed.

Trade between India and Thailand had been steadily expanding in recent years. However, in 1997, due to the economic problems faced by the East Asian region, Indian exports to Thailand declined. During the year 2010-11, the total trade between the two countries stood at US$ 7.06 billion with Indian exports standing at US$ 2.8 billion.

7.9 India and Singapore

India and Singapore have for the first time in over a decade, held a "maritime exercise" in the South China Sea. The 10 day exercise concluded recently. All previous India-Singapore naval exercises which began in 1994, were carried out off Kochi in the name and style of "Lion King" series. The latest exercise, the first of a new series, is called the Singapore-India maritime Bilateral exercise (SIMBEX-05) SIMBEX-05 was held in Singapore's "Naval Environment", as part of a natural progression of the city-state's naval exercises with India. SIMBEX-05, a continuation of whatever has been going on 'so far' under the "Lion King" series, was 'not really a war game'. It was a 'mix' of traditional navy-to-navy exercise of the 'encounter' kind and had elements of anti-piracy interdiction as also some aspects of anti-submarine operations.

However, 'anti-terrorism' was not the focus of SIMBEX-05. It was just a coincidence that the exercise was held in Singapore at about the same time as an official level meeting of the Association of South East Asian Nation's Regional Forum on confidence Building measures for maritime security. India was among the participants at the ARF meeting organised by Singapore.

8

India's Relations with Asian Neighbours

8.1 India's Relations with Japan

Exchange between Japan and India is said to have begun in the sixth century A.D., when Buddhism was introduced to Japan. Indian culture, filtered through Buddhism, has impacted on Japanese culture and thought, and this is the source of the Japanese people's sense of closeness with India. Direct exchange in the modern era, however, began only in the Meiji era (1868-1912), when Japan embarked on the process of modernization. The immediate post independence experience was no less positive, with the Tokyo tribunal, waiving of reparations and conclusion of a separate Peace Treaty.

In 1949 Prime Minister Jawaharlal Nehru donated an Indian elephant to the Ueno Zoo, in Tokyo. This brought a ray of light into the lives of the Japanese children still suffering from the aftermath of World War II. The elephant was named Indira after Nehru's daughter.

Diplomatic relations between Japan and India were established in 1952. The relationship with India was marked by a special cordiality in the early part of the post-war years. This was due to a variety of reasons, including Indian Judge Radha Binod Pal's dissenting judgment at the Tokyo International War Crimes Tribunal in favour of Japan, India's waiving of all claims for war reparations; India signing a separate Peace Treaty and India's invitation to Japan to participate in the first Asian Games in Delhi. India as the country of origin of Buddhism and Netaji and INA's Association with Japan during the war also invoke friendly feelings among sections of the Japanese society.

At the beginning of the 21st century, Japan and India resolved to take their bilateral relationship to a qualitatively new level. Both realize that the current international situation, characterized by interdependence and the advent of globalization, offers fresh opportunities to both Japan and India for enhanced engagement for mutual benefit. The foundation for this was laid when Mr. Yoshiro Mori, the then Prime Minister of Japan and Shri Atal Behari Vajpayee, the then Prime Minister of India agreed during the Japanese Prime Minister's landmark visit to India in August 2000 to establish the "Global Partnership in the 21st Century".

Today, India and Japan share a global vision of peace, stability and shared prosperity, based on sustainable development. The global partnership between Japan and India reflects a broad convergence of their long-term political, economic and strategic interests, aspirations, objectives and concerns. Japan and India view each other as partners that have responsibility for, and are capable of, responding to global and regional challenges in keeping with their global partnership.

It was agreed during the visit of the then Japanese Prime Minister Junichiro Koizumi in April 2005 that the two countries would further strengthen their cooperation and pursue an all round and comprehensive development of bilateral relations, with a particular and urgent focus on strengthening economic ties, through full utilization of the existing and potential complementarities in their economies. It was decided that both the countries would strive to develop closer dialogue and collaboration to secure peace, stability and prosperity in Asia, promote democracy and development, and explore a new architecture for closer regional cooperation in Asia.

During the visit of Japanese Foreign Minister Taro Aso to India in January 2006, the two countries agreed to further promote the Global Partnership, proceeding from a strategic perspective; cooperation in the energy sector, feasibility study survey for the Freight Corridors project, and launch of "Aso Programme" to promote people-to-people contacts, further strengthen dialogue and exchanges, close consultation and cooperation on EAS, reaffirmed the need for urgent and comprehensive reform of the United Nations.

During the visit of Indian Defence Minister Pranab Mukherjee to Japan on 25 May 2006, the two countries signed a joint statement, the first document to be signed by defence chiefs of the two countries, vowing to aim at maintaining and promoting peace and stability in Asia and the world. The statement also pledges to counter terrorism and violent radicalism and prevent the proliferation of weapons of mass destruction as common aims. It calls for regular meetings of defence chiefs, exchanges on other levels, swapping of information on international terrorism and strengthening cooperation via drills, security research and technologies. It was also agreed that the two countries would strengthen cooperation in diverse areas such as environment, energy, disarmament, non-proliferation and security, taking advantage of, and further building on, their strategic convergences.

Prime Minister of India, H.E. Dr. Manmohan Singh, paid an official visit to Japan from December 13 to 16, 2006 at the invitation of the then Prime Minister of Japan, H. E. Mr. Shinzo Abe. The Prime Minister's visit to Japan took place against the backdrop of a marked upturn in India-Japan relations, particularly since Prime Minister Koizumi's visit in 2005. Prime Minister and Smt. Gursharan

Kaur had audience with Their Majesties the Emperor and the Empress of Japan. He held extensive talks with Prime Minister Mr. Shinzo Abe of Japan, who also hosted a Banquet in honour of the visiting dignitary. He addressed a Joint Session of the Diet on December 14, 2006. Mr. Taro Aso, Minister for Foreign Affairs, Mr. Koji Omi, Minister for Finance and Mr. Akira Amari, Minister for Economy, Trade and Industry called on the Prime Minister of India. Mr. Yoshiro Mori, former Prime Minister and President of Indo-Japanese Association and Dr. Taro Nakayama, President of Japan-Indo Parliamentarians Friendship League also called on the Prime Minister of India. Mr. Yasuhisa Shiozaki, Chief Cabinet Secretary and Mr. Akihiro Ota, Chief Representative of New Komeito called on the Prime Minister of India on December 16, 2006.

The two Prime Ministers unveiled the Joint Logo and launched the India-Japan Friendship Year 2007, to be organised in both countries, and attended the inaugural event of the Festival of India in Japan on December 14, 2006. Prime Minister Dr. Manmohan Singh also addressed the business organisations of Japan at a luncheon meeting. Prime Minister Mr. Shinzo Abe received representatives of the Indian business delegation who accompanied Prime Minister Dr. Manmohan Singh.

A Joint Statement–Towards India Japan Strategic and Global Partnership was signed by the two Prime Ministers. A Joint Ministerial Statement on the launching of a Joint Task Force (JTF) to develop an Economic Partnership Agreement (EPA)/Comprehensive Economic Partnership Agreement (CEPA) between India and Japan was issued.

Prime Minister of Japan Shinzo Abe, accompanied by his spouse, Mrs. Akie Abe, visited India from August 21-23, 2007. During his visit, he called on President of India and met with PM. External Affairs Minister and the Leader of the Opposition called on JPM. JPM addressed the Members of Parliament. A 200-member strong business delegation accompanied JPM during the visit.

The first meeting of the Business Leaders' Forum was held and presented a report to two PMs. Prime Minister Abe attended the High Level Academic Exchange Forum for university collaboration, which was held with the participation of Vice Chancellors/Presidents of prominent universities of both countries.

A Joint Statement on the Roadmap for New Dimensions to the Strategic and Global Partnership between India and Japan and a Joint Statement on the Enhancement of Cooperation on Environmental Protection and Energy Security were signed by the two PMs. PM Abe visited Kolkata and attended the opening ceremony of the India-Japan Cultural Centre. Chief Minister of West Bengal called on JPM.

The dynamic growth of this relationship is reflected in the number of high-level exchanges that have taken place since last year. Our senior Ministers including Defence Minister, Finance Minister, Commerce Minister have visited Japan. Likewise, there have been a large number of ministerial visits from Japan to India including virtually all the Ministers holding key economic portfolios. There have been similarly enhanced exchanges of Parliamentary delegations and interactions at provincial and official level. There is a parallel process of business and industry in both countries taking note of the opportunities that recent economic developments in India have created for them. That has led to a very sharp increase in exchange of business delegations.

Japan and India are both in the process of globalizing, each of course in their own way, and responding to their compulsions. Ultimately, what is important is that the underlying sentiment is one of convergence rather than of competition. Healthy bilateral relations have a natural downstream flow in terms of international cooperation and in creating a positive ambience in the continent and beyond, including the reform and expansion of the UN Security Council.

Mr. Junichiro Koizumi, the Prime Minister of Japan, visited India from April 28 to 30, 2005. during his the two leaders held in-depth discussions on April 29, during which they covered the entire gamut of bilateral relations as well as regional and international issues of mutual interest. The discussions focussed in particular on adding greater substance to bilateral relations and on measures to further deepen the Japan-India Global Partnership, taking into account the steady development in bilateral relations and the far-reaching changes in the international situation, in particular the new surge of change taking place in Asia.

Japan and India share a global vision of peace, stability and shared prosperity, based on sustainable development. Shared democratic values and commitment to human rights, pluralism, open society, and the rule of law underpin the global partnership between the two countries. The global partnership between Japan and India reflects a broad convergence of their long-term political, economic and strategic interests, aspirations, objectives and concerns. Japan and India view each other as partners that have responsibility for, and are capable of, responding to global and regional challenges in keeping with their global partnership. A strong, prosperous and dynamic India is, therefore, in the interest of Japan and vice versa.

8.2 India and Mauritius

History of Bilateral Relations Given the historical links between India and Mauritius, diplomatic relations between the two countries were established even before the Independence of Mauritius. In fact, as many as eight Indian 'Commissioners' were posted to Mauritius from 1948 to 1968. [The designation of the GOI representative was changed to 'High Commissioner' after Mauritius became independent in 1968]. Moreover, non-formal contacts between India and Mauritius go back even longer in history, dating back to the early 15th Century when the uninhabited island of Mauritius was discovered by the Portuguese with the help of Indian and Arab navigators.

Thereafter, Mauritius continued to have contacts with India through successive Dutch, French and British occupation. During the Dutch period (17th Century), the links were minimal and only a small number of Indians were brought to Mauritius as slaves and workers. Contacts became more substantial during the French occupation (1715-1810) as Mauritius occupied a strategic position for French colonies in India, and contributed to France's war efforts in the Indian subcontinent during the Anglo-French wars. Indian leaders like Tipu Sultan of Mysore sent feelers to the French authorities in Mauritius, to seek their assistance against the British forces in India.

The French colony of Pondicherry played an important role in the development of Mauritius during this period, by providing skilled workforce for various projects in Mauritius. Some of the Tamil speaking sections of the present Mauritian population trace back their ancestry to this era, since their forefathers were brought to Mauritius as clerical and administrative workers by the French colonial rulers. The nature of Indian immigration underwent a complete change during the British occupation of Mauritius. Beginning from the 1820s, Indian workers started coming into Mauritius to work on sugar plantations. This trickle became an organised stream from 1834 when, with the abolition of slavery by the British Parliament, large numbers of Indian workers began to be brought into Mauritius as indentured labourers. November 2, 1834 marks the day when the ship 'Atlas' docked in Mauritius carrying the first batch of Indian indentured labourers.

This day is now observed in Mauritius as 'Aapravasi Day', a national holiday. Over the following decades, the number of Indian immigrants grew to a level where they came to constitute a majority of the population. In all, about half a million Indian indentured labourers are estimated to have been brought into Mauritius between 1834 and the early decades of the 20th Century, out of whom about two-thirds settled permanently in Mauritius. This inflow also attracted some Indian traders–mainly Gujarati Muslims–who migrated to Mauritius to cater to the market created by the specific food and clothing needs of the Indian indentured labourers.

Over time, these traders became an influential section of the population. The present Indian origin community of Mauritius comprises 68 percent of the total Mauritian population (51 percent Hindus, 17 percent Muslims), and has largely maintained its Indian cultural and religious heritage. Many of them still visit India for pilgrimage purposes.

Bilateral trade between India and Mauritius has seen growth and diversification over the past years. The official statistics of Government of India's Directorate General of foreign trade show the following trends for trade, in both directions, between India and Mauritius. Indian exports to Mauritius have traditionally been dominated by yarn for the textile sector in Mauritius. However, attempts are being made to diversify the Indian export basket to Mauritius, and to make Mauritian industry more conscious of the enhanced Indian capacity to supply a diverse range of products at competitive prices.

Under an Agreement concluded in 1974, Indian defence officers (from the Indian Navy and IAF) are sent on deputation to the National Coast Guard and the Helicopter Squadron of the Mauritian Police Force. In addition, training facilities are provided under ITEC programme to Mauritian trainees in Indian Defence Training Establishments. About 30 to 40 personnel are trained every year under this scheme. The training covers both long and short duration courses. Mauritius has also been provided with short term training teams of Indian Army officers under the ITEC programme.

Mauritius National Coast Guard was established through Indian assistance, with the gifting of INS Amar in 1974. Thereafter, in 2001 Mauritius was provided the interceptor patrol boat, INS Observer, on free lease for five years (renewed in 2006 for a further period of 5 years), and India also undertook, at its own cost, extensive repairs to Mauritius's Chilean made flagship CGS Vigilant. The Mauritius Coast Guard Vessel, CGS Guardian, has undergone its mid-life refit at Mumbai dockyard in 2005, with Government of India subsidizing about half of the expense towards this operation. Admiral Madhvendra Singh, then Chief of the Naval Staff, visited Mauritius from February 15-18, 2003, on the invitation of his counterpart. During the visit, a wide-range of subjects encompassing strategic relations were discussed, and the two sides agreed to further consolidate and strengthen bilateral cooperation.

Indian Naval ship *Savitri* visited Mauritius on January 14-16, 2004. Two Indian Coast Guard ships, Sarang and Veera, equipped with unique capabilities for maritime law enforcement, visited Mauritius on January 26-29, 2004. India's Naval ship Tabar, a modern multi-purpose naval destroyer, also visited Mauritius on July 21-24, 2004.

Sagar Kanya-India's first deep sea Oceanographic Research Vessel (ORV)– visited Mauritius from January 18-22, 2004, and conducted several surface and sub-surface oceanographic observations.

8.3 India and Philippines

After the independence of the Philippines in 1946 and that of India in 1947, the two countries established formal diplomatic relations on November 26, 1949. In August 2001, the Philippines solicited Indian support to their candidature to UNSC for 2004-05. As a gesture of goodwill, India decided to defer its candidature for UNSC and agreed to support the Philippine candidature. The first Security Dialogue was held on 12th March, 2004 in Manila.

The Government has given its approval for signing of an Agreement between India and Philippines for cooperation in the field of tourism. This Agreement shall remain in force for 5 years and shall be automatically renewed for the same period until terminated with the written consent of the parties through diplomatic channels.

It has been agreed that both countries shall create favourable conditions for the development of long-term cooperation in the field of tourism for the mutual benefit of the two countries. India and Philippines shall, in accordance with the laws and internal regulations in force of each other's country encourage the application of simple procedures for their citizens travelling to the other country for tourism purposes.

The Philippines Signed Nine Bilateral Agreements with India recently during Arroyo's visit to India, including a framework agreement for bilateral trade. The series of agreement signed with India includes those on:

- Defence,
- Health and medicine,
- Energy security,
- Agriculture,
- Tourism, and
- Culture.

It is proposed that both the countries would jointly combat global terrorism and take up joint exercise in non-combat areas.

Bilateral merchandise trade between the two countries in 2010-11 was valued at US$ 1312.12 million, out of which India's was US$ 882.74 million while its imports from the Philippines was only US$ 429.39 million. India's major exports consisted of frozen buffalo meat, iron and steel, vehicles, oilseeds and olea and rubber and articles thereof. India's imports from the Philippines consisted of parts of electronic integrated circuits and micro assemblies, mineral fuels and mineral oils, newsprint paper and paperboard and optical instruments.

Stressing the need to bridge the gap in trade balance which was weighed heavily in favour of India, Macapagal-Arroyo suggested that India import fashion garments and consumer products from the Philippines. She said that whenever a comprehensive agreement is signed, India needed to take care of Philippines trade concerns in view of its size and GDP growth which is much lower as compared to India.

She also disclosed that the Indian government has agreed to extend US$ 50 million credit line to the Philippines through the Exim Bank to support its trade and industry particularly in the area of health and medicines.

The two countries have also agreed to set up a joint monitoring group, which will closely keep a watch on the implementation aspects of agreements signed here so that further areas of joint cooperation are identified to push and integrate the trade and economic ties between India and the Philippines.

Elaborating on pharmaceuticals cooperation, the Philippines President said that Indian industry should open up manufacturing units in her country for providing low cost medicines for its population and also export to other countries. She disclosed that the State Trading Corporation of India has signed an accord with the Philippines International Trading Corporation to export US$ 35 million affordable medicines to the Philippines. Two Indian pharma companies have also signed an agreement with their counterparts in the Philippines.

Macapagal-Arroyo also urged the Indian industry to invest in power transmission projects in the Philippines. She expressed her willingness to replicate Indian experience of producing bio-fuel from Jatropha and ethanol from sweet sorghum.

She also suggested that India attract investments from Philippines construction industry. The Philippines President also invited the Indian industry to invest in dairy sector and meat processing. An agreement has been reached with India to supply live buffalo and genetic material for buffalo breeding. She also invited the Indian film industry to take advantage of the scenic beauty of her country. She said that her country has already relaxed visa norms for Indians.

Speaking on the occasion, Indian minister of state for defence, MM Pallam Raju emphasised the need for promoting trade and cultural ties with the Philippines as according to him the country has strategic importance for India in the entire ASEAN region.

Joint venture cooperation is already on process between the two countries so that their age old ties are cemented and India and the Philippines emerge as leading trade partner in the ASEAN region. The Philippines provided for huge opportunities in the areas of film and BPO and ad film making and therefore a special task force should be formed so that cooperation in this specialised field could be enhanced under mutual beneficiary conditions.

India is keen on building of special relationships between India and the Philippines in the area of pharmaceuticals, arguing that India has an edge over it and Philippines requires India's help. Therefore, emphasis should be laid on this area to exploit its potential to the maximum.

8.4 India and Afghanistan

With the fall of the Taliban, India saw its chance to reassert its influence in the country, particularly as many Afghans were openly unhappy with Pakistan's support of the Taliban. Delhi was also keen to widen its appeal beyond the Tajik and Uzbek communities which dominate the north and reach out to the ethnic Pashtuns, traditionally close to Pakistan and who form the majority of the population. It moved swiftly to establish diplomatic posts in the country, hoping to counter the influence of its long-standing rival, Pakistan. Indeed, land-locked Afghanistan placed strategically between Central and South Asia has long been a backdrop for a Cold War-style Great Game between the two nuclear neighbours. It has done so by building close ties with the country's charismatic President, Hamid Karzai. President Karzai was a university student in India and Delhi has also quietly cashed in on his public denouncing of Pakistan's alleged support to supporters of the former Taliban regime and al-Qaeda militants.

But India has also been able to play on the goodwill it has long enjoyed among ordinary Afghans. Since the fall of the Taliban, it has pledged US$ 500m of aid in Afghanistan, focusing on building schools, hospitals and highways. It has done this despite facing difficulties transporting goods to Afghanistan via Pakistan—everything has to be shipped via Iran from the west, adding to costs and time. A large number of Indian construction workers, engineers and medical personnel have been stationed in Afghanistan, helping rebuild vital installations. It has picked projects which are economically and politically significant while loaded in symbolism.

For much of the past two decades, India has been wrong-footed in its Afghan policy. In 1979, it was one of the few countries to support the Soviet invasion of Afghanistan-a decision which made the country vastly unpopular in that country. A decade later, it continued to back the Communist-regime of President Najibullah, while Pakistan threw its entire support behind the ethnic Pashtun mujahideen warlords, particularly the Islamist Gulbuddin Hekmatyar. When the Taliban swept to power, India had no presence or influence left in the country. It countered Pakistan by strongly backing the Tajik-dominated Northern Alliance, which controlled the narrow sliver of Afghan territory north of the Shomali plains.

Delhi has been working hard to develop its ties with the new Afghan regime following the overthrow of the Taliban in 2001. Much of Indian support flowed in through Tajikistan, where it established a massive and influential embassy.

India strengthened its ties with Afghanistan after Prime Minister Manmohan Singh's historic two-day visit to the country. It is the first visit to the country by an Indian prime minister after 29 years. This visit saw the cementing of strategic and economic ties between the two countries.

During the visit, the two leaders held talks on a broad range of bilateral issues as well as regional and international issues of common concern. They expressed satisfaction at the progress in bilateral relations since President Hamid Karzai's visit to India (February 23-25, 2005) and agreed to take this relationship into a new stage of partnership. They affirmed that India and Afghanistan enjoy a warm and friendly relationship underpinned by historical ties and cultural links. The time tested friendship between the people of the two countries has strived many challenges and is today based on a shared commitment to the ideals of democracy, peace and security.

Afghanistan is engaged in a gigantic process of reconstruction and development. It is emerging from the shadow and after effects of destruction, war for nearly twenty years. It has been India's privilege to be a partner in the processes of economic reconstruction and development. India is not a traditionally donor country, but it is committed already US$ 500 million for reconstruction and development effort of Afghanistan. During this visit PM announced another US$ 50 million for the construction and development of Afghanistan. This assistance, which has reached out to almost all parts of Afghanistan, covers some of the key areas crucial for development like:

- Infrastructure.
- Roads.
- Transport.
- Electricity.
- Civil aviation.
- Social infrastructure.
- Education and health.
- Agriculture and irrigation.

India is already pursuing development projects in virtually all parts of Afghanistan, covering a wide range of sectors, including hydel power, road construction, agriculture, industry, telecommunications, information and broadcasting, education and health.

India remains fully supportive to the goal of a sovereign, stable, democratic and prosperous Afghanistan. Both leaders agreed that such an Afghanistan is also necessary for peace, security and stability in the region. The two leaders condemned global terrorism as threat to democracy and declared that there can be no compromise with those who resort to terrorism. They reiterated their commitment to work together to ensure that Afghanistan would never again become a safe heaven for terrorism and extremism.

India has admired the courageous steps taken by the Afghan Government and the people, under the leadership of President Hamid Karzai, towards the restoration of peace and the adoption of a democratic polity while addressing the challenge of economic development and reconstruction.

Prime Minister, Dr. Manmohan Singh and President Hamid Karzai, signed three bilateral cooperation agreements in the areas of:

- Healthcare,
- Agriculture, and
- Health.

These Agreements reflect the growing diversification of the ties and the potential of a mutually beneficial, multifaceted cooperation.

A new initiative on 'Small Development Projects' has been launched to work with local communities in development programmes. Following on a pilot project undertaken by the Confederation of Indian Industry in pursuance to President Karzai's visit to India earlier this year, the two Governments agreed to launch a "Skill Building Initiative" in Afghanistan in partnership with the Confederation of Indian Industry and the United Nations.

Prime Minister Dr. Manmohan Singh announced that India will adopt 100 villages in Afghanistan to promote integrated rural development by introducing solar electrification and rain water harvesting using technologies that have been developed and successfully demonstrated in India.

Prime Minister Dr. Manmohan Singh welcomed President Hamid Karzai's suggestion to make greater use of Indian institutions for training of Afghans. In order to accelerate the human resource development process, Prime Minister Dr. Manmohan Singh announced 500 scholarships for Afghan students for university education and in addition, 500 short-term training fellowships under the ITEC programme for Afghan men and women.

To support Afghanistan's steps towards democracy, both countries will expand their cooperation in building of democratic institutions, infrastructure and human capacity. India welcomes the forthcoming Parliamentary elections which mark a significant milestone in this process. The parliament house is being built by India and it has already committed US$ 25 million for the construction of the Parliament.

In this context, President Hamid Karzai conveyed Afghanistan's interest in seeking closer links with SAARC. Prime Minister Dr. Manmohan Singh welcomed this initiative and affirmed India's support for Afghanistan's engagement with SAARC. The two leaders endorsed the need for greater consultation and cooperation in a future project of a Turkmenistan gas pipeline to India that would pass through Afghanistan and Pakistan.

A Joint Statement is being issued by the two leaders, which sets out a path for the development and intensification of our relations in the years to come. The Statement reiterates the emergence of a moderate, democratic and prosperous Afghanistan is essential for peace and stability in the region.
It is not surprising, therefore, that one of the key moments of Manmohan Singh's visit was the laying of the foundation stone of the country's new parliamentary building, built by India. India which plays on its strong tradition of democracy is keen to be seen to be strengthening democratic institutions in a country, fragmented and torn by ethnic rivalries.

India and Afghanistan relations spawn over centuries and date back to ancient history. The fall of Taliban regime and subsequent establishment of Interim Authority in December 2001 led to up-gradation of Indian representation in Afghanistan from Liaison Office to Embassy in March 2002. Besides Mission in Kabul, India has four Consulates (Mazar-e-Sharif, Herat, Kandahar and Jalalabad). India's role and active engagement in Bonn Conference of 2001 was positively received. Since then, India followed a policy of high-level engagement with Afghanistan through extensive and wider ranging humanitarian, financial and project assistance and participation in international efforts aimed at political reconciliation and economic rebuilding of Afghanistan. The present level of our aid assistance is at US$ 750 million.

8.5 India and Mongolia

Diplomatic relations between India and Mongolia were established on 24 December 1955. India was the first country outside the Soviet block to establish diplomatic relations with Mongolia. India's role in securing UN membership for Mongolia is acknowledged by the Mongolian people. Mongolia also expresses its appreciation for India's support for its admission to the Non-aligned Movement (NAM) as a full member in 1991.

In February 1994, a Treaty of Friendly Relations and Cooperation was signed during the visit of President Ochirbat to India.

Then Mongolian Prime Minister N. Enkhbayar paid a State visit to India in January 2004. Three agreements were signed in the fields of Animal Health and Dairy; Space Science, Technology and Applications; and Biotechnology. Both sides also formalized the ratification of the Extradition Treaty and the Treaty on Legal Assistance in Civil and Commercial Matters.

Both the countries have taken a number of new decisions to further develop their close and friendly bilateral relations. These decisions include: launching of a new joint project for the establishment of a satellite-based e-network for tele-education and tele-medicine in Mongolia; signing of two agreements for the leasing of land and for the purchase of Chancery premises in Ulaanbaatar; signing of a Memorandum of Understanding to set up an India-Mongolia Friendship Agro Park near Darkhan city in Mongolia; signing of an agreement on visa free travel for diplomatic and official passport holders; and signing of a Protocol on the Cultural Exchange Programme for the period 2006-2008.

8.6 India and Cambodia

The first real and meaningful contact between India and Cambodia began at the forum of the Non-Aligned Movement. The Secretary of State in the Ministry of Interior, Royal Government of Kingdom of Cambodia, Shri Em Sam An visited and signed an agreement to enhance co-operation in combating trafficking of drugs and arms, terrorism and transnational crime. Both the countries have agreed that such co-operation would be in mutual interest.

The agreement also provides for widest measures of mutual legal assistance in the investigation, prosecution and suppression of crime including crime related to terrorism. The agreement also provides for facilitating prosecution of individuals and their associates engaged in crime.

The Ministry of Home Affairs, Government of India would be the nodal agency for implementation of the agreement and, on the part of the Royal Government of the Kingdom of Cambodia, the Ministry of Interior would be the nodal agency.

8.7 India and Brunei

For Brunei's independence celebrations on 23 February 1984, Mohsina Kidwai, then Minister of State for Health and Family Welfare, represented India. The Sultan of Brunei paid a state visit to India in September 1992.

The Deputy Minister of Communications of Brunei Dato Paduka Haji Yussof bin Haji Abd Hamid visited India and discussed the possibility of cooperation in the Port and Shipping sector. The two sides also explored the possibility of cooperation in the area of LNG Shipping. The visiting Minister discussed the expansion and upgradation of their Ports with Indian assistance. The two sides discussed the issues of mutual cooperation in the field of port and shipping sector paving the way for entering into a Memorandum of Understanding (MoU) between the two countries in near future.

A Memorandum of Understanding (MoU) on cooperation in the fields of culture, arts and sports between India and Brunei was signed recently in June 2008.India’s cultural interactions with Brunei have remained somewhat limited in the past as there was no Agreement/MoU with Brunei. It is hoped that with the signing of the MoU the bilateral cultural relations will get an impetus and there will be many cultural exchanges between the two countries.

The Salient Features of MoU being signed are:

Cultural Exchanges between the Cultural and Sports Institutions of the two countries.

1. The constitution of a Joint Consultative Committee (JCC).
2. The Joint Consultative Committee will meet alternately in Brunei and India.

MoU will be valid for a period of 5 years from the date of its signing and has a provision of automatic renewals.

8.8 India and South Korea

In the process of strengthening bilateral relation, India and Korea signed six MoUs for cooperation in hydrocarbon sector. These include: (1) an umbrella agreement on hydrocarbon cooperation between India and Korea, (2) on strategic underground petroleum storage facility, (3) gas hydrate related technical collaboration, (4) MoU on hydrogen and CNG, (5) MoU on hydrogen and fuel cell and (6) establishment of strategic alliance.

Government of India is in the process of building a 5 MMT underground strategic storage keeping in view the energy security of the country. This will be funded and executed through Special Purpose Vehicle (SPV) under OIDB. The Oil Industry Development Board (OIDB), is a statutory body under the administrative control of the Ministry of Petroleum and Natural Gas, Government of India. Korea Gas Corporation (KOGAS) is the world's largest LNG importer. KOGAS provides clean, safe, and convenient energy to its people. KOGAS operates three LNG terminals and a nationwide pipeline network spanning 2,579 km. ensuring a stable supply for the nation.

India and Korea signed the joint study group to achieve a comprehensive economic partnership agreement (CEPA) encompassing trade in goods and services, measures for trade facilitation, promotion, facilitation and liberalisation of investment flows, besides measures to enhance bilateral economic cooperation between the two countries. The visiting Korean Deputy Minister for Trade and Foreign Affairs Joong Keun Kim opined that the JSG would facilitate the bilateral trade. Further among the rich 30 countries belonging to the Organisation for Economic Cooperation and Development (GECD), Korea is the first country with which India has completed the JSG report.

India and Korea have decided to set up a joint task force to formulate a Comprehensive Economic Partnership Agreement (CEPA) in next 24 months. The proposed CEPA is the first one that India would have with an Organisation for Economic Cooperation and Development (OECD) country. OECD is a strong group of 30 countries.

Both countries have increased the trade target from US$ 6-7 billion till 2007-08 to US$ 15-16 billion by 2010.

At present, Korea is the fifth largest investor in India. Steel major Posco's proposal to invest US$ 12 billion in an integrated plant in Orissa is the biggest FDI in India as well as the biggest outward FDI for Korea.

The visiting President of India stressed the need to promote the bilateral ties in the field of science and technology. This was the first-ever visit by an Indian Head of State to South Korea. The President of India visualised the rise of a Pan-Asian Free Trade Area covering all major Asian economies, including India, Korea, China, Japan, ASEAN and possibly extending to Australia and New Zealand. The MoU was signed at Seoul between India's Department of Science and Technology and the Korea Industrial Technology Foundation. The MoU envisaged and stressed on sharing of work for promoting technology innovation and industrial cooperation between the two countries. Both the countries also agreed to extend cooperation and mutual assistance in customs matters.

The negotiations to conclude a Comprehensive Economic Partnership Agreement (CEPA) between India and Korea has begun with the first meeting of the India-Korea Joint Task Force (JTF). The JTF discussed the modalities of the negotiations. Seven Working Groups were formed on Indo-Korean trade negotiations dealing following areas:

1. Trade in goods.
2. Trade in services.
3. Investment.
4. Other rules and economic cooperation.
5. General provisions and dispute settlement mechanism.
6. Rules of origin.
7. Customs administration and procedures.

It may be recalled that a Joint Study Group (JSG) between India and Korea was constituted in pursuance of the announcement during President Roh's visit in October 2004. The JSG had recommended a Korea-India Comprehensive Economic Partnership Agreement (CEPA) and that the two governments appoint a Joint Task Force (JTF) to work on realizing the benefits from such a CEPA and to work out specific recommendations on the constituent elements of the CEPA. In February, 2006, the President of India had visited Seoul and announced the launching of negotiations for the CEPA between the two countries with the understanding that the negotiations would be concluded by December 2007.

8.9 India and Bahamas

India and the Bahamas have decided to enter into an Memorandum of Understanding (MoU) to explore the possibilities of cooperation in the area of Cruise Shipping.

As the Government is formulating a cruise shipping policy to make India an attractive cruise tourism destination with state-of-the-art infrastructure and other facilities at selected ports of the country, the MoU with Bahamas may give a fillip to this plan keeping in view the experience of Bahamas in this area. Bahamas is a favoured cruise shipping destination in the world and its expertise could be used as valuable signpost in the development of the Indian cruise shipping industry.

8.10 India and Singapore

A joint exercise between the Indian Air Force and Republic of Singapore Air Force would be taking place at Air Force Station Kalaikunda between 03 Jan 06 to 20 Jan 06. The Republic of Singapore would be participating with eight F-16 aircraft and IAF would be taking part with a Squadron of MiG-27s. The exercise would be called *SINDEX-06.*

The present exercise is the second in the series of such exercise. Last year a similar exercise, Sindex-04, was held at Gwalior. The infrastructure at AF Station Kalaikunda was recently upgraded to host bilateral exercises with foreign air force. Singapore has a versatile air force which operates modem aircraft and weapon systems.

The IAF has recently increased the level of cooperation with air forces of friendly foreign countries including those of USA, France, South Africa, UK, China and Russia.

President Kalam emphasised the need to give scientific temper to the diplomacy. He categorically mentioned the need to strengthen the Look East Policy of the Government and he expected a Comprehensive Economic Cooperation Agreement (CECA) to be signed with the Singapore Government. President hoped that CECA would allow for the trade between the two sides touching US$ 20 billion by 2010-up from the current level of some US$ 10 billion. Nevertheless, the President expressed his satisfaction over that our bilateral trade grew over 100 percent in the last two years. President Kalam was on tour to three countries: Singapore, the Philippines, and South Korea. He emphasised on the need to set up a "world knowledge platform".

8.11 India and BIMSTEC

The hallmark of contemporary politics is the proliferation of regional groupings of varied nature and scope. The changes that have taken place in the international field in the early nineties have created a new political and economic context for India's regional diplomacy. The challenge for India is to initiate a regional policy based on shared goals and compatible philosophies. Regional framework is being widely accepted as a strategy for meeting the challenges of the present unjust world economic order and overcoming internal structural inadequacies.

India has been late in recognizing the importance of regional organizations. For India, the first attempt at regional organization of any importance was the SAARC (South Asian Association for Regional Cooperation) formed in 1985. It comprised of the seven nations of South Asia viz., India, Pakistan, Maldives, Sri Lanka, Nepal, Bhutan and Bangladesh. But SAARC was plagued by perennial problems caused by poor Indo-Pak relations, India's uneasy relations with Bangladesh and Sri Lanka and so on. The next important attempt was BIMSTEC (Bay of Bengal for Multisectoral Technical and Economic Cooperation). It was a well planned strategy of India and a prudent extension of its 'look east' n this paper an attempt has been made to discuss the achievements of BIMSTEC and explore its long-term implications for India.

BIMSTEC was formed in June 1997. In 1994, Thailand took the explore economic cooperation on sub regional basis involving the countries of South east Asia and South Asia around the Bay of Bengal. After a number of Inter-Ministerial Consultations and with the active support of Asian Development Bank (ADB) and ESCAP, a regional economic forum was formed in 1997 comprising of Bangladesh, India, I and Thailand. At that time it was called BIST-EC i.e. Bangladesh Lanka Thailand Economic Cooperation. In December of the same year Manmar joined this organization and then a 'M' was added to it. It became BIMSTEC. It comprised the countries at the rim of Bay of Bengal. BIMSTEC's inauguration was a low-key affair in comparison to SAARC. There were only ministerial level meetings for several years. It was in the year 2004 that its first Summit took place in Bangkok in July.

It was the first overseas visit of the Indian Prime Minister Manmohan Singh since he took office after the May 2004 general elections. In February 2004, Nepal and Bhutan also had become members of BIMSTEC. The acronym no longer represented the full membership of the organization. Therefore, first Summit it was decided that the letters of the nomenclature should stand for Bay of Bengal Initiative For Multi-sectoral Technical and Economic Cooperation rather than for initials of the names of member So now this group has five countries of South Asia and two of South East Asia. It is important to note that the two countries of South re not its members are Pakistan and Maldives.

BIMSTEC was formed at the time when the process of globalisation was sweeping the world. India's economy was also opening up. World scene had changed tremendously. Soviet Union had disintegrated and the cold war came to an end. Communism as an ideology was being challenged. European Union was getting stronger by the day. With the end of Cold War, the non-aligned movement lost its relevance. China had emerged as a strong economy. WTO had been formed in 1995. SAARC, the South Asian regional organization, which was formed in 1985, was not making any headway due to mutual dissensions and mistrust of member countries. This was broadly the international and regional scenario when BIMSTEC was being conceived and formed in 1997.

A Ministerial meeting was held in Bangkok from June 4-6, 1997, where the new sub regional economic grouping was formally launched. In a declaration issued, the principles, scope and institutional mechanisms of the organization were outlined. The detailed plan of action, areas of cooperation etc were covered in a concept paper. Initially BIMSTEC identified six sectors for cooperation viz., trade and investment, technology, transport and communication, energy, tourism and fisheries. It was an attempt to tap the synergies of land and maritime contiguity in yet another geo-economic setting. The people of this region had close cultural and commercial ties throughout history. Close proximity meant that the business communities maintained active contacts with each other, in addition to cultural and social interactions and people to people contacts.

It was hoped that the inter- regional grouping will serve as a bridge between the five SAARC countries and two ASEAN countries and would have a greater potential to increase the trade among member countries by taking advantage of their geographical location in the regional of Bay of Bengal and the eastern coast of the Indian Ocean.

The Bay of Bengal community also creates options other than the SAARC in pursuing India's interests in regional economic integration. This does not necessarily mean that BIMSTEC stands in opposition to SAARC. In fact, the Bay of Bengal community could complement the efforts at SAARC to promote a free trade area in South Asia. The BlMSTEC could also act as a spur to SAARC on economic cooperation.

The BIMSTEC process marks a new phase in India's Look East policy. The Congress govell1ment led by Mr. P.V. Narsimha Rao launched this initiative towards South East Asia in the early 1990's. Mr. Vajpayee deepened the scope and substance of India's 'look east' policy to cover much of Asia, including the ASEAN, China and Japan. The first segment of 'Look East' policy focused on commercial relations and institutional links with Asia. In the second phase of the 'Look East' policy, India is aiming at political partnerships, physical connectivity.

through road and rail links, free trade arrangements and defence cooperation.

During its eight years of existence the BIMSTEC countries have cooperated in a number of areas. BIMSTEC members recognized the importance to create air, sea and land linkages. They include the open sky policy in BIMSTEC, development of roads between Thai-Myanmar-India and Thai-Myanmar-Bangladesh which will facilitate land transport from the Bay of Bengal to the South China Sea. In terms of Sea transport, there arc the coastal shipping project and India's proposal to support a feasibility study on Tavoy's deep seaport. Railway links between India-Myanmar and Thailand is also a priority. A stronger and desirable intra- regional trade is contingent upon improved transport network among BIMSTEC countries.

9

India's Relations with West Asia and Gulf Countries

9.1 India's Look West Policy

As West Asia confronts dangerous turbulence and political fragmentation, India is prepared to contribute fully to the peaceful resolution of various conflicts in the region. Finding a balance between divergent interests of regional forces has become more urgent than ever in West Asia. We know from our own experience that stability and prosperity to our west accelerates our own economic growth. India has a long record of contributing to peacekeeping missions in this region. India is all set to build on this record and help structure a cooperative security order with our many friends and partners in this region. It hopes to replicate the success in the east with a similar diplomatic thrust towards our western neighbours. Developing liberal trading regimes, better connectivity and economic integration with our north-western neighbours, Pakistan and Afghanistan, Central Asia, West Asia, and Africa are now high priorities. India is determined to become a long-term partner in the neighbourhood in the Gulf, Pak, and Africa and West Asia.

After successfully implementing a "Look East" policy to promote trade and investment with its Asian neighbours, India has adopted a similar policy toward West Asia. The UPA Government has launched the "Look West" policy, in recognition of the facts that:

1. Gulf region has become a major economic partner.
2. A home to over 4 million Indians.
3. A major source of oil and gas.

This has resulted in increased interaction, enhanced trade and economic relations and launch of negotiations towards FTA with the Gulf Cooperation Council (GCC) countries. The Government is keen to cooperate with the Gulf countries in the promotion of peace and stability in the region. It has appointed a Special Envoy for the Gulf and West Asia.

Indian stakes and interests in the Gulf region are as obvious as they are immense. Geographically, the Gulf is India's extended neighbourhood and the only link with the no less vital Central Asia, with Pakistan denying this country transit rights and Afghanistan having sunk into chaos. Historically, a relationship between the subcontinent and the Gulf goes back to ancient, pre-Islamic days. Britain controlled the Gulf littoral tightly because of its overwhelming strategic importance for the defence of India, the brightest jewel in the crown.

Remarkably, however, this control was exercised not from London but from Calcutta (now Kolkata) first and then New Delhi. Even after the end of the British rule in the subcontinent, the Reserve Bank of India was the currency issuing authority in the Gulf; in the mid-1950s this arrangement was terminated at the instance of India, not of the littoral states.

The discovery of oil in the early years of the twentieth century had boosted the Gulf's strategic and economic importance. Since the first oil shock of 1973, to say nothing of the Islamic revolution in Iran in 1979 and the first Gulf War in 1991, it has swiftly increased and is at a very high pitch today amidst the brisk competition between China, India, Japan and South Korea for securing oil and gas.

Overriding all this, in some respects, is what is sometimes called India's "manpower bonanza" in the region. Three and a half million Indians live and work in the six states comprising the Gulf Cooperation Council. In some of these countries, the Indian workers form the majority of the population.

At first Indian manpower in the Gulf consisted almost exclusively of unskilled and semi-skilled workers. Now however the proportion of professionals has gone up to 25 percent. The Indian work force in the Gulf remits home a whopping sum of US$ 20 billion a year, which, incidentally, is the vale of the Indo-Gulf trade also.

All this should normally be conducive to an active Indian role in the Gulf, especially because the entire region is within the operating radius of the Indian Navy, and to maintain the safe and smooth flow of oil is a crucial interest of not just India but also all energy-importing nations. Unfortunately, however, rude ground realities often come in the way of even the most rational scenario. Until 1970, the Persian Gulf was a British lake. Now it is an American lake with the formidable presence of at least two carrier groups in the Gulf waters and the US bogged down in Vietnam-like quagmire in Iraq and apparently hell-bent on taking some kind of military action against Iran. Pakistan-specific issues also play a small but significant part in influencing attitudes in a predominantly Muslim area where the two South Asian neighbours often bicker. More importantly this factor also affects America's willingness to let India, its strategic partner, be active in the region, except in a subordinate position to it. It prefers Indo-US maritime cooperation to centre on the Strait of Malacca rather than the Persian Gulf. Only the other day the US secretary of state announced huge military sales and aid to Gulf and West Asian countries. India, itself dependent on imports of the main weapons systems it needs, is a non-player in this arena.

Nor is this all. Until two years ago, the Chinese navy hadn't crossed the Malacca Strait. Now, there is a considerable presence of the Chinese navy in the Upper Arabian Sea. Moreover, China has acquired a major advantage over India by having the use of the Gwadar port at the mouth of the Strait of Hormuz that it has built on the Makran coast of Pakistan, its all-weather friend. The crowning irony is that even in areas such as economic cooperation between the fast-growing India and the booming countries of the Gulf—in which India can make massive contributions in IT and other sectors and the oil-rich Gulf countries can meet India's virtually insatiable needs for capital investment—little has been done.

It is not that the leaders on the two sides are lacking in imagination. Grandiose promises have been made during the visits to India of President Khatami of Iran in 2003, King Abdullah of Saudi Arabia, who was chief guest at last year's Republic Day parade, and UAE Vice President and Prime Minister Sheikh Mohammed bin Rashid al-Maktoum, the Dubai ruler, who came here recently. But they all became victims of the principal Indian weakness of being long on declarations of intent and woefully short on implementing them.

The whole of West Asian region stretching from Pakistan to the Horn of Africa via the Persian Gulf is currently in the middle of a great turbulence. The major problem areas in this arc of crisis are:

1. The collapse of the old order in the Middle East.
2. The political instability in Central Asia.
3. Iran's nuclear defiance of the international community.
4. The potential failure of the international coalition in Afghanistan amidst the resurgence of the Taliban.
5. Mounting political tensions between Kabul and Islamabad.
6. The likely break-up of Iraq.
7. And failing states in the Horn of Africa.

The common minimum programme of the congress led coalition talks about the importance of developing relations with west Asia. But the region is much more than an arena of confrontation between Israel and the Arabs. The geographical conception of West Asia has significantly expanded since the collapse of the Soviet Union and is now called the "Greater Middle East".

This region shares a long historical association with India. It is the source for India's ever expanding needs of energy. It is also huge markets for Indian goods, services and skilled manpower.

And, it is the arena for the unfolding confrontation between the impulse for political modernisation and religious extremism. This tension has naturally overflowed into the subcontinent destabilising India's own security environment.

While India's engagement with the Greater Middle East has increased in the 1990s, there is no coherent strategy as yet. India has attempted to improve relations with the central Asian states, at large. It sought to promote its energy security partnership in the Gulf and beyond and reach out to markets there. It has also sought to develop a special relationship with. Iran and intensify its role in Afghanistan. All these efforts have not added up to much. India has been able to reclaim its pre-independence primacy in the region.

The inability of India to make a strategic break through in the Greater Middle East lies in the unending political rivalry and military tension with Pakistan. The partition has amply proved this. It has effectively neutralised many of India's initiatives through its own special links to the Greater Middle East.

On the basis of comprehensive bilateral engagement with Pakistan it needs a different strategic perspective about its western neighbours. The essence lies in developing policies that will transform Pakistan from a barrier to bridge a gap to the west. India and Pakistan will be partners in the Greater Middle East.

9.2 India and Iran

India and Iran share centuries of close cultural and civilizational affinities. The two neighbouring civilizations (from the times of the Achaemenian, Sassanian, Maurya and Gupta empires) have influenced each other in the fields of culture, art, architecture and language. There was strong influence of Buddhism on the east Iranian region in those times. The interaction grew closer during the Mughal times. The Persian language became the language of the Indian elite. A new language Urdu with a strong Persian influence developed in northern India. Sufism evolved as a result of spiritual interaction between India and Iran. Taj Mahal is sometimes referred to as the *"soul of Iran incarnate in the body of India"*. Close links between the two countries have continued over contemporary times.

The close and friendly relations existing between India and Iran gained further momentum in recent years by the high level visits at the political level. India and Iran have friendly relations in many areas. There are significant trade ties, particularly in crude oil imports into India and diesel exports to Iran. Iran frequently objected to Pakistan's attempts to draft anti-India resolutions at international organizations such as the OIC. India welcomed Iran's inclusion as an observer state in the SAARC regional organization.

There is a small Indian community in Iran. There are still small Hindu temples in Bandar Abbas and Zahidan. They were built in the 19th Century by

Indian soldiers in the British Army. There are also small communities in India who trace their ancestry to Iran.

A small number of Iranian students are enrolled at universities in India. The growing Iranian film industry looks to India's Bollywood for technical assistance and inspiration. The clerical government in Teheran sees itself as a leader of Shiites worldwide including India. Indian Shiites enjoy state support such as a recognised national holiday for Muharram and are generally considered less targeted than in religiously polarized Pakistan. Lucknow continues to be a major centre of Shiite culture and Persian study in the subcontinent.

In the 1990s, India and Iran supported the Northern Alliance in Afghanistan against the Taliban regime. They continue to collaborate in supporting the broad-based anti-Taliban government led by Hamid Karzai and backed by the United States.

Institutional cooperation exists in the form of a Joint Commission headed at Foreign Minister's level. 14 meetings have so far been held, the last being in New Delhi in February 2005. Three rounds of Strategic Dialogue at the level of Foreign Secretary/Deputy Foreign Ministers have been held since October 2001 in New Delhi and Tehran.

There are several bilateral Joint Working Groups (JWGs) focussing on following sectors:

- Hydrocarbons,
- Commerce,
- Transportation,
- Agriculture,
- Rural development,
- Industry,
- Culture,
- Technology,
- Consulate affairs,
- Drugs trafficking,
- Power, and
- Telecommunications.

FICCI and the Iranian Chamber of Commerce, Industries and Mines (ICCIM) have set up a Joint Business Council.

Prime Minister Narasimha Rao paid a landmark visit in September 1993, as the first Indian PM to visit Iran since the Islamic Revolution in 1979. Iranian President Rafsanjani paid a return visit in 1995.

PM Vajpayee's visit to Iran in April 2001 was a landmark visit, which helped in fostering closer bilateral relations. The two sides signed a historic Tehran

Declaration during the visit. President Khatami visited India (Delhi and Hyderabad) from January 24-28, 2003. He attended Republic Day 2003 as the Chief Guest. Eight agreements including the Delhi Declaration and a MoU on a Road Map to Strategic Cooperation were signed during the visit. Other High Level Exchanges.

Relations between India and Iran are far-reaching and multi-dimensional. The two states have recognized that they have a lot to offer one another and have acted to expand cooperation in a number of key areas.

Given its exhaustive energy needs coupled with the lack of its own reserves, India is one of the world's largest energy importers. New Delhi and Tehran have explored various methods to get Iran's abundant hydrocarbon reserves to India. In 2005, the two nations unveiled ambitious plans for an Iran-Pakistan-India (IPI) Gas Pipeline that would run directly from Tehran to New Delhi through Pakistan. Proponents of the pipeline contend that it would not only help meet India's growing energy demands, but would also give the countries involved—especially India and Pakistan—a stake in regional peace, possibly reducing the threat of conflict between the two states. Plans to move forward with the project, however, have stalled. Iran's insistence that the price of gas being sold to India be renegotiated every five years, coupled with a dispute with Pakistan over transit fees, has prompted India to opt out of the current round of trilateral talks on the pipeline. New Delhi has said it is still interested in pursuing the deal but is likely to wait and see how the precarious political situation in Pakistan unfolds before resuming negotiations.

Political considerations have also motivated stronger Indo-Iran ties. Communal tension and violence between Hindus and Muslims have risen in some areas of India over the past decade. India's growing relationships with Israel and the United States and the domestic criticism it has engendered have prompted India to reinforce its ties with the Muslim world. Because it lies on Pakistan's western border, Iran also presents a potential strategic advantage for India.

A close political relationship with New Delhi is similarly attractive, if not necessary, for Tehran. Following Iran's designation as a member of the "axis-of-evil" in 2002, the United States has aggressively sought Iran's international isolation. Close ties with a key regional, and increasingly global, power such as India could help Iran resist its "rogue" status and overcome Washington's efforts in this regard. India has repeatedly urged a peaceful, diplomatic solution to Iran's nuclear program and has largely resisted American pressure to reduce its ties with Tehran.

The New Delhi Declaration called for the two states to "broaden their strategic collaboration in third countries," a clear reference to Afghanistan. The

Taliban's ascension to power in Kabul caused deep concern in both India and Iran. Both countries face a serious challenge from the threat of Wahhabist extremism, especially from Afghanistan. Thus, the two states welcomed the Taliban's demise in October 2001 and made Afghanistan's reconstruction and stability a common, critical goal. India and Iran have since established working groups on terrorism and counter-narcotics; both these initiatives focus on al-Qaeda. Additionally, the two countries have continued to work to counter Sunni militant threats in the region and have expressed a mutual preference for a comprehensive convention against international terrorism at the United Nations.

One of the most significant provisions of the New Delhi Declaration sought to upgrade defence cooperation significantly between the two countries. Sea-lane control and security, as well as discomfort with the emerging presence of the United States in the Persian Gulf, were partially responsible for Indo-Iranian naval exercises in March 2003 and again in 2006. Defence cooperation beyond this, however, has been sporadic and low-level. Expectations that India would assist Iran in upgrading its Russian-made defence system have not yet come to fruition. Cooperation in this area seems to represent generally strong Indo-Iranian relations rather than a broader defence alliance.

9.3 India and Israel

On September 17, 1950, India announced recognition of Israel. Ben Gurion, Israel's first prime Minister, held Mahatma Gandhi in high esteem. Soon after India's recognition of Israel, the Jewish Agency established an immigration office in Bombay. This was soon converted into a Trade Office and later a Consulate. Sporadic governmental contacts continued between India and Israel in the fifties and early sixties, including visits by former Minister Rajkumari Amrit Kaur and Israeli Ministers like Yigal Allon, Moshe Sharett and Gideon Rafael. Following decision to establish diplomatic relations, Israel opened its Embassy in Delhi in February 1992 and India opened its Embassy in Tel Aviv on 15 May 1992. Since then relations have seen rapid growth across a broad spectrum.

Since the establishment of Embassies, a large number of ministerial visits have taken place. The period since 1992 has been utilized to put in place the framework of normal state-to-state relations, including agreements and MOUs in diverse areas of cooperation. Important high level visits include the following: From Israel: FM Shimon Peres (May 1993); President Ezer Weizmann (January 1997); FM Shimon Peres (January 2002): PM Ariel Sharon (September 2003); and DPM and FM Silvan Shalom (February 2004); Deputy Prime Minister and Minister of Trade, Industry and Labour Eliyahu Yishai (December 2006); Minister of Transport and Road Safety Shaul Mofaz (March 2007); Minister of

Interior Meir Sheetrit (November 2007); Minister of Agriculture and Rural Development Shalom Simon (January 2008).

From India: Home Minister LK Advani (June 2000); EAM Jaswant Singh (July 2000); MOS (Independent Charge) for Science and Technology Shri Kapil Sibal (May 2005); MOS for Urban Employment and Poverty Alleviation Kumari Selja (September 2005); Agriculture Minister Shri Sharad Pawar (November 2005 and May 2006); Commerce and Industry Minister Kamal Nath (November 2005); MOS for Industry Ashwani Kumar (August 2007); MOS for Railways R. Velu (December 2007); and Former President Dr APJ Abdul Kalam (February 2008).

Bilateral institutional mechanisms include Foreign Office Consultations; Strategic dialogue between NSAs; JWG on Counter-Terrorism and Non Proliferation Dialogue; JWG on Defence Cooperation; JWG on Trade and Economic cooperation; Joint Committee on Agriculture Economic and commercial relations.

India-Israel bilateral trade and economic relations are progressing steadily. From a base of US$ 200 million comprising primarily of diamonds in 1992, merchandise trade has diversified and increased rapidly, reaching US$ 5283.25 million at the end of 2010-11. In 2011, India, though at the eighth place in terms of Israel's trade partner countries and the third largest trade partner in Asia, was identified by the Israeli Government as one of the four target markets for focussed trade effort. While diamonds constituted about 49 percent of the bilateral trade in 2010, India's exports to Israel in other areas have increased over the years. Major exports from India to Israel are textiles, chemicals, rubber and plastic products, machinery, base metals, prepared foodstuffs and transport equipment. Major items exported by Israel were diamonds, machinery, telecom equipment, chemical products, optical, medical and other equipment.

According to figures available from the Department of Industrial Policy and Promotion (Government of India), FDI inflows from Israel to India from April 2000 to March 2012 totalled US$ 54.15 million placing it at 41st rank (0.03 percent of total FDI inflows in India). While the initial business thrust was in diamonds, followed by agriculture, information and communication technology, biotechnology and pharmaceuticals, there is a new interest from Israeli companies in real estate, infrastructure and financial services. In recent years, Indian companies have started investing in Israel. Some of the recent Indian investments have been in the areas of irrigation equipment manufacturing, tyre manufacturing, pharmaceuticals and digital marketing etc.

Israel completed a Demonstration Farm project at IARI, PUSA. The private sector in India has also shown interest in accessing Israeli technologies and JVs have been set up for manufacture of drip irrigation systems and in the areas of floriculture and horticulture. An inter-Governmental "Work Plan" laying down the agenda of cooperative activities between two countries was signed on May 10, 2006. The Work Plan provides for collaborative research in fertigation, soil less culture for growing high value horticulture crops, cooperation in development and evaluation of energy efficient greenhouse structures, studies on recycling of domestic wastewater for irrigation, post harvest management and value addition for fruits, vegetables and dairy products, dairy development through genetic improvement utilizing germplasm from Israel, training and visiting facilities in respective institutions of the two countries, collaboration in exchange of genetic material of scientific and commercial potential, and promoting private sector collaboration.

During the visit of Shri Kapil Sibal, as the then MOS (Independent Charge) for Science and Technology and Ocean Development to Israel on May 30, 2005, the two countries agreed to establish the India-Israel Research and Development Cooperation Initiative which would inter-alia assist joint innovative technology development projects undertaken by companies from India and Israel and indicated their intention for each country to allocate up to US$ one million in accordance with their national requirements and appropriate mechanisms. The initiative has since then been operationalized and joint industrial research projects supported by the fund are in progress.

India is known in Israel as an ancient nation with strong cultural traditions, and in popular Israeli perception India is an attractive, alternative tourist destination. Israeli youth are particularly attracted to India. About 30,000 Israelis, mostly youth, after finishing military service, visit India annually. The level of understanding of and knowledge about India is growing, in some measure as a result of India's economic advancement and image as an important centre for hitech as well as the contribution of individuals like Zubin Mehta. The number of pilgrims and tourists from India visiting Israel touched 20,000 in 2007.

India and Israel have agreed to take their already flourishing military ties a few notches higher by collaborating on Research and Development projects in high tech areas, ranging from:

- Sensor,
- Electronic warfare systems,
- Long endurance,
- Combat-UAVs (unmanned aerial vehicles), and
- Missiles.

This came after the fourth meeting of the Indo-Israel joint working group on defence cooperation. It is said that cooperation in missile defence, the prospect of joint exercises, ways to tackle terrorism and intelligence-sharing figured in the parleys.

India and Israel have signed their first-ever joint weapons development contract to design and produce the Barak-II next generation air defence missiles for warships. Barak systems are configured to defend warships by automatically intercepting incoming sea-skimming missiles, aircraft and UAVs using a digital radar.

Barak-II will be jointly developed by the Israeli Aircraft Industries (IAI), the Barak Programme's Secondary Integrator Rafael and by the Hyderabad-based Defence Research and Development Laboratories (DRDL), with the two countries splitting the approximately US$ 330 million kick-off-start investment. In a phased manner, the Barak-I and the Barak-II missiles will replace the ageing Russian OSA-M and Volna RZ-31 missiles still in operation on most Indian warships.

Nine Indian warships, including *INS Viraat* and the three Delhi-based destroyers, already have the 10 km. range Barak-I system purchased in 2003. The new variant of Barak is to be developed over three years. It will be built for a targeting range of at least 50 km.

The relation between India and Israel were at a very low ebb during the Cold War as Israel was a US ally and Indian inclination was more towards Russia. However, there has been a shift in the foreign policy in the post cold war. India has in the recent past engaged Israel activity in various fields and especially defence cooperation due to political and other imperatives. Israel is now one of our largest arm suppliers. It is experiencing similar threat from terrorism. India can benefit a lot from Israeli experience in fighting the menace of terrorism.

However, despite active cooperation with Israel, India doesn't support Israeli opinion on Palestine question. It is committed to the legitimate demands of the Palestine and wants a peaceful solution to the problem so that peace and tranquillity is restored between the two nations. As yet, India has been voting Israel in the UN.

9.4 India and Kuwait

Until 1961, the Indian rupee was legal tender in Kuwait. India and Kuwait have no bilateral problems. Both are members of NAM and share common perceptions on various regional and international issues. The Amir of Kuwait His Highness Sheikh Sabah AI-Ahmad AI-Jaber AI Sabah paid a State Visit to India from June 14-19, 2006. Three Agreements were signed during the visit.

One of the Agreements signed during the visit of His Highness the Amir of Kuwait to India is the Executive Programme of the Cultural Exchanges between

India and Kuwait which will give further boost to India-Kuwait cultural relations.

The Indian Government has approved the increase of weekly seats from Kuwait by 1300. Kuwait Airways is to maintain its current schedule and capacity of 5200 seats per week while Jazeera Airways will get the additional 1300 seats per week.

9.5 India and Oman

The Consulate of India opened in Muscat in February 1955. Till 1971, the UK and India were the only two countries with a diplomatic presence in Oman. The first Ambassador of India took up his assignment in Muscat in 1973. Oman established its Embassy in New Delhi in 1972 and a Consulate General in Mumbai in 1976.

Agreements on Avoidance of Double Taxation and Promotion and Protection of Bilateral Investments provide the requisite legal framework for facilitating trade and investment flows.

The Oman-India Fertilizer Project (OMIFCO), was formally inaugurated at Sur, Oman. The OMIFCO project for which the MOU was signed in 1994 was approved by the Government of India in December, 1997. It is a Joint Venture project with equal equities between Indian and Omani entities. The Indian Equity of US$160 million is shared equally between IFFCO and KRIBHCO. The project implementation commenced from 15th August 2002 and was completed on 15th July 2005 i.e. 35 months from the date of commencement. The project envisages Urea off take at pre-determined prices for 15 years period for entire Urea by the Government of India and for Ammonia by IFFCO at fixed prices for 10 years. The plant has a capacity of 16.52 lakh MTs per annum and will help in meeting the increasing the increasing demand for fertilizers in India. The project is also being provided with manpower and technical services by both IFFCO and KRIBHCO.

Both countries agreed for enhanced interaction include the exchange of observers for military exercises and sending more officers to be trained at various Army schools of instruction. Earlier, Oman had sent military observers to witness Exercise 'Desert Strike' held in the deserts of Rajasthan in April 2006. Oman has also invited Indian military observers to witness the Gulf Cooperation Council Exercise to be held in 2007. The emerging defence cooperation with countries of the Middle East indicates that India is becoming a force to be reckoned with in the region. It also testifies that India has emerged as a regional power.

9.6 India and Saudi Arabia

King Abdullah visited India on a four-day state visit from January 24 to 27,

2006. During his visit the following agreements were signed: They were as follows:

1. The MoU on Combating Crime.
2. Agreement on Avoidance of Double Taxation.
3. Bilateral Investment Promotion and Protection Agreement.
4. Agreement for Cooperation in the field of Youth and Sports.

Saudi Foreign Minister Prince Saud Al-Faisal visited India on January 22, 2006 as a follow up to the King's visit. An Indian delegation led by Shri Arjun Singh, Human Recourses Development Minister visited the Kingdom from 29th May to 3rd June 2006. HRD Minister Shri Arjun Singh signed a Memorandum of Understanding on Scientific and Educational Cooperation between the two countries on 6 November 2006. Speaker of Lok Sabha, Shri Somnath Chatterjee visited Riyadh from 9-13 February 2007. A delegation led by Hon'ble Mr. E. Ahamed, MoS for External Affairs represented India as observers in the 19th Arab League Summit held in Riyadh on 28-29 March 2007. The Special Envoy for West Asia and the Middle East Peace Process, Ambassador C.R. Gharekhan visited Jeddah on September 8-9, 2007 during which he had detailed discussions with the Saudi Foreign Minister Prince Saud al Faisal and Secretary General of National Security Council, Prince Bandar bin Sultan.

Saudi Foreign Minister HRH Prince Saud al Faisal visited New Delhi on February 28-29, 2008. He reiterated his invitation to Hon'ble External Affairs Minister to visit Saudi Arabia at the earliest. Foreign Minister Prince Saud held discussions and delegation-level talks with EAM that dealt with the situation in the Middle East, Palestine, Iraq, Lebanon and Afghanistan. FM Prince Saud also met Hon'ble Prime Minister Dr. Manmohan Singh and discussed bilateral, regional and international issues.

Mr. Pranab Mukherjee, Hon'ble External Affairs Minister visited Saudi Arabia on April 19-20, 2008. Hon'ble EAM, who led a high-level delegation to the Kingdom, called on the Custodian of the Two Holy Mosques King Abdullah bin Abdulaziz, and the Governor of Riyadh HRH Prince Salman bin Abdulaziz al Saud. Hon'ble EAM held detailed discussions with his counterpart HRH Prince Saud al Faisal. Separately, Hon'ble EAM also met and interacted with the Indian diaspora in Riyadh. The Agreement concerning Encouragement and Reciprocal Protection of Investments (BIPPA) was ratified during the visit.

Indo-Saudi relations are multi-faceted and cordial. The 1950s and early 60s saw the visits of King Saud (1955) and Prime Minister Jawaharlal Nehru (1956). The Joint Commission for economic, trade, scientific, technical and cultural cooperation (JCM) established in 1981 between India and Saudi Arabia held its sixth session in Riyadh on April 12, 2005.

The first GCC-India Industrial Conference comprising ministerial and business delegations from the GCC States and India, was held in Mumbai on February 17-18, 2004.

In order to combat terrorism, both the countries pave decided to share intelligence-sharing. King Abdullah is the first Saudi ruler to visit India in 50 years. The visiting Saudi King Abdullah bin Abdul Aziz stressed the need to strengthen intelligence ties. Both the countries have also decided to continue to look at broadening the scope of cooperation on fighting terror and related financial crimes, especially money laundering, drugs and arms smuggling. Both the countries also signed an agreement on avoidance of double taxation, investment promotion and protection agreement in sports and youth affairs.

6 MoUs were also signed between Indian and Saudi public and private sector companies at a special session of the India-Saudi Arabia joint Business Council. India stressed and identified important sectors where the Saudi investment can be made like power, telecom, and transportation infrastructure including airports and railways.

Both the countries agreed to enter into a strategic energy partnership based on "complementarity and interdependence" and Saudi Arabia agreed to increase investments in India in oil refining, marketing and creation of storage facilities. The energy partnership envisages cooperative and joint ventures, both in the public and private sectors, in the upstream and down stream oil and gas sectors in India and Saudi Arabia besides third countries.

India and Saudi Arabia are actively cooperating in the field of science and technology. CSIR and the Saudi Arabian Standards Organisation (SASO) have an ongoing programme of technical cooperation (POC) since June 1993. Under this programme, Indian experts in different scientific areas, particularly in the field of measurement and calibration, are deputed to Saudi Arabia on regular basis. Similarly, several Saudi experts and have undergone advanced training in India. National Physical Laboratory has provided expertise and technology for two important SASO projects related to calibration and teleclock system. CSIR and the King Abdulaziz City for Science and Technology (KACST) signed a MoU for bilateral cooperation in 1997 and have an ongoing programme of cooperation, particularly in the field of space science, remote sensing and installation of Internet. Recently a three-member delegation from CSIR, NPL and CFTRI visited SASO during January 2004 and both sides agreed to renew the POC.

Saudi Arabia is the 4th largest trading partner for India. The value of two-way trade between the two countries in 2010-11 was more than US$ 25 billion. Saudi Arabia is the 11th largest market in the world for Indian exports.

Trading links between India and UAE have existed since long. Growing Indo-

UAE economic and commercial relations contributes to the stability and strength of a rapidly diversifying and deepening bilateral relationship with both sides striving to further strengthen these ties.

Indo-UAE trade, valued at US$ 180 million per annum in the 1970s, is today at US$ 67,102.26 million (2010-11), making UAE India's largest trading partner. The real impetus, however, started after Dubai positioned itself as a regional trading hub by early 1990s and about the same time, the economic liberalization process started in India.

India's exports to the UAE are well diversified with a large basket. Major items India's exports to UAE have been:

1. RMG cotton including accessories.
2. Gems and jewellery.
3. Manmade yarn.
4. Fabrics and made-ups.
5. Manufacturers of metals.
6. Cotton.
7. Yarn, fabrics and made-ups.
8. Marine products.
9. Machinery and instruments.
10. Plastic and linoleum products.
11. Tea and meat and preparations.

Similarly, major items of imports from UAE include petroleum and petroleum products, gold and silver, metal ores and metal scrap, sulphur and unroasted iron pyrites and pearls, precious and semiprecious stones.

Joint Commission: An Indo-UAE Joint Commission for Economic, Scientific and Technical Cooperation was set up in January 1975. The Joint Commission has held eight meetings so far, with the last meeting being held in September, 1994.

A Joint Business Council agreement was signed on 19th February, 2004 at Mumbai between Federation of UAE Chambers of Commerce and Industry and Federation of Indian Chambers of Commerce & Industry. Pursuant to the signing of the agreement, the first meeting of the JBC was held at Abu Dhabi on March 8th 2004.

India's current exports (2010-11) to Saudi Arabia stand at US$ 5.22 billion while imports are in the range of US$ 20.38 billion. The bilateral trade between India and Saudi Arabia is expected to touch the US$ 30 billion mark by 2012 from the current level of US$ 25 billion. There are three important aspects to the economic relationship between India and Saudi Arabia—petroleum trade, bilateral trade, and remittances.

India is very keen to encourage the 'Look West Policy' in order to solve the energy crisis.

Seven member delegation of the United Arab Emirates, led by their Under Secretary (Interior), Major General Saif Abdulla AI-Sha' afar met the Indian delegation, headed by the Union Home Secretary, Shri Madhukar Gupta on 28th and 29th May, 2007. The talks were held in a friendly and cordial atmosphere. Both the countries would need to enhance bilateral security cooperation. It was noted that discussions are underway on the agreements on transfer of sentenced persons, and on combating international terrorism, organized crime and illicit drug trafficking. It was decided that these agreements would be finalized, as far as possible, within three months.

In order to combat terrorism, both the countries pave decided to share intelligence-sharing. King Abdullah is the first Saudi ruler to visit India in 50 years. The visiting Saudi King Abdullah bin Abdul Aziz stressed the need to strengthen intelligence ties. Both the countries have also decided to continue to look at broadening the scope of cooperation on fighting terror and related financial crimes, especially money laundering, drugs and arms smuggling. Both the countries also signed an agreement on avoidance of double taxation, investment promotion and protection agreement in sports and youth affairs.

6 MoUs were also signed between Indian and Saudi public and private sector companies at a special session of the India-Saudi Arabia joint Business Council. India stressed and identified important sectors where the Saudi investment can be made like power, telecom, and transportation infrastructure including airports and railways.

Both the countries agreed to enter into a strategic energy partnership based on "complementarity and interdependence" and Saudi Arabia agreed to increase investments in India in oil refining, marketing and creation of storage facilities. The energy partnership envisages cooperative and joint ventures, both in the public and private sectors, in the upstream and down stream oil and gas sectors in India and Saudi Arabia besides third countries.

9.7 India and Lebanon

India maintained its diplomatic representation in Beirut throughout the civil war from 1975-1990 barring a brief closure for two months between August to October 1989. India consistently expressed its commitment and support for the unconditional implementation of the UNSC Resolution 425 and for the restoration of the sovereignty, unity and territorial integrity of Lebanon and the extension of the authority of the Lebanese State over the entire territory of Lebanon. India has endorsed the Middle East Peace Process for bringing about a solution to the Arab-Israeli conflict, consistent with dignity and justice. India also supported the Arab Peace Initiative adopted at the Beirut Summit held in Beirut on March 26-28, 2002.

Despite the friendly and problem free relationship, however, relations between India and Lebanon are yet to gather critical momentum. As Lebanon sets about taking control its own destiny and setting its own priorities in the aftermath of Syrian withdrawal, the time is opportune to establish fruitful, mutually rewarding cooperation in all sectors of national life including social, economic and political spheres.

There is a Cultural Agreement between India and Lebanon which was signed in April 1997 during the visit of Lebanon's Foreign Minister, Mr. Fares Boueiz for the Non-aligned Ministerial Conference in New Delhi. The agreement came into force with the exchange of instruments of ratification on February 4, 2000.

Total volume of India-Lebanon trade during 2011 was US$ 373 million as compared to US$ 13 million in 1993. Balance of trade is heavily in favour of India which has reached US$ 354 million in 2011.

Indian exports to Lebanon amounted to US$ 354 million in 2011 compared to US$ 84 million in 2003. Over half of the total import is made up of textiles and its articles and gems and jewellery. Other major items are animal products, articles of plastic.

The Indian battalion assumed its responsibilities as part of the United Nations Interim Force in Lebanon (UNIFIL) in South Lebanon in November 1998, replacing the Norwegian battalion which was withdrawn by Norway after it had served for two decades. Its responsibility is to maintain peace and security within its area of operations.

The Indian battalion also render humanitarian assistance consisting of medical assistance, veterinary aid, technical support to schools, etc. to various villages in its area of operations.

9.8 India and Palestine

India's solidarity with the Palestinian people was given voice during our freedom struggle by Mahatma Gandhi. In the early years of independent India, this policy was consolidated under the leadership of our first Prime Minister Pandit Nehru. India's empathy with the Palestinian cause and its friendship with the people of Palestine has become an integral part of its time-tested foreign policy.

Apart from the strong political support to the Palestinian cause at international and bilateral levels, India has been contributing, since a long time, material and technical assistance to the Palestinian people. With the establishment of the PNA in West Bank and Gaza Strip and the opening of the Representative Office of India in Gaza in June 1996, several areas have been identified for cooperation.

As a token of India's support to Palestinian national development, India pledged US$ 3 million as donor assistance to Palestinian National Authority. However, till now, about US$ 4.5 million has already been disbursed. Two projects have been completed in the field of higher education-Jawaharlal Nehru Library at the Al Azhar University in Gaza city and the Mahatma Gandhi Library-cum-Student Activity Centre at the Palestine Technical College at Deir Al Balah in the Gaza Strip. India provided technical and scientific books to the two Institutions. During the recent visit of President Abu Mazen to India, a donor commitment for assistance worth US$ 15 million was conveyed, to utilize which, projects are being identified.

As part of India's support to the Palestine, medical supplies and food items were formally handed over during the visit of the then Joint Secretary (WANA), Shri Rakesh Kumar, to the PNA territories in July 2001. The second lot of these medicines were delivered in January 2002. The third lot was delivered during the visit of Hon'ble Minister of State for External Affairs Shri E. Ahamed to Palestine in September 2004.

During the visit of Dr. Nabeel Shaath, Minister of External Affairs, PNA, in August 2003, Government of India announced a donation of twelve Tata Safari vehicles and medicines worth ₹ 20 million to Palestine. These were also handed over to PNA Minister for Foreign Affairs Dr. Nabeel Shaath by Hon'ble Minister of State for External Affairs, Shri E. Ahamed, in September 2004.

A Memorandum of Understanding on Cooperation between the GOI and the PLO, on behalf of the PNA, was signed on November 20, 1997. The MOU provides for promoting scientific, technical and industrial cooperation including provision of training facilities in specialized areas and undertaking of mutually agreed projects. The MOU further provides for promoting commercial and economic cooperation including institutional linkages between the Chambers of Commerce and Industry and exchange of business delegations. Further spheres include education, cultural cooperation and cooperation in the field of information.

India continues to offer eight scholarships under the GCSC of the ICCR to Palestinian students for higher studies in India. Over the years, several hundreds of Palestinian students have studied in Indian universities and institutions on their own. We have made available several slots in our academies and institutes for training of Palestinian security personnel. We have also offered several slots for training courses under the ITEC programme. The signing of a Memorandum of

Understanding by PNA External Affairs Minister Dr. Nabeel Shaath in August 2003 in New Delhi with the then MOS (EA) Mr. Vinod Khanna on Mutual Cooperation between Foreign Service Institute (FSI) and the PNA Ministry of External Affairs for, *inter alia*, provision of Indian trainers and training opportunities by FSI and thereafter a proposal for a 'Special Course for Palestine Diplomats' (SCPD) at the FSI are noteworthy in this regard. Such a SCPD was organised at the FSI from 22nd November to 17th December, 2004.

9.9 India and Gulf Cooperation Council (GCC)

GCC was established by an agreement concluded on 25 May 1981 in Riyadh, Saudi Arabia among Bahrain, Kuwait, Oman, Qatar, Saudi Arabia and UAE. The GCC countries are collectively host to the largest expatriate Indian community. The GCC offers tremendous potential for cooperation in trade, investment, energy, manpower etc. India maintains traditionally cordial relations and cooperation with the GCC.

Giving a boost to their commercial and economic ties, India and Gulf Cooperating Council signed on August 25, 2004 a Framework Agreement on Economic Cooperation to explore the possibility of a Free Trade Area between them. The Agreement was signed in New Delhi by Shri Kamal Nath, Hon'ble Minister for Commerce & Industry and His Excellency Mr Mohammed Al-Sabbah Al-Salem Al-Sabbah, the visiting Foreign Minister of Kuwait and Chair of the GCC in the presence of His Excellency Mr Abdulrahman bin Hamad Al-Attiyah, Secretary General of the Gulf Cooperation Council. A 3-member GCC negotiating team visited India and held discussions on November 19, 2004 on a broad range of issues, including the possibility of initiating negotiations towards a FTA and non-tariff barriers affecting Indian exports to the region.

So far, two meetings have been held in September 26, 2003 and September 27, 2004 involving EAM with the GCC Chairman, the Secretary General and Ambassadors/representatives from GCC countries on the sidelines of the UNGA. The political dialogue has added a new dimension to the GCC-India relations, and provided an institutional mechanism for a structured exchange of views on a regular basis for addressing issues of mutual concern.

India's growth story is now tickling the interest of the Gulf, which has aggressive investment plans for India and a target of raising bilateral trade to US$ 12 b over the next few years.

Discussions on a possible free trade agreement between India and Gulf Cooperation Council (GCC) are gaining momentum with the two sides deciding to thrash out issues like rules of origin (ROO) and differential tariffs. GCC member nations include Saudi Arabia, Oman, UAE, Kuwait, Bahrain and Qatar.

The first GCC-India Industrial Conference comprising ministerial and business delegations from the six member states of the Cooperation Council for the Arab States of the Gulf–UAE, Bahrain, Saudi Arabia, Oman, Qatar and Kuwait–and India was held in Mumbai on February 17-18, 2004.

The GCC India Industrial Conference was historic, marking the first ever structured gathering and composite dialogue forum involving GCC and India on such a magnitude. The mega event symbolized the political will on all sides to complement and reinforce the strong India-GCC bilateral relations and to further promote engagement with the GCC as a group.

The Conference under the theme 'Opportunities and Challenges in the 21st Century' focused on select priority areas covering GCC and India: (a) trade, (b) investments, (c) industrial cooperation including Small and Medium Enterprises (SMEs)/Small Scale Industries.

On the sidelines of the Conference, important bilateral agreements/MOUs were concluded between CII and the Federation of GCC Chambers of Commerce and Industry (FGCCC), as well as between Federation of Indian Chambers of Commerce and Industry (FICCI) and FGCCC. It was decided that the GCC-India Business Conference will be convened regularly on a biennial basis.

The GCC India Industrial Conference at Mumbai endorsed the GCC-India Framework Agreement for Economic Cooperation and expressed the intention of the two sides to explore the possibility for setting up GCC-India Free Trade Agreement/Area. Subsequently, India and GCC have signed a Framework Agreement for enhancing and developing the economic cooperation between them on the basis of equality and mutual interest. The GCC-India agreement was signed at New Delhi on August 25, 2004. The Agreement acted as a catalyst in India's efforts to achieve closer commercial economic and political relationship with the GCC States and would provide a frame work for private sector on both sides to enter into profitable ventures in new areas. The Second India-GCC Industrial Conference was held in Muscat (Oman) on March 25-26, 2006.

The third round of India–GCC Industrial Conference was held in Mumbai (India) on May 29-30, 2007. The first official-level meeting under the Framework Agreement was held in New Delhi on 19 November 2004 between the Ministry of Commerce and Industry from Indian side and a GCC delegation led by Dr. Yousuf Al Sadoun, GCC's Coordinator General for Negotiations. The first round of FTA negotiations between India and GCC Secretariat was held in Riyadh on March 21-22, 2006.

10

India and Central Asia

10.1 India's Policy in Central Asia

India's contacts with Central Asia dates back to antiquity. It was a multifaceted interaction enriching the history and culture of both sides. During the Soviet era Indian films and music were extremely popular. Even today they are as popular as they were before. In the contemporary reality Central Asia is considered as part of India's strategic area of interest.

In the initial years Indian interests and concerns were rooted in Pakistan and its activities in Central Asia. The break up of the Soviet Union in 1991 coincided with equally momentous developments in Afghanistan, where religious extremist forces led by B. Rabbani and supported by Pakistan seized power. Pakistan's objective supported by Saudi Arabia was to spread the religious agenda in Central Asia caused concern in India. Pakistan's goal was not simply to bring these states within the fold of hardline Islam or to gain military space for itself, but to also emerge as a bridge between Central Asia and the rest of the world. In the long term Islamabad's aim was to create a strategic integrated region extending from Central Asia to the Middle East, and from Turkey to Pakistan with itself playing the leading role. In this context the defunct Regional Cooperation Development (RCD) was revived with a new name the Economic Cooperation Organization (ECO). The Quetta Plan of 1993 envisaged building transport and telecommunication links with Central Asia. Perhaps due to lack of funds the EeO could not achieve its objective at that time.

Pakistan's efforts to win over the states of Central Asia were met with mistrust and circumspection. Instead the states of Central Asia lacking experience as well as expertise looked towards India for help and guidance in transforming their economies into a free market one, building a new political system based on liberal democracy and ensuring social stability by keeping tensions under control. Such an approach came naturally to the Central Asian leaders. The following statement of President Askar Akayev of Kyrgyzstan made during his visit to India in 1992 aptly reflects the prevailing sentiment. In his banquet speech President Akayev said, "Kyrgyzstan is looking to India as an example as it sets about restructuring its economy and socio-political system". Further he said "we categorically reject extremism of any kind...let it be neither extremism of the communist type nor of religious fanatics". Such an approach undoubtedly eased India's worry about Pakistan's activities in Central Asia. This congruence of interests has become a valuable input into building India's ties with Central Asia.

India seems to have approved the military presence of the Commonwealth of Independent States (CIS) Peacekeeping force led by Russia on the Tajik-Afghan border in 1992. At least the peacekeeping force was able to check the further advance of extremist forces. Had Tajikistan been over run, the stability of Central Asia would have been in jeopardy. Russia thus became the sole guarantor of stability in Central Asia, which was compatible with Indian interests.

On the issue of religious extremism there was further congruence of interests between India and the Central Asian States when the Pakistan backed Taliban came to power in Afghanistan. Two prominent organizations the IMU and Hizb-ut-Tehrir were active in the region. In February 1999, an attempt to assassinate President Islam Karimov of Uzbekistan was made while in Kyrgyzstan. Japanese tourists were taken as hostages. In India, militancy escalated and reached a high point when the Kargil invasion took place. Hence, we find that Indian approach to Central Asia in security matters was once again rooted in the activities of Pakistan in cooperation with Afghanistan. Therefore, India extended support the opposition, namely the Northern Alliance. The Northern Alliance was also backed by Russia, Iran, Kazakhstan, Kyrgyzstan and Tajikistan. Uzbekistan and Turkmenistan were also apprehensive of the Taliban, but opted for an approach of negotiations and engagement with the Taliban. Subsequently, when the global war on terrorism was launched by the world community led by the US, India and the Central Asian States supported this endeavour. Throughout the Nineties, Indian policy focused on the activities of Pakistan in Central Asia. It was a reactive policy.

In the early part of the twenty-first century there was a broadening the Indian strategies on security matters. While the core of India's strategic interests lay in its periphery, its own rising international profile on account of several factors, a desire to playa role in Asia led it to look beyond the South Asian region. As stated in the Annual Report of the Ministry of Defence, 2002-2003, "India's size, strategic location, trade interests and a security environment that extends from the Persian Gulf in the West to the Straits of Malacca in the East and from the Central Asian Republics in the north to the equator in the south, underpin India's security response. In view of this strategic spread it is essential for the country to maintain a credible land, air and maritime force to safeguard its security interests". Against the background of widening perception of India's strategic interests, the Central Asian context assumed a new and greater significance than before. "Relations based on a shared commitment to open and progressive societies, secularism and democracy, have been reinforced by similarity of view in the fight against terrorism.

In the sphere of defence, cooperation is taking the form of a security dialogue and training of armed forces personnel. Indeed, India seems to have taken a base in Ayni near Dushanbein Tajikistan, according to media reports. Then, Defence Minister George Fernandes' visit to Dushanbe in 2002 followed by then Prime Minister Atal Behari Vajpayee's visit to Tajikistan seems to have paved the way for Ayni air base. If true, this is a decisive measure. According to Stephen Blank, a well-known American specialist on the Eurasian region, "Russian weakness in Central Asia compounds India's immediate and long term problems there. In the short term, the chaos in Afghanistan and parts of Central Asia over which Russia might once have exerted a strong restraining influence is now free to spread southwards. In the longer term, Russian weakness in the core of Central Asia creates a vacuum especially in energy rich Kazakhstan into which China will expand". This is indeed, a thought provoking point.

The emergence of the Shanghai Cooperation Organization (SCO), a multilateral regional grouping with a focus on security and economic development issues is likely to restrict India's interaction with the Central Asian States on security and other related issues. The Russian-Chinese cooperation in the SCO has added a punch to the grouping. If in the coming years the SCO acquires its own mechanism and structure to deal with security and other issues, the role of India could be limited. Presently India has an Observer status within the organisation. In order to be effective and play its due role in the region India's status needs to be upgraded to a full member. Incidentally, the Central Asian States have supported India's case for full membership. On the other any initiative emanating from Central Asia such as President Karimov's proposal of September 1995 for holding a Permanent Seminar of the United Nations on questions of stability, security and cooperation or the Kazakh initiative on Conference on Interaction and Confidence Building Measures in Asia (CICA) have been duly supported by India.

At the bilateral level India has energised its interaction when it formed Joint Working Groups (JWGs) on counter terrorism with the Central Asian States. In 2003 India set up a JWG with Uzbekistan; and in 2004 with Kazakhstan. The purpose is to coordinate and share experience and information in areas of common concerns. A regular exchange of visits of the Groups takes place between India and Central Asian nations.

A beneficial outcome of the understanding between India and the States of Central Asia is the rising cooperation in the field of defence. Firstly, there is a possibility for exporting small arms manufactured in India to the Central Asian

States. Military Technical Cooperation Agreements with Kazakhstan, Kyrgyzstan and Tajikistan have been signed. The Russian border guards sought India's help in combating fundamentalists on the strategic border of the CIS. India provided training and extended help to the Northern Alliance in the war against the Taliban. Several high level visits in this regard have been exchanged. Secondly, India could provide technical assistance in running defence related industries of the Soviet times especially in Kazakhstan, Kyrgyzstan and Uzbekistan. Thirdly, India has been providing assistance in training personnel of paramilitary forces which could deal with the internal sources of tension. India has rich (experience in managing its extraordinary diversity.

Another area which holds tremendous promise for India-Central Asia cooperation is the energy sector. Undoubtedly India is a big market for energy and the Indian demand would go up over the years. India's dependence on import of energy is more than 70 percent, and these needs are presently fulfilled primarily from West Asia. Moreover, the issue of ensuring energy security has acquired a new urgency. Earlier the demand was less and confined mostly to the developed nations; today both developed and developing nations are in need of energy...After all as rightly observed in the Joint Statement on the New US-Russian Energy Dialogue of May 2002 that, successful development of the global economy depends on timely and reliable energy delivery Central Asia has the potential to emerge as a viable source for India. In that context, the Trans Afghan Pipeline (TAP) was a viable project, but it has not taken off. Recent reports suggest that the Asian Development Bank (ADB) has again revived the project. Possibly TAP could take off.

Since the mid-Nineties there has been a virtual scramble to secure the Central Asian energy. Leading Western multinational companies have already established their presence and secured attractive contracts. As rightly pointed out by President Vladimir Putin this is "sellers market". Russian presence in this sector is growing, while China has launched diplomacy to secure Kazakh energy, and has negotiated a substantial deal for Turkmen gas. Since the Central Asian States are landlocked the issue of pipeline infrastructure soon acquired a political dimension. The Western plan was to transport the Central Asian energy by bypassing Russia so as to reduce its leverage in the region and bolster that of Turkey...According to Ahmed Rashid, a well-known Pakistani columnist the US was supporting either directly or indirectly the Taliban. In his words, "...it became apparent to me that the strategy over pipeline had become the driving force behind Washington's interest in the Taliban which in turn was prompting counter reaction from Russia and Iran. Whether the TAP option would prove to be a viable one is difficult to say. A pipeline network could be laid along this route. Kazakhstan and Russia could utilise this route by exporting oil through barges to Iran or constructing a network from Russia to Turkmenistan via Kazakhstan".

While Indian efforts to secure energy related contracts were not vigorous, the Central Asian response to Indian efforts is also lukewarm. In 2005 India lost the bid to buy the Petro Kazakhstan to China. During Prime Minister Manmohan Singh's visit to Uzbekistan in April 2006, a Memorandum of Cooperation between the' Gas Authority of lndia Limited and Uzbekneftgaz was signed. Transporting energy whether oil or gas through a pipeline is a major concern. Another alternative for attaining energy security could be India's involvement in related areas such as acquisition of assets abroad, equity participation in producing fields and exploration and production, participation In downstream projects (refineries and petrochemicals), finalisation of long term LNG contracts and setting up of trans-national gas pipeline. This will give India an opportunity to enhance its leverage in the energy sector.

Closely linked with energy, is the question of connectivity to the region...The Central Asian region is a market for intermediate technologies, consumer goods, and infrastructure services. But Indian efforts have been stymied due to lack of connectivity with the region. In this context sustained efforts are being made to overcome this handicap. The best option would have been from Uzbekistan to Afghanistan and Pakistan and then to India, but this option is not feasible given Pakistan's reluctance to allow access through its territory. The next best alternative is a combination of sea, rail and road route. In early January 2003 during then President Khatami's visit India, Iran and Afghanistan agreed to open a new route through the port of Chahbahar on the Persian Gulf and then transport the goods by railroad to Afghanistan (Delaram) and then to Uzbekistan: India would construct the 200 km. of road in Afghanistan linking it to Hayraton in Uzbekistan. Given Uzbekistan's communication network, it could become India's gateway to Central Asia. The proposed North-South corridor whell completed would open another alternative for India. During his visit to Tajikistan in November 2003, then PM Atal Behari Vajpayee proposed the extension of road route up to Kabul and then Kunduz, Badkshan in Afghanistan and Tajikistan.

The construction of a transport corridor via Iran and Afghanistan would also lead to the development of the physical infrastructure such as power, engineering, maintenance and repair of roads, communication links etc. The sustainable development would be of immense benefit to Central Asia. In the long run, it would promote regional cooperation among the Central Asian States. The railway and road network of Uzbekistan would connect it with Kyrgyzstan, Kazakhstan and Tajikistan. Importantly, it would be an alternate avenue for Central Asian

States to connect in the southern direction towards the Indian Ocean.

At the political level India's democratic and secular credentials have endeared it to the Central Asian States.

The past linkages have acted as a bridge to the present. For the Central Asian States there is much to gain from Indian experience and expertise in building democratic institutions. India was perceived as a friendly country. It was, therefore, natural for them to look to India for assistance and guidance in their gigantic task of rebuilding new societies. Hence, President Karimov visited India prior to becoming independent, that is, in August 1991and later in 1994. President Askar Akaev of Kyrgyzstan came in 1992 followed by President S. Nugazov's visit in April 1992. President Nursultan Nazabaev was in India in 1992. India reciprocated these high level visits and there has been a regular exchange of visits. Indian-Central Asian States cooperation agenda has since expanded. All the States are an issue of crucial significance to India, the Kashmir issue has upheld the Indian contention that it should be settled at a bilateral level. On the issue of extremism and terrorism there is a high degree of congruence of view, as we have seen earlier.

It is worth noting that although the people of Central Asia are predominantly Sunni Muslims of the Hanafi School they lack the tradition of fanaticism and fundamentalism. The nomadic psyche still exercises a powerful influence on the people of Kazakhstan, Kyrgyzstan and Turkmenistan. The famous silk route exposed the people to novel ideas and new cultures, the strong and benevolent influence of Sufism and the access to modern education, science and technology during the Soviet period have all played a role in moulding a modern and a secular outlook of the Central Asian people. The people have imbibed a spirit of tolerance and benevolence. However, the present day dire economic condition, the poor quality of life and lack of openness and participatory politics, and partly because of such extremist activity has external supporters in terms of funding safe sanctuaries and training is driving some people to extremism. The people, however, want a right balance between modernity and tradition. As one perceptive observer put it, "one hånd must hold the Koran and the other a computer".

10.2 India's Relation with Central Asian Republics (CARs)

The dissolution of the Soviet Union towards the end of 1991 led to the emergence of five CARs of the former Soviet Union, namely, Kazakhstan, Kyrgyzstan, Uzbekistan, Tajikistan, and Turkmenistan, as independent countries. The strategic location of these countries at the crossroads between Europe and China and also between Russia and Iran as well as their huge and largely untapped reserves of oil and gas, lend these countries immense geo-strategic importance in world affairs.

The importance of Central Asia to India is not merely civilizational and historical, but also geopolitical and economic. Ever since these five republics of Central Asia gained independence in 1991, Central Asia has come to denote the five republics of Kazakhstan, Kyrgyzstan, Tajikistan, Turkmenistan and Uzbekistan.

In a contemporary context the significance of Central Asia–India relations has risen multi-fold. The recent years have seen a movement of resurgence of the same, but with the potential being immense, this progress needs to seek higher accomplishments.

India has vital economic and security interests in the CARs and needs to develop a comprehensive, long-term strategy to protect and promote its geo-political interest in this region. In developing an effective geo-strategy, India needs to carefully examine the complex interactions between the three major strategic players in this region, viz. Russia, China, and the USA, especially in light of the altered security situation in the aftermath of the September 11 terrorist attacks in the US and its direct military action in Afghanistan and Iraq ("The New Great Game"). The potential role of Iran and Turkey as well as the impact of future developments in Afghanistan and Pakistan on the evolving geo-political situation in the CAR region are also explored.

In terms of security interests, India needs to aggressively explore and establish security and economic cooperation agreements with the CARs both on bilateral and regional basis. In this context, the Shanghai Cooperation Organization (SCO), established in June 2001 at China's initiative, is a major geopolitical development in the region and it is in India's interest to strive to win its membership. In order to meet its current and future energy needs, Indian firms need to participate in oil and gas exploration ventures in the region, perhaps by joining the relevant international consortia. Given the security problems relating to oil and gas transit routes through Afghanistan and Pakistan, India needs to seriously examine the viability of the proposed Russia-Central Asia-China-India pipeline.

India's geo-political interests in CARs include the following:

1. Economic interests: these countries are potentially a significant source of oil and gas as well as trade and investment opportunities for India.
2. Security interests: to thwart terrorism threat via Afghanistan and Pakistan

The Central Asian Republics can provide support for:

- India's emerging status regional/global power.
- India's permanent membership of the UN Security Council.

- Counteracting adverse Pakistani propaganda.

The CARs suffer from serious dissensions within individual countries as well as among countries, arising from:

1. Border disputes.
2. Large ethnic minorities.
3. Large variations in wealth and resource endowments.
4. Bitter rivalry among the ruling elites; Lack of regional cooperation.
5. Authoritarian rulers: potential for social unrest and political instability.
6. Islamic Militancy: threat seems to have receded for now as a result of the US-led war in Afghanistan; can resurface.

Thus, the important elements of India's regional strategy regarding CAR focus on aggressively pursuing bilateral and regional agreements to promote security and business interests. Built on goodwill from close relations during the Soviet times, membership in the SCO focuses on trade and investment opportunities in the service sector, including education and training, health care, IT, and hotels. India needs to become a significant player in the equitable exploitation and distribution of the Central Asian energy resources. Indian firms need to join international consortia for oil and gas exploration in the Central Asian and Caspian region. Explore alternative oil and gas transit routes to India and viability of the proposed Russia-Central Asia-China-India pipeline needs to be seriously examined.

Commercial and economic ties between India and Central Asia are an area, where the future holds to bring greater outcomes. The level of trade and investment between the two has been much below potential. Except in a few cases, there have been no great stories of successful joint ventures or technology transfer. The entire Indian exports to CAR countries was less then 0.2 percent of its total exports and stood at under US$ 293.62 million. The imports also follow a similar picture and accounted for only 0.05 percent of the Indian imports at US$ 192.99 million.

Furthermore, India needs to take energetic steps to enhance its trade and investment levels with the CARs, which are currently insignificant. Apart from trade in goods, service sectors including Education and Training, IT-software, Health-care, and Hotels appear to be promising areas for Indian trade and investments in this region and need to be aggressively pursued.

Several key areas and sectors have been identified, which will act as the drivers of future Indian strategy for Central Asia. Some of these include the following products and services, besides the traditional and non-traditional trade areas that have existed between India and Central Asia. These product groups and services represent the "new economy sectors", while also focusing on the traditional items of trade between India and Central Asia.

The future prospects for cooperation between Central Asia and India in the field of energy security seem to be very important. This is because energy security is a basic requirement today. This region is thought to contain key global reserves. According to an estimate given by Central Asian sources, the confirmed oil deposits are between 13 to 15 billion barrels, which is 2.7 percent of all the confirmed deposits in the world. On the other hand, confirmed deposits of Natural Gas in Central Asia, are around 270 to 360 trillion cubic feet, which constitute around 7 percent of world deposits. The main oil and gas deposits in CARs are in Kazakhstan, Turkmenistan and Uzbekistan whereas Kyrgyzstan and Tajikistan have enormous hydel resources. In Tajikistan, each sq. km. of the territory has up to 2 million kw hours of hydel resources and this is a very high figure.

It has been suggested that with Indian energy consumption growth expected to be over 6 percent per annum, the country's reliance on imports, which is currently 60 percent or 75 percent million tons will double to 150 million tons per annum by 2010. Estimates suggest that India has already overtaken.

UK is the sixth largest consumer of energy and by the first half of the Century, India is also projected to be among the top five world consumers of energy. To sustain this economic growth, India will need a vast amount of energy. In this respect suggestion of creating an Asian Energy Community has been increasingly felt to bring together the main producers and consumers of oil, gas and other energy sources.

Drugs, pharmaceuticals and healthcare have emerged as a key area of cooperation between India and Central Asia, owing to the efficiency levels of the Indian industry and its cost advantage in the global market.

In the course of several policy level consultations on developing India-Central Asia ties, tourism has emerged as one of the key sectors of the economy that may serve as the vital link between the two. The doctrine behind this view says that India has emerged as a potential source of outbound tourists and the Central Asian splendour of natural and historical beauty stands to gain from the same, provided the pre-requisites of bridging the gap in perception are met. Since, the outbound traffic from India is fast increasing and the upwardly mobile section of the Indian population is more inclined to travelling abroad rather than visiting various Indian destinations, owing to the high cost of domestic air travel and its price disadvantage vis-à-vis neighbouring destinations because of the high taxes on tourism. The outbound figure stood at 4.07 million in 2001. This is further aided by the advent of eco tourism, which is a recent trend in global tourism and Central Asia is a very appropriate place to practice this type of tourism. India has air links with three Central Asian states and countries like Kyrgyzstan and Uzbekistan have been at the forefront in a bid to attract the Indian tourist.

Infrastructure has emerged as a key focus area in Central Asia and this is adequately supported by the emergence of high-momentum construction and infrastructure activity in the region. In Kazakhstan alone, this sector is slated to touch a turnover of US$ 25 billion in the next decade or so.

India seems to have realised the strategic and economic importance of the Central Asian region recently. The region's energy sources on one hand and the apprehensions about the spread of Islamic fundamentalism and the possibility of Pakistan trying to establish its influence in the region on the other. It has prompted India to make conscious efforts to strengthen and diversify relations with Central Asian states. India appreciates that CAS have expressed their belief in democracy, secularism and aversion to fundamentalism and terrorism with a view to building up an enduring partnership. India recognised that though the CAS region straddles some of the world's known richest deposits of hydrocarbon resources, the inadequacy of direct surface access to this region was a problem. The idea of trilateral understanding with Iran and Turkemenistan was to overcome the problem.

Relations between India and CAS were marked by visits of high level dignitaries from both sides from 1996 to 1999. The Indian vice-president Mr. Krishna Kant visited Kazakhstan and Kyrgyzstan in September 1996, followed by a return visit by the Kazakh President. India and Kazakhstan set up joint working groups (JWGs) for a focussed co-operation in medium and small scale industries, peaceful use of nuclear energy and defence upgradation and modernization of existing infrastructure facilities as well as training programmes in the energy sector. Other events included meeting of Indo-Kazakh joint science and technology committees, visit of Kazakh parliamentary delegation etc. Indian Airlines and Air Kazakhstan signed a code sharing agreement in September 1998 and India participated in the 7th Asia-Pacific International Trade Fair in Almaty in October 1998.

India and Kyrgyzstan maintained a stable relation with each other. There were ministerial-level visits during 1998 and 1999. Other events included holding of Kyrgyz cultural festival in India and presenting a mini dairy plant to Kyrgyzstan.

During the visit of Indian external affairs minister to Iran in February 1997, India, Iran and Turkey signed a trilateral agreement on international transit of goods which provides the legal framework for the multi-model movement of goods from India to Iran and Turkmensitan and other Central Asian member states that may join the arrangement in future and vice-versa.

India and Tajakistan maintained close political understanding and mutual co-operation. A pharmaceutical plant in Dushanbe constructed with the use of Indian credit line became operational during 1996-97. India expressed its keen interest and sympathy at efforts being made to normalise the political situation within the country and the way it dealt with the Afghanistan situation. India sent two consignments of humanitarian assistance to Tajakistan. The Tajakistan president paid a 'working visit' to New Delhi in January 1999. Both sides agreed to step up economic and commercial co-operation between the two countries.

Central Asia's richness in petroleum and gas is one of the reasons for India to be interested in that region. In August 1999, the then Indian external affairs minister, Mr. Jaswant Singh discussed with the Turkmenistan leaders the chances of tapping and exporting the energy sources of Turkmenistan, keeping in view the fact that there is insufficient access or exit westwards. Saying that pipeline to India need not necessarily pass through Afghanistan and Pakistan, he mentioned about a possible alternative route; one particularly connects the pipeline from Dhonghtabad fields of Turkmenistan exiting via Bandar Abbas in Iran.

Recently the more areas of cooperation have been explored between the two countries. India and Uzbekistan both share a border with Afghanistan and this makes co-operation and sharing of information vital for both the countries. Also, India and Uzbekistan are natural partners in combating international terrorism, religious extremism and drug trafficking. Both the countries feel that they have to tackle these threats by sharing of intelligence and their resources and establish a security partnership. Both the countries also stressed on the need of increasing economic cooperation and trade relation. He invited Indian business class and entrepreneurs to invest in Uzbekistan. The two countries also signed an extradition treaty and a "mutual assistance" agreement in addition to legal assistance in criminal matters. The two countries also signed pact in the fields of agricultural research, culture, information and mass media.

India's growing presence and role in the resources-rich and strategically significant Central Asian Region has important implications. INDIA has joined in the "New Great Game" being played out in the Central Asian Region (CAR), where fierce competition for the area's vast energy resources is intensifying. A military base has been established in Tajikistan. The base, with a handful of defence "advisers" at Farkhor, is close to the Afghan border. It is the first such Indian military facility outside the country.

The Farkhor base is also being used to funnel relief assistance that India pledged to Kabul after the Taliban's ouster last year. The military base has been useful in transporting this assistance to Kabul after India and Pakistan imposed a ban on over flights by each other last December. Large Indian military transport aircraft land at airfields near Farkhor and transfer their humanitarian merchandise onto smaller planes that ferry it to nearby Kabul, informed sources said.

The Farkhor base was set up following a bilateral agreement signed during Defence Minister George Fernandes' visit to the Tajik capital Dushanbe. It was agreed that India will train Tajik defence personnel, service and retrofit their Soviet and Russian military equipment and teach its army and air force personnel English." The Tajik armed forces are small compared to India's, but both use similar equipment like T-72 tanks and BMP-II infantry combat vehicles. The two sides will also collaborate to combat drug trafficking". Afghanistan is projected to harvest a bumper opium crop this year, which officials anticipate is likely to be smuggled out as heroin to the West via long-established routes across Tajikistan.

Tajikistan has around 47,000 army personnel and an air force with 19,000 personnel, one of the largest in the region. It flies around 190 fighter aircraft such as MiG 21s, MiG 27s, MiG 29s and Sukhoi 24s, nearly all of which are operated by the Indian Air Force (IAF). But its pilot efficiency has suffered grievously over the past eight years because of under-staffing of its combat squadrons mainly owing to poor training facilities.

India's military profile in the region-principally to counter Pakistan's influence over Afghanistan through the Taliban it raised and installed in Kabul in 1996—increased after the hijacking of the Indian Airlines flight IC-184 from Kathmandu in 1999 by Pakistan-backed terrorists to Kandahar in southern Afghanistan.

Pakistan's membership of the Shanghai Cooperation Organisation (SCO), a key regional Central Asian grouping comprising Uzbekistan, Kazakhstan, Kyrghyzstan and Tajikistan besides Russia and China, meanwhile, has surprised some members because of its previous involvement with Islamic insurgent groups. India is also being considered for the SCO that came into being six years ago to deal with border issues, combat ethnic and religious tensions in member-countries and to safeguard against the export of Islamic terrorism.

India's recent diplomatic thrust into Central Asia keeping in view its future energy requirements and strategic positioning, through bilateral visits and trade and understated military agreements with some of the Republics, is also triggered by the security realignments in the region following the Taliban's ouster. The ensuing conflict of interest in the area between India's old ally Russia and the U.S., its new found "long-term, strategic partner," and nuclear rival China is also fuelling Delhi's "forward" Central Asian policy. And though India remains powerless to engineer or overtly influence the "New Game," its size, military and nuclear capability make it a not altogether insignificant part of the complex jigsaw.

India has also launched a regional "people-to-people" initiative by inviting diplomats, parliamentarians and opinion-makers from the CAR to visit its industrial and technological centres and also interact with senior politicians, officials and businessmen.

Stressing India's proximity to Central Asia and its larger international standing, the India-Kazakhstan Joint Declaration signed by Ex-Prime Minister Atal Behari Vajpayee and President Nazarbayev stated that Delhi's membership of the SCO "would add to the strength of that organisation".

In exchange, Kazakhstan wants Indian information technology expertise to develop software parks and to start joint IT ventures.

For nearly a decade India has supplied around 30 percent of the CAR's pharmaceutical requirements. At an industrial fair at Almaty in April, Indian companies secured orders for civilian goods worth US$ 28 million. India and Kazakhstan have also established a forum to counter terrorism and for "early action" in finalising agreements in military and technical cooperation.

This 'cooperation' involves servicing and possibly upgrading Kazak military hardware which, like a majority of India's defence equipment, is of Soviet and Russian origin.

Kazakhstan's push for India's membership of the SCO with a view to diluting Chinese and Russian influence in the forum, however, has evoked a cautious reaction in Delhi. India is loath to be a part of a security forum in which Beijing is a leading player and its military and nuclear ally Pakistan, a potential associate. "Till SCO membership rules are finalised we cannot assess whether joining it will be advantageous or not for India," a senior Indian diplomat said, refusing to be drawn into any discussion on Kazakhstan's proposal to admit Delhi into the organisation.

The key to India's relations with the CAR depended largely on China's response to the U.S. military presence in the region. Vajpayee attended the two-day Conference on Interaction and Confidence Building Measures in Asia (CICA) at Almaty in June, where the issue of Delhi joining the SCO was expected to be discussed. But the visit alongside Musharraf's was overshadowed by the heightened military alert along the India-Pakistan border.

10.3 India and Tajikistan

Tajikistan, and India had discussed co-operation in the mineral sector in New Delhi recently. The Tajikistan Delegation was informed that India has very rich bauxite reserves and would like to set up smelters for alumina production outside India in countries which are surplus in power. Tajikistan has a huge hydel power potential as it abounds in water resources. 55 percent of central Asian water reserves are located in Tajikistan and a number of hydel power projects have been set up and many more are coming up. Tajikistan would welcome setting up of joint ventures with India in mining and processing of minerals.

India would favourably consider proposals from Tajikistan for setting up of joint ventures. India has achieved a fair degree of excellence in mineral exploration and would be happy to share it with Tajikistan in training or in other mode.

India and Tajikistan had inked six bilateral cooperation pacts recently. The pacts, included a Joint Declaration signed by both Tajik President Emomali Rahmonov and Prime Minister Dr Manmohan Singh.

Apart from the Joint Declaration, the other five agreements inked included:

1. MoU on energy cooperation.
2. A programme of cooperation in the field of science and technology.
3. An MoU on foreign office consultations.
4. An agreement on promoting cultural exchange programmes.
5. An MoU on Cooperation between the Indian Council of World Affairs (ICWA) and Tajik Academy of Sciences.

On 5th July 2007, India and Tajikistan had inked many bilateral cooperation pacts. The pacts, included a Joint Declaration signed by both Tajik President Emomali Rahmonov and Prime Minister Dr Manmohan Singh.

Apart from the Joint Declaration, the other four agreements inked included:

1. an MoU on energy cooperation,
2. a programme of cooperation in the field of science and technology,
3. an MoU on foreign office consultations,
4. an agreement on promoting cultural exchange programmes, and
5. an MoU on Cooperation between the Indian Council of World Affairs (ICWA) .

10.4 India and Kazakhstan

The history of civilization in Kazakhstan goes back to the Iron age. Finds of archaeologists indicate settlements in the steppe in the Neolithic and late Neolithic periods (8000-2000 B.C.) Stone implements from this era have been found in both central and eastern Kazakhstan as also in the west, on the Mangyshalk peninsula that protrudes into the Caspian sea. These finds along the rivers, lakes and foothills of mountains, attest to a predominantly settled way of life. Kazakhstans' many petroglyphs also belong to the Neolithic era. Their numbers and content reveal scenes of hunts and tribal campaigns, and depictions of sorcerers, beasts, dragons, deer, horse riders and amazons all remarkable for their expressiveness of detail and interestingly symbolic maps of the world.

Among the petroglyphs at Tamghali, there is one that depicts the cosmogony of the early Kazakh peoples. Mother earth appears reclining while the line of peoples moves over the earth under the watchful eye of Tengri, the sky deity ,and Zher-Suw, the divine consort and deity. Archaeological excavations throws light on the on the far reaching connections and trading contacts of the Kazakh peoples, the coins, statues, vases and other artifacts along the Silk Road cities reveal that they originated in India, Byzantium, Persia and China.

From around USD 80 million in 2004, bilateral trade is approximately USD 200 million in 2007. Major commodities of export from India to Kazakhstan are Tea, Pharmaceuticals, Medical equipments, Machinery, Tobacco, Valves and Consumer Items etc. Major items of import by India are asbestos, soft wheat, steel, aluminium, wool and raw hides. The major Indian presence is in Pharmaceutical and Tea markets.

India-Kazakhstan Inter-Governmental Joint Commission on Trade-Economic, Science- Technology, Industry and Cultural Cooperation The Inter-governmental Kazakh-Indian Joint Commission on Trade, Economic, Scientific, Technical, Industrial and Cultural Cooperation was established in July 1993. The First Session of this Joint Commission was held on 21-23 July, 1993 in New Delhi. The last (6th) Session in New Delhi was held on 12-13 October 2006.

During Prime Minister Vajpayee's visit in June 2002, the issue of cooperation in oil and gas sector was discussed at the highest level. An MOU was signed between ONGC (OVL) and KazMunaiGaz (KMG) in 2005. A Joint Working Group on Hydrocarbons also functions under the Joint Commission.

During President Nazarbayev's visit to India in February 2002, a keen interest was shown in the IT sector of India and a desire was expressed to seek Indian assistance in setting up a Software Technology Park in Almaty. During the visit of Minister of Industry and Trade of Kazakhstan, Adilbek Zhaksybekov in September 2004, an MOU on cooperation in Information Technology was signed. The first India-Kazakhstan IT Centre, a venture between Al Farabi national university and NIIT was set up in Almaty in May 2005. 3i-Infotech, TCS, NIIT and Aptech are successfully operating in Kazakhstan. A JWG on IT also functions at government level.

Kazakhstan appreciates the help given by India in its accession to the International North South Transport Corridor transport Agreement, signed originally by Russia, India and Iran in September 2002. The fifth meeting of the experts group and the fourth meeting of the Coordinating Council of International North South Transport Corridor was held in Astana on November 2-3, 2007. The member countries agreed on various proposals including exchange of information on cargo transportation and development of transport infrastructure.

A 12-member textile delegation led by the Minister of Textiles, Shri Shankersinh Vaghela and representing major textile export promotion councils and companies of India visited Kazakhstan on March 24-28, 2007. The delegation visited Shymkent (the site for the Special Economic Zone for development of textile cluster 'Ontustik') in addition to Almaty and Astana. Textiles Minister had meetings with the Foreign Minister, Marat Tazhin, the Minister of Industry and Trade, Galym Orazbakov, the Minister of Agriculture, Akhmetzhan Esimov and the Governor of South Kazakhstan Region, Umirzhak Shukeev. Subsequently a Joint Working Group on Textiles was formed.

Agreement on cooperation in field of tourism was signed during the visit of Prime Minister to Kazakhstan. Follow up action is being taken on the important aspects of agreement.

10.5 India and Kyrgyzstan

Historically, India has had close contacts with Central Asia, especially countries which were part of the Ancient Silk Route, including Kyrgyzstan. During the Soviet era, India and the then Kyrgyzia Republic had limited political, economic and cultural contacts. Former Prime Minister Rajiv Gandhi visited Bishkek and Issyk Kul lake in 1985. Since the independence of Kyrgyz Republic on 31st August, 1991, India was among the first to establish diplomatic relations in 1992; the resident Mission of India was set up in 1994.

Political ties with the Kyrgyz Republic have been traditionally warm and friendly. The Kyrgyz leadership has been largely supportive of our stand on Kashmir and have welcomed the ongoing peace process. Both countries have common concerns so far as the threat of terrorism, extremism and drug trafficking is concerned. Since the establishment of diplomatic relations in 1992, the two countries have signed several framework agreements, including on Culture, Trade and Economic Cooperation, Civil Aviation, Investment Promotion and Protection.

At the institutional level, Foreign Office Consultations (the Fourth Session was held in Delhi in August 2006) have provided a useful forum for exchange of views on bilateral and international issues, thereby facilitating greater understanding. An Indo-Kyrgyz Joint Commission on Trade, Economic, Scientific and Technological Cooperation set up in 1992. Four sessions of the Joint Commission have been held so far (the last being in Bishkek in September 2007), facilitating cooperation in areas as diverse as tourism, civil aviation, technical assistance, etc.

Indo-Kyrgyz trade is limited; in 2010-11, exports from India to Kyrgyzstan amounted to ₹ 101.82 crore. During the same financial year, imports from

Kyrgyzstan to India amounted to a mere ₹ 5.42 crore. Further, around 80 percent of India's exports to Kyrgyzstan comprise of readymade garments, apparel, etc. Kyrgyzstan became a party (on 15th April, 2004) to the Trilateral Transit Agreement between India, Iran and Turkmenistan (signed in February, 1997).

Among the efforts to promote bilateral trade were the holding of an India-CIS conference by the Pharmaceutical Export Promotion Council in Mumbai (March, 2006-under the Focus CIS program of the Ministry of Commerce). A high-level Kyrgyz delegation, led by the Kyrgyz Minister of Agriculture, took part in the 4th session of the Joint Business Council held in India in March, 2006.

10.6 India and Belarus

India's political ties with Belarus are de facto an extension of traditionally warm and cordial bonds of friendship between India and the former Soviet Union. There is a remarkable commonality of views shared by the two countries on almost all international and regional issues. Belarus has been supportive of India's candidature for a permanent seat in an expanded UNSC. Minsk has been invariably supporting our candidatures for various UN bodies and other international organizations as well.

India's support for its joining NAM as a full member in September 1998, and in obtaining membership of the IPU in the face of heavy odds is deeply appreciated with gratitude by Belarus. Belarus has viewed with admiration the principled stand taken by India on somewhat politically motivated Resolutions targeting Minsk on account of alleged violations of Human Rights and suppression of freedom of expression. In fact, India is recognized by Belarus as an emerging global power playing a growing and extremely constructive role on the political stage of the world in a highly effective manner.

In the economic and commercial spheres, cooperation between India and Belarus has been growing steadily right from 1992, when formal diplomatic relations between the two countries were established. Two-way trade registered a good increase from US$ 71.97 million in 2002 to US$ 603.72 million in 2009.

Belarus is the most important source for India's requirements of potash fertilizer. It offers promising market for India's pharmaceutical and chemical products, automobile and knowledge-based enterprises.

A number of Indian private and public sector companies have been showing interest in joint ventures with Belarus for manufacturing giant tyres, agro-industrial machinery, mining equipment, and heavy-duty road construction machinery.

India's exports to Belarus include electrical equipments, electronic hardware, packed medicine, pharmaceutical products, tobacco, plastic products, cotton yarn and synthetic fibre, organic dye, woollen clothes, vehicle parts and food items etc.

India's imports from Belarus include potassium fertilizers, steel rods, integrated circuits, synthetic fibres, tanned leather, twisted synthetic threads, water pumps, electrical equipment for engines etc.

Defence cooperation forms an important pillar of India's bilateral ties with Belarus. Apart from meeting our Armed Forces' needs for certain military hardware, Belarus is actively cooperating with our R&D institutions for developing advanced technologies. Belarus has also offered to repair/upgrade our defence equipment of Soviet origin, particularly, helicopters and fighter air crafts in the IAF fleet. There exists a strong political will in Minsk for raising the level of their defence cooperation with India and a Joint Working Group for the purpose was formed in April 2007.

Following Agreements have been operational between India and Belarus:

1. Agreement on Trade and Economic Cooperation.
2. Agreement on Cooperation in the sphere of Culture, Arts, Education, Mass Media and Sports.
3. Agreement on Cooperation in Tourism.
4. Agreement on cooperation in Science and Technology.
5. Agreement on Visa Free Travel by Diplomatic and Official Passport holders.
6. Memorandum of Understanding on Defence Related Technical Cooperation.
7. Agreement on the Avoidance of Double Taxation. (The Agreement is in effect from July 17, 1998 with the issue of formal notifications by the Indians and Belarus sides).
8. Protocol on Foreign Office Consultations.
9. Agreement on the Establishment of an Inter-Governmental Commission on Economic, Trade, Industrial, Scientific Technological and Cultural Cooperation.
10. Air Services Agreement.
11. Agreement for the Promotion and Protection of Investments.
12. Agreement on Cooperation in the field of Posts and Telecommunications.
13. Cooperation in the field of Quarantine and Plant Protection.
14. Mutual Legal Assistance Treaty in Criminal matters (MLAT).
15. Treaty on Extradition.
16. MoU on cooperation between EXIMGARANT and ECGC.
17. Agreement on cooperation in the field of agriculture.
18. Programme of cooperation in the field of culture, art, education mass media and press for the period 2007-09.
19. Programme of cooperation in the field of S&T for the period 2007-10.

20. Protocol on cooperation in matters of youth affairs and sports.
21. Protocol on accession of the Republic of Belarus to the WTO.

10.7 India and Turkmenistan

India is pursuing import of natural gas from Turkmenistan through the Turkmenistan-Afghanistan-Pakistan-India (TAPI) Gas Pipeline Project. The TAPI pipeline is projected to supply 90 MMSCMD of gas. Gas utilization by Afghanistan will be about to 5.0 MMSCMD during 1st/2nd year and 14 MMSCMD from the third year onward, with remaining quantity of gas propose to be equally shared by India and Pakistan on successful completion of the project. Shri Patel informed that the gas is expected to flow to India from Turkmenistan in the year 2014.

A Memorandum of Understanding (MoU) between India and Turkmenistan was signed in Ashgabat, Turkmenistan on 5th April, 2008, during the visit of Uprashtrapatiji to Turkmenistan. The objective of the MoU is to establish an institutional relationship to develop bilateral cooperation in the field of oil and gas.

India was formally admitted as a member of the TAPI Project at the 10th Steering Committee Meeting of the Turkmenistan-Afghanistan-Pakistan-India Gas Pipeline Project, which was held on April 23-24, 2008 at Islamabad. It may be mentioned that the Turkmenistan-Afghanistan-Pakistan (TAP) project was initially conceived in the year 2002. ADB is playing the role of lead facilitator for the Project. The gas is expected to flow to India from Turkmenistan in the year 2014. The Project will help to promote energy security of the participating countries and strength regional cooperation.

During the meeting in Islamabad, an Inter-governmental Framework Agreement, to facilitate implementation of the Project, was initialed by the four participating countries. The Pipeline will be executed by a Consortium. The gas will be supplied from Douletabad and other fields in Turkmenistan and the Principle of unobstructed transit of natural gas, in accordance with international norms, will be followed.

The safety and security of the pipeline and related infrastructure will be provided by concerned Governments in their respective territories. The 1,680 km. long, 56” in diameter TAPI pipeline will supply 90 MMSCMD of gas. The length of the pipeline in Turkmenistan, Afghanistan and Pakistan up to India border is 145 km., 735 km. and 800 km. respectively. Gas utilization by Afghanistan will be about to 5.0 MMSCMD during 1st/2nd year and 14 MMSCMD from the third year onward, with the remaining quantity of gas equally shared by India and Pakistan.

10.8 India and Azerbaijan

India and Azerbaizan have agreed to co-operate in several areas including gas and oil sector. Indian companies are set to play a significant role in the development of Azerbaijan's rapidly expanding oil and gas industry. This was the result of a meeting recently held between the President of Azerbaizan, Mr. Ilham Alibev and Visiting Minister of State for Commerce, Shri Jairam Ramesh at Baku. At the meeting ONGC Videsh and SOCAR, the state owned oil and gas exploration company of Azerbaijan started talks for co-operation for ONGC Videsh's investments in hydro-carbon rich Azerbaijan. To begin with, ONGC Videsh and GAIL participated in the Caspian Sea Oil and Gas Exhibition held in Baku, Azerbaijan from June 3-4, 2007. Following were the proposals between the two countries:

1. Indian Pharmaceutical Companies would consider moving beyond distribution and set-up manufacturing facilities in Azerbaijan.
2. Both setup a joint inter-governmental commission on Trade, Investment and Economic Cooperation.

   Finally, India has also offered technical assistance to Azerbaijan to facilitate its entry into the WTO.

10.9 India and Ukraine

The major commodities which are exported by Ukraine to India include chemicals, fertilizers, ferrous metals, power equipment (including for nuclear reactors), steel, steel-related equipment, aluminium, railway equipment, medical equipment, vegetable oils, paper products, electrical equipments, etc.

The major commodities, which are exported by India to Ukraine include pharmaceutical products, tobacco, coffee, tea and spices, cosmetics and toiletries, natural rubber, bovine meat, plantation crops, readymade garments, machinery and instruments, leather and leather products, cotton yarn, fabrics and other textile items, agricultural products, plastic and linoleum products, packaged edibles etc.

Under the Focus CIS Policy of the Government of India, economic and commercial activities between the two countries are likely to increase, with Ukraine being one of the seven focus countries. During the visit of the Indian President to Ukraine in June 2005, the two countries agreed to endeavour to reach a target of US$ 5 billion in total trade turnover by the year 2010. Bilateral trade between the two countries stood at US$ 2.2 billion during the year 2010-11.

Most of the Indian companies based in Ukraine are involved in trading. Drugs and Pharmaceuticals is the dominant sector, with about 30 percent of Indian exports to Ukraine accounted for by this sector. India is the second largest exporter of pharmaceutical products to Ukraine after Germany in value. Indian exports, however, are the largest in volume. A number of Indian companies like Ranbaxy, Dr. Reddy's Laboratory, Sun Group etc. have their representative offices in Ukraine. Representatives of major Pharmaceutical companies have set up the 'Indian Pharmaceutical Manufacturing Association' (IPMA).

Possibilities of cooperation exist in mechanical engineering, shipbuilding, light industry, mining, metallurgy, steel, coking industry, construction of road and rail networks in India etc. Ukraine is a well-known manufacturer of world class gas and steel turbines for thermal, hydel and nuclear power plants, compressors, transformers, pumps, motors equipment for laying power transmission lines etc. Ukraine is keen to explore new avenues of joint development of power projects in India.

The India-Ukraine Inter-Governmental Commission (IUIGC) was established in April 1994. It has so far held 3 meetings on trade, economic, scientific, technological, industrial and cultural Cooperation. The sides agreed to form two Working Groups—one on metallurgy and the other on power to open new vistas of cooperation in the fields of metallurgy and power respectively. The fourth session was held in New Delhi in 2007.

11

India's Relations with US, Russia and China

11.1 India and US

Historically, the fabled wealth and treasures of India had attracted the attention of many European adventurers who set their sail to reach this treasure house. Christopher Columbus stumbled on America in 1492 while he was searching for the shores of India. Therefore, there is, though accidental, a pleasant historic connection between India and the United Sates. The British colonization of India and America had given them certain common experiences of imperial rule that the Indian nationalist movement had drawn a lot of inspiration from the American War of Independence. For India's freedom fighters, Thomas Jefferson, George Washington and Abraham Lincoln were hallowed heroes. Of course, unlike America, India chose the path of peaceful struggle to win freedom from the British. However, the imperial legacy had linked the two countries with English as the *lingua franca* which enabled the two peoples to talk to one another directly without the intervention of jarring interpreters. Moreover, many ideas which had gone into the shaping of India's Constitution and political system had come from the United Sate. Added to it are certain common features. Both countries are large multi-cultural societies. It was also believed that the President, Franklin D. Roosevelt, had supposedly applied pressure on the British Prime Minister, Winston S. Churchill, during the Second World War to grant India freedom.

Despite the presence of many features and shared ideals conducive for forging a close friendly relationship between India and the United States, the vagaries of world politics had kept them for long in a state of 'unfriendly friends'. As a result, for more than half-a- century Indo-US relationship was punctuated by a mixture of common aspirations, divergent perceptions and continual discord, all wrapped up together.

11.1.1 Nehruvian Era: When India emerged out of a bloody partition and gained independence, its leaders were confused and nursed ideas about socialism. The USA did help India through its PL-480 scheme and former Prime Minister Jawaharlal Nehru visited U.S.A. quite a few times. But he could not generate a long-term relationship. Then, Nehru came up with his position of nonalignment, but in the days of the cold war, if a country was not a friend, the US considered it as an enemy. In 1956, the US Secretary of State John Foster called India's non-alignment as "immoral". India also chose to follow the model of a planned economy on the Soviet pattern and when it entered into a friendship treaty with USSR, the divide with USA became too vast to be bridged. As a result of Indian tilt towards USSR, America decided to cultivate its friendship with Pakistan, in order to maintain a foothold in the region. With Pakistan's joining the SEATO and the CENTO, the US preference of Pakistan in South Asia became more pronounced and since then Washington took positions supportive of Pakistan in the United Nations, as was manifested in 1957, and outside. The Mutual Defence Assistance Agreement between Pakistan and the United States, signed in May 1954, had only further deepened India's distrust in Washington on Indo-Pakistan issues.

11.1.2 Indo-US Relations in the 1970s: However, from the 1971 Bangladesh crisis, India emerged with self-confidence, prestige and power. The geo-political situation in the Indian sub-continent had also changed permanently in India's favour. Clear, it was no longer possible for the United States to maintain even the semblance of an artificial; 'parity' between India and Pakistan in any serious terms. In the changed circumstances, the United States began to view India as a major country in the region. But its close ties with Pakistan did not allow the growth of bilateral ties between India and United States any further.

Until 1971 nonalignment had a dual effect on United States policies in South Asia. On the one hand, Washington considered Indian economic and political stability necessary to prevent that important regional player from succumbing to communism and Soviet influence; hence the United States gave economic assistance and support to India during its 1962 war with China. On the other hand, India's nonalignment had led the United States in 1954 to ally itself with Pakistan, which appeared to support Western security interests. The United States-Pakistan alliance was renewed in 1959, with accompanying assurances from President Dwight D. Eisenhower to Nehru that the arms supplied to Pakistan would not be used in any aggressive war. When Pakistan and India went to war in 1965, the United States government refused to support India and suspended military transfers to both countries.

In 1971 the intertwining of the United States-Soviet, Chinese-Soviet, and Indian-Pakistani conflicts dragged India-United States relations to the nadir. That year, while Washington initiated a new relationship with Beijing, New Delhi signed a friendship treaty with Moscow to counteract United States and Chinese influence in South Asia. As the situation in East Pakistan deteriorated, India was unable to convince the United States to cease arms deliveries to Pakistan and persuade Pakistan's leaders to reach a political settlement with East Pakistan's elected representatives. Indira Gandhi's November 1971 visit to Washington failed to alter President Richard M. Nixon's pro-Pakistan stance. When war formally began after Pakistani strikes on Indian airfields in early December 1971, the United States and China voted for a cease-fire in the UN Security Council, but the Soviet Union's veto prevented any resolution from coming into effect. Washington's subsequent deployment of a naval task force to the Bay of Bengal left many in India convinced that the United States was a major security threat.

Relations between India and the United States verged on the antagonistic throughout the 1970s. After Nixon abruptly terminated US$ 82 million in economic assistance, India closed down a large United States Agency for International Development program. The Indian government also restricted the flow of American scholars and students to India. India's criticisms of United States policies in Vietnam and Cambodia increased, and it upgraded its representation in Hanoi. When the United States expanded its naval base on the island of Diego Garcia and engaged in naval exercises with Pakistan in the Indian Ocean in 1974, India saw its security further threatened. Both governments, however, attempted to limit the damage to bilateral relations. A 1973 agreement defused a dispute over United States rupee holdings by writing off more than 50 percent of the debt and directing use of the remainder to mutually acceptable programs. In 1974 the Indo-United States Joint Commission was established to insulate bilateral dealings in education and culture, economics, and science and technology from political controversy and to provide mechanisms for regular exchanges at high levels of public life.

Hopes for improved relations were expressed in 1977 when Jimmy Carter became president of the United States and the Janata Party government led by Morarji Desai took over in India. These expectations came to an abrupt end two years later when the Soviet Union invaded Afghanistan. The promulgation of the Carter Doctrine, establishment of the Rapid Deployment Force (later called the United States Central Command) and an Indian Ocean fleet, planned expansion of the naval base at Diego Garcia, and arrangements to supply Pakistan with US$ 3.2 billion in military and economic aid over five years all appeared as direct United States intervention in the countries of the Persian Gulf and Indian Ocean. These actions fuelled instability in the region and, in India's view, threatened India's security.

11.1.3 Indo-US Relations in the 1980s: The personal rapport between Indira Gandhi and United States president Ronald Reagan, established during a series of meetings in the early 1980s, enabled the two countries gradually to begin improving bilateral relations. The Reagan administration reassessed its policy toward India and decided to expand areas of cooperation, particularly in the economic and scientific realms, as a means of counteracting Soviet influence in the region. Washington also regarded New Delhi's status as the major regional power in South Asia in a more favourable light. For her part, Gandhi realized that India was unable to block United States arms sales to Pakistan, but that improved dialogue with the United States could open other areas of interaction that could benefit Indian interests. Indira Gandhi's highly successful 1982 state visit to the United States was followed by a series of high-level exchanges, including the visits of Vice President George Bush and Secretary of State George Shultz to India. In addition, in 1982 the two sides resolved their dispute concerning supplies of fuel and spare parts for the nuclear power plant at Tarapur. In 1984 the United States decided to expand technology transfers to India.

The warming trend in relations between New Delhi and Washington continued with the 1985 and 1987 visits by Prime Minister Rajiv Gandhi to Washington. Furthermore, as the United States appreciation of India's role as a force for stability in South Asia grew, Washington supported New Delhi's moves in Sri Lanka in 1987 and in Maldives in 1988. In the mid- and late 1980s, visits exchanged by the United States secretary of defence and the Indian minister of defence symbolized a modest but growing program of cooperation in military technology and other defence matters. In 1988 Washington and New Delhi finalized an accord to provide United States technology for India's light combat aircraft program and also agreed to transfer technology for the F-5 fighter. Cooperation between India and the United States in a variety of scientific fields followed the signing of a bilateral agreement on scientific and technological exchanges in 1985. Non-military technology transfers also accelerated, and in 1987 India purchased a Cray supercomputer for agricultural research and weather forecasting and accepted stringent United States safeguards to preclude military uses. Furthermore, economic liberalization measures paved the way for increased trade and United States investment in India. In 1988, the improved economic climate resulted in the conclusion of a deal for a Pepsi-Cola plant and the signing of a bilateral tax treaty. In 1989, United States investment in India reached US$ 1 billion.

In the 1980s, the Indian and United States governments had divergent views on a wide range of international issues, including Afghanistan, Cambodia, the Middle East, and Central America. Serious differences also remained over United States policy toward Pakistan and the issue of nuclear proliferation. India was repeatedly incensed in the 1980s when the United States provided advanced military technology and other assistance to Pakistan. New Delhi also found objectionable Washington's unwillingness to cut off military assistance to Islamabad despite United States concerns about Pakistan's covert nuclear program. For its part, Washington continued to urge New Delhi to sign the Treaty on the Non-Proliferation of Nuclear Weapons and, after the successful test launch of the Indian Agni intermediate-range ballistic missile in May 1989, called on New Delhi to refrain from developing a ballistic missile capability by adhering to the restrictions of the Missile Technology Control Regime. India rejected these appeals on the grounds that it had a right to develop such technology and that the Treaty on the Non-Proliferation of Nuclear Weapons and the United States-sponsored Missile Technology Control Regime discriminated against non-nuclear states.

Bureaucratic and private-sector resistance to foreign participation in the economy, infrastructure problems, bureaucratic red tape, and legal problems remained formidable obstacles to significant Indian-United States economic cooperation. In the late 1980s, India had differences with the United States over improving its legal protection of intellectual property rights, opening its markets to American service industries, and liberalizing its foreign investment regulations. In April 1991, the Office of the United States Trade Representative placed India on Washington's watch list over intellectual property rights issues. Six months later, the United States gave India a three-month grace period before imposing retaliatory sanctions against India's pharmaceutical industry for inadequate patent protection. India resisted United States pressure to adopt a less protectionist stance in the Uruguay Round of negotiations to renew the General Agreement on Tariffs and Trade (GATT).

11.1.4 End of Cold War and New Strategic Partnership: The end of Cold War and the disintegration of the Soviet Union altered much of the international alliance structures of the Cold War period. The disappearance of the Soviet Union form the global strategic framework created the necessity for India to engage with the West and the US in a more effective manner. Additional factors helped India make the painful transitions, such as the dire economic situation the country found itself in the early 1990s. The economic liberalisation that followed, and the opening of the market in India allowed great interaction between the Indian and US business communities, and this became a critical cementing factor in the bilateral relations. Other factors helped coax the US into paying India grater attention was India's rapidly expanding economy, which was beginning to rival China's, the concurrent growth of India's military capability (especially in the strategic arena), and the emergence of an increasingly vocal Indian Diaspora in the U.S.

In the early 1990s, economic reforms permitted a qualitative breakthrough in relations between India and the United States. Washington was instrumental in speeding a US$ 1.8 billion IMF credit that New Delhi obtained in January 1991 to deal with a severe external-debt-payments crisis. In 1990, India and the United States signed a double taxation pact designed to facilitate American investment in India, further breaking a thirty-year deadlock in economic relations. The United States provided only modest bilateral economic assistance in the form of food aid but was India's largest trading partner and an important source of investments and technology. In December 1990, the United States approved the export of a second Cray supercomputer for the Indian Institute of Science in Bangalore, Karnataka, although the deal fell through two years later because of India's unwillingness to accept safeguards to prevent the computer's diversion to military uses.

The Soviet withdrawal from Afghanistan in 1989 had led Washington to reassess its relationship with Pakistan, with positive ramifications for New Delhi. Without containment of the Soviet Union as the driving factor behind close Pakistani-United States ties, and concerns mounting about Pakistan's nuclear weapons program, the United States suspended military and economic assistance to that country in October 1990. New Delhi appreciated this action and was relieved in summer 1991 when the United States Congress voted not to include India in the Pressler Amendment, which forbade United States assistance to Pakistan if it violated nuclear non-proliferation criteria. Washington also took a more even-handed approach to the Kashmir problem in 1990, urging both antagonists to resolve their dispute peacefully under the terms of the Shimla Accord. Military cooperation also grew. Exchanges of senior military officials became frequent, a high-level bilateral conference on regional security affairs was held, and Minister of Defence Sharad Pawar journeyed to Washington in April 1992 to discuss arms supplies and military technology. Not only did United States navy ships make occasional ports calls in India, but the two navies conducted their first-ever joint exercise in May 1992. Indian officials came to have a greater appreciation of United States interests in maintaining a military presence on Diego Garcia and in the Persian Gulf.

11.1.5 CTBT and Afterwards: The most important fact that drew US strategic attention towards India was the non-proliferation drive in the US' post-Cold War approach to world order. The US found that India was a firm and consistent defiant in its search for a global non-proliferation regime, be it through a universal and permanent NPT or a rigid, though discriminatory, CTBT. In 1993, India and the United States appeared committed to improve relations and bilateral cooperation despite differences over India's refusal to sign the Treaty on the Non-Proliferation of Nuclear Weapons and to participate in discussions with the United States, Russia, China, and Pakistan on establishing a South Asian nuclear-free zone. Nevertheless, Washington directed its efforts to creating a climate of restraint between New Delhi and Islamabad in order to freeze or roll back their nuclear weapons programs. However, India and the United States remained wary of each other's long-term strategy regionally and globally.

Some Indian political analysts criticize the United States for following a "two-track policy." On the one hand, Washington has supported New Delhi's economic reform and has facilitated international loans to India, but, on the other, it has relentlessly pursued an agenda to force India's accession to United States non-proliferation goals and has used human rights issues to try to force India to meet Washington's political objections. Moreover, many Indians have expressed worries that, with the emergence of the United States as the sole superpower, and as the leader of a Western-dominated coalition after the Persian Gulf War, Washington might attempt to impose its own standards for democratic values, human rights, and free markets. India fears that a United States vision of a new world order not only would hurt the interests of Third World countries economically and politically, but also would damage India's drive to become a leading power in a multipolar system. Washington's decision not to place Pakistan on its list of nations that sponsor terrorism and its successful efforts in getting Russia to cancel the sale of cryogenic engines to India are seen as detrimental to good Indian-United States relations.

In the midst of increasing anti-United States political rhetoric and newspaper headlines, Indian and United States officials have seemed to agree on only one thing, that bilateral relations had reached their lowest point in two decades. Observers in both countries believe that the administration of President William Clinton places a low priority on relations with India despite the fact that the United States has become India's prime trade partner. Against this backdrop, Prime Minister Rao visited the United States in May 1994 for an uneventful round of talks with President Clinton, who encouraged India's economic reforms. Six memorandums of understanding were signed with the intent of expanding official contacts, reviewing and updating a 1984 understanding on high-technology transfer, enhancing defence cooperation, stimulating bilateral ties, and establishing a business partnership initiative.

High-level visits to India in early 1995 portended greater stability in India-United States relations. Secretary of Defence William J. Perry visited New Delhi in January to sign a "landmark agreement" on military cooperation that was seen by some local observers as a convergence in India-United States security perceptions after nearly fifty years of divergent viewpoints. Following the Perry visit was a commercial mission led by Secretary of Commerce Ronald H. Brown that also occurred in January. Agreements signed by Indian and United States businesses during the visit resulted in US$ 7 billion in contracts and investments in the communications, health care, insurance, finance, and automotive sectors.

Some of the deals consummated were intended to build the infrastructure needed by foreign firms to do business in India. In March 1995, Hilary Rodham Clinton, the wife of the United States president, toured India as part of an extensive South Asian goodwill tour. In April, Secretary of the Treasury Robert E. Rubin visited New Delhi to sign a bilateral investment protection treaty' reflecting the substantial increases in United States investment in India since 1991 and Washington's encouragement to India to apply for Agency for International Development loans.

This realisation not only brought President Clinton to New Delhi in March 2000, but also led to the broadening of Indo-US dialogue in the diverse areas of fighting terrorism, economic cooperation, science and technology policies and environment.

After India, Clinton visited Pakistan for a few hours. What happened there again went in India's favour. In an extraordinary television address to the Pakistani people, Clinton broke some of Pakistan's delusions. Under the nose of the dictator, he declared that, "the answer to flawed democracy is not to end democracy, but to improve it". That dashed General Musharraf's hope that Mr. Clinton's visit would help legitimize his rule. He went on to wreck another Pakistani hope by saying that USA would not mediate in Kashmir. Even during the Kargil Conflict also US played a three-way diplomacy forcing Pakistan to withdrew from the region and the explicit US stand that the Kashmir issue is a bilateral matter, suddenly gave boost to the indo-US relations.

To further strengthen the bridge of the indo-US relations built by President during his visit to India, Prime Minister Vajpayee paid a reciprocal visit to Washington on September 14-16, 2000. During the course of his visit, Prime Minister Vajpayee pained a glowing picture of a robust Indian economy undergoing substantive reforms, as to attract the US investment in India. He also raised the issue of growing terrorist threats in South Asia, India's dispute with Pakistan over Kashmir issue, the NPT and India's concerns.

In the post-Pokhran-II phase, these negotiations were continued between Strobe Talbott and Jaswant Singh. These dialogues made the US realize that India's security concerns in the nuclear field could no longer be wished away, that the sanctions imposed on India after May 1998 were unnecessary and irrational, and that India was a potentially powerful actor in structuring a peaceful and stable world order, particularly in Asia. The findings of the officially sponsored and academic research reports reinforced this line of thought.

11.1.6 Civil Nuclear Cooperation: India's status as a non-signatory to the Nuclear Non-proliferation Treaty has kept it from accessing most nuclear-related materials and fuels on the international market for more than 30 years. New

Delhi's 1974 "peaceful nuclear explosion" spurred creation of the Nuclear Suppliers Group (NSG)—an international export control regime for nuclear-related trade—and Washington further tightened its export laws with the Nuclear Non-proliferation Act of 1978. The July 2005 U.S.-India Joint Statement notably asserted that, "as a responsible state with advanced nuclear technology, India should acquire the same benefits and advantages as other such states," and President Bush vowed to work on achieving "full civilian nuclear energy cooperation with India." Such proposed cooperation is controversial and would require changes in both U.S. law and in NSG guidelines. India reciprocally agreed to take its own steps, including identifying and separating its civilian and military nuclear facilities in a phased manner and placing the former under international safeguards. Some in Congress expressed concern that civil nuclear cooperation with India might allow that country to advance its military nuclear projects and be harmful to broader U.S. non-proliferation efforts. While the Bush Administration previously had insisted that such future cooperation with India would take place only within the limits set by multilateral non-proliferation regimes, the Administration now seeks adjustments to U.S. laws and policies, and has approached the NSG to adjust the regime's guideline. After months of complex and difficult negotiations, the Indian government in March 2006 presented a plan to separate its civilian and military nuclear facilities as per the July 2005 Joint Statement. Shortly thereafter, H.R. 4974 and S. 2429, to waive the application of certain requirements under the Atomic Energy Act of 1954 with respect to India, were, at the President's request, introduced in the Congress.

11.1.7 Civil Space Cooperation: India has long sought access to American space technology; such access has since the 1980s been limited by U.S. and international "red lines" meant to prevent assistance that could benefit India's military missile programs. India's space-launch vehicle technology was obtained largely from foreign sources, including the United States, and forms the basis of its medium-range Agni ballistic missile booster, as well as its suspected Surya intercontinental ballistic missile program. The NSSP called for enhanced U.S.-India cooperation on the peaceful uses of space technology, and the July 2005 Joint Statement called for closer ties in space exploration, satellite navigation and launch, and in the commercial space arena. Conferences on India-U.S. space science and commerce were held in Bangalore in 2004 and 2005. During President Bush's March 2006 visit to India, the two countries committed to move forward with agreements that will permit the launch of U.S. satellites and satellites containing U.S. components by Indian space launch vehicles, and welcomed the inclusion of U.S. instruments in a planned Indian lunar mission.

11.1.8 U.S-India Security Cooperation: Security cooperation between the United States and India is in the early stages of development (unlike U.S.-Pakistan military ties, which date back to the 1950s). Since September 2001, and despite a concurrent U.S. rapprochement with Pakistan, U.S.-India security cooperation has flourished. The India-U.S. Defence Policy Group (DPG)—moribund since India's 1998 nuclear tests and ensuing U.S. sanctions—was revived in late 2001 and meets annually; U.S. diplomats call military cooperation among the most important aspects of transformed bilateral relations. In June 2005, the United States and India signed a ten-year defence pact outlining planned collaboration in multilateral operations, expanded two-way defence trade, increasing opportunities for technology transfers and co-production, expanded collaboration related to missile defence, and establishment of a bilateral Defence Procurement and Production Group. The United States views defence cooperation with India in the context of "common principles and shared national interests" such as defeating terrorism, preventing weapons proliferation, and maintaining regional stability. Many analysts laud increased U.S.-India security ties as providing an alleged "counterbalance" to growing Chinese influence in Asia.

Since early 2002, the United States and India have held numerous and unprecedented joint exercises involving all military branches. Air exercises have provided the U.S. military with its first look at Russian-built Su-30MKIs; in 2004, mock air combat saw Indian pilots in late-model Russian-built fighters hold off American pilots flying older F-15Cs, and Indian successes were repeated versus U.S. F-16s in November 2005. U.S. and Indian special forces soldiers have held joint exercises near the India-China border, and major annual "Malabar" joint naval exercises are held off the Indian coast. Despite these developments, there remain indications that the perceptions and expectations of top U.S. and Indian military leaders are divergent on several key issues, including India's regional role, approaches to countering terrorism, and U.S.-Pakistan relations. The continued existence of a non-proliferation constituency in the United States is seen as a further hindrance to more fully developed military-to-military relations.

Along with increasing military-to-military ties, the issue of U.S. arms sales to India has taken a higher profile. In 2002, the Pentagon negotiated a sale to India of 12 counter-battery radar sets (or "Fire-finder" radars) worth a total of US$ 190 million. India also purchased US$ 29 million worth of counter-terrorism equipment for its special forces and has received sophisticated U.S.-made electronic ground sensors to help stem the tide of militant infiltration in the Kashmir region. In July 2004, Congress was notified of a possible sale to India involving up to US$ 40 million worth of aircraft self-protection systems to be mounted on the Boeing 737s that carry the Indian head of state. The State Department has authorized Israel to sell to India the jointly developed U.S.-Israeli Phalcon airborne early warning system, an expensive asset that some analysts believe may tilt the regional strategic balance even further in India's favour. The Indian government reportedly possesses an extensive list of desired U.S.-made weapons, including PAC-3 anti-missile systems, electronic warfare systems, and possibly even fighter aircraft. The March 2005 unveiling of the Bush Administration's "new strategy for South Asia" included assertions that the United States welcomed Indian requests for information on the possible purchase of F-16 or F/A-18 multi-role fighters, and indicated that Washington is "ready to discuss the sale of transformative systems in areas such as command and control, early warning, and missile defence." Still, some top Indian officials express concern that the United States is a "fickle" partner that may not always be relied upon to provide the reciprocity, sensitivity, and high-technology transfers sought by New Delhi (In February 2006, the Indian Navy declined an offer to lease two U.S. P-3C maritime reconnaissance aircraft, calling the arrangements "expensive").

In a controversial turn, the Indian government has sought to purchase a sophisticated anti-missile platform, the Arrow Weapon System, from Israel. Because the United States took the lead in the system's development, the U.S. government has veto power over any Israeli exports of the Arrow. Although Defence Department officials are seen to support the sale as meshing with President Bush's policy of cooperating with friendly countries on missile defence, State Department officials are reported to opposed the transfer, believing that it would send the wrong signal to other weapons-exporting states at a time when the U.S. is seeking to discourage international weapons proliferation. Indications are that a U.S. interest in maintaining a strategic balance on the subcontinent, along with U.S. obligations under the Missile Technology Control Regime, may preclude any approval of the Arrow sale.

Joint U.S-India military exercises and arms sales negotiations can cause disquiet in Pakistan, where there is concern that induction of advanced weapons systems into the region could destabilize strategic balance there. Islamabad is concerned that its already disadvantageous conventional military status vis-à-vis New Delhi will be further eroded by India's acquisition of sophisticated "force multipliers." In fact, numerous observers identify a pro-India drift in the U.S. government's strategic orientation in South Asia. Yet Washington regularly lauds Islamabad's role as a key ally in the U.S.-led counterterrorism coalition and assures Pakistan that it will take no actions to disrupt strategic balance on the subcontinent.

11.1.9 2011 Initiative: India said there was no need to get its domestic nuclear liability law vetted by the International Atomic Energy Agency (IAEA) to ensure it complied with the Convention on Supplemental Compensation (CSC). At the U.S. State Department briefing, the spokesperson said intention behind suggesting that the Indian law be vetted by IAEA was "to make sure that we do comply with international standards on nuclear energy." The issue of Convention on Supplemental Compensation again came to life two months after United States Secretary of State Hillary Clinton had introduced it during the second strategic dialogue with her counterpart S.M. Krishna here in mid-July. The issue was learnt to have been again broached when the two leaders met at New York on the sidelines of the United Nations General Assembly. The U.S. State Department said: "There continues to be serious concern that India's nuclear liability law [Civil Liability for Nuclear Damage Bill] is not consistent with the CSC. The IAEA is an appropriate venue for clarification on issues related to the CSC, which deals with international nuclear liability. The Agency can be helpful in assisting countries in evaluating their compliance with the CSC."

The American insistence comes months before the expiry of India's self-imposed deadline of ratifying the CSC before the end of the year. American and French dissatisfaction with the Indian Nuclear Liability Law is one of the reasons for the slow pace at which their civil nuclear projects are progressing in India .Indian officials maintained that the nuclear liability law was in complete conformity with the CSC and that any pressure to adjust this law on the basis of the IAEA's opinion was not acceptable.

They reasoned that the IAEA's role was different. It can act as a depository of the CSC or a clearing house for countries filing their ratification of the treaty. But it can have no role whatsoever in panning a sovereign law. Sources said during closed door talks, the U.S. had specifically objected to Section 17(b) of the Indian law. This expands the scope of the operator's right to compensation from nuclear suppliers in case of an accident due to faulty equipment. Washington is also unhappy with Section 46, which implicitly allows accident victims to file tort claims. In this respect, officials point out that while the CSC can have the provision to bar tort claims, it was not practical because only the Supreme Court could decide regarding the compatibility or otherwise with the CSC.

India and US Agreement for Educational Institutions India and United States agreed to explore new models for educational institutions to take knowledge partnership to a higher level. This will also help in further deepening the bilateral strategic co-operation. In a Joint Statement issued at the end of the India-US

Higher Education Summit in Washington, the goals of the partnership were outlined. India is keen to strengthen teacher exchange programmes to promote development of human resources. India intends to sponsor initially up to 1500 faculty and junior scholars to leading universities and research institutes in the United States. USA issued a Travel Alert to its Citizens in India the USA issued a travel alert to its citizens in India, warning them of possible terror attacks in the country during the holiday season. The State department in its statement urged the US citizens to maintain a heightened situational awareness and a low profile and to be careful while visiting public places. The places, such as markets, trains, buses, religious sites, hotels and restaurants were defined as public places. The travel alert expired on 20 January, 2012.

11.2 India and Russia

Despite the disintegration of the Soviet Union in 1991, the relationship between India and Russia remains one of considerable importance to both countries. Since the early 1950s, New Delhi and Moscow had built friendly relations on the basis of realpolitik. India's nonalignment enabled it to accept Soviet support in areas of strategic congruence, as in disputes with Pakistan and China, without subscribing to Soviet global policies or proposals for Asian collective security. Close and cooperative ties were forged in particular in the sectors of Indian industrial development and defence production and purchases. But the relationship was circumscribed by wide differences in domestic and social systems and the absence of substantial people-to-people contact--in contrast to India's relations with the United States.

Ties between India and the Soviet Union initially were distant. Nehru had expressed admiration for the Soviet Union's rapid economic transformation, but the Soviet Union regarded India as a "tool of Anglo-American imperialism." After Josef Stalin's death in 1953, the Soviet Union expressed its hopes for "friendly cooperation" with India. This aim was prompted by the Soviet decision to broaden its international contacts and to cultivate the non-aligned and newly independent countries of Asia and Africa. Nehru's state visit to the Soviet Union in June 1955 was the first of its kind for an Indian prime minister. It was followed by the trip of Premier Nikolai Bulganin and General Secretary Nikita Khrushchev to India in November and December 1955. The Soviet leaders endorsed the entire range of Indian foreign policy based on the Panch Shila and supported India's position against Pakistan on Kashmir. The Soviet Union also supported India's position vis-à-vis Portugal on Goa, which was territorially integrated into India as a union territory by the Indian armed forces in December 1961 (it became a state in May 1987).

The Soviet Union and some East European countries offered India new avenues of trade and economic assistance. By 1965 the Soviet Union was the second largest national contributor to India's development. These new arrangements contributed to India's emergence as a significant industrial power through the construction of plants to produce steel, heavy machinery and equipment, machine tools, and precision instruments, and to generate power and extract and refine petroleum. Soviet investment was in India's public-sector industry, which the World Bank and Western industrial powers had been unwilling to assist until spurred by Soviet competition. Soviet aid was extended on the basis of long-term, government-to-government programs, which covered successive phases of technical training for Indians, supply of raw materials, progressive use of Indian inputs, and markets for finished products. Bilateral arrangements were made in nonconvertible national currencies, helping to conserve India's scarce foreign exchange. Thus the Soviet contribution to Indian economic development was generally regarded by foreign and domestic observers as positive.

Nehru obtained a Soviet commitment to neutrality on the India-China border dispute and war of 1962. During the India-Pakistan war of 1965, the Soviet Union acted with the United States in the UN Security Council to bring about a cease-fire. Soviet premier Aleksei N. Kosygin went further by offering his good offices for a negotiated settlement, which took place at Tashkent on January 10, 1966. Until 1969 the Soviet Union took an even-handed position in South Asia and supplied a limited quantity of arms to Pakistan in 1968. From 1959 India had accepted Soviet offers of military sales. Indian acquisition of Soviet military equipment was important because purchases were made against deferred rupee payments, a major concession to India's chronic shortage of foreign exchange. Simultaneous provisions were made for licensed manufacture and modification in India, one criterion of self-reliant defence on which India placed increasing emphasis. In addition, Soviet sales were made without any demands for restricted deployment, adjustments in Indian policies toward other countries, adherence to Soviet global policies, or acceptance of Soviet military advisers. In this way, Indian national autonomy was not compromised.

The most intimate phase in relations between India and the Soviet Union was the period between 1971 and 1976: its highlight was the twenty-year Treaty of Peace, Friendship, and Cooperation of August 1971. Articles 8, 9, and 10 of the treaty committed the parties "to abstain from providing any assistance to any third party that engages in armed conflict with the other" and "in the event of either party being subjected to an attack or threat thereof...to immediately enter into mutual consultations." India benefited at the time because the Soviet Union came to support the Indian position on Bangladesh and because the treaty acted as a deterrent to China. New Delhi also received accelerated shipments of Soviet military equipment in the last quarter of 1971. The first state visit of Soviet president Leonid Brezhnev to India in November 1973 was conducted with tremendous fanfare and stressed the theme of economic cooperation. By the late 1970s, the Soviet Union was India's largest trading partner.

The friendship treaty notwithstanding, Indira Gandhi did not alter important principles of Indian foreign policy. She made it clear that the Soviet Union would not receive any special privileges—much less naval base rights—in Indian ports, despite the major Soviet contribution to the construction of shipbuilding and ship-repair facilities at Bombay on the west coast and at Vishakhapatnam on the east coast. India's advocacy of the Indian Ocean as a zone of peace was directed against aggrandizement of the Soviet naval presence as much as that of other extra regional powers. By repeatedly emphasizing the nonexclusive nature of its friendship with the Soviet Union, India kept open the way for normalizing relations with China and improving ties with the West.

After the Soviet intervention in Afghanistan, Indian diplomats avoided condemnatory language and resolutions as useless Cold War exercises that could only antagonize the Soviet Union and postpone political settlement. They called instead for withdrawal of all foreign troops and negotiation among concerned parties. In meetings with Soviet leaders in New Delhi in 1980 and in Moscow in 1982, Indira Gandhi privately pressed harder for the withdrawal of Soviet troops and for the restoration of Afghanistan's traditional non-alignment and independence.

Rajiv Gandhi journeyed to the Soviet Union in 1985, 1986, 1987, and 1989, and Soviet president Mikhail S. Gorbachev travelled to India in 1986 and 1988. These visits and those of other high officials evoked effusive references to the "exemplary" (in Gorbachev's term) friendship between the two countries and also achieved the conclusion of agreements to expand economic, cultural, and scientific and technological cooperation. In 1985 and 1986, and again in 1988, both nations signed pacts to boost bilateral trade and provide Soviet investment and technical assistance for Indian industrial, telecommunications, and transportation projects. In 1985 and 1988, the Soviet Union also extended to India credits of 1 billion rubles and 3 billion rubles, respectively (a total of about US$ 2.4 billion), for the purchase of Soviet machinery and goods. Protocols for scientific cooperation, signed in 1985 and 1987, provided the framework for joint research and projects in space science and such high-technology areas as biotechnology, computers, and lasers. The flow of advanced Soviet military equipment also continued in the mid- and late 1980s.

When the Soviet Union disintegrated, India was faced with the difficult task of reorienting its external affairs and forging relations with the fifteen Soviet successor states, of which Russia was the most important. In 1993, New Delhi and Moscow worked to redefine their relationship according to post-Cold War realities. During the January 1993 visit of Russian president Boris Yeltsin to India, the two countries signed agreements that signalled a new emphasis on economic cooperation in bilateral relations. The 1971 treaty was replaced with the new Treaty of Friendship and Cooperation, which dropped security clauses that in the Cold War were directed against the United States and China. Yeltsin stated that Russia would deliver cryogenic engines and space technology for India's space program under a US$ 350 million deal between the Indian Space Research Organisation (ISRO) and the Russian space agency, Glavkosmos, despite the imposition of sanctions on both organizations by the United States. In addition, Yeltsin expressed strong support for India's stand on Kashmir. A defence cooperation accord aimed at ensuring the continued supply of Russian arms and spare parts to satisfy the requirements of India's military and at promoting the joint production of defence equipment. Bilateral trade, which had fallen drastically during the 1990-92 period, was expected to revive following the resolution of the dispute over New Delhi's debt to Moscow and the May 1992 decision to abandon the 1978 rupee-rouble trade agreement in favour of the use of hard currency.

Pressure from the United States, which believed the engines and technology could be diverted to ballistic missile development, led the Russians to cancel most of the deal in July 1993. Russia did, however, supply rockets to help India to develop the technology to launch geostationary satellites, and, with cryogenic engine plans already in hand, the ISRO was determined to produce its own engines by 1997.

Despite Yeltsin's call for a realignment of Russia, India, and China to balance the West, Russia shares interests with the developed countries on nuclear proliferation issues. In November 1991, Moscow voted for a Pakistani-sponsored UN resolution calling for the establishment of a South Asian nuclear-free zone. Russia urged India to support the Treaty on the Non-Proliferation of Nuclear Weapons and decided in March 1992 to apply "full-scope safeguards" to future nuclear supply agreements. Russia also shares interests with the United States in cooling antagonisms between India and Pakistan, particularly with regard to Kashmir, thus making it unlikely that India could count on Russia in a future dispute with Pakistan.

Rao reciprocated Yeltsin's visit in July 1994. The two leaders signed declarations assuring international and bilateral goodwill and continuation of

Russian arms and military equipment exports to India. Rao's Moscow visit lacked the controversy that characterized his May 1994 visit to the United States and was deemed an important success because of the various accords, one of which restored the sale of cryogenic engines to India.

Bilateral relations between India and Russia improved as a result of eight agreements signed in December 1994. The agreements cover military and technical cooperation from 1995 to 2000, merchant shipping, and promotion and mutual protection of investments, trade, and outer space cooperation. Political observers saw the visit of Russian Prime Minister Viktor Chernomyrdin that occasioned the signing of the eight agreements as a sign of a return to the earlier course of warm relations between New Delhi and Moscow. In March 1995, India and Russia signed agreements aimed at suppressing illegal weapons smuggling and drug trafficking. And when Russian nationalist Vladimir V. Zhirinovsky visited India in March 1995, he declared that he would give India large supplies of arms and military hardware if he were elected president of Russia.

11.2.1 Indo-Russian Relations in the 21st Century: India's ties with the Russian Federation are time-tested and based on continuity, trust and mutual understanding. There is national consensus in both the countries on the need to preserve and strengthen India-Russia relations and further consolidate the strategic partnership between the two countries. A Declaration on Strategic Partnership was signed between President Mr. Vladimir Putin and former PM Shri Atal Bihari Vajpayee in October 2000.

There are number of developments between India and Russia in the year 2000. These are:

1. Russia ratified the extradition treaty which aimed at curbing terrorism.
2. In June 2000, Indian External affair Minister (Jaswant Singh) visited Moscow and held a series of high level meeting to forge a strategic partnership.
3. Another development which greatly pleased Russia took place in July 2000 when India released the five pilots of Russian origin.
4. Both the countries signed four key defence agreements.
5. The other points highlighted by the declaration on strategic partnership between India and Russia.
6. In February 2001, the Russian Deputy PM visited India and signed a deal for supply and manufacture of the T-90s Main Battle Tanks (MBT). The deal worth US$ 650 million has been described as the "deal of the century". Under this deal three agreements were concluded under the first agreement India would immediately purchase 124 MBJs.
7. The two countries also signed an agreement for promotion of aviation safety.
8. Another notable agreement was signed by ONGC-Videsh Ltd. and Russian

state-owned company Rosneft in 2001.

It may be concluded that these deals have given a significant boost to defence cooperation between India and Russia. Russia is trying to woo India to shun its appreciation of NMD and has even offered on alternative defence system. From India's point of view the shift from technology transfer to joint production has been a major gain.

The areas of cooperation between Soviet Union and India can be reviewed in the following ways:

The areas of cooperation between Soviet Union and India can be reviewed in the following ways:

1. Soviet Union helped India in its disputes with Pakistan.
2. On a number of occasions Soviet Union supported India on the Kashmir issue.
3. She also helped India to modernize her forces after the border war of China.
4. In the defence field, ties were strengthened with India.
5. In 1993, Indo-Russian treaty was signed for defence cooperation and rupee-rouble settlement.
6. A new political dimension was provided to Russia's relations with India by joint declaration (fight for terrorism).
7. In 1996, the first agreement was signed on New Delhi Moscow hot line, and second related to educational, scientific and cultural exchanges on this occasion, Russian foreign minister asserted that Kashmir issue should be resolved within the framework of Simla Agreement.
8. Russia also promised to support India's candidate for permanent membership of the Security Council.
9. India and Russia signed a defence agreement to foster closer ties.
10. In March 1997, PM Dev Gowda visited Moscow. On this occasion, several agreements were signed which pertained to avoidance of double taxation, extradition, plant protection and sports.
11. In 1997, when Indian Defence Minister visited Russia, the two countries resolved to upgrade their relationship to the level of strategic partnership.

Indo-Russian ties in post-11 attack have taken a new turn. These two countries are strategically located in an area where new game of the 21st century is being played. The main issues are reviewed after post-11 attack between the two countries mainly on:

1. Terrorist activities.
2. Central Asian natural gas and hydro carbon resources.
3. India's interest in energy sector.
4. Military cooperation.

5. Trilateral cooperation (continue partnership with Iran and the central Asian Republics) over Afghanistan, China to combat terrorism and develop alternate energy routes.

Russia concurred with the Indian stand points on terrorism and conceded that there should be no double standards on this issue and pointed out that Pakistan must take concrete action on ending cross-border terrorism. India also has keen interest in the energy sector, which can become the source of energy in future.

A land mark was created in Indo-Russian relation in the field of defence cooperation. The foreign minister of Russia signed a number of deals with their Indian counter parts. The Agreement focussed on:

1. Supply of spare parts to soviet made Indian weapons.
2. Delivery of two nuclear submarines to Indian Navy.
3. Joint production, development and marketing of weapons systems.
4. Speedy supply of T-90 tanks and aircrafts.

Apart from these, Russia also agreed for:

- To military to military ties.
- To lease 2 Project 971 nuclear powered multi-role submarines which will join the Indian Navy.
- Signing of protocols for cooperation in warship building aviation, developing land based systems for the army.
- Strengthening of defence and security cooperation.

Russian President visited India on December 3, 2002. On this occasion, Indian PM and Russian President signed the "Delhi-Declaration" to enhance strategic cooperation" and set up a joint working group on combating terrorism and joint declaration on strengthening economic and scientific cooperation.

The joint declaration document focuses:

1. On upgrading bilateral economic relations.
2. On trade promotions.
3. On investment.
4. On new areas of cooperation.
5. On science and technology projects.

The two countries also signed eight agreements relating to Delhi declaration, MoU on cooperation in combating terrorism, MoU cooperation in the field of telecommunication.

With Russia, India has a strategic and a time-tested relationship, which has stood the challenge of a changing global and regional environment. President Putin's recent visit to India provided an opportunity to take forward these relations to a much higher level of interaction. Significant successes in the field of space and energy cooperation have strengthened the strategic nature of the relationship. The signing of 4 agreements and 6 MoUs is indicative of the breadth of India's relationship with Russia. A declaratory phase in relations between the two countries has given way to concrete steps to put substance into professed intentions. The Government is also gratified that President Putin supported India's candidature for the United Nations Security Council seat with veto power.

Russia will build more atomic power reactors in India, although there were international curbs on the scale of nuclear cooperation between the two countries. This came out after the meet between President Vladimir Putin and Prime Minister Manmohan Singh in May 2005.

Key areas of discussion were as under:

1. India's growing energy requirements for its sustained economic development and New Delhi's interest in Russian involvement in the development of nuclear power projects, as part of Indian energy security efforts.
2. Russia is currently building 2000 MW Kudankulam nuclear power plant in Tamil Nadu, which is scheduled to be commissioned in 2007. The final agreement on Kudankulam was signed in June 1998.
3. Russia is supplying two 1000VVER-type light water reactors under the Kudankulam deal inked in 1985 by the then Prime Minister Rajiv Gandhi and Soviet President Mikhail Gorbachev.
4. After the Soviet collapse the deal was revived despite strong US opposition when Moscow insisted that its joining of Nuclear Suppliers Group (NSG) in early 1990s has no retrospective implications.
5. Prikhodko conceded that "there are certain issues involving Russia's commitments to NSG" and the scale of cooperation depends on the NSG guidelines.

11.2.3 Indo-Russia Annual Summits: The two countries hold annual Summits since the year 2001. Prime Minister Dr. Manmohan Singh visited Moscow on December 4-7, 2005 for the sixth annual summit meeting. Agreements on Intellectual Property Rights, Technology Safeguards in the space sector and on Coronas-Photon research project were signed during the visit. Prime Minister Dr. Manmohan Singh also visited Moscow on 8-10 May 2005 to participate in the 60th anniversary celebrations of the Victory Day.

Prime Minister Dr. Manmohan Singh paid an official visit to Russia on 11-12 November 2007 for the last Summit meeting. PM also held a meeting with the Prime Minister of Russia, Viktor Zubkov and attended a business meeting with senior Indian and Russian trade and industry representatives.

The following documents were signed:

1. Agreement between India and Russia on Cooperation in Development and

Production of Multi-Role Transport Aircraft;

2. Letters of Exchange (on utilization of Rupee debt funds for Russian investments in India);
3. Agreement between India and Russia on Cooperation to Combat Illicit Trafficking in Narcotics, Psychotropic Substances and their Precursors; and
4. Agreement between the Indian Space Research Organization and the Federal Space Agency of the Russian Federation in the Field of Joint Moon Exploration.

During his visit to India on 25-26 January 2007, President Putin was the Chief Guest at the Republic Day celebrations. Several important documents were signed/issued during the visit—Joint Statement on the outcome of the visit signed by the two leaders; Joint Statement on peaceful uses of atomic energy; Programme of Cultural Exchanges during 2007-09; Protocol on holding "Year of Russia in India" in the year 2008 and "Year of India in Russia" in the Year 2009; Two agreements concerning Russian Global Navigation Satellite System 'GLONASS' and another one on joint satellite 'YOUTHSAT'; Memorandum of Intent on development of cooperation in the construction of additional nuclear power plant units; Protocol on exchange of information between the two customs; and Plan of major events to celebrate 60 years of establishment of diplomatic relations (on 13 April 2007). Former Russian PM Mr. Mikhail Fradkov paid a visit to India from 16-17 March 2006 and discussed bilateral relations, particularly trade and economic issues.

Following were the agreements signed during Putin's visit on January 25-26, 2007:

1. Joint Statement on the Outcome of the Official Visit of Vladimir V. Putin, President of the Russian Federation to India.
2. Programme of Cultural Exchanges between the Government of the Republic of India and the Government of the Russian Federation for the Years 2007-09.
3. Protocol between India and Russia on holding "Year of Russia in India" in the Year 2008 and "Year of India in Russia" in the Year 2009.
4. Memorandum of Intent between the Department of Atomic Energy, India and Federal Atomic Energy Agency, Russia on development of cooperation in the construction of additional nuclear power plant units at Kudankulam site as well as in the construction of Russian design nuclear power plants at new sites in the Republic of India.
5. Agreement between India and Russia on the access of the Indian Party to navigation signals of the Russian Global Navigation Satellite System GLONASS for peaceful purposes.

6. Agreement between India and Russia on access of the Indian Party to a part of the Russian Global Navigation Satellite System GLONASS Radio Frequency Spectrum.
7. Agreement between the Indian Space Research Organization (ISRO) and the Federal Space Agency on cooperation in the joint satellite project 'YOUTHSAT'.
8. Protocol between the Central Board of Excise and Customs (Republic of India) and the Federal Customs Service (Russian Federation) on exchange of information on the movement of goods and conveyances between the Republic of India and the Russian Federation.

11.2.4 India-Russia Joint Declaration on Civil Aviation: Delegations representing the Government of India and the Russian Federation met in Moscow on 14th June 2007, to discuss issues related to the cooperation between the two countries in the field of civil aviation. A mutually beneficial agreement was reached, under which the designated airlines of the two countries will continue to be permitted to over fly the territory of the other country without restrictions. Further, traffic rights were enhanced and capacity entitlements were increased from 46 to 52 weekly frequencies for both sides. The increase in flights will be to the cities of Ahmedabad and Amritsar each of which will get three additional flights from Russia.

11.2.5 Russia-India Relations in 2008: 2008 began in India-Russia relations just as 2007 ended with a bang. Close on the heels of the successful visit of the Indian Prime Minister Shri Manmohan Singh to Moscow in November 2007, Russian Prime Minister Mr. Victor Zubkov led a high-level delegation of Russian Ministers, senior officials, and businessmen to India during February 12-13, 2008. The Russian Premier inaugurated the 'Year of Russia in India' together with Prime Minister Manmohan Singh at an impressive ceremony at the ramparts of the Red Fort on February 12.

Delhi and other Indian cities will hope to see the best of Russian arts and culture in India between now and December 2008. Mr. Zubkov met Prime Minister, and called on the President and the Vice-President. He also had substantive meetings with our External Affairs Minister, Finance Minister and the Leader of Opposition in the Lok Sabha.

The Russian Premier's visit to India was also timed to coincide with the second session of the India-Russia Forum on Trade and Investment. The event witnessed the participation of over 500 business representatives from the public and private sector in both countries, and resulted in two outcomes that can be considered significant: firstly, it was decided to establish a CEOs Council which will be akin to a Joint Business Council. This should kick-start and provide effective ignition for the "B2B" interaction. It is a timely initiative since, over time, the trade relationship between the two countries will need to be determined by the burgeoning private entrepreneurs in both countries. Secondly, a joint task force (JTF) will now monitor the implementation of the recommendations of the joint study group for taking the trade and economic relations between the two countries to newer highs by removing the impediments to bilateral trade and commerce. The JTF will also examine the feasibility of a Comprehensive Economic Cooperation agreement (CECA). The trade and investment forum resulted in the Captains of Indian and Russian industry and finance coming together to discuss prospects of working together in IT, financial services, power and energy sector, and other key spheres as transport, infrastructure, metallurgy and mining. Significantly, Premier Zubkov's India visit coincided with the Russian Vneshtorgbank (VTB) and Russian telecom and services conglomerate giant Sistema inaugurating their representative offices in the Indian Capital.

All in all, the Russian Premier's visit did have a significant focus on trade and economic cooperation, and should help both countries to march in tandem in realizing the goals laid down by the political leadership in both India and Russia in further advancing their partnership. The rock-solid foundation provided by the close and friendly relations that the two countries have enjoyed over the past six decades will help businesses in both countries to similarly move forward and advance cooperation in sectors ranging from energy to aviation, and metallurgy to the power and engineering sector.

11.2.6 Trade and Economic Relations: Bilateral trade turnover is modest and stood at US$ 5.17 billion in 2010-11, out of which Indian Exports to Russia were valued at US$ 1579 million. Main Indian exports to Russia are pharmaceuticals; tea, coffee and spices; apparel and clothing; edible preparations; and engineering goods. Main Indian imports from Russia are iron and steel; fertilizers; non-ferrous metals; paper products; coal and briquettes; and cereals.

The India-Russia Inter-Governmental Commission on Trade, Economic, Scientific, Technological and Cultural Cooperation (IRIGC) has had 13 sessions so far and is co-chaired by the External Affairs Minister from the Indian side and a Deputy Prime Minister from the Russian side. There are six Joint Working Groups [WG] under the IRIGC, namely, WG on Trade and Economy [trade and financial matters], WG on Energy [oil and gas, thermal and hydel power, non-conventional energy], WG on Metallurgy and Mining [steel, non-ferrous metal, coal], WG on Science and Technology; WG on Communication and Information Technology; and WG on Culture and Tourism. The 13th of the IRIGC was held in Moscow on 12 October 2007.

The two countries have set-up India-Russia Forum on Trade and Investment at the level of the two Commerce Ministers to promote trade, investment and economic cooperation. The first Forum was held in New Delhi on 12-13 February 2007 which was attended by the Minister of Commerce and Industry and the Russian Minister of Economic Development and Trade, apart from a large number of business representatives from both side. The Minister of Commerce and Industry, Shri Kamal Nath participated in the 11th St. Petersburg International Economic Forum on June 9-10, 2007.

In February 2006, India and Russia also set up a Joint Study Group to examine ways to increase trade to US$ 10 bn by 2010 and to study feasibility of a Comprehensive Economic Cooperation Agreement (CECA). The Group finalized its report after its fourth meeting in Moscow in July 2007. It has been agreed that a Joint Task Force would monitor the implementation of the recommendation made in the Joint Study Group Report, including considering CECA.

11.2.7 Defence Cooperation: Defence relations between India and the Russian Federation have a historical perspective. Russia has been an important supplier of defence goods for several decades. Today, the cooperation is not limited to a buyer-seller relationship but includes joint research and development, training, service to service contacts, including joint exercises. The last joint naval exercises took place in April 2007 in the Sea of Japan and joint airborne exercises were held in September 2007 in Russia. There is an Inter-Governmental commission on military-technical cooperation co-chaired by the two Defence Ministers. The Seventh session of this Inter-Governmental Commission was held in October 2007 in Moscow. During the visit, an Agreement on joint development and production of prospective multi role fighters was signed between the two countries.

11.2.8 Renewal of Indo-Russia Defence Deal: India and Russia have decided to renew defence cooperation programme. The defence cooperation programme which expired in 2010 has been renewed again. India would be spending close to $ 36 billion (approximately ₹ 1.8 lakh crore) to develop and produce the GenNext fighter plane. The Indian Air Force (IAF) plans to induct between 250-300 of these fighters by 2030.

Russia still remains the largest source of Indian weapons. Russia has agreed to extend help India build the Advanced Technology Vessel (ATV) and the air defence vessel. ATV is an indigenous project for the development of nuclear submarines.

At the 5th Indo-Russian Inter-Governmental Commission (IRIGC) for military-technical cooperation meeting, both the countries decided to jointly manufacture a Multi-role Transport Aircraft (MTA) for the air forces of the two countries.

11.3 India and China

India has consistently viewed bilateral relations with China in a positive spirit. India seeks friendly, cooperative, good-neighbourly and mutually beneficial relations with China on the basis of the Five Principles of Peaceful Coexistence, mutual sensitivity to each other's concerns and equality. We remain committed to the process of dialogue to resolve outstanding differences and to build a strategic and cooperative partnership for peace and prosperity.

As early as on January 1, 1969, Prime Minister Indira Gandhi indicated at a press conference that India would be prepared to hold talks with China without any preconditions in order to seek ways of solving conflicts between the two countries.

Further exploration of Mao's intriguing signal was delayed by the outbreak of the Bangladesh War of Liberation in 1971. India and China found themselves ranged on opposite sides. India sympathized deeply with the cause of the people of Bangladesh. Millions of Bangladeshis fled to India to save their lives and honour and it became clear that they would not return to their homes unless the Pakistani occupation forces were made to leave the country. China, on the other hand, sided with its quasi-ally, Pakistan. The situation was further complicated by the fact that the Bangladesh struggle coincided with a major development on the global scene. The United States decided to form an entente with China in order to contain Soviet influence. Anxious to cultivate its new ally, the Nixon Administration went to the extent of secretly encouraging China to take military action against India, ignoring strong American public support for the Bangladeshis.

Further difficulties arose from the Chinese stance on two internal developments in India. The first of these was the designation of Arunachal Pradesh as a centrally administered territory. Beijing's negative reaction to this development reflected her territorial claims to this area. Beijing also refused to accept Sikkim's full integration into the Indian Union in 1974. Despite the fact that Sikkim never had an international personality, China took the position–the only country in the world to do so – that Sikkim was an independent state.

Because of these complications, the pursuit of improved India-China relations could only be resumed in 1976. In that year, the two countries decided to restore ambassadorial-level diplomatic ties after a gap of 15 years. India took the first step by appointing K.R. Narayanan – who later became the president of India–as its ambassador and China quickly reciprocated by posting an ambassador to New Delhi.

The next major step was foreign minister Vajpayee's visit to China in February 1979–the first high-level visit between the two countries since 1960.

Among the issues Vajpayee took up with the Chinese was the question of Beijing's assistance to certain insurgent groups operating in north-eastern India. He received an assurance from his host that this was a matter that belonged to the past. There has been no evidence since that date of any Chinese involvement with insurgents operating in India. A major irritant in bilateral ties was thus removed.

Vajpayee's visit was interrupted by a regional development. China decided to launch an armed attack against Vietnam while Vajpayee was on Chinese soil and Deng Xiaoping added to India's discomfiture by tactlessly drawing a parallel with the Chinese action against India in 1962. The Indian foreign minister had to cut short his visit in these circumstances. In many ways, Rajiv Gandhi's visit to China in December 1988 marked a turning point in India-China relations.

It was the first visit by an Indian prime minister to China since 1954 and it reciprocated, after a gap of 28 years, Premier Zhou En-lai's 1960 visit. Rajiv Gandhi's discussions with Chinese leaders significantly enhanced mutual confidence and understanding. A Joint Working Group was formed for negotiations on the boundary issue and for exploring ways of maintaining peace and tranquillity along the Line of Actual Control in the border areas. Another Working Group was set up to promote trade and investment. Agreements were signed on cooperation in cultural exchanges, on science and technology and on civil aviation. In short, steps were taken to promote all-round bilateral cooperation and to maintain a tension-free Line of Actual Control while the two sides continued to seek a peaceful solution to the border issue.

This is the basis on which India-China ties have been developed since 1988. There has been a regular exchange of high-level visits between the two countries. The Joint Working Group on border issues negotiated an important Agreement on Maintenance of Peace and Tranquillity along the Line of Actual Control. This was formally signed during Prime Minister Rao's visit to China in 1993. Another important agreement, covering military confidence-building measures along the Line of Actual Control, was signed when President Jiang Zemin visited India in 1996. Both parties have honoured these accords and the Line of Actual Control has remained free from tension. Premier Li Peng visited India in December 1991. Prime Minister Narasimha Rao visited China in September 1993 during which the Agreement on the Maintenance of Peace and Tranquillity along the Line of Actual Control (LAC) in the India-China Border Area was signed and the India-China Expert Group of Diplomatic and Military Officers to assist the JWG was set up. This Agreement provides for both sides to respect the status quo on the border, clarify the LAC where there are doubts and undertake CBMs.

11.3.1 New Rides in Bilateral Relations: Chinese Premier Wen Jiabao visited India in April 2005. During the visit, the two Prime Ministers signed a

Joint Statement which establishes a strategic cooperative partnership for peace and prosperity between the two countries. Eleven other agreements were signed. The agreement on political parameters and guiding principles for the India-China boundary question represents the successful conclusion of the first phase of the work of the Special Representatives and lays down the parameters and principles for their future discussions to explore the political settlement of the boundary question. A protocol on Confidence Building Measures was also concluded which further underpins the maintenance of peace and tranquillity along the Line of Actual Control in the India-China border areas.

During the Chinese Premier Wen Jiaobao to India, when the prime ministers of the world's two most populous countries signed 11 groundbreaking agreements. The main agreement was aimed at resolving the boundary dispute that has bedevilled relations between them for more than four decades.

The accords included improving trade and cultural ties, economic cooperation and expanding aviation links.

The agreement on political parameters and guiding principles for the India-China boundary question represents the successful conclusion of the first phase of the work of the Special Representatives and lays down the parameters and principles for their future discussions to explore the political settlement of the boundary question. The leaders of the two countries have, therefore agreed to establish an India-China Strategic and Cooperative Partnership for Peace and Prosperity.

A protocol on Confidence Building Measures was also concluded which further underpins the maintenance of peace and tranquillity along the Line of Actual Control in the India-China border areas. The two sides agreed to cooperate in the field of energy security and conservation, including among others, encouraging relevant departments and units of the two countries to engage in the survey and exploration of petroleum and natural gas resources in third countries.

11.3.2 Border Solution: The Indian Prime Minister and Chinese President met on the sidelines of the UN General Assembly. They agreed to seek a pragmatic and 'reasonable solution' to the boundary dispute on an urgent basis.

India and China will make meaningful and mutually acceptable adjustments to their respective positions on the boundary question, so as to arrive at a package settlement to the boundary question. The differences on the boundary question should not be allowed to affect the overall development of bilateral relations. The boundary settlement must be final, covering all sectors of the India-China boundary. The frontier "should be along well-defined and easily identifiable natural geographical features to be mutually agreed upon between by India and China", and interests of settled populations in the border areas will be safeguarded in any final settlement. Their dialogue will include matters related to international economic forums and institutions. China has also set up financial dialogue mechanisms with the United States, Britain, France and the European Union.

India enjoys other advantages over China. It has the largest English-speaking population on Earth–English being the lingua franca of global business.

In recent years, trade and tourism between the two countries have developed rapidly. Bilateral trade volumes reached US$ 63.1 billion in 2010-11, up 34 percent over the previous year. Indian exports during the above period were US$ 19.61 billion and imports from China constituted US$ 43.47 billion.

China has supported India becoming an observer at the Shanghai Cooperation (SCO) Organisation and attending the East Asia Summit. China has also extended its support for India's participation in the ITER nuclear project in Europe.

11.3.3 MoU in Mining Sector: India and China signed a MOU for cooperation in the mining sector.

1. to promote cooperation on research in the field of metallic and non-metallic minerals,
2. to formulate mining regulation policies, technical assistance and training programmes, and
3. to undertake joint ventures in other countries.

The MOU will be the basis of mutually beneficial exchange of information on mining investment legislation, projects on mineral exploration and exploitation, trading of mineral products, service and technologies. The areas identified for cooperation include sustainable development of mining industry, mineral resources assessment, technology transfer, training programme on geological mapping, development of geological database, mineral economics and environmental aspects related to mining.

These goals will be achieved by scholar exchanges, joint training programmes, formation of a workgroup for joint research, exchange of databank and digitized maps. The relevant organizations nominated by both sides shall sign agreements on technical assistance and collaboration to determine specific terms and conditions for implementation.

11.3.4 Year of friendship, 2006: India and China also agreed to sustain the positive momentum in their bilateral engagement on the brief review of the satisfactory and comprehensive development of trilateral relations. The major areas were discussed between the two countries. These are:

1. Trade Proliferation.
2. Economic engagement.

3. Promotion of Science and Technology.
4. Promotion of culture and education as areas of cooperation.

The India-China relationship has now entered a new phase. Both sides have also agreed that it is necessary to look for ways and means to maintain the positive momentum in the bilateral relationship from a long term strategic perspective as well as to resolve the border issue.

India and China also have agreed to jointly participate in multilateral military exercises, including those focussed on non-traditional security and increase meeting points between army personnel deployed along the Sino-Indian border. During Vij's visit, the two sides reiterated their agreement to ensure peace and tranquillity along the boundary. Both sides also expressed their desire to increase military exchanges at all levels.

A very important dimension of the evolving Sino-Indian relationship is based on the energy requirements of their industrial expansion and their readiness to proactively secure them by investing in the oilfields abroad-in Africa, the Middle East and Central Asia. On the one hand, these ventures entail competition (which has been evident in oil biddings for various international projects recently). But on the other hand, a degree of cooperation too is visible, as they are increasingly confronting bigger players in the global oil market. This cooperation was sealed in Beijing on January 12, 2006 during the visit of Petroleum and Natural Gas Minister Mani Shankar Aiyar, who signed an agreement which envisages ONGC Videsh Ltd. (OVL) and the China National Petroleum Corporation (CNPC) placing joint bids for promising projects elsewhere. This may have important consequences for their international relations.

On July 6, 2006, China and India re-opened Nathula, an ancient trade route which was part of the Silk Road. Nathula is a pass through the Himalayas and it was closed 44 years prior to 2006 when the Sino-Indian War broke out in 1962. The initial agreement for the re-opening of the trade route was reached in 2003, and a final agreement was formalized on June 18th, 2006. Officials say that the re-opening of border trade will help ease the economic isolation of the region. In November 2006, China and India had a verbal spat over claim of the north-east Indian state of Arunachal Pradesh. India claimed that China was occupying 38,000 square kilometres of its territory in Kashmir, while China claimed the whole of Arunachal Pradesh as its own.

11.3.5 Sino-Indian Relations in 2007-2008: Apart from the high-level exchanges, the bilateral dialogue mechanisms provides greater depth to India-China bilateral relations and a systemic means of facilitating enhancement and implementation of existing initiatives and identifying newer ones. The various mechanisms evolved and instituted between India and China include Strategic

Dialogue, Joint Working Group (JWG), Expert Group (EG) dealing with the boundary issues, meeting of Special Representatives (SR), Foreign Office Consultations, Security Dialogue, Policy Planning Dialogue, and the dialogue on Counter-Terrorism.

11.3.6 Trade and Economic Relations: India-China trade and economic cooperation is marked by strong political commitment of the leaderships of two countries in this regard. The structural framework of economic cooperation is continuously strengthened and expanded. This includes the Joint Economic Group, Joint Study Group to examine potential complementarities and to draw up a roadmap with recommendations, Joint Working Group (JWG) on Trade to resolve trade issues, JWG on Steel, JWG on Coal, Financial Dialogue, Civil Aviation Cooperation, etc.

Bilateral trade and economic relationship is marked by rapid growth in two-way trade; up from US$ 338 million in 1992 to US$ 63.1 billion in 2011. Indian exports to China have shown continuous positive growth since 2000 and India has a trade surplus of US$ 1.7 billion in 2004. Bilateral trade in the first five months of 2005 was US$ 7.71 billion of which Indian exports were US$ 4.62 billion and imports were US$ 3.09 billion.

During the visit of Prime Minister Vajpayee to China in June 2003, the two sides agreed to establish the India-China Joint Study Group (JSG) to examine the potential complementarities between the two countries in expanded trade and economic cooperation. The JSG submitted its report to the two Prime Ministers during the visit of the Chinese Premier to India in April 2005, in which it has identified a series of measures related to trade in goods, trade in services, investments and other areas of economic cooperation, and recommended their expeditious implementation to remove impediments and facilitate enhanced economic engagement between India and China.

The two Prime Ministers tasked the Ministerial-level India-China Joint Economic Group (JEG) to consider these recommendations and coordinate their implementation. The JSG has also recommended an India-China Regional Trading Arrangement, comprising of trade in goods and services, investments, identified understandings for trade and investment promotion and facilitation, and measures for promotion of economic cooperation in identified sectors. The two Prime Ministers agreed to appoint a Joint Task Force to study in detail the feasibility of, and the benefits that may derive from, the India-China Regional Trading Arrangement and give recommendations regarding its content.

According to Government of India statistics, about US$ 126.45 million worth of FDI inflows have been received from China for the during the period April 2000 to March 2012. As per the figures released by China's Ministry of

Commerce, cumulative Chinese investments into India till December 2011 stood at US$ 575.70 million, whereas cumulative Indian investments into China till December 2011 stood at US$ 441.70 million.

Close to 100 Chinese companies have established offices/operations in India. Many large Chinese state-owned companies in the field of machinery and infrastructure construction have won projects in India and have opened project offices in India. These include Sinosteel, Shougang International, Baoshan Iron and Steel Ltd., Sany Heavy Industry Ltd., Chongqing Lifan Industry Ltd., China Dongfang International, Sino Hydro Corporation etc.

With the growth in bilateral trade between India and China in the last few years, many Indian companies have started setting up Chinese operations to service both their Indian and MNC clientele in China. Some of the prominent Indian companies in China include Dr. Reddy's Laboratories, Aurobindo Pharma, Matrix Pharma, NIIT, Bharat Forge, Infosys, TCS, APTECH, Wipro, Mahindra Satyam, Dr. Reddy's, Essel Packaging, Suzlon Energy, Reliance Industries, Mahindra and Mahindra, Binani Cements, etc.

11.3.7 Strategic Economic Dialogue in Beijing on 26 September 2011:

India and China held their first Strategic Economic Dialogue in Beijing on 26 September 2011. India and China agreed to deepen bilateral investment cooperation, further open up markets to each other and improve the investment agreed to strengthen cooperation on energy efficiency and conservation, as well as on environmental protection. In order to promote sustainable development, the two sides agreed to cooperate in the renewable energy sector. The two sides agreed to host the next SED in 2012 in India. Strategic Economic Dialogue will increase mutual understanding and trust between India and China. Through this dialogue, both nations could share their experience to achieve economic development. Although the bilateral trade crossed 61 billion US dollars in 2011, India was left with deficit of over 40.9 billion US dollars due to accelerated exports from China.

12

India and Europe

12.1 India and European Union (EU)

EU-India relations go back to the early 1960s. India was among the first countries to establish diplomatic relations with the (then) EEC. Then bilateral agreements signed in 1973, 1981. The 1994 cooperation agreement, a wide-ranging 3rd generation agreement signed between EU and India took bilateral relations beyond merely trade and economic cooperation. Together with the Joint Political Statement signed in 1993, it opened the way for annual ministerial meetings and a broad political dialogue. Since then, dialogues have been held at different levels and at regular intervals.

The EU, which has strategic partnerships with only five other countries (USA, Canada, Russia, Japan and China) now sees India as a "regional and global leader engaging increasingly on equal terms with other world powers".

In pre-Cold War days, India had supported EU. India naturally showed keen interest in developing closer politico-economic links with the members of the EU. In fact, India tried to establish relations with EEC right from the time of its inception. In 1962, India established a diplomatic mission to the EEC.

India also signed a bilateral agreement on Jute and coir and secured duty free quotas for Indian exports of silk, cotton, handloom fabrics and handicrafts. In 1971, the EEC announced Generalized System of Preferences (GSP) for third world countries.

After the admission of Britain into the EEC in 1973, Indian trade with Britain suffered a setback. India tried to overcome this problem by signing a commercial cooperation agreement (CCA) with EEC to develop and diversify trade between India and EEC. To promote better trade relations, between India and EEC, an Indo-EEC joint commission was setup. EEC offered concessions in trade terms to India. As a result of these concessions, India's trade with EEC considerably increased.

There was four to seven fold increase in community's imports on Indian goods, precious stones and textiles. In 1976, a committee was setup by India and EEC, to select and coordinate the areas of cooperation in the field of science and technology. The committee recommended cooperation in new fields like:

1. New sources of energy.

2. Management of scientific information.
3. Environmental research.
4. Remote of natural resources.

In the meanwhile, India continued to export textiles to the EEC member on the basis of the multi-fibre agreement made under the auspices of GATT negotiations. However, the community introduced unilateral restrictions on their imports to protect their domestic industries. India naturally felt disturbed over the growing trade deficit on account of protectionist policies of the community.

In 1980, Indian trade centre was setup at Brussels to promote trade relations between India and EEC. The Indian trade centre tried to promote trade in four sectors i.e. electronics, engineering goods, leather and jute.

In 1981, India and EEC signed a new commercial and Economic cooperation agreement which covered industry, science, technology, research and development.

In 1982, the Council of EC Chambers of Commerce was setup in India to promote Industrial and Commercial Cooperation between India and EU. It particularly tried to encourage business-to-business cooperation. An Indo-EC joint business forum was created to facilitate open dialogue between the European and Indian businessmen.

With the adoption of the policy of liberalisation and globalization in the 1990s by India, the EC and India were drawn still closer. In 1992, an Indo-EU Business Forum was setup. It provided a useful forum to the Indian and European businessmen to interact with each other.

The Business Forum tried to infuse new technology and financial resources in India for upgrading infrastructure. It also discussed a plan for upgrading quality in India so that it could export goods of quality for the international market.

In 1992, India and EU signed a new cooperation agreement on partnership and development. The two countries agreed to cooperate in the fields of:

1. Energy.
2. Telecommunication.
3. Scientific research.
4. Information technology.
5. Environment.
6. Transport.
7. Natural resources.
8. Tourism.
9. Trade promotion.

This agreement was of great significance to India. Another notable feature of this agreement was that it was bilateral in nature and outside the purview of

GATT. India's trade with EU showed a steep rise during the year 1993.

In 1993, India and EU launched standards and quality programme. European Commission helped India in improving standards and quality of Indian products for the Indian food industry. In this programme, EC also agreed to provide three things: technical assistance in standards, quality control, intellectual property rights (IPR). In 1994-95, the Indo-EU trade suffered a set back following adoption of a new GSP. The previous system of ceilings and quotas were abolished and new system of modification of tariff according to the sensitivity of the product was established.

Despite the above setbacks, efforts were made to strengthen the Indo-EU trade. In 1996-97, the European business information centre was setup to encourage two way trade and investment flows between Europe and India. In 1998-99, the foreign ministers of the 15 EU member states met at Dublin and decided to set up an India Experts Group to improve internal coordination with India. In 1999-2000, the EU representatives demanded more easy access of the European goods to the Indian market. On the other hand, India expressed its concern over EU's anti dumping measures and restrictions on visa for software professionals.

In 2001-2002, a round table meeting was held to upgrade India- EU ties. As a result of this meeting the two sides agreed to setup a joint working group on terrorism as part of their efforts to deal with the menace. The other issues taken up at the round table included:

1. Social and economic aspect of globalization.
2. Foreign direct investment.
3. Science and research.
4. Diversity of regional development models.
5. Indian information technology sector.

The Commission Communication for an "EU-India Enhanced Partnership" of June 1996 was a leap forward and contributed to put the Commission in the driver's seat of EU-India relations. Council and EP endorsed the Commission approach. The Commission Communication of 16 June 2004 was another milestone, as it sets out concrete proposals to up-grade the relationship to a Strategic Partnership. Council in its conclusions of 11 October 2004 endorsed the Commission's approach.

In order to provide greater coherence and focus to all the various activities being undertaken as well as undertake new initiatives, the European Commission has prepared a comprehensive Communication outlining in detail its views on various areas in which a strategic partnership could be forged with India. This document examines sector by sector how current activities can be streamlined and new actions launched. When implemented, they will be the basis of a stronger and more intensive relationship over the entire gamut of exchanges from political to multilateral, economic to science and technology, academic, cultural and civil society.

12.1.1 India-EU Joint Commission: The 15th EU-India Joint Commission meeting took place on October 24-25, 2005 in Delhi under the chairmanship of Indian Secretary for Commerce Mr. S.N. Menon and European Commission Deputy Director General for External Relations Herve Jouanjean. The meeting, which was held in an extremely productive and cordial atmosphere, confirmed the determination of India and the EU to operationalise the commitments made in the "Joint Action Plan" adopted at the EU-India Summit of September 7. Broad agreement was achieved on issues such as the negotiation of an EU-India maritime transport agreement; discussions on an horizontal civil aviation agreement; the designation of members of the newly-established "EU-India CEO Round Table"; the EU-India dialogue on employment and social affairs; industrial policy issues; the protection of intellectual property rights; bilateral cooperation on environment and climate change; science and technology; education, civil society exchanges and cultural cooperation as well as the programming of EC development assistance in India.

12.1.2 India–EU Strategic Partnership: The strategic partnership represents a "substantive upgrading" of the bilateral relationship. The strategic partnership is based on four basic cooperation in areas covering politics, trade, culture and technology. This was elaborated on a comprehensive EU-India Action Plan for the strategic partnership and a new joint political declaration. India and European Union (EU) pledged to bolster cooperation to combat international terrorism while agreeing to expand trade and investment flows.

Condemning all acts of terrorism, India and the EU pledged to take comprehensive and sustained measures to combat the menace. They decided to intensify cooperation on issues including higher education, film production and tourism. They also resolved to step up collective action to fight proliferation of WMDs as well as the means of delivery in recognition of shared concerns of the international community. The joint statement listed a 32-point bilateral agenda and identified some key areas for implementation immediately. This would include a mechanism for dialogue on nuclear disarmament and non-proliferation.

And a new joint political declaration based on the EU's proposal on the partnership and India's response for approval at the 6th summit. They agreed to encourage holding of regular, institutionalised parliamentary exchanges, promotion of cooperation between political parties, trade unions, business associations, universities and civil societies, exchange of views and possible cooperation in conflict resolution, peace operation and reconstruction of nations.

They also agreed to set up an energy panel to coordinate joint efforts and organise joint workshops on automotive engineering, genomics and life sciences and nanotechnology.

On the political front, the partnership would involve institutionalised dialogue on disarmament and non-proliferation. Apart from this it would also contain issues such as peacekeeping, conflict prevention and post-conflict construction. In the political terms, closer cooperation is important as EU represents an important pole in a multipolar world. They also pledged to "enhance collective action to fight the proliferation of weapons of mass destruction as well as their means of delivery."

India is lobbying hard to be included in the new Generalised System of Preferences (GSP) scheme being worked out by the European Union so that it can continue to have the preferential access to the textiles market of European countries. Under the GSP, the EU offers market access to developing countries (LDCs) duty-free or at reduced import duties. The EU is working on a new GSP scheme, which will be valid for the next three years. If the EU maintains its earlier GSP qualification criteria of including countries exporting less than 12 percent of the ED's total textile imports, then India will easily fall into the category of beneficiary countries and can export at one-fifth of the existing duty rates. However, if the EU reduces the threshold limit giving in to the demands of some of its members, then India could be in trouble.

12.1.3 EU-India: Country Strategy Paper 2007-2013: India has witnessed rapid economic growth in the past decade, and it has now become one of the emerging economies in Asia. As India continues on this path, as most observers expect it to, the need for development assistance will gradually decrease, and future EC Country Strategy Papers (CSP) should increasingly focus on other areas of co-operation. This CSP (2007-2013) should therefore be regarded as transitional, showing a progressive shift from development assistance towards support to pro-poor sector reform policies and other areas of mutual interest, including economic co-operation.

India is occupying two worlds simultaneously. In the first, rapid economic growth and social changes occur. In the other, a percentage of the population appears to be left behind due to lack of good social services, low employment opportunities and few prospects. Bridging this gap will be a major challenge. With more than a billion people and one third of the world's poor, India needs rapid growth, together with strong employment creation and extended social protection, to reduce poverty and sustain income increases for its very young population. Structural reforms and social cohesion are needed to accelerate growth and substantially reduce poverty. Promoting full and productive employment is also a central objective in this respect. A major effort is still necessary if India is to meet the Millennium Development Goals (MDGs).

Therefore, India's two main challenges are:

1. Making its development more inclusive, towards an increased social cohesion and a substantial reduction of poverty, in line with the MDGs.
2. Deepening and widening structural reforms, including better governance and infrastructure, in order to improve the investment climate, boost productivity and accelerate growth.
3. EC cooperation for 2007-13 will address these challenges through a two-pronged approach:

- Assist India in meeting the MDGs by providing budget support to the social sector (health/education), encompassing best practice models in good governance, decentralised decision-making and development, including innovative methods for improved service delivery to address poverty, gender issues, institutional reforms and public sector management.
- Implement the EU-India Partnership through an ambitious Action Plan with a view to supporting India's pro-poor sector reform policies, promote dialogue in areas of mutual interest and enhance economic co-operation.

Under this Action Plan, developed between the EU and India and agreed at the 6th EU-India Summit on 7 September 2005, specific dialogues and actions are envisaged for a wide range of areas where the EU and India have jointly identified a scope for enhanced co-operation leading to better governance and policy-making. The Action Plan foresees initiating economic sectoral dialogues in a variety of sectors. It also foresees the strengthening of activities in civil society and cross-cultural cooperation, as well as academic and education exchanges.

This CSP, therefore, will focus on these two priorities, namely:

1. Support for the social sectors (health and education), and
2. Support to the economic, academic, civil society and cultural activities foreseen in the Action Plan.

12.2 India and France

India and France have enjoyed cordial and substantive ties, with regular interaction between the leadership of both countries which began intensifying since the seventies. The last decade has witnessed particular strengthening of the Indo-French relationship, and, today, a long-term partnership is taking shape between the two countries. Amongst the cultural events of significance that have taken place between the two countries, mention could be made of the Festival of

India in held in France in 1985-86; the Festival of France in India in 1989-90; the three-month long 'Seasons of France in India' in the first quarter of 2003, the first ever Picasso exhibition held in India in December 2001-January 2002 under the Indo- French Cultural Exchange programme; the two-month long festival on contemporary India, held in 2002, in the Parisian suburb of Boulogne-Billancourt showcasing the richness of Indian music, dance, cinema, art and fashion. The apex French literary public body made India the 'Country of honour' for its annual literary festival 'Les Belles Etrangères' in November 2002 and invited 20 Indian authors to travel to France for a series of lectures, panel discussions and book readings. Since the 54th Cannes International Film Festival in May 2001, when the inauguration of the first-ever India Pavilion took place, our participation in the festival is continuously increasing every year. In 2005, Minister of Culture Shri Jaipal Reddy led the delegation to the Cannes Film Festival.

Over the past few years, there has been a significant increase in exchange of visits at the highest level, set in motion by the landmark January 1998 visit to India by President Chirac, followed by several visits in both directions by senior leaders, Ministers, Parliamentarians, opinion makers, and officials. Efforts on both sides have come to increasingly focus on realising a long-term relationship, based on greater understanding and a similar vision of a multi-polar world.

An elaborate dialogue architecture has evolved in the wake of these political initiatives, and provides a framework for regular, structured consultations between France and India on a variety of issues of mutual concern. Apart from the annual consultations between the two foreign ministries at the Foreign Secretary level, France and India have also instituted a high-level *Strategic Dialogue*, a special biennial *Joint Working Group for Terrorism*, *Indo- French High Level Committee on Defence* and *Indo-French Joint Committee on Economic & Technical Cooperation.* In addition to these numerous official forums of interaction, the '*Indo-French Forum*' (which was launched in 1998, and last met in Paris on 13-14 October 2003), brings together representatives of the two countries from the fields of art, culture, science and technology, business and academia.

Over the past few years, there has been a significant increase in exchange of visits at the highest level, set in motion by the landmark January 1998 visit to India by President Chirac, a visit to France by PM Vajpayee the same year. In September 2005, Prime Minister Dr. Manmohan Singh visited France. In February 2006, President Chirac paid a State visit to India. Besides the Head of State/Head of Government visits, there have been a series of visits in both directions by senior leaders, Ministers, Parliamentarians, opinion makers, and officials. President Nicolas Sarközy also paid a State visit to India from 25-26 January, 2008.

Mr. Nicolas Sarközy, President of France accompanied by a high level Ministerial and business delegation paid a state visit to India from 25 to 26, January 2008 at the invitation of the President, Smt. Pratibha Devisingh Patil. This was his first visit to India after assuming office in May, 2007. He was the Guest of Honour at the Republic Day Parade.

During President Sarkozy's visit to India in January 2008, several Agreements in the field of Defence, Consular, Nuclear Research, Development Cooperation and Neurosciences were signed. These include the Agreement on Mutual Protection of Classified Information in the field of Defence, Agreement between India and France on Transfer of Sentenced Prisoners, Agreement between Commissariat a L' Energie Atomique (CEA) France and DAE, India for construction and operation of Jules Horowitz (JH) Reactor, Agreement between the two Governments on India-French Development Cooperation through AFD and MoU on an International Associated Laboratory in the field of Neuro Science.

Other than these numerous official fora of interaction, the 'Indo-French Forum' (which was launched in 1998, and last met in October 2006, in Paris) brings together representatives of the two countries from the fields of art, culture, science and technology, business and academia.

Prime Minister Manmohan Singh visited France en route New York to attain UNGA 60th World summit with a view that India is committed to further strengthening the privileged relations of strategic partnership with France.
India's intention is to further expand cooperation with France in the fields of

1. Trade and investment.
2. Defence.
3. Space.
4. Civilian nuclear energy.
5. Advanced science and technology.
6. Cultural and civilisational ties.

Dr. Singh had wide-ranging discussions with French President Jacques Chirac, Prime Minister Dominique Villepin, and other leaders. He also had meetings with the chief executive officers of some major French companies to apprise them of the emerging opportunities for trade and investment in India.

12.2.1 Scorpene Deal: During his visit to New York on the second leg of his tour, the Prime Minister participated in the high-level segment of events being organised by the United Nations to mark the 60th anniversary of its founding day. Various aspects of U.N. reform, including the expansion the Security Council, was on the agenda. On September 14, he addressed the General Assembly, which reviewed the implementation of the Millennium Development Goals (MDGs) adopted a decade ago.

By publicly announcing the purchase of 43 Airbus aircraft from the European consortium in which France has a substantial stake, New Delhi has sent Paris a strong message: that India counts France as one of its major strategic partners; and that closer Indian ties with the United States do not preclude a sustained political, economic, and strategic relationship with France. India announced the purchase of six Scorpene submarines from France during the Paris visit, which interestingly comes at a time when U.S. Congressmen are threatening to call for a review of Washington's landmark civilian nuclear cooperation pact with New Delhi.

12.2.2 Boosting Bilateral Cooperation: This visit is an attempt by both sides to reinforce and further cement traditionally excellent ties that appeared, these past months, to have slipped into the doldrums. Dr. Singh's visit takes place just days after an extremely successful exchange of views during the 14th edition of the Indo-French Strategic Dialogue on September 2.

While there is elation at India's desire to re-invest in the bilateral and strategic relationship, Paris is worried that New Delhi's rapprochement with Washington could diminish its own importance. Although France officially declined to comment, the U.S. State Department's remarks seeking clarification on India's stand on Iran's nuclear policy did not go unnoticed. U.S. Congressman Tom Lantos put it bluntly when he said the bold new Indo-U.S. strategic partnership "is predicated on reciprocity."

French officials are at pains to point out that France is not at all put out by the nuclear pact India signed with the U.S. France has been pushing for a similar special regime for India by the Nuclear Suppliers' Group on condition that it meets certain obligations that would align it with the non-proliferation regime (separating its civilian and military nuclear programmes, placing its civilian facilities under International Atomic Energy Agency safeguards, and adhering to the Additional Protocol on civilian nuclear facilities). France has worked within the NSG to strengthen India's claims for special status. So the India-U.S. pact is seen as a source of hope since any relaxation in NSG rules would allow French companies such as Areva or Cogema to compete for contracts to build nuclear reactors in India.

France hoped that the change in government in New Delhi would lead India towards greater multilateralism and distance it from the U.S. The reverse proved to be true. India has a definitely pro-American attitude and the deepening of Indo-U.S. ties is very significant. American logic in zeroing in on India as a strategic partner was not difficult to understand, as India is the perfect counterweight to China.

What is true of the Indo-French relationship is that it has come a long way in the past 15 years, especially in the way in which India is perceived in France. There was a time when Indian embassy officials despaired of seeing a single positive story on India in the news media. Now barely a day goes by without comment and news reports on India, not so much about its internal political situation as about its emerging economic prowess.

India has become a favourite destination of students wishing to do internships in international companies. The country's overall visibility in French minds has shot up despite the fact that business ties, although in progression, can hardly said to be flourishing when compared to other EU countries such as Britain or Germany. France comes 9th on the list of foreign investors (March 2012) and two-way trade between India and France totalled € 4.7 billion during January-December 2011. The balance of trade remains in India's favour.

A great fillip was given to commercial ties with a flurry of contracts being signed recently, especially in the private sector. IndiGo, Spice and Kingfisher Airlines were the stars of the Paris Air Show, totalling up orders upwards of US$ 12 billion for Airbus. Renault, Alcatel, Lafarge, Saint Gobain, and other companies have recently struck major deals to produce in India, both for an expanding local market as well as for exports.

But while there is scope for deeper and closer contacts in all fields—cultural, commercial, strategic—India is not unaware of France's limited role as a world power. French concerns about India have also been heightened by the fact that President Chirac has been weakened as a result of the French rejection of the European Constitution both within France and within Europe.

France also promised to leave "no stone unturned" to enable India to meet its civilian nuclear needs, a euphemism for a gradual dismantling of the restrictive Nuclear Suppliers Group (NSG).

Both the leaders issued a joint statement during the visit. In the statement France acknowledges for the need for full international civilian nuclear cooperation with India and will work towards this objective by working with other countries and the NSG and by deepening bilateral cooperation. France appreciated India's strong commitment to prevent weapons of mass destruction (WMD) proliferation and the ongoing steps it is taking in this regard. In this context, both countries will also work towards conclusion of a bilateral nuclear cooperation agreement. The two countries also agreed to work on "a framework agreement on defence cooperation," besides the promised dismantling of the NSG regime.

12.2.3 Commercial and Economic Relations: France is the 6th largest economy of the world and an important member of the G-8. Its technological strengths make it the leader in sectors such as aviation, space, food processing, transport, railways and agricultural research.

France is ranked 5th in the list of India's trading partners among EU countries (after the UK, Belgium, Germany and Italy). Indo-French bilateral trade has been growing over the years. Indo-French trade, at € 7.46 billion in 2011, is still below the potential.

Electrical equipment, aeronautical and space construction products, measuring and control equipments, iron and steel products, equipment for emission and transmission of sound and image, mechanical equipments, organic chemical products, para-chemicals, general and special usage machines, equipment for reception and recording of sound and image, etc.

A range of goods and services from the small and medium sector, garments, textiles and leather exports constitute a major share of India's exports to France. Non-traditional items like organic chemicals, refined petroleum products, metallic products, food products, gems and jewellery and para-chemical products are gaining ground.

Foreign Direct Investment (FDI) approved from France from April 2000 to March, 2012 was of the order of US$ 2.92 billion. The number of technical and financial collaborations approved with France is 915. France is the 9th largest foreign investor in the period April 2000 to March 2012. Indian investments in France have also been growing. Indian companies are active in IT, pharmaceuticals and plastic industry in France.

Cooperation in the field of science and technology comes within the purview of Indo-French Joint Committee for Scientific and Technological Cooperation (IFJCSTC). Along with the Indo-French Cultural Exchange Programme (IFCEP), the two agreements fall within the larger umbrella of the Indo-French Commission for Cooperation in the fields of Science, Education and Culture. The Indo-French Centre for the Promotion of Advanced Research (IFCPAR) was established in New Delhi in 1987 as a joint and equally funded project. It supports and finances joint research projects, bilateral workshops, seminars and exchange visits. An active programme of cooperation exists between the Centre for Scientific and Industrial Research (CSIR) and the French National Centre for Scientific Research (CNRS). A cooperation agreement also exists between the CNRS and the Department of Biotechnology of the Government of India. The long-standing cooperation between ISRO and the French Space Agency CNES in the exploration and research into the peaceful uses of Outer Space is an outstanding example of scientific collaboration. The current focus in this area is on new initiatives for setting up joint laboratories and projects in emerging technologies like water sciences, medical research, climatology, nano-technology, bio-technology and information technology. Recent examples of fruitful interaction include the Sixth Joint Working Group between the Indian Council of Medical R Medical Research and the French Institut National de la Santé et de la Recherche Medicale.

12.3 India and Netherlands

Recorded bilateral contacts between India and the Netherlands go back several centuries, and include the first voyage to the Indian Ocean by Cornelius Houtman in 1595-96 as well as by two other Dutch ships reaching India in 1597. The first recorded agreement between the two countries, of November 11, 1604, was between the Dutch East India Company and the Zamorin of Calicut, to form an alliance against the Portuguese military presence in India. In subsequent years, although the Dutch had trading outposts, with administrative control, on both the western and eastern coasts of India, the largest one being at Cochin, they did not try to further extend their territorial control, and the Dutch historians today assume that the Dutch in the 17th and 18th centuries did not want an empire in India. Moreover, their attention had begun to shift to the campaign to set up a colonial empire in Indonesia.

Independent India was, in Dutch eyes, a developing country and a sturdy democracy, but one struggling with several political, social and economic problems. While Dutch interest in India picked up in the mid-70s, it was only after the 1990s, when Indian economic liberalization programme gathered momentum that the Dutch began to focus on India. Prime Minister Wim Kok's visit to India in November 1999 signalled this renewed Dutch political interest in India. Impressed by India's sustained economic growth over the past several years and the evident sophistication of many sectors of the Indian economy, such as IT, bio-tech, space research and satellite technology, Dutch government and business circles have, despite their innate caution, began to move systematically towards expanding trade, investment and technological cooperation.

During 2002-03, the Netherlands commemorated the 400th anniversary of the establishment of relations with India, with a series of trade-related and cultural events both in the Netherlands and in India, including seminars on the impact of globalisation and on water management, a major conference on agro-processing, a modern dance drama, a visit to India by the top Dutch chamber music orchestra, and an exhibition of Dutch paintings from Indian collections. The two countries hold regular Foreign Office Consultations to discuss bilateral relations and regional and international issues. The last round of such consultations was held in

New Delhi in October 2003.

12.3.1 Important Bilateral Treaties and Agreements: Various agreements, which constitute a comprehensive framework for economic cooperation, are operational between India and the Netherlands. These include Air Services Agreement (May 1951), 1898 Treaty for the Mutual Surrender of Fugitive Criminals (effected in 1971), an Agreement on Economic and Technical Cooperation (February 1983), an MoU on Cooperation in Agriculture and Animal Husbandry (September 1990, June 1984), a Cultural Agreement (May 1985), an MoU and an Agreement on Scientific Cooperation (July and November 1985 respectively), a Convention for the Avoidance of Double Taxation and Prevention of Fiscal Evasion (July 1988), an Agreement for the promotion and protection of investments (November 1995), and an MoU on Investment Promotion (February 2004).

12.3.2 Bilateral Trade and Investment Cooperation: The bilateral trade between India and Netherlands has increased by 250 percent in the past five years (2006-2011) from US$ 3.83 billion to US$ 9.60 billion. Exports from India to the Netherlands in these five years have increased from US$ 2.67 billion to US$ 7.75 billion while Dutch exports to India increased from US$ 1.15 billion to US$ 1.85 billion percent. Netherlands now ranks 6th in the list of countries in terms of cumulative FDI inflows into India during the period April 2000 to March 2012 with total inflows amounting to about US$ 7.10 billion.

12.4 India and Germany Relations

In 1951, India was among the first four countries to establish diplomatic relations with the Federal Republic of Germany (the erstwhile West Germany) and was among the few countries to have supported German unification from the early stages. Both countries adopted an "Agenda for Indo-German Partnership in the 21st Century" during the visit of FM Joschka Fischer in May 2000. During the visit of Chancellor Schroeder in October 2001, the two countries agreed on building a 'strategic partnership'. It was agreed that there would be an annual Summit at the Heads of Government level. Prime Minister Dr. Manmohan Singh visited Germany from April 22-25, 2006 and jointly inaugurated the Hannover Trade Fair with German Chancellor Dr. Angela Merkel on April 23, 2006, in which India was the Partner Country. A bilateral Defence Cooperation Agreement was also signed on September 7, 2006 by the then Raksha Mantri, Shri Pranab Mukherjee, and the German Defence Minister, Dr. Franz Josef Jung, during the former's visit to Germany from September 5-8, 2006. Chancellor Merkel paid a state visit to India from October 29-November 1, 2007 at the invitation of Prime Minister Dr. Manmohan Singh.

12.4.1 Political Relations: Following World War II, India was the first country to end the state of war with Germany and among the first to grant the Federal Republic of Germany diplomatic recognition. It demonstrated sympathy and support for German reunification. India regards united Germany as an important partner in its quest for a new political role in the region and the world. Mutual high-level visits have given relations a considerable impetus.

Both countries are seeking to expand bilateral relations further, particularly in the economic sphere, and to cooperate in international bodies, for a reform of the United Nations, for example. The Indo-German consultation group, convened by Prime Minister Rao and Federal Chancellor Kohl in 1991 and constituted in Bonn in 1992, makes recommendations for the development of bilateral relations. The group holds annual meetings alternately in Germany and India, the latest in Hamburg in September 2004. There has been an Indo-German friendship group in the German parliament since 1971; the Indian parliament followed suit in the spring of 2003, setting up the Indo-German Parliamentary Forum. Further fields for deeper bilateral relations are set out in the Agenda for Indo-German Partnership in the 21st Century signed by both foreign ministers in May 2000.

The highlight of Indo-German bilateral relations was the state visit by German Chancellor Gerhard Schroeder to India between October 28-November 2, 2001. During the visit both sides availed the opportunity to review various facets of bilateral relationship and assess the rapidly evolving security situation in Afghanistan. Four loan agreements were signed for solar energy, fertilizer, polio and drinking water between Government of India and the KFW of Germany during the visit. The interaction between Indian and German CEOs both in New Delhi and in Bangalore were extremely useful for expanding mutually beneficial economic and commercial ties, particularly in IT and infrastructure. Germany and India have agreed to have regular bilateral annual summits.

The "Agenda for Indo-German Partnership in the 21st Century", a vision statement which provides a concrete plan for upgradation of bilateral relations through enhanced political exchanges, security dialogue, trade and investment, cultural exchanges and cooperation to combat international terrorism, drug trafficking and trade in arms, was adopted during the first visit. The primary focus of the second visit was the inauguration of the Festival of Germany in India.

12.4.2 Development Co-operation: Germany's development cooperation with India is a major component of German foreign policy and an important element of the two countries' bilateral relations. Despite economic advances and the successful fight against hunger and endemic disease, India faces problems with severe disparities between rich and poor, urban and rural areas and the resulting inadequate access to health care or education for large parts of the population. These deficits are a permanent impediment to development targets at the desired rate throughout the country. So there are still numerous intervention points for specific cooperation to improve people's living standards.

In its efforts to make its development cooperation efficient and give it a clearer profile, the German government has agreed with the Indian government on the following priorities:

1. Environment, conservation of natural resources.
2. Energy.
3. Health.
4. Economic reform (financial and private sectors).

Indo-German cooperation is conceived as a multisectoral approach aimed at poverty alleviation, the goal being to curb poverty by 50 percent by 2015.

Germany's development cooperation measures are carried out by the *Deutsche Gesellschaft für Technische Zusammenarbeit GmbH* (GTZ) and the *Kreditanstalt für Wiederaufbau* (KfW Group) on behalf of the Federal Ministry for Economic Cooperation and Development (BMZ) in coordination with the Federal Foreign Office. GTZ concentrates on Technical Cooperation (advisory services) and KfW on Financial Cooperation (investment projects). Because development cooperation with India cannot be divorced from economic and political developments in the country, many projects are carried out in close cooperation with business associations (chambers of commerce) and self-help organizations of small and medium-sized business.

On the political front, the German government is open to initiatives for developing regional, cross-border cooperation with neighbouring countries, catering also for the experience of other developing nations, in a South-South cooperative effort. Development policy dialogue at government level takes place in the annual intergovernmental negotiations.

12.4.3 Economic Relations: The Indo-German Joint Economic Commission set up in the early 1980s deals with matters of bilateral trade and investment under the joint chairmanship of the Federal Minister of Economics and Labour and the Indian Minister of Finance. Important work is also carried out by the working groups on coal, tourism and infrastructure.

The main Indo-German economic agreements include:

1. Double taxation agreement, which came into force on 19 December 1996.
2. Agreement on the promotion and protection of investments, which came into force in July 1998.
3. Exchange of notes on the protection of German investments in India of 15 October 1964.

4. Trade agreement of 31 March 1955.
5. Agreements on cooperation in scientific research and technological development of 1971 and 1974.

12.4.4 Bilateral Trade: Germany is India's fifth largest trading partner and the largest trading partner in Europe and accounts for about 3 percent of our global trade.

Indo-German two-way trade which had remained static at € 5 billion during 2001-2003 has dramatically rose to € 15.44 billion in 2010. The principal commodities accounting for the increase were engineering goods, textiles, leather products and pharmaceuticals.

Indo-German trade reached US$ 18.65 billion in 2010-11 up 18.5 percent over 2009-10. Indian exports were US$ 6.75 billion (+24.8 percent) and imports were US$ 11.89 billion (+15.2 percent). In 2010-11, bilateral trade increased by 19 percent to US$ 18.65 billion.

During the visit of Federal Chancellor Gerhard Schroeder to India in October 2004, the two Heads of Government had stated that efforts would be made to double two-way trade from € 5 billion to € 10 billion by 2010. As per the above statistics, the two-way trade has already surpassed € 10 billion target of 2010 to reach the € 15 billion mark. The visit of PM Dr. Manmohan Singh for the Hannover Trade Fair in April 2006 gave a further boost to trade and economic cooperation between the two countries.

The major items of exports to Germany are:

1. Engineering goods.
2. Textiles and leather goods.

Major items of imports are:

1. Machinery, chemicals and pharmaceuticals.
2. Knowledge-based industry (IT, biotech).
3. Entertainment.
4. Healthcare, pharmaceuticals.
5. Engineering goods, fresh fruits and processed food stuffs, floriculture etc.

Value addition and diversification in traditional areas such as cotton, silk, leather, sports goods, toys and Christmas decorations are areas for growth.

12.4.5 German Direct Investment: German approved investment in India, which averaged € 200 million annually in the nineties, has declined in recent years as a result of the sluggish performance of the German economy, Germany's preoccupation with the integration of East Germany and the priority attached to Eastern Europe as well Germany's focus on China in the Asian region. Actual investments from Germany were US$ 133.1 million in 2001, US$ 138.1 million in 2002 and US$ 78.8 million in 2003, US$ 158.2 million in 2004 and US$ 1,622 million during 2011-2012. In terms of approved investments during April 2000 to March 2012, Germany ranked eighth with cumulative FDI approvals amounting to US$ 4.62 billion.

The top sectors attracting German investment into India are:

1. Electrical equipment, and
2. Metallurgical industry.

The top sectors attracting technology transfer during the same period were industrial machinery and electrical equipment.

There are now some signs of greater German interest in India with the big German companies stepping up their existing investments and several new players entering the Indian market. Many German companies such as Bosch, Siemens, Daimler Chrysler have had a presence in India for a long time. A new and welcome trend is of Indian investments in Germany.

Bharat Forge Limited (BFL), Ranbaxy, Samtel, Hexaware Technologies, NIIT, Wockhardt, Graphite India Limited and most, recently Dr Reddy's laboratories, have either acquired German companies or started their own subsidiaries in Germany.

12.4.6 S&T Cooperation: In Europe, India enjoys most active cooperation in science and technology with Germany. There are presently more than 150 joint S&T research projects.

There is an exchange programme (PPP) launched by DST and DAAD to encourage collaboration between young scientists. Another initiative is to provide opportunity every year for 25 young Indian scholars to meet with Nobel Laureates in Lindau.

Additionally, for 2006 Economics Nobel Laureates meeting 8 young economists were invited. There has been ongoing cooperation in the field of space. India has launched two German satellites in the late 1990s and 2001. India has agreed to participate in the EU Galileo satellite navigation system. Daimler Chrysler India and CSIR have successfully collaborated in production of bio-diesel from Jatropha plants.

During the visit of Chancellor Schroeder in October 2004, a Science Circle networking Indian and German scholars and research institutions was inaugurated and an MOU signed between the Max Planck Institute and the Department of Science and Technology. In pursuance of this MOU, 8 partner groups were set up in 2005-06. During the visit, it was also agreed to set up Joint Working Groups (JWG's) on Environment and Energy and Bio-medicine. Several other important MoUs such as between DSTand DFG; ICMR and Helmholz Association; DBT and FZJ, UGC and DAAD have recently been signed. New proposals/initiative include: LAPAN-TUBSAT, a 55 kg. micro satellite that was recently launched onboard Indian PSLV as a piggy back payload.

Further, a German proposal for participation in the Indian Moon mission Chandrayaan 1 has been accepted by ISRO. India has become a signatory to the multi-national MOU to set up the Euro 700 million heavy ion and antiproton accelerator facility (FAIR) in Darmstadt. An Indo-German liaison office on infectious diseases research was established in Hyderabad. An office of the German Research Council has been opened in New Delhi. During the visit of Prime Minister Manmohan Singh in April 2006, both sides agreed to work towards the establishment of an Indo-German Scientific Research and Technology Centre at an early date.

The German Minister of Education and Research visited India on 6-8 February, 2007. Under the German Presidency of the EU, an Indo-EU S&T Ministerial conference was held in Delhi. This was the first ever EU S&T Ministerial Conference held outside the EU. The India-EU Science Ministerial Conference could cover India's S&T relations with Europe, including those with member states, Issues for EU-India cooperation–Energy, Environment, ICT, Research Infrastructure, Two-way mobility of Researchers; India's interface with European Technology Platforms (ETP) & related Pilot Joint Technology Initiatives.

12.5 India and UK

Relations between India and the UK are close. Frequent and frank high level bilateral consultations have helped to sensitise the UK leadership on a range of issues of concern India. The Joint Declaration—'Towards a new and dynamic partnership' adopted during PM's visit to UK on September 20, 2004 (based on the New Delhi Declaration issued during PM Tony Blair's visit to India in January 2002) would upgrade bilateral relations through a comprehensive strategic partnership. As envisaged in the Joint Declaration, PM Tony Blair visited India on 6-8 September 2005 in his capacity as EU President for the EU/India Summit and also in a bilateral capacity. This was the third meeting between the two Prime Ministers since our PM assumed office in May 2004. The bilateral Summit was held on September 8 in Udaipur, a day after the 6th India-EU Summit.

12.5.1 India-UK Strategic Partnership: India and the UK share a Strategic Partnership. The two Sides underscored their commitment to the Strategic Partnership launched in 2004 and reaffirmed their shared conviction in the values of democracy, fundamental freedoms, pluralism, rule of law, respect for human rights and multilateralism in the international political and financial architecture as the means to tackle global challenges effectively. The close bilateral relationship has already led to growing cooperation in global affairs and substantial expansion in the bilateral engagement in multiple fields. Building on the achievements of the 'New Delhi Declaration' (2002) and 'India-UK Joint Declaration' (2004), the two Sides commit themselves to strengthening and deepening the comprehensive Strategic Partnership that exists between the two countries, which is underpinned by growing economic ties and the presence of a large Indian Diaspora in the UK.

12.5.2 Economic and Commercial Ties: Bilateral economic linkages are strengthening through increased trade and investment flows. The UK is the third largest cumulative investor in India. India has emerged as one of the largest investors in the UK, including several major acquisitions, reflecting the maturing nature of the bilateral economic partnership. The UK is among India's important global trading partners. The two Sides acknowledged the potential for greater collaboration especially in hi-tech (ICT, life sciences, nano-technology etc.), research, advanced manufacturing, infrastructure, energy, healthcare, agricultural products and processed foods, higher education and other service sectors.

Both sides took note of the outcome of the 4th meeting of the India-UK Joint Economic and Trade Committee (JETCO) held in London on 13 December 2007. This meeting reviewed various aspects of bilateral trade and received valuable feedback from businesses on both sides on measures that could further enhance bilateral trade and investment flows. India and the United Kingdom agreed to cooperate in developing collaboration between Small and Medium Enterprises (SMEs), entrepreneurs and venture capitalists. The Prime Ministers welcomed the meeting of a CEOs' Round Table and Entrepreneurs' Summit of Indian and UK business leaders in Delhi. In the light of the rapidly growing trade and economic relations and the rapidly evolving pattern of international competitive advantage, both governments acknowledged the considerable potential for bilateral trade, investment and services. They noted the importance of improving market access through liberalization and facilitating movement of professionals across a broad range of sectors of interest to both sides.

Both sides took note of the large opportunities in the infrastructure sector, in the context of the massive infrastructure development programme being undertaken in India. Facilitating the flow of information on the infrastructure projects being undertaken would encourage business partnerships. Both sides agreed to take forward proposals for the establishment of a capacity building programme in India for public-private partnership in infrastructure with UK support.

India and the United Kingdom noted the role played by people of Indian origin in Britain. Through their hard work, dynamism and entrepreneurial talents they have made an enormous contribution to the strengthening of bilateral ties.

12.5.3 Education: The two Sides noted the traditionally close ties between the two knowledge societies in the field of Higher Education. They recognised that the UK-India Education and Research Initiative (UKIERI), launched in April 2006, was playing an important role in fostering such contacts. They further noted the huge expansion planned in the Indian Higher Education sector which would increase the gross enrolment ratio by 5 percentage points and include the establishment of a range of central government institutions of excellence including 8 new Indian Institutes of Technology (IITs), 7 new Indian Institutes of Management (IIMs), 5 Indian Institutes of Science Education and Research and 30 new Central Universities. It was agreed that both sides would forge a closer partnership in the field of Higher Education, for further developing education and skills to the mutual advantage of the students and faculty of both countries.

While exploring new avenues of collaboration to further deepen the cooperation, the two Sides agreed to initiate specific measures to collaborate in the field of higher education. In particular they agreed: to establish an Education Forum to work towards an early conclusion of an Education Partnership Agreement; to enter into a Memorandum of Understanding on an India-UK Higher Education Leadership Development Programme to develop leadership skills in Indian and UK universities; to establish a Programme, under UKIERI, to support faculty development in key Indian universities with participation of leading UK academics; to develop further student and faculty exchange programmes and partnerships with a commitment of further funding from the UK government; and to promote pro-actively links between British Universities and the premier educational institutions in India including collaborating for the establishment of at least one new Indian Institute of Technology, one new Indian Institute of Science Education and Research and one Central University proposed in the Eleventh Five Year Plan.

The latter would be taken forward through a meeting between a British delegation, including Vice Chancellors and their Indian counterparts later in the year. They further agreed to work towards mutual recognition of degrees, diplomas and other academic qualifications supported through greater co-operation between the relevant UK and Indian authorities. The two Sides agreed to the further development of UK/India collaboration on English Language Training. The two Governments recognize the strong interest of higher educational institutions of both countries to work together to further their global educational objectives.

12.5.4 Research, Science and Technology: India and the UK see considerable potential for growth in Research, Science and Technology collaboration. They share the vision for further strengthening their partnership through new and existing initiatives and agree to widen discussion to all research funding bodies in both countries through the India-UK Science and Innovation Council mechanism. The UK's proposal to establish a Research Councils UK (RCUK) office in India is a welcome development that would lead to enhanced collaboration between the two countries.

Underlining the importance for further developing Research and S&T cooperation, India and the UK shall establish a Science Bridges Initiative to build institution to institution relationships on equal partnership with joint funding under the principle of parity. RCUK will contribute £ 4 million with a matching grant from Department of Science and Technology (DST) India to promote this initiative. The UK and India also agree to support a further round of UKIERI awards designed to establish networking links between Indian and UK education and research institutions with the UK committing £ 2 million over 3 years and DST agreeing to match this funding on a parity basis. DST and the Engineering and Physical Sciences Research Council (EPSRC), UK also agreed to collaborate on the initial phase of development of major projects in select research areas.

12.5.5 Civil Nuclear Cooperation: The two Sides strongly emphasised the potential of civil nuclear energy to be a safe, sustainable and non-polluting source of energy, which could make a significant contribution to meeting the global challenge of achieving energy security, sustainable development, economic growth, and limiting climate change. The UK supports the India-US civil nuclear co-operation initiative with all its elements, including an appropriate India specific exemption to the Nuclear Suppliers Group Guidelines. As two countries with advanced nuclear technology, India and the UK agree to promote co-operation in civil nuclear energy and will work expeditiously towards a bilateral agreement for this purpose, in line with their strong commitment to non-proliferation. The two sides will also continue to encourage their scientists to develop closer links and to co-operate in research in this field. The two sides also welcome the opportunity for their scientists to work together in the context of ITER.

12.5.6 Climate Change: India and the UK recognise the need to find effective and practical solutions to address concerns regarding climate change and its implications for human kind. These would include mitigation and adaptation strategies in a manner that supports further economic and social development in particular of developing countries. Long-term convergence of per capita emission rates is an important and equitable principle that should be seriously considered in the context of international climate change negotiations. They expressed satisfaction over the successful outcome at Bali that reaffirmed the relevance of the United Nations Framework Convention on Climate Change (UNFCCC), including its provision and principles, in particular the principle of common but differentiated responsibilities and respective capabilities.

The process established under the Bali Road Map should aim for enhanced implementation of the UNFCCC and give due weight to issues of concern to developing countries, in particular those relating to addressing adaptation, technology, and financing arrangements. In the field of bilateral cooperation on climate change, the two Sides expressed satisfaction over the announcement of a UK-India Agreement on the second phase of UK-India Climate Change Impacts and Adaptation Study.

The UK and India are convinced that development of the international carbon market is important for the future and wish to explore new approaches to market related investment that offer the potential to drive technology transfer. The two Sides shall work towards the success of the second Phase of a project aimed at identifying the barriers to low carbon technology transfer. They will also collaborate on a project piloting implementation of programmatic CDM in India this year to jointly explore the potential of this to facilitate up-scaling of carbon market investment in accordance with India's future development priorities. Both sides recognised the importance of Research and Development collaboration on low carbon energy technologies and welcomed the broadening dialogue between the two countries on clean coal technologies and other power generation technologies.

12.6 India and Switzerland

India and Switzerland signed a Memorandum of Understanding on Intellectual Property, on August 07, 2007. The MoU would benefit closer cooperation between the two countries in fostering the protection and promotion of intellectual property rights. The implementation of this memorandum will be jointly by the Office of the Controller General of Patents, Designs and Trade Marks, Department of Industrial Policy and Promotion under the Ministry of Commerce and Industry, Government of India and the Swiss Federal Institute of Intellectual Property.

As per the MoU, a Joint Committee will be set up to develop a dialogue on issues of intellectual property that will encompass:

1. Exchange of views, information and experiences regarding the protection of intellectual property at the national level.
2. Dialogue related to international issues concerning intellectual property.
3. Serve as a forum for consultations to address specific issues in the area of intellectual property in the bilateral relations of the Parties.

4. Development of continued institutional cooperation for regular technical exchanges between intellectual property institutes in the two countries.
5. Exchange of experiences between India and Switzerland in training on intellectual property.
6. Development of appropriate modules and curricula for such trainings.
7. Joint studies on specific intellectual property issues.
8. Exchange of experiences and best practices regarding the raising of public awareness on the role of intellectual property rights.
9. Discuss strategies aimed at preventing the manufacture, distribution, sale and consumption of counterfeit and pirated products as well as at raising public awareness of the damages caused by counterfeit and pirated products.
10. Exchange of experience and dialogue on cooperation in the area of protection of geographical indications.
11. Exchange of experience and dialogue on cooperation in the area of protection of traditional knowledge.

Both sides agreed that the Joint Committee would meet once a year in India or Switzerland alternately.

India and Switzerland have signed the Executive Programme of Cooperation (POC) for the period 2006-2010 within the framework of the umbrella agreement on cooperation in the fields of S&T signed during the visit of the then President Couchepin to India in November 2003.

The broad areas of Indo-Swiss joint cooperation are:

1. Basic and applied sciences.
2. Technology and engineering.
3. Research and development etc.

Seven leading Indian Institutions of S&T and EPFL and ETH have concluded an academic alliance for cooperation in various areas. The Programme of Cooperation (PoC) signed during the visit envisages joint research projects specifically in life sciences, information technology and application and nano science and technology. The PoC seeks to promote exchange of ideas and skills through visits by scientists and specialists, technical workshops and seminars, establishment of joint Indo-Swiss labs and centres in areas of mutual interest, training of your scientists and twinning of institutions. The discussions during the visit also covered the proposal for the establishment of Centres of Excellence especially in the areas of micro-engineering at IIT Delhi and micro-electronics at IIIT Allahabad in collaboration with EPFL. The need for developing programmes integrating research and development with industry was also emphasized. It was agreed to develop an industrial R&D programme. A roadmap in this direction will be prepared jointly by first quarter of next year. Rights to intellectual property created as a result of joint research and projects will be governed by the special provisions which form an integral part of the Executive PoC. Both Switzerland and India attach to S&T as a catalyst for change and for strengthening and expanding bilateral relations. With India's vast pool of skilled manpower and Switzerland's world renowned technical institutes, there clearly exists a synergy for broadening and deepening cooperation in this area.

12.7 India and Sweden

Relations between India and Sweden can be described as stable, friendly and multi-dimensional based on a shared history of common perceptions on issues related to democracy, development, climate change and even disarmament. This desire for enhanced relations found expression in several important Ministerial and Parliamentary delegations. The Swedish King visited India in November 2005 as member of a delegation from the Royal Society of Engineering Sciences to study economic developments in India. Trade and investment are now becoming the principal drivers of the India-Sweden engagement. Areas identified for cooperation are IT, telecommunications, biotechnology, environmental technologies and automotive industry.

12.7.1 Bilateral Investment Protection Agreement (BIPA): BIPA was signed on July 4, 2000 between Sweden and India. It provides for national and most favoured treatment of investments and guarantees for free transfer of profits and capital in case of phasing out an investment, as well as full compensation in case of expropriation and similar measures.

Avoidance of Double Taxation Agreement, signed between the two governments in end-June 2000, provides for national and most favoured treatment of investments and guarantees for free transfer of profits and capital in case of phasing out an investment, as well as full compensation in case of expropriation and similar measures. It also has provisions related to arbitration and conciliation.

12.7.2 Sweden-India Business Council (SIBC): Pursuant to the visit of Confederation of Indian Industry and the efforts of the Indian Embassy, a Sweden-India Business Council has been established to enhance trade and investment cooperation. It now has a membership of over 100 Swedish companies, including SMEs.

Federation of Indian Chambers of Commerce and Industry (FICCI) had set up a Joint Business Council in collaboration with the Swedish Trade Council (Exportrådet), the last session of which was held in June 1995 in Stockholm.

15th Session of the Indo-Swedish Joint Commission for Economic, Industrial, Technical and Scientific Cooperation is due to be held. 14th JCM was held on

April 1-2, 2003 in New Delhi.

12.7.3 Commercial and Economic Relations: Trade and investment are now becoming the principal drivers of the India-Sweden engagement. Indo-Swedish bilateral trade has grown by 8 percent in 2010-11 and stands at US$ 2.2 billion. Swedish investments into India are just under US$ 1 billion and there is growing Indian investment into Sweden. A large number of Swedish MNCs have had a long presence in India. Their numbers are growing as Swedish companies look not only for manufacturing hubs but rely increasingly on offshore IT operations and R & D in India. The traditional reluctance of small and medium enterprises to enter India appears to be wearing out due to the inherent cost benefits and the large market. India has emerged as Sweden's 19th largest export market and third largest trade partner after China and Japan in Asia. Recognising the booming trade and investment opportunities in India, the Swedish Trade Council opened its second office in India in Bangalore and Trade Minister Ewa Björlilng inaugurated the third office in March 2008 which is to be set up in Mumbai.

12.7.4 Investments: Sweden with its large number of MNCs has had a very long presence in India. Ericsson, which started supplying telecom switches to India in 1903 inaugurated its R&D facilities in Chennai in February 2006 as well as its second manufacturing facility in Jaipur in March 2005. In January 2007, Ericsson announced its intention to invest US$ 500 million in the next five years in India. Swedish Match had established its facility (WIMCO) as early as in 1926. Since then other Swedish companies like SKF, Atlas Copco, DeLaval, Volvo, ABB, Astra Zeneca, etc. have expanded their operations in India. Scania, Europe's number four heavy truck maker, has also entered into an agreement with L&T for building tipping trucks. Retail giants like IKEA are also keenly watching the opening of the retail sector in India.

There has been traditional reluctance on the part of Swedish small and medium industries to come forward to invest in India, but in recent years these industries are also exploring India due to inherent advantages of cost benefits and a growing market. At present, there are over 100 Swedish joint ventures wholly owned subsidiaries in India. However, Swedish investment in India is far below the perceived potential. Around 15 major Indian IT companies have their representative offices in Sweden and their cumulative exports are estimated at US$ 400 million.

Indian pharma companies like Dr. Reddy, Biocon, Kemwell and Ranbaxy have also either formed collaborative relations or are looking to tie up or establish joint R&D facilities in Sweden. This trend has permeated beyond IT and pharma sector and a recent entrant is Bharat Forge, which acquired the Swedish firm Kjilsta AB in 2005. In 2006, Wipro acquired 100 percent equity of the Sweden-based Hydrauto Group AB for a consideration of USD 31 million.

Recognizing the transnational drive of Indian corporations, the Swedish government has joined the race for attracting Indian investments in Sweden. A special allocation of US$ 195,000 was made to the Invest in Sweden Agency (ISA) to create interest in India for Sweden and Swedish expertise.

12.7.5 S&T Cooperation: MOS for Science and Technology, Shri. Kapil Sibal visited Stockholm in December 2005 to sign a bilateral S&T Agreement. His counterpart, Minister for Culture & Education, Leif Pagrotsky visited India in April 2006, to explore further collaborations between India and Sweden. Steady progress is being made on cooperation following the signing of the S&T Agreement. The Department of Science & Technology (DST) in coordination with VINNOVA–A Swedish Governmental Agency for Innovation Systems have held a number of exchanges, seminar.

12.8 India and Austria

India and Austria has signed an Agreement on Science and Technology Cooperation recently. Under this Agreement both sides will encourage and support the development of direct scientific-technological cooperation between national institutions, Academies of Sciences, schools of higher education, research centres for science and technology and other institutions. According to the Agreement the Indo-Austrian Joint Committee shall be set up for scientific and technological cooperation.

Major Highlights of the Agreement are as under:

1. Exchange of Scientific and Technological Information.
2. Documentation and Publications, Exchange of Scientists.
3. Experts and Implementation of Bilateral-Projects of Mutual Interest.
4. Exchange of Scientists and Experts for Consultations.
5. Symposia and Special Studies.
6. Support to Joint Scientific-Telelogical Events.
7. Other Scientific Programmes.

12.9 India and Italy

On February 14, 2007 11 MoUs were signed between various Indian and Italian companies primarily from the auto sector (3) followed by two each in the defence and electronics, oil and gas, banking and finance and education sector. The MoUs were signed in the presence of the visiting Italian Prime Minister, Romano Prodi, who acknowledged the increase in bilateral trade between the two countries while adding that India has to offer easier market access to Italy on a reciprocal basis. He also pleaded for a reduction in peak customs tariff.

Besides these 11 MoUs, the country witnessed the largest foreign delegation (400 single entrepreneurs from Italy) from any overseas country with 2000 one-to-one B2B (Business-to-Business) meetings in Kolkata and Mumbai. Italy has also created a €300 million "Go India Fund" with a view to assisting Italian small and medium businesses (SMBs) to set up operations in India. Romano Prodi arrived in India on February 9, on an official mission. The week-long visit had numerous B2B meetings with Indian businessmen.

Within three months of the decision of the India-Italy Joint Commission, the India-Italy Joint Working Group (JWG) on Infrastructure has been established and has met for the first time here on 15 February, 2007. The broad goal of the JWG is to widen the India-Italy economic relationship by facilitating trade and investment flows in the infrastructure sector. One of the major outcomes of the 17th Session of India-Italy Joint Commission for Economic Cooperation held in Rome in November 2006 was the agreement to set up an India-Italy Joint Working Group on Infrastructure.

Both sides presented the opportunities and expertise available in the infrastructure sector. Identification of joint pilot projects was discussed and projects in the highways and power sector have been identified for further participation by both sides.

12.9.1 Cultural Exchange Programme: India and Italy signed a cultural exchange Programme (CEP) of cultural cooperation for the years 2007-2009. The CEP envisages cooperation in education, arts and visual events, archives, libraries and publishing, cooperation in the fields of restoration, preservation and protection of cultural heritage, information, radio and television cooperation and cooperation in tourism and youth affairs and sports.

Both the countries agree to cooperate in order to counter illicit trade in works of art with preventive, repressive, and remedial measures in accordance to the respective national legislations, and in accordance to the obligations ensuing the 1970 UNESCO International Convention on the Means of Prohibiting and Preventing Illicit Import, Export, and Transfer in Ownership of Cultural Property, and taking into account the principles of the 1995 UNIDROIT Convention on Stolen or Illegally Exported Cultural Objects.

They also agree to cooperate in protection of submerged cultural heritage according to their respective legislation regarding submarine archaeology, and considering the principles contained in the 2001 UNESCO International Convention on the Protection of Underwater Cultural Heritage. The two Parties may develop bilateral co-operation in the field of the protection of intellectual property and copyright, and explore the possibility of co-operation between the respective relevant government bodies in this area.

The two countries will encourage contacts and co-operation between their respective universities, institutions of higher artistic, musical education and other institutions of higher education through the signing of agreements and conventions, the exchange of teachers, data and information, as well as through the implementation of common research projects, seminars and conferences.

12.10 India and Portugal

India and Portugal signed an extradition treaty on January 11, 2007. The treaty was signed between Prime Minister Manmohan Singh and visiting Portuguese President Anibal Cavaco Silva. The treaty provides for exchange of criminals taking shelters in each other's territory. The other provisions of the treaty are seizure of the property of criminals and terrorists, prosecution of fugitives, handing over of criminals and terrorists to the host country and suppression of a variety of crimes.

12.11 India and Poland

The First Session of the Indo-Polish Commission on Economic Cooperation was held on May 27 2008 in New Delhi. The meeting highlighted the positive investment climate in India as also the investment opportunities in various sectors. A Protocol was signed to resolve to cooperate in several spheres of mutual interest. It was decided that both sides would facilitate exchange of business delegations and interactions besides participation in trade fairs and international exhibitions in order to help create a mutually beneficial partnership, particularly in

1. Automobiles.
2. Automotive components.
3. Healthcare.
4. Pharmaceuticals.
5. Coal.
6. Food processing.
7. Non-conventional energy.
8. Electrical equipments.
9. IT and e-Governance.

Wide range of issues including bilateral trade and investments and cooperation in industrial and scientific fields between the two countries were taken up during the session. It was emphasized that the level of economic engagement between the two countries, in terms of trade and investment relations, should increase. India's export to Poland was US$ 676.43 million in 2010-11 while its import was US$ 386.04 million. India has received FDI of US$

51.84 million from Poland so far (April 2000 to March 2012). Some of the major Polish companies that have investments in India are TZMO S.A. and Polfarma. Prominent Indian names in Poland are Videocon, Ranbaxy, Mittal Steel, Reliance Industries etc.

Following Poland's accession to the European Union in 2004, India and Poland signed a new Agreement in Budapest on 19th May 2006 whereby it was decided to establish the Joint Commission afresh to discuss the development of, identify new possibilities for and draw up suggestions and proposals for economic cooperation. This meeting on 27th May 2008 is the first session after signing of the Agreement.

12.12 India and Greece

On April 28, 2007 the President of India and Prime Minister of Greek have discussed the foreign issues between the countries for future development. India and Greece have proposed to double their bilateral trade to over 1 billion by 2010 with India asking Athens to actively participate in its infrastructure projects to remove the trade imbalance between the two side. The core competence of India and Greece can be identified by a joint task team which will enable establishment of collaborative ventures for synergising the strengths of two nations leading to the· design, development, production and marketing of products and systems in the world market.

Greece is indeed very good at infrastructure building, so Greece and India will be partners in creating infrastructure. The country could be a good partner for India's infrastructure quest. Greece has keen interest in India's shipping and tourism sectors and sought air connectivity between the two countries at the earliest.

12.13 India and Finland

India and Finland propose to step up the level of bilateral trade, which is none considered for below the potential, despite having risen by 56 percent to US$ 1901 million in 2010-11 over the previous year. This was indicated at a meeting between the Union Commerce and Industry Minister Kamal Nath and the visiting Finland Foreign Trade and Development Minister Paula Lethomaki who came along with an official delegation. During the first six months of the current financial year, bilateral trade between the two countries has already registered a growth of 45 percent. An official release says Finland is an important member of the European Union and is generally supportive of an open trade regime. It adds that the two ministers discussed bilateral and multilateral issues.

The Union commerce Minister reiterated India's commitment to the multilateral trade system and appreciated the role played by the European Union in arriving at consensus that resulted in Framework Agreement on August 4, 2004 in Geneva, providing guidelines for further negotiations in the World Trade Organisation.

India also sought active support of the European Commission is developing modalities on the principles contained in the Framework agreement, including reduction of all trade distorting domestic support and elimination of all forms of export subsidies in agriculture.

The areas having potential for Joint Ventures include food processing, electronics and software as well as paper, forestry and telecommunication.

India reiterated its commitment to the multilateral trade system and appreciated the role played by the European Union in arriving at a consensus that resulted in the Framework Agreement in August, 2004.

The products which have potential for boosting Indian exports to Finland include granite, marble and tiles, fruits and vegetables. The areas having potential for joint ventures include food processing, electronics and software as well as paper, forestry and telecommunications.

12.14 India and Romania

Bilateral political relations between India and Romania are warm and friendly. The deepening of democracy in Romania since 1989 has strengthened shared values. India and Romania work together at multilateral forums. Regular foreign office consultations are held to assist and coordinate policies.

12.14.1 Trade and Economic Co-operation: Romania was involved in major Indian projects such as the oil refinery at Guwahati, the thermal power plant at Singareni, the Mangalore pelletizing plant, the Durgapur agglomeration plant and the Hyderabad tractor plant. In 1993, an Agreement on Trade and Economic Cooperation was concluded, envisaging trade in hard currency to replace the earlier clearing system.

Bilateral institutional mechanisms to promote trade and economic cooperation include Joint Commission at the Government level and Joint Business Council at the level of businessmen.

The 16th Indo-Romanian Joint Commission was held in New Delhi in October 2003, concurrently with the last session of the Joint Business Council. Inter-sessional consultations for the Indo-Romanian Joint Commission were held in New Delhi in March 2005.

An MoU on cooperation in the oil and gas sector was initialled on the occasion. In recent years India-Romania trade turnover has been as During the calendar year 2007, trade grew by 69 percent compared to 2006. India and Romania have identified information technology, pharmaceuticals, energy, metallurgy and heavy industries, as sectors for special focus. Twenty-one Indian textile companies participated in an Indian Textile Exhibition held in Bucharest in 2004 and sixty-five companies in 2007. 40 Indian companies participated in Romania's largest trade fair [TIBCO] in Bucharest in 2005. A CII Exhibition with about 40 participants was organized in June 2007.

12.15 India and Czechoslovakia

Agreements signed after 1993: The following agreements have been signed between India and the Czech Republic since 1993:

1. Agreement on Cooperation in the field of Culture, Education and Sciences;
2. Agreement on Promotion and Protection of Mutual Investments;
3. Protocol on Foreign Office Consultations;
4. Air Services Agreement;

Vaclav Klaus, President of the Czech Republic categorically indicated that his country is going to support India in its demand for a permanent seat on the United Nations Security Council. Both the countries have extended their cooperation in the field of Space, Information Technology and defence. In the IT field, there would be possible tie-ups with other IT companies. On defence deals, India may get more hunting rifles.

12.16 India and Denmark

India and the visiting Denmark's Prime Minister, Anders Fogh Rasmussen, have signed a joint agreement covering sectors such as environment and biotechnology. Denmark had protested the nuclear test conducted by India and then the relations deteriorated. India and Denmark has close cooperation in the energy sector. This visit has further cemented the relations. Denmark has invested heavily in India over the past few years.

The two sides have found that the proposed timing for the visit was not optimal. The Indo-Danish relationship is strong and excellent and is moving into a new phase which is focused on political dialogue and economic cooperation. The visit of Danish Prime Minister will highlight this evolution. India and Denmark will continue their endeavours to establish a new cooperation framework in areas of mutual interest like ICT, biotechnology, maritime transport, double taxation and the establishment of a joint commission. India and Denmark look forward to the visit of the Danish PM to India at an early date.

12.17 India and Iceland

The Government has approved its ex-post facto approval to the Agreement signed on October 19, 2005 between India and Iceland on cooperation in the fields of culture and education. The salient features of the Agreement are as under:

1. Exchange of representatives of universities, institutions and organizations in the fields of culture and education; (b) Scholarships for study and research; and
2. Organizing of bilateral workshops, seminars, training programmes and exhibitions.

The Government has approved the signing of air services agreement between India and the Republic of Iceland to ensure better air links. The essential features of the ASA will be:

1. Both countries shall have the right to designate as many airlines as they wish;
2. Either country may revoke, suspend or limit the operating authorization or technical permission of an airline designated by the other country under given conditions.
3. As per the agreement to be signed the designated airlines of Iceland shall be able to fly from any point in Iceland to any two points in India via any two intermediate points and to any two beyond points.
4. Similar facility will be accorded to the designated airlines of India.
5. The designated airlines of each country may at their option omit points on any of the above routes.

India and Ireland enjoy friendly and cordial relations as a result of the bonds established during their freedom struggles. These have been strengthened over the years. Formal diplomatic links were established in 1947. India opened an Embassy in Dublin in 1951.

India and Ireland signed three agreements on cultural, scientific and technological cooperation. This was signed by India and Irish Prime Minister Bertie Ahem. On the scientific and technological cooperation front a MoU was signed between the Indian National Science Academy and the Science Foundation of Ireland. The Irish Bio-Industry Association (IBIA) and the India-based Association of Biotechnology Led Enterprises (ABLE) signed a MoU during the visit Ireland Prime Minister Bertie Ahem. This is the first step to improve collaboration between the biotech sectors in the two countries. An Agreement on Cultural Co-operation signed during the visit, facilitating exchanges between professors, experts, academics, artists and journalists, etc. Besides these agreements, the delegates also explored opportunities related to software services, engineering, health care, food, and construction and consumer products.

12.18 India and Luxembourg

India enjoys warm friendly relations with Luxembourg. There are no outstanding political issues between the two countries. Luxembourg supports India's candidature for Permanent membership of the UNSC. Bilateral Agreement on Health was signed on April 15, 1996 in India and the Cultural Agreement was signed in September 1996. The Bilateral Investment Protection Agreement (BLEU) was signed in November 1997. The Bilateral Air Services Agreement was signed in January 2001.

12.19 India and Spain

Diplomatic relations between the two countries were established in 1956 and the bilateral relations are very cordial and friendly.

India and Spain agreed to institutionalise the process of political dialogue at various levels, commensurate with the expanding bilateral relationship. The two sides would also work towards forging business partnerships in the following priority sectors: energy, tourism, food processing, automobiles, environment, information technology and infrastructure. They agreed to work towards closer cooperation in the defence sector, including the possibility of joint research and development.

Both sides look forward to the inauguration of the Cas a de la India building in the City of Valladolid in Spain in November 2006, and to the next civil society dialogue under the aegis of Casa Asia and Indian Council of World Affairs, scheduled to be held in India in October 2006.

The two sides agreed to further promote cultural and academic exchanges between the two countries and expressed their willingness to support and facilitate the increase in the number of Spanish lecturers in Indian Universities in the following years and took note with satisfaction of the announced opening of a Cervantes Institute in New Delhi in 2007.

13

India and Africa

13.1 Indian Policy towards Africa

India gave its support for the Independence movements in African countries. It tried to associate Asian struggle for declaration with those of African countries and worked effectively to create world opinion against colonialism.

The emergence of Afro-Asian Group at the United Nations after 1949 was an expression of common aspirations of the Asian and African people. Later when India, Egypt and others sponsored the Non-Aligned Movement, many African countries joined it to strengthen the Afro-Asian solidarity.

India had opposed the South African policy of apartheid even before its independence. In the post -independence era, it worked for the elimination of racial discrimination and apartheid in South Africa at all international fora. India imposed a total ban on all imports and exports from South Africa and at last the efforts culminated in success. With African President F.W. Declark finally deciding to end the policy of Apartheid, and with the endorsement of new interim South African constitution on November 17, 1993, White minority conceded equal rights to the nation's long suffering black majority after three centuries of oppression. Nelson Mandela, who symbolised the struggle against apartheid was on May 9, 1994, elected President of a new multilateral South-Africa to lead a government of national unity. India was represented by its vice-president Mr. K.R. Narayanan at the celebrations.

India has also been increasingly collaborating economically with the African countries which have been of mutual benefit to both. India has secured some of the world's biggest contract in Africa for construction of sophisticated airports in arid areas. India has procured contracts for the construction of hospitals, irrigation dams etc. in many countries of Africa.

India has also contributed to the economic development of Africa through transfer of technology. India has fully sympathised with the aspirations of the African people to attain self-reliance. India has transferred technology in various forms such as direct foreign investment in the extractive sectors like petroleum, mining and export, agriculture and industry etc. Trade has been the other mechanism for transfer of technology embodied in goods and services. However, India's trade with African countries has not been large and continued to be stagnant during the period 1960-70, and even after that. Further, this trade has been mainly confined to some countries of Africa like viz. Nigeria, Sudan, Kenya, Tanzania, Ghana etc.

However, with the diversification of market economy according to new trade demands as Indian government is stressing, there are full chances that our trade will improve with Africa, which has an indefinite scope to grow. Further, India has always been providing credit to the African countries to meet their demands.

Another form of transfer of technology has been there in the joint-ventures. India has been associated with a large number of joint industrial ventures and turn key projects in Africa. At present, India is involved in over fifty joint ventures with various African countries. Recently, Indian Oil and Natural Gas Corporation (ONGC) announced India's largest joint venture for oil exploration in Sudan.

In addition, India has also provided extensive facilities for the training of the local people so that they may be able to play an active role in the management and development of various projects. Training facilities have been provided to personnel of these countries in India. In addition a number of experts have been sent to various African countries. After the African countries gained independence, India and the African countries took identical stand on various international issues. They expressed full faith in the policy of non-alignment and peaceful coexistence. On the wider economic issues like North-South Dialogue also they have worked in complete co-operation and have come to accept the need of closer horizontal co-operation between the undeveloped countries.

Apart from bilateral assistance to various African countries, India has also tried to assist African countries through International organisations.

Thus, in 1979, India gave a grant of ₹ 50 lakh to United Nations Trust Fund for African Development and this earned India the distinction of being the first non-African developing country to contribute to this fund. India has also participated in peace keeping mission of United Nations and its agencies.

The peace keeping mission of Indian army in Sierra Leone was quite sad as the peace-keeping forces under the guard of U.N. instead of co-operating started altercating among themselves and India was persuaded to call its forces from peace keeping mission from Sierra Leone.

However, the global scenario is changing very fast. Africa is emerging as a market for large investment and growth prospects. Thus India has decided that apart from its friendly overtures, it will also search for market, joint ventures and trade related possibilities in Africa with more stress on diversification of our international market in context of our continuing sliding position of our exports and position in international trade.

More intimate relations between India and Africa developed only with the coming of the Western powers and the dawn of the merchant capitalist's era, when the colonial labour and a large number of Indian labourers were taken to South Africa, Mauritius and West Indies to work on sugar plantations. A large number of Indians were taken to Uganda for subordinate and technical services. In fact the Indian provided most of the middle level services and they played a prominent role in the economic life of East African countries. Generally, the relations of Indians with the Africans were cordial but often frictions also appeared in their relations.

India extended full support to the African people in their struggle against colonial domination, racial discrimination etc. In this regard Mahatma Gandhi played a vital role and organised agitation against racist policies of South African Government. After the attainment of independence by Indian the nationalist movements in Africa gathered further momentum and it would not be wrong to say that Indian independence blazed the liberation for the countries of Africa.

13.1.1 India and Liberation Struggle in Africa: India has consistently supported the Liberation Movements in various African countries and took up the cause of the African countries in the United Nation, the commonwealth Conferences and other international forums. First, India tried to impress on the United States that the Trusteeship System should be worked in the interest of dependent people and there should not be any parcelling out of territories on the basis of strategic needs. India also insisted that the Trusteeship powers must supply regular information to the United Nations Organization regarding the measure taken by them or proposed to be taken by them with a view to expedite the grant of independence or self-government to the trust territories.

India was the first country to take up the question of apartheid and racial discrimination practised by the South African regime. India raised the question or racial discrimination being made by South African government against the people of Indian origin in South Africa constituted a violation of the fundamental human right.

India has also tried to assist the African countries through international organizations. Thus in 1979 India gave a grant of ₹ 50 lakh to United Nations Trust Fund for African Development, and thus earned the distinction of being the first non-African Developing country to contribute to this fund. India also joined African Development Bank and thus participated in the various projects funded by the African Bank.

Outside the United Nations also India extended full support to the African liberation movements and various organizations founded for the purpose. India particularly showed great appreciation for the Organization of African Unity (O.A.U.) set up in 1963, which endeavoured to create conditions to find an

African solution to the African problem. As India did not seek any privileged position in relation to the African countries it did not take part in the liberation movement and tried to channelise its aid chiefly through the O.A.U.

13.1.2 Economic Assistance to Africa: India did not merely extend support to the African countries in their struggle for freedom but also provided economic assistance during the struggle and after independence, primarily with a view to ensure stability and economic prosperity in the African continent, and to strengthen their hard won independence. India provided special assistance to countries like Mauritius, Tanzania, Zambia, Nigeria, Libya and Algeria. It set up joint commissions of economic and technical cooperation with these countries. These commissions hold periodical meetings and try to promote cooperation by identifying new areas of economic activity.

Both India and African countries profess faith in the policy of non-alignment. They adopted this policy because they wanted to preserve their newly won freedom and independence.

India has also been increasingly collaborating with the African countries which have been of mutual benefit to both. India has secured some of world's biggest contracts. India also got a contract to construct world's most sophisticated airport in an arid area. India has procured contracts for the construction of hospitals, houses and irrigation dams in Libya.

India has fully sympathized with the aspirations of the Africans to attain self-reliance. Trade is one of the mechanism for the transfer of technology embodied in goods and services. India has also contributed to the economic development of Africa through transfer of technology. India's trade with the African countries has not been large and continued to be stagnant during the period 1960-70.

India has provided funds and foodstuffs at the time of drought. It also made available expertise and technical assistance in the development of agriculture along modern lines and development of irrigation facilities so that these problems can be tackled on long term basis. India has also showed its solidarity with various African countries at the time of their distress and provided them with every possible assistance. India has also extended assistance to various African countries in the development of non-conventional energy sources, rural electrification solar energy and wind power.

Despite her tight financial position India has made available to several African countries enormous amounts as credit on most reasonable terms. It offered credit between ₹ 5 to ₹ 10 crore to countries like Tanzania, Mauritius, Mozambique, Zambia, Uganda, Sudan etc. for purchase of India manufactured goods such as textiles and engineering goods, tractors, motor cycles, buses, trucks, bicycles etc.

India has maintained very intimate relations with Africa since the day of independence. She not only extended full support to the liberation movements in different African countries and took the cause of African countries at the United Nations and other international forums, but also extended every possible help to these countries to enable them to make quick economic.

As a result she has earned the gratitude of the African countries and is held in high esteem by most of them. The one issue which has tended to strain India's relations with some of the Africa countries is the problem of Indians settled in Africa. This problem arose because the East African countries Kenya, Uganda and Tanzania expelled a large number of Indians from their countries. These Indians went to East Africa during the British rule and played an important role in the economic development of these countries during the colonial period. They provided the missing links or artisan skills, subordinate services and trading talents which the white settlers found uneconomical to supply and for which the Africans were as yet not fit. The lead in the expulsion of the Asians was taken by President Idi Amin.

Soon thereafter, Kenya and Tanzania also took certain measures which resulted in substantial exodus of the Asians from these countries. In 1975, President Banda of Malawi expelled several hundred Goans and asked Asians to wind up their business in the countryside and concentrate only in three large towns of Lilongwe, Blangyre and Zomba by March, 1977. Thus, the Asians had to face rough weather in Africa. They were eliminated from Africa but British did not welcome them even though they held valid British passports. Even India was not quite enthusiastic to receive them.

This rough treatment meted out to Indians in some of the African countries should not give the impression that the Indians have been excluded from African countries. In fact, more and more Indians are now going to the African countries because of the better economic opportunities available there. For example, in Nigeria and Ghana, the number of Indians has considerably increased.

India as Chairman of the 9 member Africa Fund Committee took concrete initiative and formulated definite project and measures to attain the objectives of the fund. Apart from contributing ₹ 500 million to the AFRICA Fund, India appealed to other countries and agencies to contribute to the fund. The Fund was also anticipated to provide assistance to the frontline states in development of their infrastructure, particularly transport and port facilities as alternatives to the existing facilities passing through South Africa and reduce their dependence on the racist regime. As a result, about US$ 256 million dollars were collected for the fund. The African fund was instituted at the initiative of Prime Minister Rajiv Gandhi at the Harare Summit of Non-aligned Nations, with a view to strengthen the economic and financial capability of the frontline states to fight the apartheid regime of Pretoria and to support the liberation movements in both Africa and Namibia in their unrelenting struggle against racist and colonist oppression.

13.1.3 Changing Indian Outlook towards Africa: First, on the political side, there has been an end in sight to some of the debilitating conflicts that have ravaged the continent. The conflict in the Democratic Republic of Congo, often referred as Africa's world war, has abated considerably.

Similarly, Rwanda, Sierra Leone, Liberia and Ivory Coast have moved out of the conflict zone. In Sudan, after years of negotiations, the Comprehensive Peace Agreement (CPA) was signed between southern rebels and the Sudanese government in 2005.

At the same time, there is a move towards Africans taking charge of their own destiny. This is reflected in the African Union's (formed in 2002) steps towards conflict resolution. The continent is also embracing the value of democracy and good governance.

Some two-thirds of African states have conducted multi-party elections in recent years. Similarly, 24 countries have taken their promises of good governance seriously and signed up for the African Peer Review Mechanism (APRM), which is an offshoot of the New Partnership for Africa's Development (NEP AD) initiative launched by African countries in 2001.

Second, on, the economic plane, there is a transformation underway ill the continent. About 20 countries have averaged a growth rate of over 5 percent during the past decade. According to the latest IMF World Economic Outlook, the average growth rates for Sub-Saharan Africa were around 5.8 percent in 2007. While rising crude oil and other non- fuel commodity prices may explain the high growth rates of some of these economies, the implementation of radical structural adjustment programmes mandated by the IMF may be the real factor for the steady performers.

From the geo-strategic perspective, there has been a perceptible rise in the importance of Africa for New Delhi. First, India's growing energy needs have forced it k> diversify its oil imports. In the past, India has been dependent on West Asia for its oil imports. In recent years, India, like the US and the other major powers, has recognised the energy potential of African countries. Currently, around 24 percent of India's crude oil imports are sourced from Africa (including North African countries). Indian national oil companies like the Oil and Natural Gas Corporation Videsh Limited (OVL) have invested in equity assets in Sudan, Ivory Coast, Libya, Egypt, and Nigeria, Nigeria Sao Tome Principe Joint Development Area and Gabon. Private sector companies like Reliance have also invested in equity oil in Sudan. Essar has procured exploration and production blocks' in Madagascar and Nigeria. India has recently completed a US$ 200 million project to lay a pipeline from Khartoum to Port Sudan on the Red sea.

Second, there is a growing recognition of the fact that countries on the eastern coast of Africa abutting the Indian Ocean from South Africa to Somalia-fall under India's maritime strategic neighbourhood. It has been acknowledged that insecurity in the Indian Ocean region is growing, given the existence of fundamentalist, terrorist, and militant, separatist or extremist organisations and criminal syndicates involved in trafficking in drugs, arms and humans; and piracy. The growth in incidents of piracy in Somali waters in particular threatens the security of the Sea Lanes of Communications (SLOCs). The Indian Navy has been active in its diplomacy in the Indian Ocean, providil1g maritime security cover during the African Union Summit in 2003 and the World Economic Forum in 2004 in Mozambique.

New economic initiatives launched by the African governments like the New Economic Partnership for African Development (NEPAD) have also attracted the interest of Indian investors. There is a growing realisation that African economies are at a stage of development when India could offer the most appropriate technology and products at competitive prices. A recent study by the Federation of Indian Industry and Commerce (FICCI) points out that it is "high time India took a pragmatic assessment of the business opportunities offered by Africa." The success of the four India-Africa project partnership conclaves held in New Delhi since 2005—the last one attracted 606 African delegates from thirty three countries, and around 152 projects worth US$ 10.5 billion were negotiated - is an indication of Indian industry's growing interest in Africa.

13.1.4 Opportunities in Africa: India and Africa together make up nearly a third of humanity. Politically, both share similar world views—they acknowledge the growing North South divide, identify with issues like reforms in institutions of global governance, and face similar challenges of instability and conflict. It is therefore quite natural that countries from Africa and India have come together to collaborate in multiple areas:

One of the priority areas for India is developing partnerships in the human resource development process in Africa. In the last forty or more years, India has extended US$ 1 billion worth of assistance in this sector in Africa through the Indian Technical and Economic Co-operation Programme (ITEC). This has involved deputation of Indian experts in a number of African countries as well as providing training to Africans in Indian institutions. Over 1000 officials and 15,000 African students receive training in India annually. The challenge is to take this partnership beyond government to the business and corporate levels.

This would involve undertaking a needs analysis of each African country as a unit and for Africa as a whole. Finally, it would involve formulation 6f common human development training, techniques and methods.

The Indian pharmaceuticals industry leads the effort in the developing world in terms of technology, quality and' range of medicines. Over the years, India had Africa have dealt with the scourge of communicable disease like malaria, TB and HIV-AIDS. Collaborative research and development partnerships between Indian and African pharma majors would be mutually beneficial. Several Indian pharma and healthcare companies have invested in Africa like, Ranbaxy Laboratories, Cipla Limited, Aurobindo Pharma and Emcure Pharmaceuticals.

The Indian government, private sector IT and telecom companies have recognised the potential investment opportunities available in this sector in Africa. African governments have shown interest in accessing Indian assistance to bridge the digital 'divide. India has already made a vast, contribution through building the Pan-African E-Network, which will connect all 53 nations of the African Union through satellite and fibre optic network. The network will connect 5 universities, 53 learning centres, 10 super specialty hospitals and 53 remote hospitals in India and Africa. Leading infotech firms like Tata Consultancy and HCL, NUT and Aptech have launched operations across Africa. One of the largest M&A deals worldwide in 2010 was the acquisition of the telecoms operations of Zain (Kuwait) in 15 African countries by the Indian mobile operator Bharti Airtel, for US$ 10.7 billion.

The majority of African countries are looking for ways and means to fortify their food security. To achieve this, they would like to replicate the Indian "green revolution model" in Africa. Specific areas of collaboration could range from provision of agricultural inputs, agro processing and watershed 'management. A few Indian companies like the Kirloskar Brothers Ltd. and Water and Power Consultancy services (WAPCOS) are, already engaged in water management projects across Africa.

African countries have identified expansion of power projects as one of the priorities in recent years. Opportunities thus exist for Indian companies for setting up power plants that includes laying transmission lines, sub-station structures and railway electrification structures. Indian public sector companies like Bharat Heavy Electronics Limited (BHEL) and private sector firms like Tata Power, Kalptaru Power lines, KEC International, Mohan Energy Corporation and others are making inroads in this sector across Africa. In the alternative energy sector, India's Suzlon Energy and Mohan Energy Corporation are offering wind energy based solutions. In the hydrocarbon sector, apart from acquiring equity assets, Indian firms have invested in refineries. Essar Energy Overseas has invested to acquire stakes in Kenya and Egypt.

13.2 India and Nigeria

India and Nigeria have cordial and friendly relations, marked by mutual respect and understanding. There are no contentious issues between the two. India established a diplomatic mission in Nigeria in 1958, even before Nigeria became independent in 1960. This year we are celebrating the 50th anniversary of establishments of bilateral relations. Both countries have been in the forefront of the worldwide anti-colonial and anti-apartheid struggle. Similarities in colonial struggle, ethnic diversity and geo-political situation have created affinity and mutual goodwill between the two countries. Both India and Nigeria are members of UN, NAM, G-15, G-77 and the Commonwealth and have collaborated at various international organizations. Both share common perspectives on international political, social and development issues and these have manifested in various meetings at UN, WTO, etc. Nigeria is strongly opposed to all forms of terrorism.

With a population of 140 million and considerable revenue from oil exports, Nigeria is the largest trading partner of India in Africa. Bilateral annual trade turnover exceeds US$ 8 billion.

Indo-Nigerian relations gained momentum with the State Visit of President Olusegun Obasanjo to India in January 2000 as Chief Guest at the 50th Republic Day celebrations and the visit of the then EAM to Nigeria in March 2000 to co-chair the Third Session of India-Nigeria Joint Commission. In May 2003, the Minister of State for Commerce and Industry visited Lagos to Chair the Conference of Commercial Representatives of Western Sub-Saharan Africa. Former Nigerian Foreign Minister, Mr. Oluyemi Adeniji, visited India from October 28-30, 2003 to co-chair the Fourth Session of the Joint Commission and again visited in May 2006 when he had meeting with Hon'ble MoS (AS) Shri Anand Sharma.

The Hon'ble Prime Minister, Shri Atal Behari Vajpayee, visited Nigeria in December 2003 to participate in the Commonwealth Heads of Government Meeting (CHOGM-2003).

Hon'ble Prime Minister Dr. Manmohan Singh paid an official visit to Nigeria from October 14-16, 2007. This was the first bilateral visit after Pandit Nehru in 1962. During the landmark visit of Hon'ble Prime Minister of India Dr. Manmohan Singh (first bilateral visit after 45 years) the two sides elevated their relationship to a strategic partnership level through "Abuja Declaration" that lays down roadmap for future intensive and extensive cooperation. During the visit of Hon'ble Prime Minister of India, an Abuja Declaration on Strategic Partnership was issued and MoU between Foreign Service Institute and the Nigerian Foreign Service Academy, MoU between Indian Council for World Affairs (ICWA) and Nigerian Institute of International Affairs, MoU on Defence Cooperation and Protocol for Foreign Office Consultations were signed. Other key agreements like Trade Agreement, DTAA, BIPPA, S&T, ICT cooperation, MLAT etc are expected to be signed within the next six months.

Prime Minister Dr. Manmohan Singh paid an official visit to Nigeria from 14-16 October 2007. Agenda on bilateral relations between India and Nigeria are linked by common historical experiences and in the contemporary context are united in the desire to work towards democratic pluralism, tolerance, economic development and social justice.

13.3 India and Senegal

Both are members of the Non-Aligned Movement and GIS. Senegal has also extended its support to India's candidature for permanent membership of the UN Security Council. The Government has approved the signing and ratification of a Bilateral Investment Promotion and Protection Agreement with the Republic of Senegal.

Bilateral Investment Promotion and Protection Agreements (BIPA) have been signed by the Government of India till date with 57 countries since negotiations commenced in 1994. Agreements have also been finalized with eight other countries and negotiations are in progress with another 25 countries. These negotiations have been conducted on the basis of a negotiating text approved by the Steering Committee on Economic Reforms.

The Model India Text of BIP A was formulated by an Inter Ministerial Group which incorporated Indian sensitivities while taking note of several other such bilateral agreements negotiated earlier. The salient features of this Text include, inter-alia, the definition of Intellectual Property Rights (IPRs) which is to be defined in accordance with domestic laws.

This was perceived as being important, for the agreements reached in the Uruguay Round to allow developing countries a ten-year transition period to adopt the provisions of Trade Related Intellectual Property Rights (TRIPS). It provides for extending National Treatment and Most Favoured Nation (MFN) treatment of foreign investments, in addition to MFN treatment for investors. Expropriation and nationalization are to be restored to only on a non-discriminatory basis and subject to the payment of compensation.

Repatriation of all returns from investment is to be allowed without unreasonable delay and on a non-discriminatory basis. In respect of disputes between an Investor and the host Government, as well as between the two Governments, a dispute resolution mechanism including an international arbitration procedure is prescribed.

13.4 India and Sudan

India and Sudan have maintained cordial and friendly relations since the latter's independence in 1956. An Indian Liaison Office was set up in Khartoum in April 1955, months before Sudan's independence on January 1, 1956. Over 30,000 Sudanese have graduated from Indian universities and several Sudanese girls are named Hind. Indian films are the rage. There is much warmth and goodwill for India.

India-Sudan relations go back in history to the time of the Nilotic and Indus Valley Civilizations. There is evidence of contacts and possibly trade almost 5,000 years ago through Mesopotamia. The ancient Kush kingdom of Sudan, just south of the first Nile cataract (modern Aswan), reached its apogee some 2,000 years ago. Its pre-eminent deity Apedemak, associated with war, is depicted in the famous temples of Naqa (30 km. east of the Nile) as a triple headed god emerging from a lotus. Some archaeologists claim Indian influence through the ancient Red Sea port of Adulis.

Dozens of Indian soldiers sleep in the Commonwealth Cemetery in Khartoum, having laid down their lives in the Second World War. The first Sudanese Parliamentary elections in 1953 were conducted by Shri Sukumar Sen, India's Chief Election Commissioner (the Sudanese Election Commission, formed in 1957, drew heavily on Indian election literature and laws). In April 1955, the interim Prime Minister of the Sudan Ismail Al Azhari and several Ministers transited through New Delhi on their way to Bandung for the first Afro-Asian Relations Conference. At the 1955 Bandung Conference, the delegation from a still not independent Sudan did not have a flag to mark its place. Taking out his handkerchief, Jawaharlal Nehru wrote "Sudan" on it, thus reserving a place for Sudan in the international community.

Bilateral relations were boosted with the historic visit of Rashtrapatiji to Sudan in October 2003 and the entry of OVL in Sudan's oil sector. Institutional frameworks such as the Joint Ministerial Commission and Foreign Office Consultations have been set up.

13.4.1 Commercial and Economic Relations: India sells manufactured goods, machinery and equipment, transport equipment, chemicals and pharmaceuticals, foodstuffs, wheat, textiles, etc. India buys raw hides and skins, cotton, leather, ores and metal scrap.

Although there are over 50 companies with Indian capital in Sudan, bilateral economic relations reached an inflection point in 2003 with India's decision to invest US$ 750 million in the oil sector. ONGC Videsh Limited (OVL) acquired 25 percent of the shares of Sudan's biggest oil consortium Greater Nile Petroleum Operating Company (GNPOC). In May 2004, OVL acquired stakes in Blocks 5A and 5B from OMV of Austria. OVL also funded and built a 741 km. multi-product pipeline from Khartoum Refinery to Port Sudan Export Terminal. Completed in August 2005 two months ahead of schedule, it was formally dedicated to the nation in December 2005.

Since 2003, India Sudan bilateral trade has increased six times. India is the 2nd largest exporter to Sudan. India is everywhere through the ubiquitous Bajaj auto rickshaws, found in all towns and cities. The entry of Maruti cars in July 2006, the return of Tata buses and trucks in August 2006 and the launch of Mahindra Scorpio sports utility vehicle and Bolero pickup trucks in December 2007 have increased Brand India visibility.

Several Indian companies are now active in Sudan including TCIL, ITI Limited, RITES, BEL, IRCON, BHEL, Progressive Construction Ltd, Kirloskar Brothers, Kalpataru Power, Mohan Exports, Jaguar Industries, Angelique International and L&T.

In October 2007, Water and Power Consultancy Services (India) Ltd. (WAPCOS), won a consultancy contract from the World Bank administered Multi Donor Trust Fund for a US$ 40 mn water and electricity supply project to various cities in South Sudan under the Sudan Emergency Transport and Infrastructure Development Project for Ministry of Housing, Land and Public Utilities, Government of Southern Sudan, Juba.

India has laid the foundation-stone for a mega power project at Kosti in the White Nile State of Central Sudan recently. This 500 MW Thermal Power Project will be built in 44 months by Bharat Heavy Electricals Ltd. (BHEL) for US$ 457 million, of which India has extended a concessional line of credit of US$ 350 million. The Kosti project, when completed, will be the single largest power project in Sudan. Given its strategic geographic allocation, the project will cater to power needs of all the regions of Sudan. Thus it is conceived as a national integration project for Sudan. The ONGC and BHEL, India's two leading Public Sector Undertakings were already working in Sudan. ONGC completed its 741 km. multi-product pipeline project in August 2005, two months ahead of schedule.

In November 2007, Tata International Ltd. finalized a locomotives contract with Sudan Railways Corporation.

To give a sustained focus to India-Sudan trade relations and achieve 100 percent annual growth, the Mission has a non-exclusive five-plus-one commercial policy since October 2005. The five priority sectors in which India can respond to Sudan's developmental requirements are infrastructure (including transport), agriculture, human resource development, information and communications technologies, and small and medium industries. The "plus-one" is commercially viable investment in the energy sector (oil, electricity, gas). To achieve this, the Embassy has formulated a Target and Introduce Programme (TIP) under which one new Indian product is introduced every semester.

Enterprise India Advantage Sudan, the first ever exclusive exhibition of Indian products and technologies relevant to Sudan's developmental needs, was organized by the Mission in Khartoum over five days in August 2006 and business worth over US$ 100 mn was discussed.

13.5 India and Botswana

India-Botswana established diplomatic relations in 1966. Immediately after the latter's independence, The Indian High Commission was established in Gaborone in May 1987.

India is looking forward for enhanced export of services relating to Information Technology and construction industry to Botswana as part of its efforts to increase bilateral trade with that country. President of Botswana, Festus G. Mogae visited and expressed his desire for greater partnership.

India was keen to share its knowledge and experience in the field of information technology with developing countries like Botswana so as to develop a sustained partnership in technology transfer and development.

India prefers to be associated with the diversification of the economy of Botswana especially in the fields of agriculture, textiles, health, tourism, development of small and medium enterprises and institution building for channelising development finance to the entrepreneurs. Botswana is known for its sound management of rich natural resources.

India and South African Customs Union (SACU) are working towards finalizing a Preferential Trade Agreement (PTA) which would provide further opportunities to strengthen bilateral trade between India and Botswana. Botswana has been given high priority under the "Focus: Africa" programme of the government to increase its trade in the region.

13.6 India and Angola

India and Angola have traditionally enjoyed close and friendly ties dating back to pre-independence era of Angola. India set up its resident mission in Luanda in September 1986 and Angola its Embassy in New Delhi in 1992. ONGC Videsh Limited had failed to get 50 percent stake in Angola's offshore Block 18 oilfield after the African country's national oil company, Sanagol, exercised its pre-emption rights.

India will make a fresh attempt at entering Angola for oil exploration. An Indian delegation is preparing to visit Angola recently. The delegation would try to broad base India's economic relationship with Angola by also focusing on other sectors. Railway reconstruction through expertise from Rites Ltd would be on the agenda. The offshore Block 18 has 50 percent participation from British Petroleum which is also the operator of the block. Angola is a key player in Africa's oil industry both as a major producer and exporter. It is the second-largest producer in the Sub-Saharan Africa after Nigeria. Its oil reserves are estimated at 5.4 billion barrels.

13.7 India and Kenya

Talks on review of Bilateral Air Services Agreement Indian Civil Aviation delegations visited Nairobi to review their Bilateral Air Services Agreement, with the objective of liberalizing the existing arrangements and allow for greater and better connectivity for the benefit of the travelling public.

Both sides agreed to remove seat restrictions on routes between the two countries. Any capacity aircraft can now be used. Kenyan carriers previously had the right to fly on from Mumbai and carried traffic to Bangkok and Hong Kong. They can now do so to one more destination in Asia. Indian carriers will also be able to fly on to one additional African destination beyond Nairobi, besides Dar-es-Salaam and Johannesburg.

It is expected that the new agreement will greatly facilitate tourism and business linkages between Kenya and India, and further consolidate the friendly relations between the two countries.

The presence of a sizeable number of people of Indian origin in Kenya, numbering about 75,000, is a keystone to Indo-Kenyan structural relationship. I believe wealth is created by the people. The role of entrepreneurs in an economy including knowledge-based economy is most vital. Indian community, because of its history, culture and long tradition of entrepreneurship has contributed to Kenya's economic development. It can also provide an additional link between India and Kenya in the fields of commerce and industry and education, especially in professional education including information technology.

Terrorism, carried out in the name of religion has been casting a long and dark shadow on the face of humanity for over two decades. World community realized this dramatically on 11th September. India and Kenya have suffered from gruesome and dastardly acts of terrorism on their soils. India has been faced with repeated acts of cross-border terrorism spilling the blood of innocent men, women and children over the last two decades. We remain committed to secularism, peace and goodwill, we remain determined to wipe out the scourge of terrorism from India. We are heartened by the encouragement and support we receive from all countries dedicated to peace and goodwill.

13.8 India and Congo

India and Congo are considering steps to boost bilateral trade, which is not encouraging at present although there is a huge potential for two-way trade in the area of both goods and services. In order to boost trade, it was necessary to promote not only export of merchandise but also of services. This may cover induction of professionals and skilled labour from India, support to Indian IT and construction companies to get contracts in Congo. India could share with Congo its experience and expertise in the development of small and medium enterprises (SMEs), agriculture, tourism, health etc.

From the Indian perspective, Republic of Congo offers a possibility of entering into its promising petroleum sector. The revenues generated by sustained high international prices of oil are also beginning to provide the country with resources to invest in a number of socio-economic developmental activities. This, in turn, creates a market for Indian exports. The country is also rich in minerals and other natural resources like timber. These, along with the energy sector, offer potential areas of participation for India. At present, the two-way trade between India and Congo is a negligible US $ 790 million (2010-11).

13.9 India and Ethiopia

Emperor Haile Selaise visited India in 1956 and 1968. President Haile Mariam Mengistu visited India in 1983 to attend the NAM Summit and in 1985 for a state visit.

The 4th India-Ethiopia Joint Trade Committee meeting (JTC) was held in New Delhi on 5th June 2006. It has called for expanding the existing areas of trade and investment between India and Ethiopia and also to find new areas of cooperation between the two nations.

The JTC proposed that different Indian Delegations would visit Ethiopia in the next 60 days to look for possibilities. These would include delegations of:

1. National Institute of Information Technology (NIIT)-for IT training in Ethiopian educational institutes;
2. Infrastructure Leasing and Financial Services (IL&FS)-to explore possibilities in Infrastructure project in Ethiopia by Indian Companies;
3. BHEL – to explore long term partnership in Energy;
4. Council of Leather Exports- to explore possibility of sourcing raw hides and skins from Ethiopia and a Delegation of Tea Board for cooperation and

development of Ethiopian Tea Sector.

13.10 India and South Africa

India had been in the forefront of the international community in supporting the anti-apartheid struggle in South Africa ever since Mahatma Gandhi started his Satyagraha movement in South Africa a century ago. India was the first country to sever trade relations with the apartheid Government in 1946, and imposed a complete—diplomatic, commercial, cultural and sports—embargo on South Africa. India worked consistently to put the issue of apartheid on the agenda of the UN, NAM and other multilateral organizations and for the imposition of comprehensive international sanctions against South Africa. The ANC maintained a representative office in New Delhi from the 1960s onwards.

Following the commencement of talks between the South African Government and the ANC, India's relations with South Africa were restored after a gap of over four decades, with the opening of a Cultural Centre in Johannesburg in May 1993. Formal diplomatic and consular relations with South Africa were restored in November 1993 during the visit to India of the then South African Foreign Minister Pik Botha. A Consulate General was thereafter established in Johannesburg. The Indian High Commission in Pretoria was opened in May 1994, followed by the opening of the Consulate General in Durban in the same month. Since Parliament in South Africa meets in Cape Town, a permanent office of the High Commission was opened there in 1996.

Against the background of India's consistent support to the antiapartheid struggle, there has been a steady consolidation of our close and friendly ties with South Africa, both bilaterally and through the trilateral IBSA Dialogue Forum. A number of bilateral agreements have been concluded between the two countries since the assumption of diplomatic relations in 1993 in diverse areas ranging from defence, culture, heath, human settlements, public administration, science and technology and economic cooperation.

President Pratibha Patil visited Cape Town on April 24, 2008; President Thabo Mbeki, visited India from April 7-9, 2008 to participate in the India-Africa Forum Summit in New Delhi; Prime Minister Dr. Manmohan Singh went to South Africa to attend the 2nd IBSA Summit in October 2007. India and member countries of the South African Customs Union (SACU)-South Africa, Namibia, Botswana, Lesotho and Swaziland have signed a framework agreement for a preferential trade agreement.

The government has recently concluded an extradition treaty and a pact on mutual legal assistance with South Africa at the end of the sixth Joint-Ministerial Commission meeting. Two sub-committees to oversee IT and Communication, and human resource development relations between the two nations have also been established.

The Pan-African e-initiative involved the creation of a distance education network, telemedicine and VVIP connectivity. Fifteen countries, including South Africa, are likely to participate in the initiative. The African Union had chosen Adis Ababa (Ethiopia). The trilateral India-Brazil-South Africa (IBSA) which includes India, Brazil and South Africa initiative has already proved to be effective especially in the field of tourism, civil aviation and small and medium enterprises.

The India-South Africa Joint Commission at the level of Foreign Ministers was set up in 1994 to identify areas of mutually beneficial cooperation. The 7th session of the Joint Ministerial Commission was held in Pretoria on February 21-22, 2008 for which EAM Shri Pranab Mukherjee visited South Africa, together with a high level delegation. During the visit, three new Agreements on:

- Customs cooperation,
- S&T, and
- Visa free travel for diplomatic and official passport holders, were signed.

On June 6, 2003, the Foreign Ministers of India, Brazil and South Africa met in Brasilia and agreed to set up a Dialogue Forum for regular consultations on such matters. Two Summits have been held so far. India hosted the 4th meeting of the Trilateral Commission on July 16-17, 2007 and the 5th Trilateral Ministerial Commission Meeting took place in South Africa on May 11, 2008. Currently a total of 16 sectoral Working Groups have been established in areas as diverse as health, agriculture, education, human settlements, science and technology and defence. India hosted the 3rd IBSA Summit on October 15, 2008.

India and South Africa have a common approach on many global issues, including the future of multilateralism, South-South Cooperation and multilateral trade negotiations. This has led to fruitful cooperation in the UN, NAM, Commonwealth, IOR-ARC, WTO, G-77, G-20 and the New Asian-African Strategic Partnership (NAASP).

India has strongly supported the objectives of New Partnership for Africa's Development. A sum of US$ 200 million have been committed for this purpose to be utilized through credit lines, grants etc. Its utilization has begun with some major projects in Angola, Senegal and Mali etc.

The Indian Government's International Technical Cooperation Programme (ITEC) has been a useful medium of promoting cooperation in development of human resources. South Africa has utilized about 500 slots since 2000. Due to increase in utilisation, the number of slots allocated to South Africa has been almost doubled from 55 to 100 in 2006, as agreed during Prime Minister's visit in

October 2006.

In the field of higher education, a number of South African universities are establishing links with counterpart institutions in India. We have facilitated the process by hosting the Vice Chancellor of the University of KZN in September 2007 and the Vice Chancellor of Witwatersrand University in November 2007. Visit of the Vice Chancellor of the Cape Town University in on the anvil. The University of Witwatersrand has decided to set up a Centre of Indian Studies in Africa which will be launched in September 2008. This would be first 'India focus' centre in Africa.

Defence is an important area of cooperation. A Defence Cooperation Agreement was signed in September 2000 during the then Raksha Mantri's visit to South Africa. It has provided the framework for further strengthening cooperation in this sector.

13.11 India and Gabon

On November 3, 2006, the meeting was held between India and Gabon. The equatorial African Republic of Gabon has shown interest in India's participation in the exploration and exploitation of its mining resources. This came out during the discussions between the Minister of Mines and the President of the Republic of Gabon.

The President mentioned that Gabon is rich in mineral resources like manganese, petrol, diamond, gold, lime stone and columbium. It has got the second largest resources of manganese ore. It exports petroleum and manganese to different countries. The Republic seeks cooperation of the emerging economic powers like India for exploring and exploiting its mineral reserves.

13.12 India and Ivory

After a long gap of 9 years, the second meeting of the Indo-Côte d'Ivoire (Ivory Coast) Joint Trade Committee was held in New Delhi. A delegation of 110 members from Côte d'Ivoire including 3 Senior Ministers and led by the Foreign Minister of Côte d'Ivoire Mr. Youssouf Bakayoko is in India and met with Shri Jairam Ramesh, Minister of State for Commerce and other officials.

Shri Jairam Ramesh drew attention to the emerging importance of Africa in India's foreign economic policy and a special role that West Africa is now occupying. He identified hydrocarbons and diamonds as two areas where India is actively exploring investment opportunities in West African countries. Shri Ramesh spoke about the activities of ONGC Videsh in Côte d'Ivoire where it has already invested US$ 12 million for oil and gas exploration and will now seek to expand its activities there.

It was pointed out that while the volume of two-way trade between India and Côte d'Ivoire in 2005-06 was only US$ 350 million and was confined mostly to rice from India and raw cashews from Côte d'Ivoire, the real success story of India in the Côte d'Ivoire lies in investment. Indian companies announced their intentions to invest close to US$ 1 billion in the Côte d'Ivoire spread over the next 5 years in the mining sector. In the last ten years, the total amount of announced Indian FDI abroad is around US$ 10 billion. Bilateral trade between the two stood at US$ million in 2010-11.

The Côte d'Ivoire delegation expressed their keenness for Indian support to start an IT-cum-Technology Park in Abidjan, named after Mahatma Gandhi. Shri Ramesh promised all support and assured the Côte d'Ivoire delegation of India's seriousness in getting this technology park operational at the very earliest, as also for increasing the lines of credit from India to Côte d'Ivoire and scholarships to its students in India under the on-going ITEC programme. 50 such scholarships have been extended to Côte d'Ivoire and this will now be enhanced to 65. In the 1980s, the development economics community had lauded the economic miracle of Côte d'Ivoire and expressed the hope that the on-going ethnic conflict there would end soon. India has assured full assistance in the rebuilding and reconstruction of Côte d'Ivoire.

14

India and Latin America

14.1 India's Policy towards Latin America: An Overview

India has recognized ambassadorial relations with most of these countries and cultured reasonably good relations. India has traditionally maintained very friendly relations with the countries of Latin America. The continent of Latin America comprises of 43 countries broadly falling in three areas-Central America, the Caribbean and South America. Central America comprises of Mexico, E1 Salvador, the Honduras, Nicaragua, Costa Rica, Belize, Panama, and Guatemala. The Caribbean area comprises of Cuba, Jamaica, Haiti, the Dominican Republic, Bahamas, Puerto Rico, Grenada, Antigua, Barbuda, the commonwealth of Dominica and Dutch Antilles. South America, loosely described as Latin America, comprises of Guinea, Venezuela, Colombia, Ecuador, Peru, Bolivia, Chile, Argentina, Uruguay, Paraguay, Brazil, Surinam and Guyana. Several factors prompted India to develop intimate relations with Latin American countries. In the first instance, India felt greatly perturbed over voting by the Latin American countries in the Security Council on the question of Kashmir. The partisan position taken by Argentina on the Kashmir issue in the Security Council that Pakistan armed forces should remain in Kashmir at a time when the council was engaged in demilitarizing the area, greatly disturbed India and prompted it to improve relations with Latin American countries.

The economic considerations also prompted India to cultivate more intimate relations with countries of Latin America. The various studies undertaken by Indian Institute for Foreign Trade (IIFT), Indian Council for Research in International Economic Relations (ICRIER), Federation of Indian Chambers of Commerce and Industry (FICCI), the Confederation of Indian Industry (CII) etc. indicated that there existed abundance of opportunities for trade and investment in several major Latin American countries.

In fact the main objective of India's foreign policy towards Latin America has been to strengthen and deepen the existing relationship and to impart to it a greater economic content.

In recent years a number of high level visits have been exchanged between leaders of India and countries of Latin America which resulted in the conclusion of a number of agreements between the two in areas of mutual interest. In May

2000, India's Minister of State for Commerce and Industry (Omar Abdullah) paid a visit to Argentina and tried to secure market access for Indian products, particularly pharmaceuticals, to Argentina. In August 2000, India's Minister of State for External Affairs (Ajit Kumar Panja) also paid a visit to Argentina and held discussions on wide range of bilateral and international issues, including the possibility of the entry of Indian pharmaceutical products into the Argentina market.

India requires to strengthen its economic and commercial ties with Venezuela. A delegation consisting of representatives of ONGC (Oil and Natural Gas Commission), Reliance Petroleum, Nagarjuna Fertilizers, Diamond and Gem Development Corporation etc. paid a visit to Venezuela and sought to strengthen economic ties. In fact for the first time Venezuela agreed to supply oil to India by shipping 5 million barrels of heavy crude oil to reliance Petroleum. The India delegation during its visit to Venezuela explored the possibility of utilizing Venezuela technology for extraction of heavy crude in Rajasthan.

To promote closer economic relations with Chile, India's Minister of State for Commerce and Industry, led a CII (Confederation of Indian Industry) delegations to Chile in May 2000. During this visit the idea of a Free Trade Agreement between the two countries was discussed in details. In November 2000, the first round of discussion on a Bilateral investment promotion and protection agreement between India and Chile was held at New Delhi. India also completed a bid to develop intimate relations with Mexico. In June 2000, a meeting of the Telecom sub-commission of the Joint Commission was held at Mexico City to review the memorandum of understanding on the subject. The two countries also made a bid to simplify the visa arrangements for Indian visitors—both tourists and businessmen to Mexico.

In December 2000 PDVSA, Venezuela's largest oil company offered to ONGC six blocks for exploration and production of oil. It may be noted that it was for the first time that Venezuela offered oil field concessions to a foreign company outside the international tendering procedure. In October, 2000, a 14-member Venezuelan Software delegation paid a visit to India and signed a memorandum of understanding with the Electronics and Software Export Promotion Council. In view of the growing relationships between the two countries India gifted medicines worth US$ 20,000 to Venezuela when natural calamity struck that country.

Decolonisation means there is end of colonialism and imperialism. Decolonisation is the product of 20th century. As a result of the process of decolonisation, a large number of territories which were formerly under the control of various colonies, gained independence. It is particularly a post-World

War II phenomenon. In the post-World War-I period, the spread of nationalism in the colonial areas of Asia posed a serious challenge to the colonial rule. The process of decolonisation did not start this period. It was only in post-II World War period that the process of decolonisation was greatly speeded up.

From the very beginning, the UN started playing an important role in speeding up the process of decolonisation. There are number of steps being implemented by UN to upgrade the process of decolonisation. There are number of resolutions have been passed for speedy development. The main resolutions behind decolonisation are:

1. Bandung conference 1955.
2. Granting of independence to the colonial countries and people-1960.
3. Special committee on Decolonisation 1961, 1962, 1966, 1967, 1969 and 1972.
4. UN General Assembly adopted a declaration of Namibia in 1978.
5. UN General Assembly adopted at its 39th Session (1984-85) a series of resolutions an decolonisation.
6. UN and non-aligned movement (1990-2000) stand for international decade for the eradication of colonialism.

All these above resolutions are being made by UNO to end colonialism in the 21st century. It is evident from above resolution that the UN has played a commendable role in the process of decolonisation.

14.2 Impacts of Decolonisation

There are number of impacts of decolonisation an international community. The impacts are:

1. It is a society of sovereign states.
2. The size of the international community has expanded.
3. The emergence of a large number of new countries and their entry into the UNO has exercised profound influence on the international relations.
4. International society is multi-layered.
5. Nationalism is also a motivating force for human behaviour due to decolonization.
6. Regional organisation concerning EEC, Latin America, America Middle East, South-East Asia, African unity etc. played important role in making international society economic.
7. Decolonisation has developed new institutional devices–coalitions, block, international organizations in order to meet new challenges.
8. Interdependence of the world has greatly increased.
9. Numerous powerful cross national actors have also increased.

10. International trade union and consumer protection group have also increased. Environmental protection group has also increased.
11. Personality of the world leaders have also shaped the dimension of international society (for example, Bush, Kofi Annan etc.).
12. The discussion now shifts from the micro-level study to the macro level study.
13. The international system has changed from European to global. In 1994, at Bretton Woods, IMF and the World Bank were established.

14.3 India, Latin America and Caribbean

The Government has also intensified relations with Latin America and the Caribbean both at the bilateral level and with the regional groups. Ministerial visits of Foreign Ministers of Mexico, Venezuela, Suriname and the visit of Shri Rao Inderjit Singh, Minister of State, to Panama, Colombia, Dominican Republic and El-Salvador has maintained high-level interaction with the countries of the region. India's commonalities with Brazil have continued to grow as both collaborate on Security Council reform and the WTO. The process of finalizing Preferential Trade Agreement (PTA) with MERCOSUR (Brazil, Argentina, Uruguay, and Paraguay) is on course and negotiations are being held with Chile.

14.4 India-Brazil-South Africa (IBSA)

In March 2004, the India, Brazil and South Africa (IBSA) conducted their first-ever Trilateral Commission meeting at New Delhi. At the New Delhi Summit, the Forum decided that no new member would be allowed. China, Russia and Egypt have shown their interest to join the Forum. The Forum has aimed at encouraging cooperation in poverty alleviation, coordination at the World Trade Organisation, increase in trilateral trade and cooperation in defence matters.

The total trade between the two countries, India and Brazil was US$ 7.5 billion during 2010-11. Of this, US$ 3.97 billion were Indian exports and US$ 3.54 billion were Brazilian imports to India.

Both the countries are working closely in the G-20 alliance in the WTO agriculture negotiations. Both countries are also representing the G-20 in meetings of the G-4 and FIPs (Five Interested Parties) on WTO matters.

Brazil has the world's most competitive agri-business centre. In fact, besides being big producer of fruits, Brazil has emerged also as the world's largest exporter of beef and poultry, soya, orange juice, coffee and ethanol.

India and South Africa have signed an agreement to develop mutually-beneficial relationship in merchant shipping and related maritime transport matters on the basis of sovereign equality and reciprocity.

The agreement shall be renewed automatically for successive periods of one year unless terminated by either party giving six months written notice in advance.

India has already signed a framework agreement with MERCOSUR, which will provide a preferential trade regime to India-Brazil trade.

The India, Brazil and South Africa (IBSA) is going to be a big force to be reckon with. With a combined population of more than 1.2 billion, nearly US$ 1.6 trillion domestic market and foreign trade of US$ 30 billion, the IBSA grouping is in a position to emerge as a strong player.

1. Trade between India on the one hand and Brazil and South Africa on the other will double in coming years.
2. India's trade with Brazil by the fiscal 2010-11 stood at US$ 7.5 billion and its trade with South Africa was at US$ 11.25 billion.
3. Indian exports to Brazil were US$ 3.97 billion against its import of US$ 3.54 billion. Similarly, India's exports to South Africa stood at US$ 3.98 billion against its imports of US$ 7.14 billion in 2010-11.

14.5 India-Brazil-Argentina

Argentina, Brazil and India which have submitted their joint proposal on the Non-agriculture Market Access (NAMA) negotiations at the World Trade Organisation (WTO) recently, have managed to win the support of some members including Kenya, Malaysia and the Caribbean group of countries. It is also said that apart from Argentina, Brazil and India (ABI), there are large number of developing countries which shares ABI objective of opposing the Swiss Formula of tariff reduction.

The Swiss Formula is a harmonising method designed to narrow the gap between high and low tariffs. If implemented it would require developing countries with high tariffs to bring about stiffer cuts than developed countries which have relatively lower average tariffs. The ABI proposal has suggested a "Swiss-type" tariff reduction formula based on the average tariffs of members. The formula would enable countries with higher average bound tariffs to reduce tariffs less steeply than countries with lower average bound tariff.

The logic behind the tariff formula proposed is that Doha mandate talks about less than full reciprocity for developing countries which has to be incorporated in the formula itself. Therefore, a formula which imposes lesser reduction burden on developing countries should be absolutely valid.

Securing the energy security India is increasingly eyeing on Latin America as a potential source of oil security. Venezuela's President Hugo Chavez during his visit to India in the first week of March offered oil fields to ONGC Videsh Ltd (OVL) and also expressed interest in the long term supply of oil to India's large and growing market. President Chavez's offer is part of his own strategic policy of market diversification for Venezuelan oil to reduce dependence on the United States market.

The entry of OVL in the rich Venezuelan market is an important breakthrough. This will also help India learn the technology for upgrading extra-heavy crude, which has been found by Oil India Ltd in Rajasthan.

Besides Venezuela, other countries in the region such as Mexico, Ecuador, Colombia, Argentina, Trinidad and Tobago, Cuba and Suriname offer opportunities, in varying degrees, for acquisition of oil and gas assets by India. Mexico, which had kept foreign companies out of its energy sector so far, is now opening up for foreign participation, particularly in deep sea exploration and production. The Mexicans need foreign funds and technology to fill the gap in their own resources and capacity. Further, the new state energy company of Argentina, ENARSA, has formed partnerships with Petrobras (state oil company of Brazil) and PDVSA (Venezuelan state oil company) for exploration of about 50 blocks and will be open to Indian companies too. Trinidad and Tobago is expected to call for international bids this year for three offshore and one onshore oil and gas blocks. The Indian companies could consider the option of tying up with Latin American and multinational companies in these ventures.

14.6 India-Mercosur

The Government has given its approval for signing of five Annexes of the Preferential Trade Agreement (PTA) between MERCOSUR and India. It will facilitate the ongoing endeavour to strengthen trade and economic relations between MERCOSUR and India. The signing of the annexes to the PTA with MERCOSUR will pave the way to implement the Preferential Trade Agreement as the first step towards negotiating ultimately a Free Trade Agreement. This will boost our trade to MERCOSUR in particular and Latin America in general.

MERCOSUR is a trading block in Latin America comprising Brazil, Argentina, Uruguay and Paraguay. It has Chile and Bolivia as its associate members. MERCOSUR was formed in 1991 with the objective of facilitating the free movement of goods, services, capital and people among the four member countries. It became a Customs Union in 1995. MERCOSUR has become a successful market of about 200 million people, representing about US$ 1 trillion of GDP and US$ 190 billion of trade. It is the fourth largest integrated market after the European Union (EU), North American Free Trade Agreement (NAFTA) and ASEAN.

India had a total trade of US$ 1416.65 million with MERCOSUR during 2003-2004. Indian exports to MERCOSUR were approximately US$ 566.96 million during 2003-04 and imports from MERCOSUR were around US$ 849.69 million during the same period. The region still has a huge potential for Indian exports as Indian share is just 0.83 percent of the global imports of MERCOSUR. Indian major items of exports to MERCOSUR are drugs, pharmaceuticals and finc chemicals, transport equipment, inorganic/organic/agro-chemicals, cotton yarn and cotton and manmade fabrics, made-ups, readymade garments, dyes, intermediates and coal tar. The major imports into India from MERCOSUR are edible oils (primarily soya), metalliferous ores, metal scrap and non-electrical machinery.

14.7 India and Chile

Diplomatic relations between Chile and India officially started in the year 1959. Since the restoration of democracy in 1990, Chile has emerged politically the most stable, economically the most dynamic, and socially the most cohesive nation in South America.

The Government has approval for signing the Preferential Trade Agreement (PTA) between Chile and India. It will facilitate the ongoing endeavour to strengthen trade and economic relations between the Republic of Chile and the Republic of India. The signing of PTA with Chile will pave the way to implement the Preferential Trade Agreement as the first step towards negotiating ultimately a Free Trade Agreement. This will boost our trade with Chile in particular and Latin America in general.

A PTA provides for exchange of tariff concessions on a limited scale between two countries/groups of countries, both in terms of coverage (number of products) and depth of concessions (percentage of tariff reductions, i.e. Margin of Preference offered).

Fixed tariff preferences are fixed Margins of Preference offered by an importing PTA partner on specific products, which are applied to the Most Favoured Nation (MFN) import duty to arrive at a reduced import duty for the exporting PTA partner.

Both the countries have signed a preferential trade agreement in a bid to increase bilateral trade and investment. This was a first step towards an Indo-Chile free trade agreement. The Agreement provides tariff preferences ranging from 10 to 50 percent on 178 products to Chile and a similar range of preferences on 296 items to India. The 296 items cover about 91 percent of the goods being exported by India to Chile. The Chilean goods to get preference cover about 98 percent of the country's exports to India. The Indian products to benefit from the agreement include textiles, chemicals, pharmaceuticals, engineering and agricultural machinery. Chilean products to face lower tariff barriers in India include newsprint, cellulose, fish meal, copper, wood-boards and salmon.

1. In 2010-11, total trade between India and Chile stood at US$ 2,100 million.
2. Chile is the leading producer of copper in the world. The two sides discussed wide range of issues of mutual interest. These included issues of bilateral interest, the reform of the Security Council, interest in increasing bilateral trade, scientific cooperation, and negotiating a Free Trade Agreement.
3. Chile expressed its continued support to the candidature of India as a permanent member of the UNSC.

15

India and North America

15.1 India and Canada

Canada will support India in the ongoing negotiations in the World Trade Organisation (WTO), especially in the key areas of agriculture and services. Canada urged that the Bilateral Investment Promotion and Protection Agreement between India and Canada be expedited as it had been pending for too long and could lead to huge increase in inflows of Canadian foreign direct investment (FDI) into India.

Bilateral Investment Promotion and Protection Agreement would also provide an effective mechanism for resolving outstanding investment related issues between the two countries. The agreement is currently under discussion between the two delegations.

India raised the issue of export of Indian ayurvedic drugs to Canada in the light of the health warning issued recently by the Canadian authorities against the use of some ayurvedic medicinal products especially from India on alleged grounds of high metallic content and pointed out that there had never been any complaints against Indian ayurvedic products. It was agreed that the matter would be looked into by experts on both sides. Among other trade issues, the Canadian side flagged the issue of import of Canadian pulses which is at present subject to system of annual permits and urged a stable policy framework which would help Canadian exporters.

Indo-Canadian bilateral trade amounted to US$ 5.21 billion in 2011, of which India's exports to Canada were valued at US$ 2.58 billion and India's imports from Canada were US$ 2.63 billion. As far as investment is concerned, cumulative FDI from Canada to India stood at US$ 383.63 million during the period April 2000 to March 2012.

15.1.1 Cooperation in Diamond Mining: India and Canada have agreed to explore the possibility of cooperation in the field of diamond mining on a mutually beneficial basis. The visiting Minister of Economic Development and Trade, Joseph Cordiano mooted the idea of investing in diamond mines in Canada for sourcing of rough diamonds which could be then cut and polished in India for exports. India has already emerged as the top exporter of cut and polished diamonds in the world.

Although annual bilateral trade between India and Canada had grown significantly over the last few years US$ 2.88 billion in 2006-07 to US$ 3.39 billion in 2010-11. India's share in Canada's imports is only about 0.5 percent. India is the 37th largest source of direct investment in Canada, with more than half of the Indian investment there being in pulp and paper.

Canada and India have entered into a collaboration that envisages development of a new wireless technology to link remote and rural areas. It paves that way for the researchers from the two countries to work together for coming out with viable and efficient technologies in broadband wireless networking.

A formal agreement has been signed by the communication research centre, Canada and India's centre for Development of Telematics (C-DoT). The Convergence of views between the countries is providing communication links for rural and remote areas. It also paved the way for the collaboration.

Much like in Canada, the Indian Government is also focussing on improving infrastructure for rural and remote areas. Rural areas in both the countries face significant challenges for which technology may provide some answers. There is realisation that the cost of establishing current infrastructure technologies, such as laying fibre opticables to rural areas, could often be prohibitive.

Under the agreement, the CRC and C-DOT will be looking at the potential uses of a new technology developed in Canada Microwave Light organised network or Milton. This technology is a low cost wireless "last while access solution. The technology takes broadband Internet from a central fibre optic cable and distributes it wirelessly through an antenna network over an area of several kilometres.

The proposed MoU between the C-DOT and the CRC would go a long way in developing technologies suitable for the borming broadband application market including those for rural masses.

Canada and India would be able to sort out differences on civilian nuclear cooperation over time. It has been revealed that the Canadian nuclear agency had offered help to India in a matter of hours after the tsunami struck the country on December, 26. Canada had a long relationship with India in the nuclear field. India and Canada had agreed to work with third countries to develop a tsunami early warning system. A joint statement issued after talks said the two Prime Ministers underlined the need for a strong and sustained international response to such adversity and welcomed coordination of relief efforts resulting from their participation in the "core group".

15.2 India and Mexico

India and Mexico have surprising similarities in geo-climatic conditions, biodiversity, ancient civilizational centres, physiognomy, cultural and family values, European connection during the colonial period and a somewhat similar politico-economic approach in the post-Independence periods.

Indo-Mexican relations have historically been characterised by friendship, goodwill and commonality of views on a wide range of global issues. The two countries have traditionally cooperated in the context of the UN, GIS, disarmament and multilateral trade policy issues.

India and Mexico signed a Memorandum of Understanding (MoU) on cooperation in the field of Micro, Small and Medium Enterprises. The MoU provides for cooperation in the development-of trade between Micro, Small and Medium Sized Enterprises (MSMEs) of both sides, exchange of information on best practices for the promotion and development of MSME's international trade and device strategies, practices and procedures to facilitate trade between MSMEs of the United Mexican States and the Ministry of Small Scale Industries and Ministry of Agro and Rural Industries, Government of India.

The objective of this Memorandum of Understanding is to establish the basis for cooperation between the sides to increase and strengthen commercial ties between the two sides for achieving mutually beneficial economic development and employment generation.

The sides will promote and facilitate the development of cooperative relationship between Mexican and Indian service providers and resource partners and share information on the programmes, products and services that each provides to its MSMEs.

Relevant service providers in India include Small Industries Development Organisation, National Small Industries Corporation, National Institute for Entrepreneurship and Small Business Development, National Institute for Small Industries Extension Training, Indian Institute of Entrepreneurship, Khadi and Village Industries Commission and Coir Board; whereas in Mexico PRIMER CONTACTO (Entrepreneurial Advice and Support Centre "First Stop Shop"), SIEM (Mexican Entrepreneurial Informative System) and CIPI (Industrial Policy Intersecretary Commission) will be among the partners. The two sides will jointly evaluate and share information in order to facilitate joint ventures, licensing, sub-contracting and commercial alliances and distributorship opportunities between Mexican and Indian MSMEs.

On May 21, 2007 India and Mexico signed the number of relevant agreements on Bilateral Protection and Promotion of Investments. Finance Minister of India P. Chidambaram and Mexican Minister of Economy Dr. Edward Sojo signed the agreement for the future results of the investment flow. Outcome of the Agreement:

1. The Agreement seeks to promote and protect investments from either country in the territory of the other country with the ultimate objective of increasing bilateral investment flow.
2. It requires each country to encourage and create favourable conditions for investors of the other country to make investments in its territory and to admit investments in accordance with its laws.
3. The Agreement would remain in force for a period of ten years and is expected to serve as a catalyst in boosting investment flows between the two countries.
4. The term investment includes every kind of asset including intellectual property rights in accordance with laws and regulations of the country in which the investment is made.
5. Principles of Most Favoured Nation Treatment and National Treatment (NT) have been asserted in the agreement.
6. It also provides for free repatriation of funds of an investor of either country.
7. In the last decade the bilateral trade has grown almost 5 times and has reached the level of almost US$ 3.3 billion.
8. The investments in Mexico by the investors of Indian origin have also crossed US$ 1.5 billion.
9. The country also has emphasized that given the fact that Mexico 'is a member of important free trade associations including the NAFTA.
10. This Agreement will certainly be remembered as one of the most important Treaties, which India has signed in recent times.
11. The rapid growth of bilateral trade and Indian investments in Mexico and assured that the Indian investors would be provided with all possible incentives and comfort in establishing and reinforcing their investments in Mexico.
12. India and Mexico have also maintained close collaboration at the UN bodies and other international fora, including WTO, G-15, G-20 and group of mega bio-diverse countries.

16

India and Oceania

16.1 India and New Zealand

India and New Zealand have traditionally enjoyed cordial and friendly relations based on common linkages of Commonwealth, parliamentary democracy, English language and sports. However, despite the New Zealand Government's sharp reaction to India's nuclear tests in May 1998 resulting in somewhat lukewarm relations for some time, both the countries maintained their normal relations. New Zealand has unveiled a slew of measure to attract more Indian students to the country. Recently, the New Zealand Education Minister Trevor Mallard has inked a pact with his Indian counterpart, Arjun Singh, to expand the existing education relationship between the two countries.

The Education Cooperation Arrangement envisages New Zealand amending its visa policies to become an attractive destination for Indian students. One of the incentives is that international students, who have graduated from a course that would gain points under the skilled migrant category, will be eligible for a six-month work permit.

16.1.1 Educational Pact

1. On completion of the course in New Zealand, the student will be qualified for a six month work permit.
2. School students and some English language students will be eligible to work part time while studying.
3. Working hours for those eligible have been increased to 20 hours a week during term from the current 15 hours.
4. Those in 12 month course or longer will get to work full-time over the summer.
5. Spouses of those studying in an area of absolute skill shortage, post-graduate students will be eligible for an open work permit valid till spouse's course competition.

Negotiations for a Free Trade Agreement (FTA) between India and New Zealand have commenced. The first round of talks was held in Wellington on April 7-8, 2010 and four other rounds have since been held in August 2010, October 2010, March 2011 and June 2011.

16.1.2 India-New Zealand Cooperation Sectors:

- Education.
- Telecommunications.
- Bio-technology.
- Information technology.

New Zealand agricultural technology, biotechnology and infrastructure engineering all have a big potential role to play in helping India lift food production. Bilateral trade in 2010 stood at NZ$ 1268 million between New Zealand and India, but there is a large untapped potential for increasing it. There were tariff and technical barriers for New Zealand agriculture products in India. These include sanitary and phyto-sanitary restrictions, besides the customs procedures.

16.2 India and Australia

The pre-cursor of Consulate-General of India first opened in Sydney as the Trade Office in 1941. The first Indian High Commissioner reached Canberra in 1946.2007 will not be met if the issue of non-tariff barriers (NTBs), particularly the sanitary and phyto-sanitary measures and technical barriers, to trade in Australia were not tackled.

India stands to benefit from the facilitation of Australian investment particularly in areas such as energy and resources, infrastructure development, food and agricultural processing and services.

Tourism promotion, eco-tourism, sharing expertise and a tourism business forum formed the basis for an action plan for fast-tracking tourism growth between India and Australia. Both the countries jointly promoted the 2006 Melbourne Commonwealth Games and 2010 Delhi Commonwealth Games which significantly increased the tourist flows.

Both the countries have agreed to establish a bilateral eco-tourism-working group to identify joint research and training projects. The sides agreed that Australia would host an Australia-India Tourism Business Forum for this purpose in Melbourne during the 2006 Commonwealth Games besides interaction time to time.

The sides identified eco tourism as an area of vital interest to both countries and agreed to establish an eco-tourism working group for this purpose. Indian tourism to Australia is forecast to grow at an average 14 percent per year for the next decade and Australia tourism to India has grown by 22 percent in the last 12 months.

Australia has gradually started to occupy an important position in India's foreign policy. Australia is nudging the UK as India's second largest foreign higher-education provider. Gold is now Australia's main export to India at a value of well over US$ 2.1 billion. Australia now supplies 25 percent of India's gold market; Australian coking coal is used in more than 50 percent of steel produced in India. India is the world's sixth largest energy consumer. Considering this Australia may be very helpful. Australian LNG can be of enormous use for the Indian requirement.

The India-Australia Coal and Mining Forum is a joint initiative by the Indian and Australian Governments. The Forum aims at enhancing the collaborative relationship between both the countries to stimulate increased information exchange and joint projects, provide an opportunity for industry to showcase expertise and capabilities and bring Indian and Australian industry, research institutions and governments together.

The Forum will focus on topics of shared interest including investment, regulation, sustainable mining, mining technology services and equipment, coal blending and washing facilities, clean coal technologies, coal mine methane, technical cooperation, skill development and education.

16.2.1 Cooperation in Oil Sector: India and Australia discussed the possibilities of further enhancing cooperation in the hydrocarbon sector. The two sides felt the need for having criss-cross investment by the companies from India and Australia, in both the countries.

Shri Deora while referring to the existing cooperation in various areas of oil and gas sector said that the companies from the two countries could take greater advantage of investment opportunities available in both countries. He referred to the possibility of importing LNG from Western Australia as well as Indian companies picking up more equity oil as part of India's plans to add E&P properties abroad.

Similarly, the cooperation in developing Coal Bed Methane (CBM) projects offer significant possibilities to build upon the participation of Arrow Energy, an Australian company, in the third CBM round which concluded recently. He also invited Australian companies which have strong R&D base in oil and gas sector to set up facilities in India.

Mr. Carpenter informed that Western Australia is a significant source of supplying natural gas particularly the Liquefied Natural Gas (LNG), for which India is also emerging as a an attractive market. The new projects for enhancing LNG capacity in the country are being implemented to increase this from about 16 million tonnes to about 50 million tonnes. He also invited Indian investment in the exploration and production of hydrocarbon in Western Australia.

India and Australia on June 23 2008, reviewed the bilateral Framework Dialogue between the two Foreign Ministers and underlined a strong bond and enduring shared interests that underpin their growing relationship.

The External Affairs Minister, Mr. Pranab Mukherjee, met with his Australian counterpart Stephen Smith here and reaffirmed that the two countries were committed to take bilateral talks to a new and high level. Reviewing the Framework Dialogue mechanism, which held its last meeting in 2005, Mr. Mukherjee and Mr. Smith welcomed the diversification and strengthening of political links between India and Australia. The two ministers also emphasised that regular high-level political contact would continue to underpin bilateral relations.

On his maiden visit to Australia, Mr. Mukherjee said this would provide another opportunity for continuing dialogue with Canberra. Mr. Mukherjee welcomed Australia's bid for a non-permanent UNSC seat for the 2013-2014 term and noted India would follow Australia's initiatives in appointing an envoy to explore how an Asia-pacific community as suggested recently by Canberra be evolved overtime to respond to the emerging opportunities.

Australia had recently mooted the idea of forming a Asia-Pacific grouping, on the lines of the European Union, to deal with political, security and economic challenges. India, Australia to step up bilateral trade, investment flows march 2 2007. India and Australia have resolved to step up bilateral trade and investment flows substantially, while taking due note of the increasingly diverse and considerably large nature of the bilateral trade and economic relationship.

This is indicated in the agreed minutes of the 10th India-Australia Joint Ministerial Commission (JMC) meeting, which were signed on March 1 2007 by the Union Commerce and Industry Minister, Mr. Kamal Nath, and the Minister for Trade of Australia. Both the Ministers voiced satisfaction at the rapid spurt in bilateral goods and services trade between India and Australia and the significant increase in the commercial presence of Indian and Australian companies in each other's markets. Indo-Australian trade stood at US$ 17.66 billion in 2010-11 registered a record increase from just US$ 1.4 billion in 2001-01. In 2010-11, India's exports to Australia were valued at US$ 2.05 billion and Australia's exports to India were placed at US$ 15.58 billion.

India is emerging as Australia's fastest growing trading partner. The meeting also took note of the immense potential for investment flows between the two countries. India and Australia also agreed to promote bilateral investment, including in the energy, mining, infrastructure, food processing, telecom, information and communications technology, tourism, biotechnology and financial sectors.

While India shared information about steps taken by it to ease foreign direct investment regulation including sectoral caps and simplification of procedures,

Australia informed New Delhi of the establishment of Invest Australia offices in both Mumbai and New Delhi to enable Indian investment in Australia.

17

India and the UN System

During the Cold War, India's participation in the UN was notable for its efforts to resist the imposition of superpower disputes on UN General Assembly debates and to focus international attention on the problems of economic development. In the early 1950s, India attempted unsuccessfully to help China join the UN. India's mediatory role in resolving the stalemate over prisoners of war in Korea led to the signing of the armistice ending the Korean War. India chaired the five-member Neutral Nations Repatriation Commission while the Indian Custodian Force supervised the process of interviews and repatriation that followed. The UN entrusted Indian armed forces with subsequent peace missions in the Middle East, Cyprus, and the Congo (since 1971, Zaire). India also served as chair of the three international commissions for supervision and control for Vietnam, Cambodia, and Laos established by the 1954 Geneva Accords on Indo-china.

Although not a permanent member of the UN Security Council, India has been elected periodically to fill a non-permanent seat, and during the 1991-92 period served in that capacity. In the early 1990s, New Delhi supported reform of the UN in the hope of securing a permanent seat on the Security Council. This development would recognize India's position as the second-largest population (possibly the largest in the early twenty-first century) in the world, with an economy projected by some to become the fourth largest, after China, the United States, and Japan, by 2020.

India also has served as a member of many UN bodies—including the Economic and Social Council, the Human Rights Commission, and the Disarmament Commission—and on the board of governors of the International Atomic Energy Agency. In addition, India played a prominent role in articulating the economic concerns of developing countries in such UN-sponsored conferences as the triennial UN Conference on Trade and Development and the 1992 Conference on the Environment and Development in Rio de Janeiro.

17.1 India's Role in UN Peacekeeping

Time and again, India has risked the lives of its soldiers in peacekeeping efforts of the United Nations, not for any strategic gain, but in the service of an ideal. India's ideal was, and remains, strengthening the world body, and international peace and security.

Indian troops have taken part in some of the most difficult operations, and have suffered casualties in the service of the UN. Professional excellence of the Indian troops has won universal admiration. India has taken part in the UN peacekeeping operations in four continents. Its most significant contribution has been to peace and stability in Africa and Asia. It has demonstrated its unique capacity of sustaining large troops commitments over prolonged periods. Presently, India is ranked as one of the largest troop contributors to the UN. India has also offered one brigade of troops to the UN Standby Arrangements. Over 55,000 Indian Military and Police personnel have served under the UN flag in 35 UN peace keeping operations in all the continents of the globe.

India provided a paramedical unit to facilitate withdrawal of the sick at wounded in Korea. After the ceasefire, India became the Chairman of the Neutral Nations Repatriation Commission. One brigade group of the Indian Army participated in the operation in Korea, authorized by the UN General Assembly through Uniting for Peace resolution. Indian troops provided guards for the prisoners of war. The Chairman of the Neutral Nations Repatriation Commission was Lt. Gen. K.S. Thimmaya and the Commander of the Custodian Force to take custody of the Prisoners of War (numbering over 22,000) was Maj. Gen. S.P.P. Thorat.

India also contributed to peace in the Middle East. The United Nations Emergency Force (UNEF) was created in 1956 following cessation of hostilities between Egypt and Israel. India provided an infantry battalion, which accounted for the bulk of the UN force. Over 11 years, from 1956 to 1967, more than 12,000 Indian troops took part in UNEF. Pursuant to the Geneva Accord, an International Control Commission (ICC) for Indo-China was set up in 1954. India was the Chairman of the Commission, which implemented the ceasefire agreement between Vietnam, Laos, Cambodia and France. India provided one infantry battalion and supporting staff until the ICC was wound up in 1970. The UN faced one of its worst crises when war between the government and the secessionist forces broke out in Congo. The UN operation in the Congo, ONUC, was unique in many ways. The operation involved heavy casualties. It was also the first time that the UN undertook an operation in an intra -State, rather than an inter-State conflict. The operation upheld the national unity and territorial integrity of the Congo. The Indian contingent lost 39 men in action in the Congo. The performance of the Indian troops was distinguished by their discipline, self-restraint and humanitarian concern.

Indian Army provided a Force Commander and observers for the Observer

Mission in Yemen in 1963-64 (UNYOM). India also participated in the UN operation in Cyprus (UNFICYP). India provided three Force Commanders to UNFICYP, Gen. K.S. Thimmaya, Lt. Gen. P.S. Gyani and Lt. Gen. Dewan Prem Chand. The UN set up a Military Observer Group to monitor the situation on Iran-Iraq border. India provided military observers during the period 1988-90.

Following the end of the Gulf War, the UN established the UN Iraq-Kuwait Observer Mission (UNIKOM). Indian observers continue to participate in the operation. UN operation in Namibia is considered one of the success stories of the United Nations. Lt. Gen. Prem Chand of India was the Force Commander. Indian military observers in Namibia were responsible for the smooth withdrawal of foreign troops, elections and subsequent handing over of the authority to the government.

UN established the ONUMOZ to restore peace and conduct elections in Mozambique. India provided a large contingent of staff officers, military observers, independent headquarters company, and engineering and logistics company. The operation has ended successfully. In recent times, one of the biggest peace keeping operations which was completed successfully was the UN operation in Cambodia. India provided an infantry battalion, military observers and a field ambulance unit.

India has also regularly sent military observers to various UN operations. This includes ONUCA (Central America) in 1990-92, ONUSAL (El Salvador) in 1991 and UNOMIL (Liberia) in 1994. The UN Operation in Somalia is considered one of the most difficult and challenging operations the UN has ever attempted. Indian naval ships and personnel were involved in patrolling duties off the Somali coast, in humanitarian assistance on shore, and also in the transportation of men and material for the United Nations. The UNOSOM II operation involved peace enforcement under Chapter VII. The objective was humanitarian relief. The Indian contingent successfully combined the often conflicting roles of coercive disarmament and humanitarian relief to the civilian population.

With stand-alone capacity, the Indian brigade had operational responsibilities for one-third of Somalia viz. 1,73,000 square kilometres area of responsibility, the largest ever held by any contingent. Inspite of such large areas of operations, there were minimum civilian casualties in the area of responsibility of the Indian contingent. The Indian contingent dug a large number of wells, constructed schools and mosques, and ran mobile dispensaries and relief camps, which provided veterinary care, and medical and humanitarian relief to a large number of Somalis and their livestock. In spite of suffering casualties the Indian contingent exercised utmost restraint in firing in self defence. It also organized and carried out rehabilitation and resettlement of thousands of refugees and helped to repatriate them to their homes. The Indian contingent played a vital role in reviving the political process by organizing reconciliation meetings. The last remaining units of the Indian contingent were repatriated from Somalia on board Indian naval ships from Kismayo port. India demonstrated its capacity to provide an integrated force, comprising land and naval forces as well as air support.

India provided a contingent comprising one infantry battalion and support elements to the UN assistance mission in Rwanda to help ensure security for the refugees, and to create conditions for free and fair elections. After successful completion of the assignment, the Indian contingent was repatriated in April 1996. The Indian army has participated in the successive phases of the UN mission in Angola since 1989. The Indian contingent comprised one infantry battalion group, one engineer company, staff officers and military observers. The contingent has made a sizeable contribution towards construction of quartering camps. The Indian contingent was also involved in rebuilding bridges over the Conga, Rio Quisaju, Rio Mugige and Rio N'hia Rivers. One high risk task was the demining of the main arterial road connecting Lobito and Huambo and repairing a 60 mile stretch of the road. The Indian contingent has also built a 3,300 feet airstrip at Londuimbali. The Deputy Force Commander was an Indian army officer. India also participated in the UN Observer Mission in Angola (MONUA), which succeeded UNAVEM III.

The Chief Military Observer of the UN Observer Mission in Sierra Leone (UNOMSIL) was also an Indian army officer. India provided a medical unit and civilian police personnel to UNOMSIL. After the upgradation of the UN Mission in Sierra Leone in November-December 1999, India provided two infantry battalion groups, a quick reaction company, a field engineering company, a level III medical facility, a special forces company, an artillery battery, transport and attack helicopters and the backbone of the force headquarters in Freetown. Maj. Gen. V.K. Jetley was the first UN Force Commander in Sierra Leone.

India has also provided an infantry battalion to the UN Interim Force in Lebanon (UNIFIL). The Force Commander of UNIFIL is Maj. Gen. L.M. Tewari. India is also currently participating in the UN Mission in Ethiopia and Eritrea (UNMEE) with an infantry battalion, a Force Reserve Company and a Field Engineer Construction Company.

Recent peacekeeping operations have tended to be multi-dimensional, and include police monitors and election observers. India has contributed police personnel and election observers to the UN peacekeeping operations in Cambodia, Mozambique and Angola. India provided 123 police personnel to UN mission in Haiti (Phase II). India has also provided police monitors for the UN

International Police Task Force in Bosnia and Herzegovina, Sierra Leone (UNOMSIL), Western Sahara (MINURSO) and Kosovo (UNMIK). In addition, two companies of CRPF have deployed in UNMIK as Special Police units. The Police Commissioner of MINURSO is an Indian Police Officer, Mr. O.P. Rathor. India sent Lt. Gen. Satish Nambiar, as the Force Commander of UNPROFOR in former Yugoslavia in 1992-93.

India has also provided senior staff to assist the UN Secretary-General at the UN Headquarters. Major Gen. I. J. Rikhye served as Military Advisor to the UN Secretary General from 1960 to 1969.India also hosted a UN Regional Training Workshop for Peacekeeping Operations in New Delhi during January 20-26, 1996 in which 17 countries of the Asia-Pacific region participated. Mr. Kofi Annan, the then Under Secretary General for Peacekeeping visited India in this connection. India also held an International Seminar on UN Peacekeeping in March 1999 in which over 70 countries participated. The United Services Institution (USI) of India hosted another seminar in New Delhi in September 2000 in collaboration with the Swedish National Defence College. A Centre for UN Peacekeeping (CUNPK) was set up under the aegis of USI in New Delhi in 2000. UN Secretary General Kofi Annan visited the Centre in March 2001 during his visit to India.

India has considerable experience in demining activities and has made significant contributions to the de-mining work in various missions in Rwanda, Mozambique, Somalia, Angola and Cambodia. Experienced Indian Army Engineers have been employed for training of selected personnel from the host countries to execute mine clearance programmes as also to generate awareness of the problem among the local people. Indian Army has also undertaken mine clearance projects in support of repatriation and rehabilitation programmes of the UNHCR.

India has also provided opportunities for training to military officers from different countries. India has, at present, army training teams in six countries: Seychelles, Laos, Mauritius, Botswana, Zambia and Bhutan. India has also offered diverse courses to service personnel at various military training institutions across the country. This includes officers from Bangladesh, Bhutan, France, Germany, Japan, Jordan, Kazakhstan, Kenya, Korea, Laos, Malaysia, Maldives, Mauritius, Myanmar, Namibia, Nepal, Nigeria, Oman, Saudi Arabia, Singapore, South Africa, Sri Lanka, Sudan, Tanzania, Thailand, UAE, UK, USA, Vietnam, Zambia and Zimbabwe. Cadets from countries such as Maldives, Palestine, Bhutan, Nepal, Sri Lanka and also many African States receive pre-commission training at the National Defence Academy, Khadakvasla and the Indian Military Academy.

India continued to participate actively in the UN Peace Keeping Operations. During 1996-97, around 1,100 Indian troops, staff officers and military observers were stationed in Angola. Indian police observers were deputed to UN International Task Force (UNIPTF) in Bosnia and Herzegovina. Indian peace-keepers are also deployed in the UN Special Mission in Haiti (UNSMIH). India actively contributed to the debate and decisions of the Special Committee on Peace Keeping Operations.

India called for expansion in both non-permanent and permanent members' categories and for objective criteria for the selection of new permanent members. India remains opposed to a selective expansion of the UN Security Council and believes that any piece-meal or temporary solution that does not provide for adequate representation of developing countries in both permanent and non-permanent members category may lead to a weakening of the UN itself.

India reiterated its call in support of an International Convention to Combat Terrorism. The resolution on Terrorism adopted in the 51st session of the UN General Assembly (UNGA) includes the consideration of the elaboration such a Convention. Along with this Resolution, a new Declaration to supplement the 1994 Declaration on Measures to Eliminate International Terrorism was also adopted. The new Declaration is aimed at governing the abuse of right to asylum of refugees turned terrorists.

17.2 Disarmament and International Security

Since independence, India has consistently pursued the objective of global disarmament based on the principles of universality, non-discrimination and effective compliance. Given the horrific destructive capacity of nuclear weapons, India has always believed that a world free of nuclear weapons would enhance both global security and India's own national security. Thus India has always advocated that the highest priority be given to nuclear disarmament as a first step towards general and complete disarmament.

As early as 1948, India called for limiting the use of atomic energy for peaceful purposes only, and the elimination of atomic weapons from national armaments. India was the first country to call to an end to all nuclear testing in 1954. This was followed up in subsequent decades by many other initiatives, for example, on the Partial Test Ban Treaty, and the call for international negotiations on nuclear non-proliferation. In 1978, India proposed negotiations for an international convention that would prohibit the use or threat of use of nuclear weapons.

This was followed by another initiative in 1982 calling for a "nuclear freeze" i.e. prohibition on the production of fissile material for weapons, on production of nuclear weapons, and related delivery systems. At the special sessions of the United Nations General Assembly on disarmament, India put forward a number of serious proposals including the 1988 Comprehensive Plan for total elimination of weapons of mass destruction in a phased manner. It was a matter of regret that the proposals made by India along with several other countries did not receive a positive response and instead, a limited and distorted non-proliferation agenda, meant above all to perpetuate nuclear weapons was shaped.

India was compelled by considerations of national security to establish and adopt a policy of keeping its nuclear option open while it continued to work for global nuclear disarmament. India's nuclear capability was demonstrated in 1974. India exercised an unparalleled restraint in not weaponising its nuclear capability. It is relevant to recall, that during this period, when we voluntarily and totally desisted from testing, over 35,000 nuclear weapons were developed through a series of tests by states possessing nuclear weapons. This has happened even as Article VI of the Non-Proliferation Treaty committed the Nuclear Weapons States, party to the NPT, to take steps in good faith for nuclear disarmament. India was obliged to stand apart on the CTBT in 1996 after having been actively engaged in the negotiations for two and a half years precisely.

In 1996, India continued to play a leading role in various multilateral disarmament fora-the Conference on Disarmament (CD) at Geneva, the UN Disarmament Commission (UNDC) and the First Committee of the UNGA. In the Conference on Disarmament, India followed its consistent and principled stand on the Comprehensive Nuclear Test Ban Treaty (CTBT).

India had visualized the CTBT as part of a step by step process of global nuclear disarmament, leading to the complete elimination of all nuclear weapons within a time bound framework. India also believed that the objective of CTBT was not merely to end test explosions but to end the qualitative development and refinement of nuclear weapons whether through explosive or other means. Concrete Indian textual proposals on amendments to CTBT were tabled on 26 January 1996.

As the Indian proposals were not taken on board, India made a definitive statement on 20 June 1996 that it could not subscribe to the CTBT in its existing form as it was not conceived as a measure towards universal nuclear disarmament and was not in India's national security interest. Following the assessment of the Chairman of the Ad hoc committee that his draft was the best attainable text, India opposed the adoption of the draft Treaty by the Ad hoc Committee and its submission to the CD Plenary. Subsequently, India also opposed the transmission of the Special Report by the CD to the 50th UNGA, as there was no consensus on the draft treaty text. In the resumed session of the 50th UNGA, Australia moved a resolution seeking adoption of a draft treaty text identical to the non-consensus draft treaty negotiated in Geneva. In the voting on the Australian resolution on 10 September 1996, India, along with Bhutan and Libya voted against the resolution. In a suo moto statement made in Parliament on September 11, 1996, the Minister of External Affairs reiterated that India would maintain its opposition to the treaty and not sign it in its present form. He also stated that India would continue to take initiatives in the UN and other fora in keeping with India's consistent and principled policy of achieving progress towards the goal of a nuclear weapon free world which would enhance India's security as also global security.

On September 3, 1996, India deposited its instruments of ratification of the Chemical Weapons Convention (CWC). India maintains that the CWC is a significant milestone in multilateral disarmament negotiations in both its negotiating process and its non-discriminatory character and provides a valid model for future disarmament agreements. India will now set up a National Authority and take steps towards enacting domestic legislation for implementation of the activities prescribed under CWC.

India, as a State Party to the Biological Weapon Convention (BWC), participated actively in the deliberations of the Ad hoc Group meetings of the State Parties. The Indian delegation continued to support strengthening of the Convention and the unimpeded transfer and exchange of biotechnology for peaceful purposes for creating a non-discriminatory and transparent regime.

As a State Party, India participated in the Review Conference of the Convention on prohibition or restrictions on the use of certain conventional weapons, which may be deemed to be excessively injurious or to have indiscriminate effects. India supports the move towards complete ban on anti-personnel land mines, which should be universal and non-discriminatory; and this needs to be carried out in a phased manner since many countries use mines as weapons of defence along long borders.

In the First Committee of the United Nations, the Indian Resolution on "Convention on Prohibition of Use of Nuclear Weapons" was adopted with 83 votes in favour, 27 against with 24 abstentions. Another Indian Resolution on "The Role of Science and Technology in the context of International Security and Disarmament" was adopted with 81 votes in favour, 38 against with 24 abstentions. Based on the NAM Cartagena Summit, India continued to co-sponsor the Resolution on "Nuclear Disarmament", which was adopted with 87 votes in favour, 39 against and 20 abstentions.

At various international fora, India continued its principle opposition to the various Ad hoc export control regimes and called for their conversion into universal, transparent, non-discriminatory treaties.

17.3 India as Non-permanent Member

India's latest election, with the highest number of votes cast in the United Nations General Assembly, to serve a two-year term as non-permanent member of the Security Council commencing in January 2011 was a worthy development that should prompt informed appreciation of its importance. On the one hand, the election, no doubt, is a clear recognition of the long and rich reputation our country has earned in the U.N., besides being an acknowledgment of the growing importance India continues to gain in matters of multilateral governance. On the other hand, it could be dismissed as being too little too late a development to quench India's vexatious thirst for status of a permanent member. What are the opportunities and challenges awaiting India in its new role? How is the non-permanent membership relevant to pursuing our aspiration for permanent membership? A useful basis for such speculation should be a stock-taking of the patterns in India's performance in the United Nations Security Council (UNSC) on the occasions when it served as a non-permanent member previously.

At the San Francisco Conference where U.N. structural architecture was finalised, India not only supported the need for permanent members in the UNSC, but also persuaded the powerful countries to accept an eligibility criteria for election to the non-permanent membership category. No comparable criteria guided the selection of permanent members, while the non-permanent members are to satisfy tough criteria of contribution to peace and equitable geographical representation. Our approach to the U.N. is characterised by, to borrow Jawaharlal Nehru's words, "wholehearted co-operation" through full participation "in its councils to which her geographical position, and contribution towards peaceful progress entitle her." How tough, nevertheless, is the route to non-permanent membership became clear from the fact that, after establishment of the U.N., it took four years for India to enter the UNSC through the election route. Inclusive of the ensuing stint, India has to its credit only seven terms (mostly) representing the Asian region in a span of 65 years.

17.4 India Edges Closer to Permanent UN Seat

A permanent seat in United Nations Security Council (UNSC) is no longer a pie in the sky for India with U.S. President Barack Obama formally endorsing the candidature of this Asian giant with 1.2 billion people. The five permanent Security Council members have the power to veto United Nations resolutions and this fact is at the heart of reforms to meet the power realities and equations of the 21st century.

So far, however, only China, which rivals India for power in Asia, has shied away from openly voicing support for India's bid for a seat at the UNSC.

Beijing's response to Obama was guarded. "We hope all parties can have democratic and patient consultations to reach a package of consensus on the issue," an official spokesman was quoted as saying. "China values India's status in international affairs and understands India's aspirations to play a greater role in the U.N."

India's apprehensions may be seen in an intervention of Hardeep Singh Puri, Permanent Representative of India to the United Nations, at the informal meeting of the plenary on the intergovernmental negotiations on equitable representation in the membership of the Security Council on June 28, when he called on permanent members to look beyond national interests. Permanent members are expected to act in such a manner that transcends narrow national interests when dealing with issues relating to international peace and security. It is, therefore, important that the category of permanent membership reflects contemporary realities and includes adequate representation from all regions of the world.

India's optimism in being able to swing for itself a permanent seat in the UNSC, over other contenders, notably Japan, Germany and Brazil, stems partially from the fact that it gained a record 187 votes in the October elections for non-permanent seats. Out of the 191 countries one abstained and three member-states polled against India. India demonstrated its acceptability again, last week, when it won 164 votes for a seat on the U.N. General Assembly's advisory committee on administrative and budgetary questions, while Japan received 140 votes and China 130.

18

India, WTO, IMF, World Bank and ADB

18.1 India and World Trade Organization (WTO)

The WTO came into existence on 1 January 1995 after the conclusion of the Uruguay Round of Multilateral Trade Negotiations. The WTO aims at the liberalization of word trade India is a founder member of the World Trade Organization (WTO), a successor to the multilateral treaty-General Agreement on Tariffs and Trade (GATT) which was set up in 1947. All the member countries are required to apply fair trade rules covering commodities, services and intellectual property. The members are also committed to lower tariffs on industrial goods, abolish import duties on a variety of items, progressively abolish quotas on garments and textiles, reduce trade-distorting subsidies and import barriers. The members are expected to implement agreements on intellectual property and rules for civil aviation, telecommunications, financial services and the movement of labour. The provisions of Uruguay Round Agreement shall become part of the global trade law in 2004.

In terms of the built in agenda of GATT 1994 for periodic review negotiations of the existing agreements, the WTO decided to hold a Ministerial Conference at Seattle (USA). However, the meeting was shadowed by protests by various non-governmental organizations and individuals who blocked avenues of possible talks. This convinced development nations like USA that the interests of the developing countries can no longer be ignored. India opposed the idea of new round of trade talks on the ground that most countries are still in the process of implementing GATT provisions. Further there are several issues like agriculture, financial services, maritime services, infotech services etc. on which the Uruguay Round itself mandated further negotiations. It was further emphasized that many developed countries have failed to provide the developing countries special concessions which were agreed upon in the Uruguay Round. In other words the WTO has a large unfulfilled agenda which must be addressed before it ventures into a new round of trade negotiations. The developed countries on the other hand insisted that the talks should go beyond the immediate agenda at hand and include new issues like labour standards, environment and e-commerce. In view of the different views of the developed and developing countries the Seattle Meet could not arrive at a consensus and was suspended after 36 hour of discussion.

18.1.1 Benefits to India:

1. The reduction of domestic subsidies and barrier is likely to up world price of agricultural products which would benefit India. As a result India's earnings from agricultural export would greatly increase.
2. The Uruguay Round of Agreement has strengthened rules relating to anti-dumping, subsidies and counter veiling measures, safeguards and disputes settlement, which is likely to ensure greater security and predictability of international trading system. This would operate in favour of India.
3. The implementation of the Uruguay Round of Package has added between 213 and 274 billion US dollars annually to the world income. A large part of this income is in the area of clothing, agriculture, forestry and fishery products. Since India's potential export competitiveness lies in these product groups, it can be logically concluded that India will obtain large gains in these sectors.
4. The phasing out of quota regime by 2005 is likely to give a fillip to the export of Indian extensible benefits India. It is anti-fertility that India alone will not benefit from this provision.

18.1.2 Disadvantages:

1. The creation of WTO has continuously eroded the authority and jurisdiction of the nation-states by permitting the WTO to enact laws relating to protection of patents, trademarks and copyright; conservation of exhaustive natural resources; restrictions on export of domestic materials; laws and regulations essential for the acquisition and distribution of products in short supply.
2. The working of WTO so far has given rise to a feeling among the developing countries that the developed countries have cheated them. While the developing countries have been forced to open up their markets to the developed countries, the latter have circumvented their obligations and adopted protectionist measures.
3. There has only been a marginal increase in Indian exports, in fact there would hardly be any liberalization of our textile exports till 2005. The reduction of tariff on good is also not likely to benefit India much as the number of goods of export interest to India is very small.
4. The agreements on Trade Related Intellectual Property Rights (TRIPs) and Trade Related Investment Measures (TRIMs) are also likely to work to the disadvantage of India.
5. The Uruguay Round has tried to protect the interests of the multinational corporations and developed countries by making stringent provisions regarding intellectual property rights. In fact intellectual property rights

protection is anti-competition and anti-liberalization. It virtually tantamount to legalizing the 'monopoly' of multinational corporations (MNCs).

6. The Agreement on Trade Related Investment Measures (TRIMs) is also pro-developed countries in so far as it is mainly concerned with provisions for elimination of trade related investment measures which are designed to protect the interests of foreign investors in the developing countries.
7. The trade and non-tariff barriers put up following the formation of WTO has given set back to the exports from developing countries like India. A study made by the policy division of the Union Commercial Ministry of India found that the multi-fibre agreement (MFA) put up by USA and European Union have acted as a major barrier against textile exports from India.
8. The working of WTO shows that US has been able to exert undue influence on its working. Often it took unilateral action against the countries which undermined its trading interests; conveniently bypassing the multilateral system. What is worse, the developed countries have demanded inking of trade with labour standards.
9. Again attempt on the part of developed countries to link trade with environments is also not quite fair. In poor countries like India provision of safe drinking water deserves a higher priority because large number of people dies due to dysentery. It would be unfair to divert the fund which can be utilized for the above purpose, for checking pollution.

In conclusion, it can be said that the experience of the working of WTO indicates that the more powerful and developed countries have been guided by selfish considerations and have tried to promote their own interests. They have hardly paid attention to the advantages of free trade or globalization etc.

18.2 India and International Monetary Fund (IMF)

India is a founder member of IMF and has made use of different financial and other During the period 1980-1990, on account of the large trade deficit the reserve position of India became quite difficult which compelled India to borrow from IMF. In fact the debt service ratio of India rose sharply from 9.3 percent in 1980 to 28.8 percent in 1990. In the second quarter of 1988 India's balance of payment position became so precarious that it was left with reserves which could barley meet the import requirements for 45 days. The situation grew still worse after the Gulf War. The problem was further complicated due to fall of emigrant remittances, massive withdraw as of NRI deposits, fall in India's credit rating which made commercial borrowings difficult, etc. the situation reached a crisis position in June 1991 when the country had reserves which were barely enough to meet the imports for two weeks. At this juncture the government was left with no other choice but to borrow from IMF. It may be noted that it was not only India who approached IMF for assistance; several other countries have also been approaching IMF. In fact even the National Front Government headed by V.P. Singh, and the Chandrasekhar government had also taken loans from IMF, and there was nothing wrong with the decision of Narsimha Rao Government to seek IMF Assistance.

India is not the only country to have introduced the above reforms. Several other countries like China, USSR and countries of East Europe have already carried out such reforms. Some critics have expressed the apprehension that the policy of economic liberalization adopted by India will lead to the dominance of Indian economy by multinationals and large house in India and lead to ruin of same firms. However, these apprehensions are well-founded and can certainly be prevented if the government pays its role properly.

India first approached IMF for assistance in 1957-58 when its foreign exchange reserves fell sharply. In fact India's balance of payments remained quite precarious until 1968-69 which obliged India to make several draw also from the IMF. It has been alleged that in 1966 India devalued rupee on the advice of IMF to correct the balance of payments disequilibrium. Thereafter also India borrowed from the IMF on several occasions. India resorted to major borrowing from the IMF in 1980s to meet the crisis situation arising due to potential fall in the balance of payments. This situation arose because of the surge in the oil import bill and trade deficit in 1980-81. Though the foreign exchange reserves of India were still at a comfortable level it entered into an extended agreement with IMF under which India could draw SDR 5 billion over a period of three years. India took this step as precautionary measures and clarified that I may not draw the whole amount as the economic condition would improve. Actually India withdrew only 3.9 billion under Special Drawing Rights (SDR), in view of improvement in reserve position of the country.

India is one of the founder members of the Bretton Woods institutions viz., the International Monetary Fund (IMF) and International Bank for Reconstruction and Development (IBRD) which were set up in 1945. While the International Monetary Fund was designed to tackle the problem of international liquidity and to achieve international monetary stability, the IBRD, or the Bank was set up to help the reconstruction and development of various notional economies by providing long-term capita assistance.

The International Monetary Fund came into existence in December 1945. Its chief objectives are:

1. To promote international monetary cooperation through a permanent institution which provides the machinery for consultation and collaboration

on international monetary problems.

2. To promote exchange stability, to maintain orderly exchange arrangements among members and to avoid competitive exchange depreciation.
3. To facilitate the expansion thereby to the promotion and maintenance of high levels of employment and development of the produce resources of all members as primary objectives of economic policy.
4. To give confidence to members by making the Fund's resources available to them under adequate safeguards, thus providing them with opportunity to correct maladjustments in their balance of payments without resorting to measures destructive of national or international prosperity.
5. To assist in the establishment of a multilateral system of payment in respect of current transactions between members and in the elimination of foreign exchange restriction which hamper the growth of world trade.

The money for the fund comes through contributions made by the members. Each member contributes twenty-five percent of its share in gold and the remainder in the currency of its country.

The organization of the IMF consists of a Board of Governors, Executive Directors and a Managing Director. There is also other staff to assist the organizations. The real powers are vested in the Board of Governors. The members of the Board are appointed for a term of 5 years. The members of the Fund have not been accorded equal status. The votes have been given to the members according to the weightage of their contributions. Thus USA and UK enjoy a weightage of 33 and 14 percent respectively. The executive directors constitute the executive body of the IMF. It consists of 20 members (originally 12). The five Directors are sent by the member states who contribute the largest quotas, while the others are elected by the Board of Governors. In electing these members due consideration is given to the geographical representation. The executive directors meet twice or thrice in a week and are responsible for the operation of the fund throughout the year. The Managing Director is the chief of the organization and enjoys a position identical to the one enjoyed by the Secretary General. The main responsibility for the proper working of the Fund mainly rests with him. He is also responsible for the appointment of the staff of the Fund.

During the initial years the IMF could not work as per plan because most of the nations did not move towards multilateral payments system envisaged by the Fund. The 'dollar problem' also compelled the European countries to impose strict restrictions on import of goods from USA. But after the establishment of the European Payments Union in 1950 (Under which the European states provides a clearing system by which defects with one country could be balanced by surplus with the other), the Fund introduced the system of 'stand-by-credits'. In the post-suez crisis years the fund was increasingly used to meet the strain.

It also included the adoption of the principle of non resident convertibility by a number of governments in 1958 under which pound string could be freely converted outside the sterling area into gold dollars or other currencies. The IMF also increased the quotas and credit facilities. In 1968 the Fund introduced the scheme of Special Drawing Rights to solve the problem of liquidity. The Fund also introduced the scheme of compensatory financing and financing of buffer stocks to increase assistance to the poor countries. In the wake of hike in the prices of oil in 1973 which created the problem of balance of payments deficits in most of the industrial and developing countries, the Fund took special measures to assist the governments in difficulty and made available necessary money at low rates of interests.

Thus in the course of time the International Monetary Fund has come to play a vital role. According to Luard, "The degree to which the Fund's policies have evolved over the years, especially in the successful introduction of SDR system have brought a greater willingness to acknowledge its capacity to evolve with the time. Its technical abilities and the quality of its staff have been doubted."

It may be observed that domestic mismanagement of the economy as well as the wrong economic policies of the past were responsible for the economic crisis. Whatever be the reasons, it cannot be denied that the crisis was indeed deep. This warranted not only external assistance but also demanded radical masseurs to rejuvenate the economy. Some critics raised objections to the conditions imposed by the IMF, but these conditions were in no way different from the conditions imposed on other borrowers. In fact as per guidelines of IMF a country making use of the resources of the Fund is required to carry out an economic policy programme which aims at achieving a viable balance of payments position over an appropriate period of time.

It has been alleged that recently India carried out economic reforms at the instance of the IMF-World Bank. These reforms include devaluation of currency; reduction in the fiscal and budgetary deficit; reduction of abolition of subsidies; reduction in customs duties and import liberalization; rationalization of public sector pricing; liberalization of foreign investment; industrial policy reforms redefining the role of the public sector and privatisation; liberalization of capital issues; reduction in the statutory liquidity ratio; and convertibility of rupee. It may be noted that these reforms were also being demanded by the economists and experts within the country.

The reforms introduce by the governments since July 1991 broadly fall into four categories (i) measures which aim at better domestic economic management and economic disciplines; (ii) measures which aim at accelerating economic growth, particularly industrial growth; (iii) measures aimed at improving the trade and payment position; and (iv) measures aiming at simplification of procedures. India could not introduce these reforms earlier despite persistent demand from experts because the environments were not favourable. It was found opportune to introduce these reforms in 1991, not only because the crisis situation so demanded, but also because the climate of reforms pervaded all around the world.

It has been contended that economic reforms carried out in India are likely to give rise to several transitional problems. Some of these problems can be listed as under.

1. Firstly, the cut in government expenditure is likely to lead to further unemployment. However, it cannot be denied that fiscal discipline is essential for the future of the country.
2. Secondly, monetary discipline is also like by to lead to further unemployment. But no body can deny that such monetary and fiscal discipline is essential to keep the prices under control.
3. Thirdly, the policy of economic liberalization is likely to create problems for several industrial units. No doubt in many cases the important duties are still above 50 percent but the domestic industries shall not be able to withstand the foreign competition. It is desirable that instead of seeking protection the Indian Companies should try to face competition through better management and techniques.
4. Fourthly, industrial restructuring is likely to lead to reduction in labour force and cause unemployment. This is, however, essential to improve productivity and reduce costs. In the larger interest of the country it is not desirable to follow the policy of employment protection, especially in view of the international competition. It is also desirable that the government changes its policy towards sick units. As one writer observed it would be a social crime to give artificial respiration to unviable sick units sustaining heavy losses on a perpetual basis.
5. Fifthly, the increase in prices due to devaluation, reduction of abolition of subsidies, and rationalizations of prices is likely to give rise to inflationary forces. This would pose a serious challenge for the government to keep the prices under control.

However, the nation must learn to face these transitional problems keeping in view the long-term interests of the country. It is true that some Latin American countries had to suffer serious consequences during the transitional phase and their per capita income fee considerably. But gradually they returned to the normal path of growth. In case of India American countries and after the transitional period the Indian economy would emerge strong. The World Bank experts have also expressed the view that the Indian economy would be one of the most dynamic in the world by the turn of the century.

18.3 International Bank for Reconstruction and Development (IBRD)

Though the Bank was set up in December, 1945, it recognized as a specialized agency of the UN only in November 1947.The International Bank for Reconstruction and Development (IBRD) popularly known as World Bank, was set up for the purpose of assisting the less developed countries and regions in their development. One of the main considerations with the statesmen in creating this Bank was that in the wake of World War II a large number of independent countries made their appearance. But most of these countries were at a very low level of development. The developed countries realized that in view of the interdependent nature of the world economy it was their duty to tackle the problem of underdeveloped regions. They thought this action desirable in their national interest too. The IBRD was created for this purpose. It may be noted that the membership of the Bank is open only to the sovereign states.

Article 1 of Bretton Woods Agreement which created the Bank specifies the following purposes of the IBRD.

1. To conduct its operation with due regard to the effect of international investment on business conditions in the territories of members.
2. To promote private foreign investment by means of guarantees.
3. To arrange the loans made or guaranteed by it in relations to international loans through other channels.
4. To assist in the reconstruction and development of territories of members by facilitating the investment of capital for productive purposes.
5. To promote long-ranged balanced growth of international trade and maintenance of equilibrium in balance of payments by encouraging international investment.

The organization of IBRD consists of Board of Governors, the Executive Directors and the President. While all powers of the Bank are vested in the Board of Governors, the Board of Governors elect a Chairman every year. Each member has 250 votes, plus an additional vote for each share of the capital stock held by the nation which he represents. As countries like USA hold large number of shares they come to exercise great influence. The Board of Governors appoints a body of Executive Directors Consisting of five members. The President is the ex-official Chairman of the Executive Directors. These Executive Directors are appointed by the five largest stock-holders and not all the members. The

President is the chief Executive Officer of the Bank. He is assisted by other members of the staff.

The chief function of the Bank is to raise the levels of productivity.

1. In initial stages the Bank gave money only for reconstruction purposes but after Europe and Asia got rehabilitated, the Bank started giving loans for development purposes.
2. Thus, it gave loans to Chilean government for development of hydro-electric power and water resources; to Mexico for electric power development; to Brazil for expansion of hydro-electric power and telephone installations; to India for reconstruction and development of state owned railways and to Turkey for development of major ports and construction of grain storage facilities.
3. The Bank lends funds at moderate rate of interest to the countries which will have no difficulty in repaying the loan. Even after the loan has been granted the Bank can make sure that the money is being used as per terms of the contract.

In 1956, the International Finance Corporation was set up as an affiliate of the World Bank. The Corporation was expected to provide assistance to private enterprises projects in developing countries on commercial terms. The other important steps taken in this direction included the setting up of a special fund in 1958 and International Development Association 1962. All these organizations provided fund at very soft terms. However, certain critics have alleged that during these years the Bank advanced loans mainly to the advanced countries and the less developed countries could not get any benefit. The main reasons for this cautious approach on the part of the Bank have been put by Professor Luard, "It was extremely conscious of the history of the war year when a number of developing countries in difficulties had defaulted on their loans. It was concerned to reassure those investing in the Bank's bonds about the soundness of its lending policies. Conceived as a 'bank' it felt it necessary to think like a bank and talk like a bank. It applied strict banking nations to all projects, requiring firm assurance on the one hand that the projects themselves were sound, and on the other than the governments would not default on repayments."

A change in the Bank's policy took place after Woods took over as President. The Bank showed tendency to take greater risks. It not only lent money to the manufacturing industries but also advanced funds to India for the purpose of financing its imports. The Bank also rendered advisory services to the Member states. It sent Missions to make comprehensive surveys of the economies of a number of countries with a view to advise them regarding fixation of priorities of different sectors of production. The Bank sent such missions to countries like

India, Pakistan, Iraq, Jordan, Thailand, Ceylon etc. It also trained officials of various member states to enable them to implement the technical programmes more effectively.

It is often complained that by playing safe, the bank has disappointed those 'who had counted on it as the major outside source of help to countries unable to finance their recovery'. It finances only those projects which involved permanent addition to production capacity and where interest and repayment of loan could be easily foreseen. This was due to propounders position of USA, which determined the Bank's policy and decisions.

18.4 India and Asian Development Bank (ADB)

Asian Development Bank is one of the several regional development banks which have been established to assist the developing countries of the respective regions. The various regional development Banks include the African Development Bank, the Caribbean development Bank, Inter-American Development Bank, and Asian. Development Bank (ADB). Like the other regional banks ADB has also been very responsive to the special needs of the countries of Asia. The ADB was set up in December 1966 under the auspices of the United Nations Economic Commission for Asia and Far East (ECAFE) to foster economic development of the Asian countries. The Bank has its headquarters at Manila. The ADB is dependent for its funds on contributions by developed countries like Japan, Canada, West Germany, Australia etc.

The main objectives of ADB include:

1. Promotion of investment in ESCAP regions of pubic and private capital for development;
2. Utilization of the available resources for financing development, giving priority to those regional sub-regional or national projects and programmes which contribute to the harmonious economic growth of the region as a whole;
3. Greater priority to be given to alleviation of poverty and protection of environments;
4. Provision of assistance to private sector to improve productivity and efficiency; and
5. Bank works with developing countries to lay down framework of policy for efficient use of available human and capital resources.

The adoption of poverty reduction as a strategy gave primacy to ADB's fight against poverty. ADB continues to carry out activities to promote economic growth, develop human resources, improve the status of women, and protect the environment, but these strategic development objectives now serve its poverty reduction agenda. Its other key development objectives, such as law and policy reform, regional cooperation, private-sector development, and social development, also contribute significantly to this main goal.

ADB consulted its various stakeholders—central and local governments, nongovernmental organizations, the academic community, development agencies, and funding agencies—in preparing its poverty reduction strategy. Two- and three-day workshops were held for this purpose in Bangladesh, People's Republic of China, India, Indonesia, Kyrgyz Republic, Nepal, Philippines, Sri Lanka, and Viet Nam. Consultations were also held over the Internet.

The consultations identified lessons learned from poverty reduction efforts in each country, examined emerging strategies, and explored ways in which the new ADB strategy could best support national efforts and priorities. The key findings were summarized in the ADB publication Reducing Poverty: Major Findings and Implications.

The various consultations and other preliminary efforts at drafting ADB's poverty reduction agenda culminated in the Manila Social Forum from 9 to 12 November 1999 at ADB headquarters. At the forum, which had strong support from the World Bank, high-level representatives from around the world discussed the new social policy agenda arising from the transition from central planning to market economies and globalization in Southeast, Central, and East Asia.

Among the topics discussed at the forum were the following:

1. Inclusive labour markets.
2. The decentralization of social services to rationalize social public expenditure.
3. The role of the private sector in job creation, governance, and poverty reduction.
4. The new challenge of urban poverty.
5. The building of proactive social safety nets.

The forum brought out the need to re-examine solutions that were valid before globalization in the mid-1990s. Social safety nets have to be established, and public systems built up. The state must be made increasingly responsible for transparency and good governance and for an enhanced role for stakeholders. Good governance must also be given greater emphasis by international finance institutions.

19

Indian Diaspora

19.1 India and Non-resident Indians (NRIs)

Pravasi Bharatiya Divas aims at bringing the expertise and knowledge of the Indian overseas community to India and integrating it into India's development process. Pravasi Bharatiya Divas is focused to highlight networking opportunities and collaborating them to confer a mutual developing platform. Generating this synergy to excel together towards a bright India along with the Indian overseas community is what Pravasi Bharatiya Divas 2007 proclaims with its head held high.

19.1.1 Non-resident Indians (NRIs) and Persons of Indian Origin (PIO): A Non-Resident Indian (NRI) is an Indian citizen who has migrated to another country, a person of Indian origin who is born outside India, or a person of Indian origin who resides outside India. Other terms with the same meaning are overseas Indian and Expatriate Indian. In common usage, this often includes Indian born individuals (and also people of other nations with Indian blood) who have taken the citizenship of other countries.

A Person of Indian Origin (PIO) is usually a person of Indian origin who is not a citizen of India. For the purposes of issuing a PIO Card, the Indian government considers anyone of Indian origins up to four generations removed, to be a PIO. Spouses of people entitled to a PIO card in their own right can also carry PIO cards. This latter category includes foreign spouses of Indian nationals, regardless of ethnic origin. PIO Cards exempt holders from many restrictions applying to foreign nationals, such as visa and work permit requirements, along with certain other economic limitations.

The NRI and PIO population across the world is estimated at over 30 million (not including Pakistan, Bangladeshi and Sri Lankan diasporas). The Indian government recently introduced the "Overseas Citizenship of India (OCI)" scheme in order to allow a limited form of dual citizenship to Indians, NRIs and PIOs for the first time since independence in 1947. It is expected that the PIO Card scheme will be phased out in coming years in favour of OCI.

19.2 Indians in US

Indian immigration to North America started as early as 1890s. A Sikh-

Canadian community has existed in Abbotsford, BC Canada for over 100 years. The 1911 Gurdwara (Sikh Temple) on South Fraser Way in Abbotsford is Canada's, and perhaps North America's, oldest extant Sikh Temple. Emigration to the U.S. also started at the same time in the late 19th and early 20th century, when some of the Sikhs arriving in Vancouver found that the fact that they were subjects of the British Empire did not mean anything in the Empire (Canada) itself and they were blatantly discriminated against, some of these pioneers entered the U.S or landed in Seattle and San Francisco as the ships that carried them from Asia often stopped at these ports. Most of these immigrants were Sikhs from the Punjab region in British India which is now divided between India and Pakistan.

They were referred to in the U.S. as *Hindus* (due to a common American misconception that everyone in India was a Hindu and also for want of a term that distinguished these immigrants from Native Americans who were also called Indians). Due to a restriction on immigration of their women from India, which was banned under the racist immigration laws passed by the US government in 1917 at the behest of California and other states in the west, that had seen a large influx of Chinese, Japanese and Punjabi immigrants during and after the gold rush. As a result a large number of these men married Mexican women in California. A fair number of these families settled down in the *Central Valley* in California as farmers, and continue to this day.

These early immigrants were denied voting rights, family re-unification and citizenship. In 1923 the US Supreme Court in United States v. Bhagat Singh Thind case ruled that people from India (at the time, British India, e.g. South Asians) are aliens ineligible for citizenship in became a citizen a few years later in New York—Bhagat Singh Thind was a Sikh from India settled in Oregon, he had earlier applied and been rejected in Oregon. After World War II family re-unification was allowed again for people of non-white origin after being banned for almost half a century and they were given the right to vote. A large number of the men that arrived before 1940's were finally able to bring their families to the US, most of them settled in California and other West coast states.

Another wave entered the U.S. in the 1950s, 1960s, 1970s and 1980s. A large proportion of them were Sikhs joining their family members under the new colour-blind immigration laws and professionals or students that came from all over India. The Cold War created a need for engineers in the defence and aerospace industries, many of whom came from India. By the late 1980s and early 1990s Gujarati and South Indian immigrants outnumbered Sikhs or Punjabis as new arrivals, though all communities had pretty much even representation in overall Indian-American numbers.

The most recent and probably the largest wave of immigration to date occurred in the late 1990s and early 2000 during the Internet boom. As a result, Indians in the U.S. are now one of the largest among the groups of Indian diaspora, numbering about 3 million. In contrast to the previous sets of Indians who entered the US workforce as taxi drivers, labourers, farmers or small business owners, the latest set went on to be very successful financially thanks to the hi-tech industry, and are thus probably the most well off community of immigrants. They are well represented in all walks of life, but particularly so in academia, information technology and medicine. There were over 4,000 PIO professors and 84,000 Indian-born students in American universities in 2007-08. The American Association of Physicians of Indian Origin boasts a membership of 35,000. In 2000, Fortune magazine estimated the wealth generated by Indian Silicon Valley entrepreneurs at around US$ 250 billion.

Though the Indian diaspora in the US is largely concentrated in metropolitan areas such as Philadelphia, Atlanta, Chicago, Dallas, Los Angeles, New York, San Francisco, Detroit and Houston, almost every state in the US has a community of Indians.

19.3 Indians in Canada

According to Statistics Canada, in 2006 there were 962,665 people who classified themselves as being of Indian origin. The term "East Indian" or Indo-Canadian is most commonly associated with people of Indian origin, since the term Indian in Canada has commonly been used to refer to the Aboriginal Canadians and still continues to be used to describe them, causing much confusion. In addition, the term Indian is also occasionally applied to people from the Caribbean (West Indians), also called Indo-Caribbeans. Out of this population, 42 percent are Hindu, 39 percent are Sikh, and the remainder are Muslim, Christian, Jain, Buddhist, or no religious affiliation. The main Indian ethnic communities are Punjabis (who account for more than half the population) as well Gujaratis, Tamils (Indian as opposed to Sri Lankan), Indo-Caribbeans (numbering approximately 200,000), Keralites, Bengalis, Sindhis and others.

The first known Indian settlers in Canada were Indian army soldiers who had passed through Canada in 1897 on their way back home from attending Queen Victoria's Diamond Jubilee celebration in London, England. Some are believed to have remained in British Columbia and others returned there later, along with other Punjabi Indians who were attracted to the possibilities for farming and forestry. They were mainly male Sikhs who were seeking work opportunities. Indo-Caribbeans, descendants of the Indian indentured workers who had gone to the Caribbean since 1838, made an early appearance in Canada with the arrival of the Trinidadian medical student Kenneth Mahabir and the Demerara (now Guyana) clerk M.N. Santoo, both in 1908.

The first immigrants in British Columbia, allegedly faced widespread racism from the local White Canadians. There were race riots that targeted these immigrants, as well as new Chinese immigrants. Most decided to return to India, while a few stayed behind. The Canadian government prevented these men from bringing their wives and children until 1919, another reason why many of them chose to leave. Quotas were established to prevent many Indians from moving to Canada in the early 20th century. These quotas allowed fewer than 100 people from India a year until 1957, when the number was increased to 300. In 1967, all quotas were scrapped, and immigration was based on a point system, thus allowing many more Indians to enter. Since this open door policy was adopted, Indians continue to come in large numbers, and roughly 25,000-30,000 arrive each year (which now makes Indians the second highest group immigrating to Canada each year, after the Chinese).

Most Indians choose to immigrate to larger urban centres like Toronto, Montreal, and Vancouver, where more than 70 percent live. Smaller communities are also growing in Calgary, Edmonton and Winnipeg. Indians in Vancouver are from diverse locations in India, such as Punjab, Gujarat, Tamil Nadu, Andhra Pradesh and Kerala. Little India. Indians in Vancouver mainly live in the suburb of Surrey, but can also be found in other parts of Vancouver. The vast majority of Vancouver Indians are of Sikh origin and have taken significant roles in politics and other professions, with several Supreme Court justices, three Attorneys General and one provincial premier hailing from the community.

19.4 Indians in UK

The Indian emigrant community in the United Kingdom is now in its third generation. As an immigrant group, people of Indian origin have been remarkably successful. Indians in the UK, are the largest community outside of Asia percentage wise, and the second largest population wise, only surpassed by the United States.

A remarkable collection of the oral history of the British NRIs is available on Britain's leading NRI website History Talking.com. It's a web radio where you can listen to some of the leading NRIs living in the UK.

Stereotypes about Indians have now moved from their being bus-conductors, waiters, and small shopkeepers to their being doctors, lawyers, accountants and successful businesspeople.

Increasingly, the second and third generation of Indians has started inter-marrying with the rest of the population. This has caused tension between the "old traditional Indian parents" and the "new generation UK Indians". Many third generation Indians are combining the British and Indian cultures. Third generation Indians tend to have broader knowledge and range of experiences than previous generations which often conflicts with the views of the older more traditional parents or grandparents. As a result some of the new generation of Indians do not want to marry other stereotypical Indian men/women.

Indian culture has been constantly referenced within wider British culture, at first as an "exotic" influence in films like *My Beautiful Laundrette*, but now increasingly as a familiar feature in films like *Bend It Like Beckham*. Indian food is now regarded as part of the British cuisine.

According to the April 2001 UK National Census, there are 1,051,800 people of Indian origin in the UK. Hindus comprise 45 percent of the population, Sikhs 29 percent, Muslims 13 percent, Christians nearly 5 percent with the remainder made up of Jains (15,000), Parsis (Zoroastrians), Buddhists and those who stated no religion. 2005 Estimates state 2.41 percent of England's population as being Indian (not inc. Mixed race) which is around 1,215,400. Following continuous trend (including those of mixed Indian ancestry), in 2008 there are likely to be well over 1,600,000 Indian people in the UK.

19.5 Indians in Australia

It is said that the first Indian had come to Australia as part of Captain Cook's ship Before roads and road transport were developed, many Indians had come to Australia to run camel trains. These Indians were called Afghans and kept the communication and supply line open between Melbourne and the centre of Australia. They would transport goods and mail via camel in the desert. Some of the earliest Punjabi arrivals in Australia included Kareem Bux who came as a hawker to Bendigo in 1893, Sardar Beer Singh Johal who came in 1895 and Sardar Narain Singh Heyer who arrived in 1898. Many Punjabis took part in the rush for gold on the Victorian fields.

Indians also entered Australia in the first half of the 20th century when both Australia and India were still British colonies. Indian Sikhs came to work on the Banana Plantations in Southern Queensland. Today a large number of them live in the town of Woolgoolga (a town lying roughly half-way between Sydney and Brisbane). Some of these Indians, the descendants of Sikh plantation workers, now own banana farms in the area. There are two Sikh temples in Woolgoolga. One of which even has a museum dedicated to Sikhism. A large number of Britons and Anglo-Indians born in India migrated to Australia after 1947. These British citizens decided to settle in Australia in large numbers but are still counted as 'Indian' Nationals in the census. The third wave of Indians entered the country in the 1980s, after the demise of the white Australia policy. After the policy was abolished many Indian teachers and doctors settled in Australia. Another big influx began with the IT revolution.

Large numbers of Indian software professionals arrived in Australia from 1976 onwards. After successive military coup's in Fiji of 1987 and 2000 a significant number of Fijian-Indians migrated to Australia as such there is a large Fijian-Indian population in Australia. Fijian-Indians have significantly impacted the character of the Indian community in Australia. While most earlier Indian migration was comprised primarily with educated professionals, the Fijian-Indian community was also comprised largely with professionals but also brought many small business owners and entrepreneurs.

The current wave of Indian migration is that of engineers, tool-makers, Gujarati business families from East Africa and relatives of settled Indians. Starved of government funding, Australian education institutes are desperately recruiting full fee paying overseas students. Many universities have permanent representatives stationed in India and other Asian countries. Their efforts have been rewarded and a new influx of Indian students entering Australia. The total number of student visa's granted to Indian students for the year 2006-2007 were 34,136 a significant rise from 2002-2003 when 7,603 student visa's were granted Indiàn students.

According to the Australian Bureau of Statistics, 87 percent of Punjabis residing in Australia are aged under 50 and over 83 percent of the population are proficient in English. Many in the community are Hindu and Sikh, while there also smaller number of Christians and Muslims. There are about 260,000 Indians living in Australia.

19.6 Indians in New Zealand

Indians began to arrive in New Zealand in the late eighteenth century, mostly as crews on British ships. A small number deserted; the earliest known Indian resident of New Zealand was living with a Māori wife in the Bay of Islands in 1815. Numbers slowly increased through the nineteenth and twentieth centuries, despite a law change in 1899 which was designed to keep out people who were not of 'British birth and parentage'. As in many other countries, Indians in New Zealand dispersed throughout the country and had a high rate of small business ownership, particularly fruit and vegetable shops and convenience stores. At this stage most Indian New Zealanders originated from Gujarat. Changes in immigration policy in the 1980s allowed many more Indians, Pakistanis and Bangladeshis into the country, and the 1987 and 2000 military coups in Fiji caused a large increase in the number of Fijian Indians coming to New Zealand.

Notable Indian New Zealanders include former Dunedin mayor Sukhi Turner, cricketer Dipak Patel, singer Aaradhna, and current Governor General Anand Satyanand.

19.7 Indians in Singapore

Indians in Singapore-defined as persons of South Asian paternal ancestry - form 9 percent of the country's citizens and permanent residents, making them Singapore's third largest ethnic group. Among cities, Singapore has the one of the largest overseas Indian populations.

Although contact with ancient India left a deep cultural impact on Singapore's indigenous Malay society, the mass migration of ethnic Indians to the island only began with the founding of modern Singapore by the British in 1819. Initially, the Indian population was transient, mainly comprising young men who came as workers, soldiers and convicts. By the mid-20th century, a settled community had emerged, with a more balanced gender ratio and a better spread of age groups.

Singapore's Indian population is notable for its class stratification, with disproportionately large elite and lower income groups. This long standing problem has grown more visible since the 1990s with an influx of both well-educated and unskilled migrants from India, and as part of growing income inequality in Singapore. Indians earn higher incomes than Malays, the other major minority group. Indians are also significantly more likely to hold a university degree than these groups. However, the mainly locally-born Indian students in public primary and secondary schools underperform the national average at major examinations.

Singapore Indians are linguistically and religiously diverse, with Sikhs and Hindus forming small majorities. Indian culture has endured and evolved over almost 200 years. By the mid to late 20th century, it had become somewhat distinct from contemporary South Asian cultures, even as Indian elements became diffused within a broader Singaporean culture. Since the 1990s, new Indian immigrants have increased the size and complexity of the local Indian population. Together with modern communications like cable television and the Internet, this has connected Singapore with an emerging global Indian culture.
Prominent Indian individuals have long made a mark in Singapore as leaders of various fields in national life. Indians are also collectively well represented, and sometimes over-represented, in areas such as politics, education, diplomacy and the law.

19.8 Indians in Malaysia

Malaysia has the largest overseas Chinese and overseas Indian groups outside

China and India. Most Indians migrated to Malaysia as plantation labourers under British rule. They are a significant minority ethnic group, making up 9 percent of the Malaysian population. Most of these are Tamil but some Malayalam-and Telugu-speaking people are also present. They have retained their languages and religion-80 percent of ethnic Indians in Malaysia identify as Hindus. Hinduism in Malaysia diverges from mainstream (post-Vedantic Hinduism: its main feature is Mother-goddess (Amman) worship; caste deities, tantric rituals, folk beliefs, non-Agamic temples, and animal sacrifice are its other characteristics. Deepavali and Thaipusam are the main festivals and are national holidays along with other festive seasons like Chinese New Year and Christmas. However, there is an increase in agamic worship in Malaysia, due to the efforts of the Malaysian Hindu Sangam and several notable Hindu organisations in Malaysia.

There is also a small community of Indian origin, the Chitty, who are the descendants of Tamil traders who had emigrated before 1500 AD, and Chinese and Malay locals. Considering themselves Tamil, speaking Malay, and practicing Hinduism, the Chittys number about 2000 today.

19.9 Indians in Indonesia

Though there are no official figures, it is estimated that there are around 50,000 PIOs/NRIs living in Indonesia of which the Indian expatriate community registered with the Embassy and our Consulate in Medan numbers around 5000.

Indians were first brought to Indonesia by the Dutch in the 19th century as indentured labourers to work on plantations located around Medan in Sumatra. While the majority of these came from South India, a significant number also came from the North. The Medan Indians included Hindus, Muslims and Sikhs. They have now been in Indonesia for over four generations and hold Indonesian passports. While local statistics continue to suggest that there are some 40,000 PIOs in Sumatra, the vast majority are now completely assimilated in Indonesian society, though some elements of the Tamil, Sikh and Bihari Communities still maintain their cultural traditions.

The Indian Diaspora also includes several thousand Sindhi families who constitute the second wave of Indian immigrants who made Indonesia their home in the first half of the 20th century. The Sindhi community is mainly engaged in trading and commerce.

Among these communities, Tamils and to a lesser extent Sikhs were primarily engaged in agriculture while Sindhis and Punjabis mainly established themselves in textile trade and sports business.

Due to economic factors, most traders and businessmen among PIOs have over past decades moved to Jakarta from outlying areas such as Medan and

Surabaya. Almost half the Indian Community in Indonesia is now Jakarta based.

The inflow of major Indian investments in Indonesia starting in the late 1970s drew a fresh wave of Indian investors and managers to this country. This group of entrepreneurs and business professionals has further expanded over the past two decades and now includes engineers, consultants, chartered accountants, bankers and other professionals.

The Indian community is very well regarded in Indonesia, is generally prosperous and includes individuals holding senior positions in local and multinational companies.

There are six main social or professional associations of the Indian PIO/NRI community in Jakarta. Gandhi Seva Loka (formerly known as Bombay Merchants Association) is a charitable institution run by the Sindhi community and is engaged mainly in educational and social activities. The India Club is a social organization of PIO/NRI professionals. An Indian Women's Association brings together PIO/NRI spouses and undertakes charitable activities. There is a Gurudwara Prabandhak Committee in Jakarta and Sindhis as well as Sikhs are associated with Gurudwara activities The Economic Association of Indonesia and India (ECAII) brings together leading entrepreneurs from the Indian community with the objective of promoting bilateral economic relations, but has been largely inactive. Finally, there is the Indonesian Chapter of the Institute of Chartered Accountants of India (ICAI).

19.10 Indians in Philippines

There approximately 125,000 and more Indians and Indian Filipinos who are PIOs/NRIs on a whole living all over in the Philippines. Most are concentrated in Manila, Cebu, and Davao, and even in places like Iloilo, and other major cities and small towns of the named 11 islands. Indians have been in the Philippines from the 4th century A.D. to the 17th century A.D. Making Hinduism and mixture of Buddhism the main religions before the onset of Islam and Catholicism by the Arab and Spaniards. Even today, a lot of illegal Indians from India are smuggled in to the Philippines for a better life.

Indians from Chennai, Tamil Nadu, India also came with the British expedition against Manila that took the city from the Spaniards and occupied Manila and the area around Cainta and Rizal between 1762 and 1763. A lot of them refused to leave, mutinied and married local Filipino women, which explains why a lot of Filipinos around Cainta, Rizal are Indian descendants. A lot of Indians there have intermarried with Filipinos, more so than in neighbouring countries like Indonesia, Malaysia, Singapore, mainly cause those populations are mostly Muslim, and the Indians there feel uncomfortable marrying Muslims in their host countries. During the 30s and 40s, a lot of Indians and Indian Filipinos lived in the provinces in the Philippines, and even Davao which at the time had have and still a lot of Japanese and Japanese Filipinos. When the economy of the Philippines was based out of Manila, a lot of them moved there—which also explains why today half of the Indian and Indian Filipino community are now based.

Most of the Indians and Indian Filipinos in the Philippines are Sindhi and Punjabi, but there is also a big Tamil population as well. A lot of them are fluent in Tagalog and English, as well as the local language of the provinces and islands of where they live. A lot of them are very prosperous middle and rich class (especially the Hindus) with there main jobs selling clothing. But there is also a lot of them are poor, mostly the Sikhs who mostly sell things and collect intersets, hence 5-6. Most of the Indians and Indian Filipinos are Hindu and Sikh, but have assimilated into Filipino culture and some are Catholic. There are 2 main Hindu and Sikh temple in Manila, and Hindu temples all over the Philippine provinces as well.

19.11 Indians in the Middle East

There is a huge population of Indians in the Middle East, most coming from Kerala and other south Indian states, especially in the oil rich countries neighbouring the Persian Gulf. Most moved to the Gulf after the oil boom to work as labourers and for clerical jobs. Indians—all foreigners, in fact—in the Gulf do not normally become citizens however. They retain their Indian passports since most of the countries in the Gulf do not provide citizenship or permanent residency.

One of the major reasons why Indians like to work in the Gulf is because it provides incomes many times over for the same type of job back in India and its geographical proximity to India. The Indian Diaspora makes up a good proportion of the working class in the GCC. In 2005, about 40 percent of the population in the United Arab Emirates were of Indian descent.

Gulf Cooperation Council (GCC) states include Saudi Arabia, Kuwait, Bahrain, Qatar, United Arab Emirates and Oman. NRI population in these GCC countries is estimated to be around 6,000,000 (2006-2007), of which over 1,500,000 stay in the UAE. Majority of them originate from Kerala, Andhra Pradesh, Karnataka and Tamil Nadu. NRI population tends to save and remit considerable amount to their dependents in India. It is estimated such remittances may be over USD 10 Billion per annum (Including remittances by formal and informal channels in 2005-2006).

19.12 Indians in Mauritius

Outside of India itself, Mauritius is the only country where people of Indian Origin form the vast majority (not including Guyana, Trinidad and Tobago where Afro-Trinidadian and Indo-Trinidadians have equal populations, or Fiji where the Indo-Fijians once formed the majority but not today). The people are known as Indo-Mauritians, and form about 70 percent of the population. The majority of them are Hindu (77 percent) and a significant group are Muslims (22 percent). There are also some Christians, Baha'is and Sikhs, but the Baha'i and Sikh populations do not add up to even 1 percent of the population. Various Indian languages are still spoken, especially Tamil, Marathi, Bhojpuri, Hindi and Urdu, but most Indo-Mauritians now speak a French-based Creole language at home, as well as French in general fields. Finding an Indo-Mauritian who exclusively speaks an Indian language is very rare.

19.13 Indians in South Africa

Most Asians in South Africa are descended from indentured Indian labourers who were brought by the British from India in the 19th century, mostly to work in what is now the province of KwaZulu-Natal (KZN). The rest are descended from Indian traders who migrated to South Africa at around the same time, many from the Gujarat area. The city of Durban, has the largest Asian population in sub-Saharan Africa, and the Indian independence leader Mahatma Gandhi worked as a lawyer in the city in the early 1900s. South Africa in fact has got the largest population of people of Indian descent outside of India in the world i.e.: born in South Africa and not migrated, compared to the U.S. Most of them are fourth to fifth generation descent. Also, In the Natal area alone, there has been over 20 Temples built over the last 140 years of indenture, as stated by the Sun Newspaper. They mainly belong to the Hindu (the largest) and Muslim religious groupings. Indian Languages such as Tamil, Telugu, Hindi and Gujarati are still retained, normally by the older generation and Generation X, creating semi speakers, as indicative of the census. In such temples, degrees of Hinduism Vary, from Vaishnavism, inaugurated by ISKCON and The divine life society to more classical, where at some instances, Animal Sacrifice is performed.

19.14 Indians in East Africa

Before the larger wave of migration during the British colonial era, a significant group of South Asians, especially from the west coast (Sindh, Surat, Konkan, Malabar and Lanka) regularly travelled to East Africa, especially Zanzibar. It is believed that they travelled in Arab, Maratha (Coonagee Angria) and Portuguese vessels. Some of these people settled in East Africa and later spread to places like present day Uganda. Later they mingled with the much larger wave of South Asians who came with the British. Indian migration to the modern countries of Kenya, Uganda and Tanzania started nearly a century ago when these were part of British East Africa. Most of these migrants were of Gujarati or Punjabi origin. Their number may have been as high as 500,000 in the 1960s. Indian-led businesses were (or are) the backbone of the economies of these countries. These ranged in the past from small rural grocery stores to sugar mills. In addition, Indian professionals, such as doctors, teachers, engineers, also played an important part in the development of these countries. After independence from Britain in the 1960s, the majority of Asians, as they were known, moved out or were forced out from these countries. Most of them moved to Britain, or India, or other popular destinations like the USA and Canada.

19.15 Indians in Madagascar

Indians in Madagascar are descended mostly from traders who arrived in 19th century looking for better opportunities. The majority of them came from the west coast of Indian state of Gujarat known as Karana (Muslim) and Banian (Hindu). The majority speak Gujarati, though some other Indian languages are spoken. Nowadays the younger generations speak at least three languages including, French or English, Gujarati and Malagasy. A large number of Indians are highly educated in Madagascar, particularly the younger generation, who try to contribute their knowledge to the development of Madagascar.

19.16 Indians in the Caribbean

From 1838 to 1917, over half a million Indians from the former British Raj or British India, were brought to the British West Indies as indentured servants to address the demand for labour following the abolition of slavery. The first two shiploads arrived in British Guiana (now Guyana) on May 5, 1838.

The majority of the Indians living in the English-speaking Caribbean came from eastern Uttar Pradesh and western Bihar, while those brought to Guadeloupe and Martinique were mostly from, but not only, from Andhra Pradesh and Tamil Nadu. A minority emigrated from other parts of South Asia, including present-day Pakistan and Bangladesh. Other Indo-Caribbean people descend from later migrants, including Indian doctors, Gujarati businessmen and migrants from Kenya and Uganda. A vague community of modern-day immigrants from India is to be found on Saint-Martin/Sint Maarten and other islands with duty-free commercial capabilities, where they are active in business.

Indo-Caribbeans are the largest ethnic group in Guyana, Suriname, and Trinidad. They are the second largest group in Jamaica, Saint Vincent and the

Grenadines and other countries. There are small populations of them in Bahamas, Barbados, Belize, French Guiana, Grenada, Panama, St. Lucia, Martinique and Guadeloupe.

The indentured Indians and their descendants have actively contributed to the evolution of their adopted lands in spite of many difficulties. Jamaica has always celebrated the arrival of the East Indians in Old Harbour Bay on May 13th. In 2003, Martinique celebrated the 150th anniversary of Indian arrival. Guadeloupe did the same in 2004. These celebrations were not the fact of just the Indian minority but the official recognition by the French and local authorities of their integration and their wide-scale contribution in various fields from agriculture to education, politics, and to the diversification of the Creole culture—thus, the noted participation of the whole multi-ethnic population of the two islands in these events.

19.17 Significance of Indian Diaspora

The utility of the Indian diaspora for India lies in the fields of economy, polity and socio-cultural areas. Within the economy, investment and expertise of the Indian diaspora forms the much needed lifeblood for our developing economy. Whether it is the Resurgent India Bonds or Indian Millennium Deposits, the NRlsl PIOs have been an important source of capital. During the last decade, the trend of NRI/PIO contribution to our economy has gone through a change in nature. The contribution by the Indian diaspora has changed from remittances and return of savings abroad to FDIs.

Investment by the Indian diaspora constitutes about 9 percent of the total FDl to the country. On the political front, countries like the USA and the UK have recognised the Indian diaspora as critical vote banks—A fact which provides them the power to influence political opinion in favour of Indian Government in their respective countries. The list of Indians who have made it big in foreign countries is endless, be it Sir Swaraj Paul (UK), Ujjal Dosanjh (Canada) or L.M. Mittal (U.K.). In the Silicon Valley the Indian technocrats have made great contributions in the field of Information Technology. Vinod Khosla (Co-founder Sun-microsystems), Sabeer Bhatia (Hotmail), Naveen Jain (Infospace), K.B. Chandrashekar (Exodus) and Sanjeev Sidhu (i2tech) are few such names.

Many among the Indian diaspora have started 'giving back' what they feel they owe 'to their country of origin. The Puspawati Loomba Trust, founded by Raj Loomba of Britain funds the education of children of poor widows in India. In Gujarat, Dr. Kiran C. Patel from the USA and his wife have set up a 50-bed hospital serving 100,000 villagers. In the wake of the Gujarat earthquake, they constructed hospitals and schools. London based L.N. Mittal who has a personal fortune of US$ 3 billion has set up the LNM foundation to carry out philanthropic work, specially in India. Their contribution varies from providing proper drainage facilities in Rajasthan villages, offering scholarships to bright local students, donating a mobile medical van, setting up of ₹ 36 crore INM Foundation Institution of IT, and donating ₹ 10 crore to Mumbai's SNDT University.

While on the face of it, the above examples seem to portray the presence of a strong urge among the Indian diaspora to contribute to the Indian economy the picture is not so rosy. It is in this context that the high level committee under Dr. L.M. Singhvi has found that India can learn a few lessons from China. The lessons from China are the need for flexible labour laws an deficient administrative procedure. While the Indian diaspora contributes only 9 percent of the total FDIs that India receives, in China it is more than 50 percent. In numbers, the Chinese diaspora is one of the largest in the world, forming the biggest immigrant group in Canada, USA and Australia. Like the Indians they are among the most successful ethnic groups In the Silicon Valley. The need of the hour, therefore, is to tap the potential of our diaspora like the Chinese do.

The advantage is mutual. India gains by attracting NRI investments, forming a powerful global lobby of investors, and making use of their collective managerial and trading skills. This would reinstate the feeling of pride in the mother country. The flip side is equally attractive NRls need more opportunities to invest and like the Chinese expatriates would prefer that to be in the country of their own origin. The PIOs are also worried about the cultural identities of their children. This they feel could, be addressed by having more in" teracti6n and business with their roots.

The sheer potential of the Indian diaspora can be understood when we see that mere 20 mn Indian diaspora have a total annual income of about US$ 160 bn whereas India with a population of 1014 mn have an national income of US$ 454 bn which means NRI per capita is US$ 8,000 per annum while the Indian citizens per capita is US$ 448 per annum while the NRls/PIOs do want to contribute in the Indian economy at a scale much higher than the present they face many hurdles.

Bibliography

Bibliography

Agwani, M.S., "West Asia: Humiliation Far from Home," *World Focus* (New Delhi), January 1985.

Ajami, Fouad, "Third World and World Order," *Alternatives* (New Delhi), Vol. II, 1976.

Albert and Roberta Wohlstetler, *Controlling the Risks in Cuba* (Adelphi Papers, No. 17, April 1965, The Institute of Strategic Studies, London).

Alexeyev, A., "The Political Situation in Pakistan", *New Times,* No. 51, 1951.

Allison, Graham and Zelikow, P., *Essence of Decision: Explaining the Cuban Missile Crisis*; New York: Longman, 1999.

Andrew W. Cordier, "Methods and Motivations of Dag Hammerskjold," A.W. Cordier and K. Maxwell, eds., *Paths to World Order* (NY, 1967).

Arnold Wolfers, "The Actors in International Politics" in David S. McLellan et al., eds., *The Theory and Practice of International Relations* (New Delhi, 1977).

Arthur Lall, *Modern International Negotiation: Principles and Practices* (New York, N.Y., 1966).

Arthur S. Lall, *How Communist China Negotiates?* (New York, 1966).

Ausland, John C. and Col. F. Richardson, "Crisis Management: Berlin, Cyprus, Laos," *Foreign Affairs* (New York), January 1966.

Ayoob, Mohammed, "Pakistan's Trade Relations with the Soviet Union", *International Studies,* Vol. 11, No. 1, July 1969.

B.K. Srivastava, "Foreign Policy Issues in the 1976 Presidential Election," *Foreign Affairs Reports* (New Delhi), Vol. 26, No. 3, March 1977.

Bandyopadhyaya, Jayantanuja, "The Non-aligned Movement and International Relations," *India Quarterly* (New Delhi), April-June 1977.

Baral, J.K. and J.K. Mohapatra, "Sino-Indian Peace Efforts, *Foreign Affairs Reports* (New Delhi), May 1982.

Baral, J.K., "Paris Talks on Vietnam and American Diplomacy," *International Studies* (New Delhi), July-September 1975.

Baral, J.K., *The Pentagon and the Making of US Foreign Policy* (New Delhi, 1978).

Barton, Sir William, "Pakistan's Claim to Kashmir", *Foreign Affairs* (New York), Vol. 28, No. 2, January 1950.

Baxi, Upendra, *The Future of Human Rights*, Oxford University Press, New

Delhi, 2002.

Bell, Coral, "The October Middle East War: A Case Study in Crisis Management during Detente," *International Affairs* (London), October 1974.

Burton, J.W., *International Relations: A General Theory* (Cambridge, 1965*)*.

Campbell, John C, "Negotiating with the Soviets," *Foreign Affairs* (New York), Vol. 34, 1956.

Carl Sagan, "Star Wars Won't Work," *Mainstream,* 21 September 1985.

Chandra, Aashis, *Human Rights and Conflict Resolution*, Rawat Publications, New Delhi, 2000.

Charles F. Hermann, *International Crises: Insights from Behavioural Research* (New York, 1972).

Charles O. Lerche, Jr. and Abdul A. Said, *Concepts of International Politics* (Englewood Cliffs, N.J., 1963).

Chaterjee, Bandana; (2004), "Women and Politics in India", in Rakhahari Chatterjee (ed.) *Politics India: The State Society Interface*, South Asian Publishers, New Delhi.

Chaudhri, Mohammed Ahsen, "Pakistan and the Soviet Bloc", *Pakistan Horizon,* Vol. 9, June 1956.

Chayes, Abram. *The Cuban Missile Crisis, International Crisis and the Role of Law*; Oxford University Press, 1974; 2nd ed., 1987.

David P. Forsythe, "United Nations Intervention in Conflict Situations Revisited; A Framework for Analysis," *International Organization,* Vol. 23, No. 1, Winter 1969.

David Singer, "Inter-Nation Influence: A Formal Model," *American Political Science Review,* Vol. 57, June 1963.

Dean Acheson, *Present at the Creation: My Years in the State Department* (New York, 1969).

Deutsch, Karl W., *The Analysis of International Relations* (Englewood Cliffs, 1968).

Divine, Robert A,. *The Cuban Missile Crisis*; New York: M. Wiener Publishers,1988.

Elmer Plischke, *The Conduct of American Diplomacy* (New York, 1961).

Ernst B. Hass et al., *Conflict Management by International Organizations* (Morristown, New Jersey, 1972).

Finnemore, Martha. 2003. *The Purpose of Intervention: Changing Beliefs about the Use of Force*. Cornell University Press.

Flathman, Richard E. 1980, *The Practice of Political Authority: Authority and the Authoritative,* Chicago University of Chicago Press.

Forbes, Geraldine (1999), *Women in Modern India*, Cambridge University Press,

New Delhi.

Frederic Hartmann, *Relations among Nations* (New York, 1963).

Gabriel Almond, *The American People and Foreign Policy* (New York, 1950).

Giaham T. Allison, *The Essence of Decision: Explaining the Cuban Missile Crisis* (Boston, Mass., 1971).

Gilpin, Robert, (1975), *U.S. Power and the Multinational Corporation: The Political Economy of Foreign Direct Investment*. New York: Basic Books.

Gilpin, Robert (1981), *War and Change in World Politics*. New York: Cambridge University Press.

Girija Shah and K.N. Gupta, *Human Rights: Perspective Plan for 21st Century,* Diamond Pocket Books, New Delhi, 2002.

Godelier, Maurice, and Marilyn Strathern, eds. (1991), *Big Men and Great Men: Personifications of Power in Melanesia.* New York: Cambridge University Press.

Haas, E.B., et al., *Conflict Management by International Organizations* (Morris-Town, New Jersey, 1972).

Hameed, Syeda Saiyidain, "The Plight of Women", R.M, Pal (ed.) *Protection of Human Rights: A Critique*, Indian Social Institute, New Delhi, 1999.

J.K, Baral, "American Policy in Vietnam from 1945 to 1960; Myths and Realities," *Political Scientist* (Ranchi), Vols. 14-16, July-December 1977 to January-June 1980.

J.W. Burton, *International Relations: A General Theory* (Cambridge, 1965),

Jasjit Singh, "Geopolitics and Superpower Rivalry in Indian Ocean, *Strategic Analysis,* Vol. 8, No. 8, November 1984.

Jawaharlal Nehru, *India's Foreign Policy: Selected Speeches September 1946-April 1961* (The Government of India, The Ministry of Information and Broadcasting, Publication Division).

Jaya Krishna Baral, "US Involvement in Vietnam: From Cold War to 1960," *China Report* (New Delhi), Vol. 12, No. 3, May-June 1976.

K. Subrahmanyam, "Nuclear Colonialism without Disguise," *Times of India, Sunday Review,* 25 August 1985,

K. Subrahmanyam, "The Legacy of Hiroshima: Four Decades of Nuclear Terror," *Times of India,* 7 August 1985.

K. Subrahmanyam, *Indian Security Perspective* (New Delhi, 1982).

Lifschultz, Lawrence, "Afghanistan: The Not-So-New Rebellion," *Far Eastern Economic Review* (Hong Kong), 30 January 1981.

Mishra, K.P. and K.R. Narayan, eds., *Non-alignment in Contemporary International Relations* (New Delhi, 1981).

Mohammad Shabbir (ed.); *Quest for Human Rights,* Rawat Publications, Jaipur,

2005.

Morgan, P.M., *Theories and Approaches to International Politics* (San Ramon, Calif., 1972).

Morgenthau, Hans J, *Dilemmas of Politics* (Chicago, 1958).

O.N. Mehrotra, "NATO and 'Star Wars' Programme," *Strategic Analysis,* No. 6.

Pearson, Lester B., *Diplomacy in the Nuclear Age* (Toronto, 1959).

Pope, Ronald R., *Soviet Views on the Cuban Missile Crisis: Myth and Reality in Foreign Policy Analysis*; University Press of America, 1982.

R.B. Montoya, "International Development Issues: Five Views," *India International Centre Quarterly* (New Delhi,), Vol. 6, No. 1, January 1979,

R: E. Hopkins and R.W. Mansbach, *Structure and Process in International Politics* (New.York, 1973).

Rao, D.B., *Human Rights and the United Nations*, Part-I & II, Discovery Publishing House, New Delhi, 2001

Seymore M. Hersh, *The Price of Power: Kissinger in the Nixon White House* (Summit Books, New York, 1983).

Sharma, Kumud; (1994), Women's Studies in India; Academia and Action, in J.S. Grewal and Hugh Johnston (eds), *The India-Canada Relationship: Exploring the Political, Economic and Cultural Dimensions*, Sage, New Delhi, 1994.

Shiva, Vandana; (1989), Staying Alive: Women, Ecology and Development, Zed Press, London.

Shrivastava, B.K., "Foreign Policy Issues in the 1976 Presidential Election" *Foreign Affairs Reports,* Vol. 26, 1977.

Sidney B. Fay, "Balance of Power", *Encyclopaedia of the Social Sciences* (New York, 1937), II.

Sridharan, Indhrani, Practicing Human Rights: A Feminist Perspective, C.J. Nirmal (ed.), *Human Rights in India*, Oxford University Press, New Delhi, 2002

Tanter, R. and R.H. Ulman, eds., *Theory and Policy in International Relations* (Princeton, 1972).

Tanter, Raymond, "Dimensions of Conflict Behaviour within and between Nations," *Journal of Conflict Resolution,* March 1966.

Thomas C. Schelling, *The Strategy of Conflict* (Cambridge, Mass., 1960).

V.M. Nair, "Havana Summit Shows up Non-aligned Decisions," *Mound Table* (London), Issue 277, January 1980.

Venkataramani, M.S., "The Ford-Kissinger Safari in Angola", *Foreign Affairs Reports,* September-October 1976.

Waltz, Kenneth W., *Man, the State and War* (New York, 1959).

Warner R. Schilling, "The Politics of National Defence: Fiscal 1950," in Schilling et al., *Strategy, Politics and Defence Budgets* (New York, 1962).

Willets, Peter, *The Non-aligned Movement: The Origin of a Third World Alliance,* 1978.

William Appleman William, *The Tragedy of American Diplomacy* (New York, 1959).

Zbigniew Brzezinski, *Power and Principle: Memoirs of the National Security Adviser* 1977-1981 (New York, 1983).

Index

Index